Multicultural Assessment

PRINCIPLES, APPLICATIONS, AND EXAMPLES

Multicultural Assessment

PRINCIPLES, APPLICATIONS, AND EXAMPLES

Richard H. Dana
Portland State University

LEA
LAWRENCE ERLBAUM ASSOCIATES, PUBLISHERS
2005   Mahwah, New Jersey   London

Lawrence Erlbaum Associates, Inc., Publishers
10 Industrial Avenue
Mahwah, New Jersey 07430
www.erlbaum.com

Cover design by Kathryn Houghtaling Lacey

Library of Congress Cataloging-in-Publication Data

Dana, Richard H. (Richard Henry), 1927–
    Multicultural assessment : principles, assessment, and examples /
Richard H. Dana.
        p.   cm.
    Includes bibliographical references and index.
    ISBN 0–8058–5200–X (alk. paper)
    ISBN 0–8058–5650–1 (pbk.)
    1. Minorities—Psychological testing—United States. 2. Personality
assessment. 3. Ethnopsychology. I. Title.
    RC473.P79D363 2005
    155.8—dc22   2004056213

Books published by Lawrence Erlbaum Associates are printed on acid-free
paper, and their bindings are chosen for strength and durability.

Printed in the United States of America
10 9 8 7 6 5 4 3 2 1

Contents

II Multicultural Interpretation

III   Practice Examples

Preface

If you are reading this preface, you are probably currently taking a graduate assessment course, or have completed assessment training, or practice as a professional psychologist. You may wonder why these courses contain little that is relevant for assessment practice with all those persons who are not included in normative data and represent many multicultural populations resident in the United States as well as refugees, students, and other sojourners from many, many foreign countries. This book tries to answer your question.

Multicultural assessment distinguishes between what clinicians now understand about standard instruments and familiar populations and what remains to be known from research and experience that is relevant for high-stakes assessment practice with unfamiliar populations. This book attempts to uncover and articulate what we neither know nor practice with assurance at this time. Current assessment training assumes that our instruments and our service delivery processes are universal and people are more similar than different. This book emphasizes how differences can be examined using standard instruments.

As clinicians, we approach ethnic minority individuals in the United States as well as persons from other countries needing our informed professional understanding with our American values and training that has prepared us very well for understanding and treating persons who are similar to ourselves (i.e., predominantly White and middle class) in problems in living, emotional distress, and psychopathology as defined by our psychiatric nomenclature. These habitual professional practices fall short, as our clients present problems stemming from different worldviews and health–illness beliefs, acculturation status, and cultural/racial identities. This book recognizes standard assessment training as necessary but insufficient preparation for applications of these instruments with the 40% of our client population who are ethnic and cultural minorities. Our older instruments were not designed explicitly for these new clients, and the research basis for practice that has been so carefully assembled requires reformulation and an altered focus of attention to serve these new clients equitably.

This book provides an initial overview of multicultural assessment to augment cultural awareness and increase sensitivity to interpretive bias. General and instrument-specific guidelines for practice with multicultural populations provide one approach to reduce bias. The suggestions and procedural recommendations contained in this book ultimately require a research foundation to provide consensual, low-inference, group-specific, and test-specific interpretive standards for using standard assessment instruments in multicultural practice. For me, these guidelines and their contextual elaboration represent a conspicuous hope and an explicit invitation to psychologists to provide the necessary research foundations and practice examples permitting the development of multicultural assessment standards and their incorporation into the American Psychological Association ethics code.

Textbooks designed for graduate courses in multicultural assessment are not available despite my expectation that *Multicultural Assessment Perspectives for Professional Psychology* (Dana, 1993) would stimulate a number of similar, introductory books. Unfortunately, the Dana (1993) book was not suitable for use as a graduate assessment training text because it contains only background psychometric information on instruments and cultural populations at an undergraduate level. Although the *Handbook of Cross-Cultural and Multicultural Personality Assessment* (Dana, 2000d) is currently being used as a text for some multicultural assessment courses, that volume was designed as a general reference for multicultural personality assessment training and does not provide details on culture-specific, instrument-specific, and clinically relevant interpretive issues. Finally, the linkages between assessment and intervention suggested by *Understanding Cultural Identity in Intervention and Assessment* (Dana, 1998e) have not directly affected multicultural assessment practice in the absence of an explicit context for this practice employing standard instruments.

This new book is the outcome of teaching assessment courses, doing assessments as a practitioner, and conducting research with the three most frequently used standard personality-psychopathology tests—the Rorschach (Rorschach, 1942), the Minnesotsa Multiphasic Personality Inventory (MMPI; Hathaway & McKinley, 1943), the MMPI–2 (Butcher, Dahlstrom, Graham, Tellegen, & Kaemmer, 1989), and the Thematic Apperception Test (TAT; Murray, 1943)—for over 50 years (for a professional autobiography and personal assessment history, see Dana, 2004). This book provides a multicultural assessment model employing cultural knowledge in a proximal manner during training and practice. *Proximal* refers to the direct examination of cultural issues affecting test performances rather than proxy measures and inadequate ethnic glosses describing ethnic minority populations.

I assume that students, practitioners, and other readers are competent in administration, scoring, and interpretation of the Rorschach Comprehensive System (CS) and the MMPI–2 in compliance with available normative data and research and, in addition, have some background and experience with general interpretive procedures for the TAT. Prospective readers include several professional audiences: (a) students in advanced assessment courses including those on clinical inference and multicultural assessment, (b) practicum and internship supervisors, and (c) psychologists providing assessment services to multicultural populations.

Assessment courses in professional psychology programs primarily offer training in a relatively small number of standard tests/methods and may not meet internship expectations in numbers of reports, demonstrated competencies, and skills using particular tests and assessment batteries. Psychometric issues, research methodologies, and exploration of the conduct of assessment training are infrequently addressed. Moreover, although some programs offer an advanced elective or clinical inference course in multicultural assessment, there are few available courses explicitly combining standard and multicultural assessment training (see Dana, 2002d).

As a consequence of these training restrictions, assessment services are now inequitable for many clients because cultural knowledge per se is underutilized to reduce bias in assessment training, research, and practice. The existing norms for standard instruments are of limited applicability for responsible assessment practice with ethnically diverse U.S. populations as well as with foreign nationals, students, sojourners, and refugees. Moreover, there are no available standards for assessment practice with these populations, although recent guidelines for multicultural practice include an assessment overview (American Psychological Association, 2003), and the new American Psychological Association ethics code includes Standard 9.06 that "requires psychologists to take into account in their reports the situational, personal, linguistic, and cultural differences that may influence test scores and interpretations" (Knapp & VandeCreek, 2002, p. 305).

This book has three distinct components. Part I provides a framework for multicultural assessment training using three standard instruments. This framework for multicultural competence training is contained in the first four chapters. Standard assessment training is a necessary foundation for multicultural assessment practice that includes attempts to reduce sources of bias, particularly of interpretation bias, by adaptation of standard instruments for conservative applications (chap. 1, this volume). Specific knowledge of worldviews and belief systems (chap. 2, this volume) provides a transition from the prevailing assumption of universal personality-psychopathology dimensions in standard assessment instruments toward an equal focus on the role of cultural differences in assessment practice. Potential cultural malpractice issues require an examination of assessment bias and cultural competence (chap. 3, this volume) including a counseling psychology rationale for multicultural competence training coupled with advocacy for multicultural research standards and the development of general and assessment-specific guidelines (chap. 3, this volume). Earlier guidelines provided precursors for assessment-specific guidelines containing desirable elements in multicultural competence in assessment practice (chap. 4, this volume).

Part II is designed to bridge the gap between standard assessment training and multicultural assessment practice. Four chapters describe orientation questions and moderators (chap. 5, this volume) as well as instrument-specific guidelines for stepwise procedures with standard instruments (chaps. 6, 7, and 8, this volume). These instrument-specific procedures, except for including orientation questions, differ remarkably. Although the Rorschach CS may be considered as a test or a method, I prefer the method label because the assessor assumes primary control of interpretation, ultimately relying on high inference procedures despite the presence of a carefully elaborated scoring system with a compelling research history (chap. 6, this volume). The MMPI/MMPI–2, a low-inference test remarkably intact despite profound psychometric advances and an absence of theoretical preconceptions, requires greater interpretive caution with multicultural populations. For that reason, essentially low-inference, data-bound interpretation relying on psychometric issues and supplemented by extratest, high-inference considerations is recommended (chap. 6, this volume). Although "special corrections" for the MMPI/MMPI–2 have been deplored by some test-oriented psychologists, chapter 7 (this volume) provides a detailed and constructive response to their legitimate demands for a clear rationale and descriptions of how multicultural interpretation can be accomplished with standard tests.

I recall vividly that students in my first clinical inference course experience (California School of Professional Psychology–San Diego, 1999) specifically requested stepwise, instrument-specific, and culture-specific guidelines for multicultural assessment. At that time, I was unable to provide even tentative and preliminary guidelines. This book represents a belated appreciation of their awareness and communication to me that multicultural assessment sorely required a modus operandi that begins by asking new questions of standard instruments and subsequently includes guidelines for practice or "proposals for discussion" as suggested by Fernandez-Ballesteros et al. (2001).

Part III presents a small number of multicultural practice applications employing cultural information. Contributors use their culture-specific styles for multicultural interpretation of assessment findings with standard instruments. These chapters contain culture-specific assessment exemplars and were prepared independently of the contents of this book. Data sets are included as examples in these chapters as well as procedures for using moderators in test and interview format and other cultural information as a basis for the preparation of responsible assessment reports. Gerrian Wuts provided a case study of the use of the MMPI–2 English-language version in Singapore (chap. 9, this volume). Johanna Tiemann examined the interpretation of Spanish and English Rorschach CS and TAT protocols (chap. 10, this volume). Ailsa Aguilar-Kitibutr provided a case study of a Filipino American using the CS, TAT, and MMPI–2 (chap. 11, this volume). Stamatia Daroglou described Rorschach CS usage with Greek urban and rural individuals (chap. 12, this volume). One of these contributing authors was a student in my first multicultural assessment course (Ailsa Aguilar-Kitibutr). I served on the dissertation committees of two others (Gerrian Wuts and Stamatia Daroglou). The fourth (Johanna Tiemann) presented a paper at the Society for Personality Assessment convention that provided the basis for her chapter.

It should be noted that I experienced extreme difficulty in persuading professional psychologists to write chapters for this book. At least five others persons desired and attempted to provide chapters but unfortunately did not prevail. The contributed chapters thus expose a limited range of multicultural applications rather than realize my original hope of including the four major cultural groups and uniformly incorporating case examples including the three standard instruments in each chapter. Nonetheless, as exemplars, these chapters represent distinctive styles of report writing and reliance on different instruments as well as varying approaches to interpretation.

Acknowledgments

My professional life since retirement in 1989 has been enabled, supported, and encouraged directly by the Regional Research Institute (RRI) and indirectly by the Graduate School of Social Work, Dean James Ward, and Portland State University. I particularly want to acknowledge Barbara Friesen who permitted me to participate in a Minority Cultural Initiative Project as part of her Research and Training Center Grant, 1989 to 1991. William Feyerherm, now Vice-Provost for Research and Graduate Studies, made it possible for me to remain immediately following this project. Finally, Nancy Koroloff, RRI Director, has been responsible for my continuing presence here across the years and provides a continuous welcome and awareness of my activities. This book, as well as the three preceding books (Dana, 1993, 1998e, 2000d), could have neither been conceived nor prepared without the aegis and scholarly sanctuary provided by these individuals. Ron Talarico and Jennifer Williams, Assistants to the Director, have been unstinting in their daily facilitation and patient resolution of my minor crises and embroglios. Terell Avery and Ivan Hernandez, Network Sub-Administration and Technical Support, have immediately, frequently, and graciously solved my computer headaches and tolerated my abysmal ignorance of things my grandson has known since he was 6. Art Emlen, RRI Director when I first arrived in 1988, now shares his office, his good nature, and his profound experience in an adjacent professional world with me. Finally, Denise Schmit is facilitating the production of this book by dealing with references and indexes as she did so competently for the earlier LEA Handbook.

Although I am the sole author of chapters 1 through 8, a small number of individuals have been responsible for the professional motivation and perseverance that culminated in this book. Bob Malgady was responsible for a paradigm shift in thinking about research and clinical practice by accepting the null hypothesis and thereby assuming the presence of cultural influences until otherwise demonstrated. Stan Sue could not readily comprehend the initial rendition of the Multicultural Assessment-Intervention Process model in my 1993 book and encouraged me to do better. Nancy Hansen provided some immediate model clarifications and improvements for her Fielding students. Mike Conner and Jim Allen developed the present flow chart format used for assessment practice subsequently adapted for embedding cultural issues in services and service delivery in California community mental health centers and facilitating research with the model. Giuseppe Costantino and colleagues, including Bob Malgady, designed a new instrument, Tell-Me-A-Story, to replace the Thematic Apperception Test (TAT) with culture-specific pictures and a reliable scoring system. This immense contribution, conforming to my 1993 criteria for cross-cultural assessment instruments, compelled me to include the TAT in this book as a basis for comparison. Finally, across many years, Jim Allen shared assessment research and practice ideas, pertinent particularly to Native Americans and Alaska Natives; in symposia, enabled me to teach multicultural and consumer-oriented assessment courses; and our recent paper (Allen & Dana, 2004) contributed directly to chapters 6 and 7 of this book.

My students at the University of La Verne, California School of Professional Psychology–San Diego, and University of Alaska, Anchorage are responsible for communicating clearly to me that instrument-specific and culture-specific guidelines were feasible and necessary. Nonetheless, preparation of instrument-specific guidelines in chapters 6, 7, and 8 (this volume) was particularly difficult for me across the years beginning in 1998, and culture-specific guidelines have not materialized to date.

Drafts of these three chapters were examined, carefully reviewed, and critiqued by Professor Carl-Erik Mattlar (chap. 6, this volume), Dr. Dave Nichols (chap. 7, this volume), and Dr. Sharon Jenkins (chap. 8, this volume). I am indebted to these individuals because their instrument-specific sophistication, specialization, and objectivity enabled them to identify historical inaccuracies, misstatements, and omissions in these chapters. These experts should not be held responsible, however, for the structure or logic of the interpretive recommendations in these chapters stemming from my 50-year academic perspective rather than practitioner, research specialist, or major contributor to the extensive literature on each instrument. I am also grateful for the tolerant and informed feedback on chapter 7 (this volume) provided by Dr. Jose Cabiya at a June 4, 2004 presentation to his cadre of doctoral practicum supervisors at Carlos Albizu University, San Juan, Puerto Rico.

I

A Framework for Multicultural Assessment Training

Standard and Multicultural Assessment

This chapter describes standard and multicultural assessment or personality and psychopathology. For the purposes of this book, *standard assessment* refers to practice with the most frequently utilized objective and projective instruments—the Rorschach (Rorschach, 1942), the Thematic Apperception Test (TAT; Murray, 1943), and the Minnesota Multiphasic Personality Inventory (MMPI; Hathaway & McKinley, 1943), although standard assessment also includes a broader range of instruments encompassing eight practice areas and the 50 most frequently applied measures (Camara, Nathan, & Puente, 2000). Training for competence in a relatively small number of these instruments has been an essential ingredient in Boulder model scientist practitioner and more recent Vail model professional programs (see Dana & May, 1987, pp. 1–75; Dana, 1992b). However, assessment training in some programs has been diluted by the omission of required courses for undergraduates in psychological testing and for graduate students in psychometrics and test theory.

Multicultural assessment refers to assessment applications of all standard instruments in concert with interview and other test/method sources providing additional information necessary for multicultural competence. Applications of standard instruments with ethnic minority populations for which these measures were inadequately constructed and normed requires not only knowledge about these populations derived from research and clinical experience but an explicit recognition of the strengths and limitations of each instrument vis à vis assessment bias. This chapter describes remediation of assessment bias and reviews psychometric components and supplemental adaptations essential for multicultural applications of standard instruments. This chapter continues with communication of assessment findings in psychological reports and concludes with a description of a checklist for examining the report contents.

STANDARD ASSESSMENT

Psychometric psychology and experimental psychology of Euro-American origins were embodied in Boulder Model scientist-practioner training (Raimy, 1950). Psychometric psychology was legitimized during compulsory assessment instruction using tests as the primary means of describing human beings. A *test* consists of an objective measure of behavior that is standardized to ensure uniformity of procedures and includes norms from a large, representative sample with demonstrated reliabilities and validation on independent external criteria (Anastasi & Urbina, 1997). In addition to test criteria, standard assessment uses established interpretation procedures and reports prepared for consumers and other audiences. Psychologists increasingly preferred tests with objective scores, low-inference interpretations, and normative data rather than techniques or clinical methods necessitating high-inference interpretation. As a consequence, a nomothetic focus gradually replaced an earlier idiographic assessment preoccupation with individual differences premised largely on acceptance of a psychoanalytic frame of reference for research and practice.

Standard assessment currently employs a process that identifies problems, selects and implements information-gathering methods, integrates relevant information sources, and reports conclusions and recommendations using referral-based information in specified areas (Groth-Marnat, 2003):

1. Descriptions or formulations of the pattern of current behaviors.
2. Causes of the behavior observed.
3. Changes that can be anticipated in these behaviors over time.
4. Ways in which these patterns may be modified.
5. Patterns and areas of deficit.
6. Resources and strengths of the person. (p. 20)

Beutler and Groth-Marnat (2003) recommended acquisition of information during an assessment process employing an interview; a small, selected number of standard tests to examine historical background, cognitive functioning, emotional functioning, interpersonal–intrapersonal functioning, diagnosis, prognosis and risk; and client strengths and resources evaluated within psychiatric, general medical, legal, vocational, and psychological contexts. Quantitative and qualitative data from both fixed and flexible test batteries are used to maximize clinical judgments in psychological report format including feedback to clients for integrative assessment of adult personality.

Historically, assessment training has included psychological testing courses for many undergraduates as well as exposure to graduate courses in psychometric theory. There is now limited coverage of validity and reliability in approximately two thirds of graduate programs and test development is reviewed in less than one half of programs (Childs & Eyde, 2002), and norming, test/item bias, classical test theory, and item response theory are presented in only 20%, 15%, 15%, and 5% of courses, respectively. Even these minimal requirements have now disappeared in many professional programs, and contemporary assessment training typically consists of several graduate courses in the technology of standard test applications. Standard assessment also relies almost exclusively on low-inference interpretation of test scores. Such interpretation is predicated on the presumed adequacy of test construction, the development of representative normative data, and on the quality, breadth, and sophistication of empirical research documenting the intended uses for the test with all populations in the United States. Standard assessment is now compartmentalized by paradigms represented by particular tests (Wiggins, 2003) applied within intellectual and neuropsychiatric, objective and projective personality, behavioral, and industrial/organizational areas (Hersen, 2003).

Standard assessment training has decreased in quality, intensity, and scope during the last 20 years (Dana, 1992b, 2003a). Usage of some of the most widely used tests and methods including the Wechsler scales, Rorschach, TAT, and the MMPI–2 (Butcher, Dahlstrom, Graham, Tellegen, and Kaemmer, 1989) has decreased due to managed care assessment restrictions (Piotrowski, 1999; Piotrowski, Belter, & Keller, 1998) and the American Psychological Association Division 12 Presidential Task Force (1999) recently deemphasized projective assessment training. Moreover, internship settings have reacted by noting that too few assessment reports are prepared during graduate training for competence (Stedman, Hatch, & Schoenfeld, 2001). Assessment training with these standard instruments is now augmented during internship (Clemence & Handler, 2001).

Standard assessment practice has also been eroded by an increasing managed care preference for brief, symptom-focused diagnostic instruments (Piotrowski, 1999) and compensation of only approximately two hours of time for administration, scoring, interpretation, and report preparation, although a standard test battery requires a minimum preparation time of four hours (Camara et al., 2000). Sanchez and Turner (2003) suggested that standard tests and test batteries may be replaced by very limited assessment in managed care settings, a prediction that augurs continuing deficiencies in graduate assessment training with standard instruments and also promotes expectations for dramatic alterations of the prevailing assessment model in the public sector (see Dana, 2003a).

Cronbach (1949) and others have described major Rorschach limitations as a result of failure to address psychometric issues of test construction and validation research. Many of these early criticisms have been responded to by the design and conduct of increasingly rigorous validity research on the Rorschach Comprehensive System (CS; Exner, 1969), MMPI/MMPI-2, and TAT (e.g., Meyer et al., 2001). These instruments continue to be the most widely used measures of psychopathology and personality both nationally and internationally and are taught in a majority of professional programs (Camara et al., 2000; Childs & Eyde, 2002; Muniz, Prieto, Almeida, & Bartram, 1999).

Relatively clear preferences continue to exist among professional psychologists for employing either objective tests or projective methods with different client populations in varied practice contexts (Piotrowski, 1999). For example, health psychologists use objective tests exclusively; clinical psychologists use both objective tests and projective methods. Psychologists who assess adolescent and child clients in schools still favor high inference projective methods coupled with low inference intelligence tests (e.g., Kamphaus & Frick, 2002; Knopf, 1986). Clinical and health psychologists favor low-inference interpretation or relatively literal descriptions of the meaning of test scores.

Recently, there has been a gratuitous and prolific assault on the scientific integrity of the standard projective methods described in this book by a number of psychologists who assume an exclusively critical stance and demand a moratorium on teaching and practice with these instruments (e.g., Garb, Wood, Lilienfeld, & Nezworski, 2002; Lilienfeld, Wood, & Garb, 2001; Lohr, Fowler, & Lilienfeld, 2002). A sustained and constructive professional responsiveness to these allegations (e.g., Meyer & Archer, 2001; Viglione & Hilsenroth, 2001; Weiner, 2001; Weiner, Spielberger, & Abeles, 2002) has refuted allegations of pseudoscience by providing new evidence that these instruments are indeed legitimate scientific products and documenting the present usage of time intensive, clinician-administered tests and methods with mainstream populations. Many now feel that personal motives, nonscientific values, and prejudicial attitudes help to fuel this assault (Lerner, 2002; Smith, 2002), although it may also represent a continuing absence of consensus among professional psychologists concerning the nature and function of assessment science.

This chapter addresses this controversy by advocating continued usage of standard instruments for cross-cultural/multicultural assessment training/practice augmented by a careful reexamination of research literature and normative data for bias and use of culturally responsible interpretive strategies as well as new instruments. In this new usage for ancient tools, the validity of standard assessment instruments, scores, and normative data for multicultural populations cannot be assumed but must be demonstrated in each instrument for separate scores as well as for each cross-cultural/multicultural application.

MULTICULTURAL ASSESSMENT

Standard assessment and multicultural assessment represent somewhat different perspectives on the nature of psychological assessment practice. Both standard and multicultural assessment, whether accomplished with objective tests or projective methods/tests, share common roots in the statistical and methodological procedures responsible for development and application of these instruments. Both domains also stem from strong personal convictions by assessors concerning the relative merits of either low-inference or high-inference interpretation. Both domains also share differences and similarities with behavioral assessment and compete with behavioral assessment for professional and public favor and preference (Barrios & Hartmann, 1986).

Multicultural assessment adheres to an ethical mandate for moving beyond cultural sensitivity toward cultural competence. Multicultural competency begins with the demonstration of respectful behaviors toward clients on the basis of cultural knowledge, the recognition of assessor competency boundaries, and an emphasis on the skills needed to foster trusting relationships and interpret responses within a cultural context. Assessors must possess a depth of knowledge concerning the culture/ language of clients for whom services are provided as well as an awareness of available resources for acquiring information about persons in the contexts of diverse cultures.

Because standard assessment focuses on a select mainstream, middle-class population of predominantly Euro-American origins, large population segments are not represented adequately by normative data, leading to distortions and omissions in test interpretation. Social classes are frequently described from a six-class White perspective in the United States that includes 15% in capitalist and upper-middle classes, 30% each in middle and working classes, and 25% in the working poor and under classes (Gilbert & Kahl, 1987). This structure has been inappropriately generalized to encompass all other cultural/racial groups. For example, African American reality designates a three-class structure differing in income, occupation, and educational representation from the six White social classes (Bass, 1982; Myers, 1982; Stricker, 1980). These African American classes include a single upper class (10%), with middle (40%) and lower classes (50%), each with three subgroups including 13% of nonworking poor. This system is further complicated by the fact that the three lower middle classes dwell in segregated urban neighborhoods! To what extent this class structure has been perpetuated over time requires empirical documentation. There is certainly a somewhat enlarged upper class now, although many segregated neighborhoods have been maintained.

Differences in language proficiency may also occur across samples. Often there is no attempt to evaluate the possible effects of limitations in language skills on communication during the assessment process. Assessees from different cultural/racial groups, especially those of lower class origin and limited educational experience, also have increased difficulty due to relatively less familiarity with standard tests and instruments. Similarly, administration bias can occur because of an assessor's age, gender, social class, or social etiquette.

A multicultural assessment paradigm including explicit and detailed cultural knowledge for understanding personality and recognizing psychopathology in these varied populations is now mandatory. Malgady (1996, 2000) has recommended a reversal of the null hypothesis to recognize that because culture exerts an abiding influence on all aspects of human lives, cultural influences must always be evaluated. Applying the cultural null hypothesis with each instrument and client population invites a systematic examination of data prior to interpretation. Cultural issues can be systematically examined during assessment by employing the multicultural assessment-intervention process (MAIP) model (e.g., Dana, 1997a, 1998a, 2000a, 2001a, 2001b; Dana, Aragon, & Kramer, 2002) to make explicit Malgady's (1996, 2000) strategy for cultural hypothesis testing. The MAIP model provides a long-term remedy for cultural bias consistent with Malgady's (1996, 2000) demand for radical change in the contemporary role of cultural issues in assessment. This model identifies questions posed at critical points and suggests how culturally relevant information can be incorporated and embedded in the assessment process. These questions, identified and discussed in chapter 4 (this volume), encourage acceptance and exploration of client cultural differences until the relevance of such differences are ruled out by specific information or become integumented within the assessment process.

Multicultural assessment serves all assessees by recognizing the personal nature of assessor preferences for instruments and interpretations levels with an awareness that sound applications are dependent on the psychometrics of particular instruments and the credibility of their cross-cultural research histories. Thus, a continued application of both objective tests and projective techniques is recommended for multicultural assessment, although some of these instruments have significant limitations in addition to their positive contributions for multicultural assessment practice. These different kinds of instruments also have complementary relations that invite incremental validity studies within a training-research rubric permitting objective evaluations of competence in preparation of assessment reports.

Multicultural assessment is dependent to an even greater extent than standard assessment on adequate psychometric knowledge for selection of relevant tests and methods. First, assessors have assumed, without empirical justification, that their standard tests are genuine "etics," or universal in their applications. Standard tests, however, are by-products of a Euro-American, culture specific or emic construction of reality including both explicit rules for test development and implicit consensus on how these rules are applied in the various steps of the research enterprise (for criticism of these applications, see Okazaki & Sue, 1995, 2000; Sue, 1999). Second, these standard tests are thus culture-specific measures applied as if they were culture general and universal. Thus, these tests have been more accurately described as pseudo, derived, or imposed etics, although Berry (1969, 1989) has recommended the term *imposed etic*, which I use consistently in this book to encompass these labels. Research that unequivocally demonstrates cross-cultural equivalence is required for a test to be described as a genuine etic (Dana, 1993, 1998e, 2000c).

Multicultural assessment demands critical and informed attention to each step in test construction and all areas of application to understand the extent to which each test is appropriate, fair, and useful for describing personality characteristics or psychopathology in a particular individual from a given culture. Gross psychometric inadequacies and limited supportive, cross-cultural, construct validation research provides a strong impetus for augmenting low-inference tests with high inference projective techniques using explicit guidelines for increasing the reliability of high-inference interpretation. Multicultural assessment training, therefore, must include careful attention to various ways for increasing the reliability and validity of high-inference interpretation using projective techniques.

Although multicultural assessment courses are available in many programs (Childs & Eyde, 2002), students are rarely exposed to the psychometric deficiencies of standard assessment instruments that perpetuate biased applications with multicultural populations. To reduce bias, professional psychology training for multicultural practice should integrate cultural perspectives and issues in all courses and supervised experiences. Students also have insufficient empirically derived knowledge of cultural/racial groups per se and also generally lack awareness that cultural issues permeate each phase of ethnic minority research (i.e., planning, definition of variables, selection of measures, selection of participants/sampling/cooperation, linguistic/construct/metric equivalence, research design, and interpretation of data; Sue & Sue, 2003).

The remainder of this chapter provides a closer examination of major multicultural assessment training issues. The sections that follow include remediation for bias by clinicians during service delivery, in tests/methods, and the *Diagnostic and Statistical Manual of Mental Disorders* (4th ed. [*DSM–IV*]; American Psychiatric Association, 1994), and then reexamine the multicultural relevance of reliability, validity, and normative issues. A variety of careful test/method adaptations to increase reliability of interpretation are examined. Finally, a section on communicating assessment findings begins with a research history of psychological reports as assessment products including ethical issues in feedback and a rationale for responsible and ethical feedback. Some advantages and limitations of formats for the preparation of multicultural assessment reports are discussed as well as systematic generic procedures for the preparation of competent psychological reports adapted for multicultural assessment courses.

REMEDIATION OF BIAS

The objective of the interpretation approach described in this book is to reduce various sources of bias resulting in assessment practices that can be unfair, discriminatory, and potentially unethical. Table 1.1 summarizes

TABLE 1.1
Assessment Bias: Sources and Suggested Remedies

Locus	Source	Remedy
Clinician	Ethnocentricism Racism Prejudice Stereotyping	Examine own identity Immersion in another culture Training Supervision
Service delivery	Anglo style social etiquette: Impersonal, formal, task-oriented	Culture-specific styles
Tests/techniques	Anglo emics or imposed etics used as etics	Cross-cultural equivalence in language (translation), constructs, and metric/scalar
DSM–IV	Anglo emic symptoms, syn- dromes, and disorders used as genuine etics	Cultural formulations Culture-bound disorders

Note. DSM–IV = Diagnostic and Statistical Manual of Mental Disorders (4th ed.). From "Projective Assessment of Latinos in the United States: Current Realities, Problems, and Prospects," by R. H. Dana, 1998d, *Cultural Diversity and Mental Health, 4,* p. 166. Copyright by American Psychological Association. Adapted with permission.

several sources of bias among clinicians during the service delivery process, in assessment tests/methods, and in descriptions of psychopathologies provided by the *DSM–IV* (American Psychiatric Association, 1994). Each of these sources of potential bias has potential remedies to reduce or minimize the impact and effects on multicultural clients. It should be noted that these sources of bias are limited to assessment. For a discussion of bias at several levels, including practitioner, practice network/program, and community, I refer readers to Snowden (2003).

Clinician Bias

Bias among clinicians is typically inadvertent, denied, and often below thresholds of awareness. The most blatant bias occurs by stereotyping groups as inferior and in acceptance of invidious group comparisons with Euro-Americans on the basis of comparative research that identifies groups by ethnic glosses (Trimble, Helms, & Root, 2003) and omits relevant matching criteria (Azibo, 1988). Bias of a more subtle nature has been uncovered in research demonstrations of "social stereotypy . . . in survey findings, hospital admissions, and diagnostic decision-making during encoding of data and distortions that accompany information retrieval" (Dana, 2001a, p. 108). Blind faith in either low- or high-inference interpretation potentially creates opportunities for bias in the psychological reports of persons from multicultural populations in the form of stereotypy, caricature, and dehumanization (Dana, 1999b) as well as overpathologizing or underpathologizing, described by López (1989).

Careful self-examination by students of their own cultural/racial identities is necessary within a training context that includes diversity of students and faculty. An understanding of the self as a cultural construction prior to assessment training (Dana, 1998b, 1998e) can provide the beginnings of ethnorelativistic thinking and behaviors described by J. M. Bennett (1986).

Clinician bias also occurs during test/method administration, a source of control over the process because all examiners learn to administer a test/method to all examinees using the same directions without embellishment or alteration. Standard directions are designed as unambiguous, consensual statements operationalizing the administration procedures. If administration procedures are not consistent, the assessment instrument is not a "test" but a technique or method. For example, TAT cannot properly be considered a test without the use of standard verbatim directions during administration by all examiners (e.g., Dana, 1982) in addition to other criteria. Additionally, *eisegesis*, an intrusion of examiner personality into the interpretation of high-inference techniques such as the TAT, can also provide inadvertent bias, although explicit training procedures can be employed for understanding and minimizing personal eisegesis (Dana, 1966).

Service Delivery Bias

Bias in service delivery typically occurs in the absence of awareness and experience with culturally credible and appropriate service delivery etiquette. The behavioral component of test administration must be consistent with social etiquette expected by the client. Whenever the service delivery style is discordant with client expectations, attention, interest, and subsequent task orientation may falter and affect the entire response process and interpretation procedures. The use of culturally acceptable service delivery styles is necessary for cultural competence in administration of instruments (Sue & Zane, 1987). I describe client expectations for credible examiner social etiquette to be observed with major cultural/racial populations in chapter 4 (this volume).

Test/Method Bias

Bias occurs in the adequacy of each test/method for use with specific multicultural populations as well as in the selection of particular instruments for use with clients. Recent reviews have examined bias reduction by demonstrating the inclusion of cultural issues as proximal rather than distal variables and extending applications of standard instruments with cross-cultural and multicultural populations using the Rorschach CS (Allen & Dana, 2004; Ephraim, 2000a), MMPI/MMPI–2 (Holden, 2000), and the TAT (Dana, 1999a, in press-b; Ephraim, 2000b; Rossini & Moretti, 1997). Reducing bias in test scores as well as in their interpretation is a primary objective of multicultural assessment training.

   Selection of Tests/Methods.   Multicultural assessment currently relies on imposed etic instruments in practice, although emic instruments are available for African Americans (Jones, 1996) and an etic–emic rationale is used with the TAT (e.g., Ephraim, 2000a, 2000b, in press). Etic–emic conceptualizations or combinations of universal categories and culture-specific diagnostic criteria and personality constructs can result in employment of imposed etics and available emics with multicultural clients. At present, however, such combinations are infrequent, although providing an avenue for employing psychometrically respectable multicultural instruments.

   Emic knowledge provides a context for using assessment data within the psychometric properties of standard instruments and clinical utility research. This knowledge should be provided primarily by available emic instruments and is especially necessary to comply with assessment preferences and needs of specific cultural/racial populations.

Cross-Cultural Equivalence. Bias in test/method adequacy can only be detected by a detailed understanding of the methodological requirements for cross-cultural equivalence. This knowledge provides a frame of reference for examination of actual research demonstrations of equivalence for a particular test or technique employed with specific client populations of interest (e.g., Allen & Dana, 2004; Allen & Walsh, 2000: Cuellar, 2000; Dana, 2000c; Van de Vijver, 2000). Cross-cultural equivalence of the tests/methods selected for an assessment client has several distinct and necessary dimensions—linguistic/translation, construct, and metric/scalar equivalence (Allen & Walsh, 2000).

The imposed etic nature of many standard tests has been largely ignored historically, and these tests were administered in a second language, English, or translated literally. Because translations can be accomplished in a systematic manner (e.g., Brislin, 1976; Butcher, 1996b), linguistic equivalence in the form of systematic translations using accepted rules/strategies became the sine qua non of psychometric equivalence, at least for Butcher (2001) who asserted that "careful translation is perhaps the most crucial aspect of assuring that a psychological test adapts effectively across a different language culture" (pp. 621–622). Nonetheless, linguistic technologies, although necessary, can only provide an incomplete and partial demonstration of equivalence. The more substantial and fundamental construct and metric/scalar equivalence demonstrations remain underutilized (Allen & Dana, 2004; Dana, 1993; Van de Vijver, 2000).

Construct validation for applicability of constructs in tests constructed in one culture and applied in another culture necessitates empirical demonstrations of underlying dimensions of personality and psychopathology. Because constructs are language specific and culture specific, three relevant research questions may be framed: (a) Does the construct exist in the second language/culture of application?; (b) if the construct does exist in a second culture, then does this construct have the same components as in the culture of origin?; and (c) finally, is there cross-cultural similarity/identity of the subjective experience in which the construct is embedded? The answers to these three questions are complex, and have not been sufficiently documented by available empirical research but amenable to cross-cultural investigation.

Statistical procedures for examining cross-cultural construct equivalence assume equal importance with knowledge of the psychometrics of test construction, validation, and norms (Allen & Walsh, 2000; Cuellar, 2000). Factor analysis is the predominant approach to cross-cultural construct validation due to relative ease of application, although other approaches are considered to be more adequate (Irvine & Carroll, 1980).

Metric/scalar equivalence requires that scores on a scale measure the same behavioral quality cross-culturally, and bias is found in dissimilar psychometrics such as score distributions and ranges of scores in different cultures. Item bias, or differential item functioning, and unequal item endorsement across groups is noted, as it affects MMPI/MMPI–2 interpretation.

DSM Bias

Bias in *DSM–IV* can be addressed directly by training to increase reliability of clinical diagnoses using a stepwise procedure following an assessment model such as the MAIP and by supervised experience in the preparation of cultural formulations for multicultural populations. Proficiency in recognizing culture-bound disorders and preparing cultural formulations by all clinicians is now mandatory for culturally competent clinical diagnoses (Dana, 2001a, 2002a).

PSYCHOMETRIC COMPONENTS

This general introductory statement on sources of bias is followed by more detailed description of psychometric components essential for multicultural applications of assessment instruments. Table 1.2 summarizes issues pertinent to reliability, validity, and norms.

Reliability of Tests, Scales, Scores, and Scoring

Explicit scoring procedures break down the response process into components or scores. The reliabilities of these test scores indicate several different aspects of consistency: First, test–retest reliability suggests anticipated consistency of the same test over particular time periods. Second, alternate form reliability indicates the equivalence of parallel test forms. It should be noted that only one form of the Rorschach is generally available in the United States, although other sets of inkblots are available in Canada, Japan, and Switzerland; the Holtzman Inkblot Test (Holtzman, Thorpe, Swartz, & Herron, 1961) has a parallel form. The MMPI/MMPI–2 also lack parallel forms, although available short forms have had limited research examination (e.g., Hoffmann, Dana, & Bolton, 1985). The TAT has competing forms for different populations (e.g., African Americans, Plains Indians) requiring redrawing the standard Murray cards and the design of new cards with differing interpretive criteria for scoring and interpreta-

TABLE 1.2
Psychometric Components of Multicultural Assessment

Component	Definition	Instrument
Reliability		
Test–retest	Two administrations	Consistency versus change
Alternate form	Two forms	HIT only
Internal consistency	Relationship of items to scale (part–whole)	All
Interrater	Scoring agreement	CS/TAT
Standard error of measurement	Scale reliability correction	MMPI–2
Reliability of differences	Scale intercorrelation correction	MMPI–2
Validity		
Content	Content accuracy judgment; item operational adequacy	All
Criterion oriented	Relations to external correlates: outcomes and other measures	All
Construct	Examination of underlying dimensions	All
Norms		
National	Match groups on all relevant participant variables	All
Local	For isolated groups	Infrequent Native American examples
Cultural/racial	By group—extreme within-group variability	Impractical
Acculturation status	Traditional acculturation status	Recommended

Note. HIT = Holtzman Inkblot Test; CS = Comprehensive System; TAT = Thematic Apperception Test; MMPI–2 = Minnesota Multiphasic Personality Inventory–2.

tion. Third, the reliability/consistency of items is referred to as *internal consistency*. Fourth, agreement among scorers, or *interrater reliability*, is not used with objective tests because clerical error in scoring is considered to be minimal. However, interrater reliability is mandatory for the Rorschach and TAT whenever these instruments are used with scoring variables. Students should learn Rorschach CS and TAT scoring to preestablished agreement criteria using scoring exercises, with feedback, to provide equal practice on scores occurring with high and low frequencies as a safeguard against errors in interpretation resulting from faulty scoring.

The practical function of test reliability is to provide estimates of an examinee's true score on the basis of the adequacy of test construction and validation. Either internal consistency reliability, particularly Cronbach's alpha, or test–retest reliability may be used to calculate a standard error of measurement (*SEM*). However, internal consistency reliability is preferred whenever the numbers of items are consistent across scales, and each item makes an equal contribution to the total score, although alpha coefficients increase with numbers of items. Test–retest reliability is preferable whenever a scale (e.g., MMPI/MMPI–2 clinical scales) has several item clusters and/or scales have different numbers of items. *SEM* provides information on the range within which an examinee's true score would appear as a function of test or scale reliability using an infinite number of test administrations. This range is calculated in standard deviation units under the normal curve. For practical purposes, a range of 1 *SEM* is considered sufficient for estimating the range within which a true score would occur. This information has been available with standard intelligence tests, but such data has only infrequently been applied to objective tests such as the MMPI/MMPI–2 and to my knowledge has not been used with the CS or Tell-Me-A-Story Test (TEMAS; Costantino, Malgady, & Rogler, 1988). Routine usage of *SEM* scale information is strongly recommended for all MMPI/MMPI–2 interpretation (see chap. 7, this volume) and particularly whenever multicultural examinees are excluded from norms or included in a nonrepresentative fashion as well as those who fit the norms poorly due to social class or other variables.

In addition, whenever a test has two or more separate scales or dimensions considered together for interpretive purposes, the extent of overlap between each pair of scales must be calculated using a statistic designed for this purpose, the reliability of differences (*SEdiff*). Whenever the scales are orthogonal or devoid of any overlapping contents, then the difference between the two scales may be interpreted literally within the context of *SEM* coefficients calculated for each scale. However, whenever the item content of two scales overlaps, the magnitude of overlap will determine the probable range of error that may be present in comparing scores on the two scales. *SEdiff* serves to delineate the point separation between scales necessary for independent interpretation. The validity of interpretations for scores of highly intercorrelated scales, ostensibly measuring distinct personality/psychopathology dimensions, are suspect in any objective test unless these scores have minimal overlap in item contents using the *SEdiff* statistic.

Test Validity

Geisinger (1988), who summarized available standards (American Psychological Association, 1985) indicated that "test validity refers to the appropriateness, meaningfulness, and usefulness of inferences that are made on the basis of the scores on the test in question" (p. 26). Test validity thus provides evidence for the adequacy of the research process undergirding test interpretation. Test validity is specific to the purposes for which a test or test score is used as exemplified by content validation, criterion-oriented validation, and construct validation. *Content validity* includes expert judgment of the personality or psychopathology content adequacy and the operational adequacy of test items and materials. *Criterion-oriented validity* provides correlational evidence (i.e., magnitude and significance level) for test adequacy in predicting measurement outcomes or relatedness to other measures of the same content. For example, a psychopathology measure used cross-culturally should demonstrate consistent predictive validity for specific interventions applied to different cultural/racial groups. In other words, the possibility of differential prediction should always be investigated. However, information on cross-cultural content and criterion-related validation of standard tests is seldom available.

Content- and criterion-related validity provide evidence for construct validity; this information is fragmentary and incomplete without an independent focus on *construct validation*. Thus, it is always necessary to establish construct equivalence in the absence of previously demonstrated universality of particular constructs. If the constructs were universal, not as posited by theory alone but demonstrated unequivocally by empirical methods, then establishing construct equivalence would be unnecessary. However, in spite of evidence that some constructs in standard tests such as extraversion and introversion, independence and collectivism, as well as repression and sensitization may be universal, any presumption of cross-cultural generality is insufficient without an empirical test. This is also true even when the construction of a particular test (e.g., TEMAS) is predicated on the assumption of equivalence. As part and parcel of construct equivalence, any test constructed in English for use in the United States must be translated following standard rules for adequacy of translation. Moreover, the translation by bilingual/bicultural translators must survive subsequent demonstrations of equivalence for the monolingual/ monocultural target population.

Construct validation becomes necessary whenever the universe of content or criterion is inadequate to define whatever is being measured (Cronbach & Meehl, 1955). As the previous examples illustrate, construct validity has proven difficult to establish and was once likened with whimsical intention and accurate anticipation of subsequent research difficulties to "measuring a floating cloud with a rubber band in a high wind " (Shneidman, 1959, p. 261). Among several methods of establishing construct validation, the convergent-discriminant paradigm developed by Campbell and Fiske (1959) has been systematically extended to examine cross-cultural equivalence by using culture-syntonic measures of the same construct (Irvine & Carroll, 1980). Several other methods including factor analysis and experimental demonstrations of construct elements have also been used to demonstrate cross-cultural construct validity, although these alternative methodologies provide demonstrations that are also equivocal and incomplete.

I include several examples of construct validation using different methodologies to illustrate method limitations and difficulties of research. There are blatant national differences in composition of the depression construct that provide a rationale for mandatory construct validation prior to international use and subsequent cross-cultural generalization of findings from depression measures developed in the United States (Dana, 1993). First, a cross-cultural construct validation study using a standard measure of depression provides an illustration of the emic nature of this construct and illustrates the necessity for equivalence demonstrations prior to assuming the adequacy of measures in another cultural setting (Brandt & Boucher, 1986). Second, an example of the introversion construct, or Rorschach M, was examined using independent laboratory methods for definition and critique of construct components (Dana, 1968a; Dana & Cocking, 1968). Although these studies have suggested some positive findings, there were also difficulties inherent in the research process.

Depression, as construed for psychiatric diagnosis in the United States more than 50 years ago, is an emic construct measured by the MMPI/ MMPI–2 Depression scale. The description of the psychiatric criterion condition, depression, has changed over time across *DSM* editions (see Castillo, 1996). Moreover, depression is also conceptualized differently in various languages using specific vocabularies to describe the cultural meanings of the experience and does not appear to be a universal construct.

Emotional words characterizing and providing a cluster labeled as depression were found in Japan, Indonesia, and Sri Lanka, although identification of clusters labeled as depression in Malaysia, Korea, Australia, and Puerto Rico was infeasible and existing depression clusters differed in complexity (Brandt & Boucher, 1986). In the United States, depression was relatively noncomplex with characteristic sadness. Alienation, shame/ guilt, and anxiety were only peripherally related. However, in Japan, depression was very complex, primarily manifested by anxiety, pain, misery, and feelings of sadness-loneliness, regret-repentence, and being bored-lacking but associated with 10 other more peripheral emotional states.

Thus, depression measured by the MMPI/MMPI–2 scale cannot be construed as synonymous with depression in Japan. Although the depression construct does exist in Japan, their construct is much broader in definition and enriched by numerous components differing markedly from attributes experienced in the United States. To describe a Japanese individual as depressed as a result of a significant MMPI/MMPI–2 scale elevation literally invests him or her with dubious psychopathology and may foster a conspicuous distortion of cultural humanity by caricaturing the constellation of affect meanings that embody and identify the construct.

The Center for Epidemiological Studies Depression scale (Radloff, 1977) has four original factors described as depressed affect, positive affect, somatic and retarded activity, and interpersonal relations. However, either three factors (Manson, Ackerson, Dick, Barton, & Fleming, 1990) or two highly correlated factors appeared (Dick, Beals, Keane, & Manson, 1994) with different tribal samples of Native Americans and Alaska Natives. In reviewing this literature, Allen (1998) indicated that the lack of factorial invariance among various Indian groups suggested tribal and geographic differences in how depression is experienced and identified. These construct validation findings have emphasized the persistence of culture-bound disorders characterized by narrow clusters of behaviors identified in different tribal settings as "feeling worthless," "totally discouraged," "being killed by melancholy," and *wacinko* (i.e., mild to severe reactive depression; Dana, 1998e). Given the failure to demonstrate cross-cultural construct equivalence for depression, imposed Euro-American etic measures applied in Indian communities or urban populations are unlikely to yield accurate *DSM* diagnoses or contribute to effective interventions for traditionally and marginally acculturated persons as well as for some bicultural individuals.

The introversion construct, exemplified by M or human movement as part of the Rorschach extraversion–introversion experience balance, has been presumed to be etic or universal. Converging research evidence for hypothesized M components included delay, time sense/estimation, intelligence, creativity, fantasy, and interpersonal relations and were reviewed to provide independent and empirically derived descriptions (Dana, 1968a). Validation of these components was attempted using a Brunswik Lens Model paradigm (Dana & Cocking, 1968) with graduate student judges subjectively weighting scores on M component tasks for comparison with M percentages derived from Rorschach records of college students. The results suggest that intelligence and fantasy were major M ingredients, although the other four components also contributed to a lesser extent. These studies have articulated the complexity of the Rorschach M score as well as some difficulties inherent in construct validation. These findings apply most directly to college student participants and judges during the late 1960s. Generalizing these findings to noncollege individuals, multicultural populations, or mental health clients is hazardous without replication. Note that some evidence does exist to support the assumption that this construct is a universal dimension of personality (Dana, 1993). For example, factor analysis has been used to establish the cross-cultural construct equivalence of Rorschach introversion–extraversion (Dana, Hinman, & Bolton, 1977). Nonetheless, more recent empirical evidence within an international and methodologically sound Rorschach CS research context is also necessary to document the universality of Rorschach dimensions including extraversion–introversion (Allen & Dana, 2004).

Sources of Interference With Reliability and Validity

In a recent assessment text, Domino (2000) asked, "What can interfere with the validity of a particular test score?" (p. 444) and devoted an entire chapter to issues of faking, test anxiety, and "testwiseness" that have particular resonance for multicultural assessment. Cronbach (1946) discussed response sets or item and response formats potentially resulting in consistently different responses to test items. These response sets included a penchant for gambling or risk taking that can yield omitted responses, caution, and neutrality in self-report tests. Inclusiveness, or voluntary control over numbers of responses as in the Rorschach, leads to specification of minimum and maximum numbers of responses. Acquiescence, or yea saying, displaces test-taking uncertainty but tends to inflate the validity of false items while decreasing the validity of true items. Directions specifying speed versus accuracy, overtly or implicitly present in sentence completions or the TAT, may limit or enlarge the content available for interpretation. The TAT particularly is affected by a lack of consensus on standard directions such that inadvertent response sets for organization and story dimensions may be communicated with unknown effects on contents and subsequent interpretation. Later, social desirability or faking good, opposition/deviation or faking bad, and inaccurate self-presentation were added and stimulated efforts to incorporate measures of response bias, comparisons of self-report measures with independent bias measures, and demonstrations of scale susceptibility to faking. Two potentially separate domains of bias were noted historically with some disagreement regarding overlap and definitions. These domains represent conscious or unconscious response sets or error variance in content scores as well as unconscious response styles or selection of a response category independently of the content to create reliable variance from stylistic personality measures. Although there has been controversy concerning the magnitude of bias contributed by response sets, response styles, testwiseness, and anxiety, the fact that these sets/styles can potentially introduce bias in tests and methods is generally accepted. The meager research on these bias sources in specific multicultural populations and particular interpretation concerns with each standard test will be examined in chapters 6, 7, and 8 (this volume).

Normative Data

The development of norms as a basis for interpretation of intelligence test scores was predicated historically on the assumption that matching standardization subjects on all relevant variables was necessary. Nonetheless, conventional wisdom, cost-effectiveness, parsimony, and minimization of differences across persons dictated selection of only a few salient variables that typically included age, gender, residence (urban–rural), geographic location, and education. However, only research demonstrations can unequivocally identify the numbers of relevant critical matching variables. Azibo (1988) recommended mandatory matching of research participant groups on a large number of relevant variables in comparative studies. These relevant variables include generation, cultural orientation status, or racial identity stage in addition to ethnicity or race as well as social class using adequate criteria for different cultural and racial groups as necessary (Dana, 2000c).

The norms for major standard assessment tests are all less than ideal because participants are not identified with sufficient care, precision, and detail to permit accurate correspondences with assessment clients. These norms also describe sophisticated, privileged, primarily middle-class persons (Lonner & Ibrahim, 2002). Standard tests typically have "high-stakes" outcomes in educational, employment, or clinical settings for multicultural assessment clients. As a consequence, responsible attention to the goodness of fit between the person who is an examinee and participants who compose the available test norms is mandatory. For multicultural clients, ethnicity, social class, and acculturation/racial identity status are major issues in evaluating the adequacy of normative data. Norms adequately reflecting the multicultural nature of the population for standard tests, acculturation/racial identity status norms, and even local norms are ultimately mandatory for standard tests in addition to a continued development of culture-specific or emic instruments as well as single domain instruments (Dana, 2003a).

There are practical reasons for lack of support by the assessment establishment for culture-specific and/or ethnicity-specific norms on standard tests in the United States. There are a very large number of major ethnic groups, and the cost of restandardizing even a small number of tests would be prohibitive. Moreover, there are three major groups of Hispanics—Cuban, Mexican, and Puerto Rican—plus large numbers of persons from many other Latin American countries. Each of these groups has major within-group differences. Similarly, for Asian Americans, Native Americans and Alaska Natives, there are many hundreds of tribal affiliations with diverse linguistic origins and migration patterns. Culture-specific norms would effectively mask the extreme range of these within-group differences. This is analogous to the use of representative norms that obscure subgroup differences for some standard tests.

Acculturation Status and Racial Identity Status Norms

Special norms, either derived from cultural orientation status or simply norms of local origin, also can serve to reduce pathology bias and misdiagnosis. These norms can complement existing norms for standard tests and the use of dual norms for multicultural assessment is analogous to Caldwell's (1997) recommendation for use of both MMPI and MMPI–2 norms. Similarly, because English is now the global lingua franca and the basis for international communication, it will become an ethical assessment obligation and necessity for tests to be available both in English and in translated versions or preferably equivalent national emic versions (Dana, 2003a).

The development of these norms is desirable and ultimately necessary to minimize confounding with psychopathology and documented on the MMPI/MMPI–2 for African Americans (Whatley, Allen, & Dana, 2003), Asian Americans (Sue, Keefe, Enomoto, Durvasula, & Chao, 1996), Native Americans and Alaska Natives (Hoffmann et al., 1985; Pollock & Shore, 1980), and Latinos (Montgomery & Orozco, 1985; Whitworth & McBlaine, 1993). Although similar confounding on the Rorschach and TAT may affect scores, ratios, and interpretations, documentation is not yet available for these projective methods.

Acculturation status measurement using moderator variables is necessary for individuals who may not be sufficiently assimilated to mainstream society in the United States for application of available norms. Assimilation involves acceptance of dominant society values coupled with rejection of the original culture. For these individuals, norms from standard tests are generally applicable and may be applied with confidence because assimilation requires loss or abandonment of an original culture, successful adaptation to the exclusive use of English, and behaviors that represent mainstream society in the United States. Assimilation usually occurs only after several generations of residence in the United States and may always be incomplete because individuals actively choose to maintain cultural/ national ties including language and customs.

A practical and ethical solution to the dilemma of inadequate norms for multicultural populations lies in developing norms for each standard test that reflect acculturation and racial identity (Dana, 2000c, 2003a). There has been greater attention to acculturation status than to racial identity status. However, the two may assume equal importance during assessment as a consequence of recent literature that has demonstrated that matching clients and clinicians for language, ethnicity, racial identity, and client preference is a complex issue related to the adequacy of clinical diagnosis, intervention procedures, and their outcomes in reducing distress and contributing to quality of life.

Arnold, Montgomery, Castanada, and Longoria (1994) provided an example using acculturation status as a performance correlate on standard neuropsychological tests. This normative enterprise is feasible at the present time as a consequence of the documented generality and importance of acculturation status and racial identity status as measured by moderator variables in test format.

This proposed solution emerges from the history of acculturation research and development of instruments to measure acculturation status or what I referred to as cultural orientation (Dana, 1993). A variety of acculturation strategies are used by individuals in the process of adapting to the demands of a new culture. Acculturation strategies have been described as values that either maintain an original cultural identity or permit and enhance acquired relations to the dominant society (Berry & Sam, 1997). These strategies are introduced descriptively here, presented within the MAIP context and discussed in greater detail as moderator variables in chapter 4 (this volume), Table 4.1.

All multicultural immigrant groups share involvement in an acculturation process requiring choices or preferences for acculturation outcomes that include assimilation, biculturality, marginality, and traditionality. The acculturation process occurs most forcibly and rapidly among children of immigrant persons who attend school and acquire a peer group within the host culture. However, acculturation is always difficult and may not be a voluntary choice, especially for refugees. Culture permeates the person as a source of pride, strength, and vitality as well as a personal rendering of what is involved in being a human being that involves values, beliefs, modes of thought, affects, language, and behaviors that are identified with ethnicity or race. These tangibles and intangibles of personhood can persist across many generations with even minimal support, modeling, and nourishment.

Biculturality implies personal integration by maintenance of two sets of values representing the original and acquired cultures. Biculturality involves relatively equal, balanced, and situationally separate life styles that are enacted with comfort, fidelity, and continuity by an individual (e.g., Chinese Americans). Biculturality can also involve an attempt to blend both cultures in daily life by exposing original cultural values to public scrutiny while preserving language and family values relatively intact at home. Hispanics/Latinos frequently favor a blend, although there is often a preference for mainstream or original identity demonstrated by using the Acculturation Rating Scale for Mexican Americans–II (ARSMA–II; Cuellar, Arnold, & Maldonado, 1995).

Marginality precludes unequivocal acceptance of either set of cultural values. Marginality implies a variable mixing of both traditional and mainstream behaviors, a frequently idiosyncratic solution that may serve an individual well in specific situations but may appear somewhat asynchronous in either traditional or mainstream settings. Marginality has been associated with lack of opportunity, often due to poverty or residence location, to learn behaviors that are entirely consistent and acceptable in either cultural context. Marginality, particularly among African Americans, implies an absence of any clear cultural tradition and being trapped by the "victim system" because of poverty and racism (Pinderhughes, 1982). It should be noted that both racial identity status and acculturation status identification are relevant for some African Americans. Relatively large numbers of persons in several major cultural/racial groups including African Americans, Hispanics, Native Americans and Alaska Natives have a happenstance marginality that may serve them poorly in relationships, education, and occupation by providing increased opportunity for exposure to the mental health or criminal justice systems (Dana, 1998e).

Finally, traditional persons are those who have retained their original cultures relatively intact by language maintenance in contexts of familial and residential propinquity that sustain and perpetuate their cultural values and behaviors. Traditionality provides separation from the dominant society that is often residential while maintaining original cultural values. For these persons and for many marginal and some bicultural persons as well, the norms for standard tests often have limited applicability. In fact, the use of these norms can lead to interpretations that pathologize or dehumanize persons and at best invoke caricature and stereotypy in assessment reports.

ADAPTATION OF STANDARD TESTS/METHODS

Whenever a test is adapted in any manner including administration directions and etiquette, translation, or other alterations, it is mandatory to know whether the reliability estimates have been affected. A premise of the multicultural assessment approach I advocate here is that whenever an examinee does not fit the available normative data for the test, then some adaptation of that test is required. The use of "fit" here includes cultural/racial origin, first language, social class, and education. Moreover, if the examinee's ethnic group has not been sufficiently sampled in terms of adequate numbers or representative proportions in the normative data (e.g., MMPI–2 Hispanics, Native Americans, and Alaska Natives), adaptation may also be required. Nonetheless, adaptation of the assessment process is an ethical necessity with the process and data of many multicultural clients.

Nonetheless, there are unknown effects of these adaptations on reliability estimates, and recommendations for these supplements to MMPI/MMPI–2 interpretation are controversial (Dana, 1995, 1996a, 1996b; Velasquez, Butcher, Garrido, & Cabiya, 1996). Adaptation can represent either personal, informal, and subjective "tinkering" or become part and parcel of an informed and responsible critique (Dana, 2000b). Personalized tinkering to reduce bias and maximize fairness, although widespread and accomplished in the interests of client welfare, cannot result in development of an empirical basis for accepting or rejecting specific adaptations and practices. Nonetheless, consistent and replicable adaptations may reduce test bias and will continue to be applied and examined due to a conspicuous absence of adequate norms or supportive research on cross-cultural construct and metric equivalence.

Moderator variables, special norms, special scales, response sets/styles, translations, culture specific service delivery styles, and interpretation guidelines are recommended forms of adaptation for applications of tests/methods with multicultural populations (Dana, 1995, 2000c, 2003a). Extratest information from moderator variables is necessary to determine the extent of acculturation or cultural orientation status using test or interview content prior to administration of any assessment instruments. Whenever the cultural orientation status is assimilated or bicultural, adaptation may not be necessary unless a bicultural examinee requests specific adaptations either in the form of translated instruments, emic instruments, or services in a first or primary language. In addition, I reiterate that examiners must always practice a social etiquette in assessment service delivery that is credible for clients and thereby fosters and maintains task orientation.

Special scales for the MMPI–2 can provide culture specific descriptive information for groups not included in the standardization. Translations of tests for immigrant non-English speakers and second-language English speakers after determining the client's level of comprehension for spoken and written English may be necessary. For populations who speak nonstandard American English as a legally required first language, equivalents for some test items may be necessary for comprehension (see Wuts, 2002).

Uniform practice of low-inference interpretation with all standard assessment instruments is ultimately desirable and necessary in professional assessment practice. However, at present, strict adherence to low-inference interpretation is only feasible with reasonable fidelity using assessment data from multicultural persons who conform with available normative data in gender, age, ethnicity, generation in United States, cultural orientation status, racial identity stage, social class, educational level, primary language, and urban–rural residence.

The objective of using adaptations is to increase the reliability of subsequent interpretations by putting in place a number of incremental steps between data and inference (for some MMPI/MMPI–2 adaptations, see Dana, 1996b). A hierarchal model consisting of observational and/or test data, trait adjectives, and generalized description illustrates how high-inference or observational personality data can be processed during the clinical inference process to increase reliability of interpretation (Dana, 1970; Dana & Handzlik, 1970). In this example, reports from a standard personality data source generated by students were compared with an exemplar report generated from application of this model. My goal was to approximate low-inference interpretation by imposition of specific guidelines for low-inference instruments lacking relevant norms and for high-inference instruments without consensual scoring systems. In chapters 6, 7, and 8 (this volume), I suggest interpretive steps for the Rorschach/Rorschach CS, MMPI/MMPI–2, and TAT.

COMMUNICATION OF ASSESSMENT FINDINGS

In this section, I examine the communication of assessment findings beginning with reports as assessment products examined in early surveys as an impetus for subsequent research on the contents and utilities of psychological reports. A research literature on feedback has illustrated the relevance of an assessment credo emphasizing the nature, benefits, and ethical responsibilities of feedback. I follow a methodology for utilizing the contents of students' reports competence training by a review of psychological report preparation with suggestions applicable to reports describing multicultural assessees.

Psychological Reports as Assessment Products

A review of ten 1954 to 1974 surveys of assessment reports (Dana, 1982, chap. 10) found differences in quality, adequacy of sampling, and return rates although there was consensus in report deficiencies in communication style and contents. All professional consumers desired descriptions of behavior and dynamics in matter-of-fact, unambiguous, jargon-free reports providing clear distinctions between assessment data and inferences.

This review (Dana, 1982, chap. 10) was followed by an examination of published reactions to these surveys in research studies exploring methodology, adequacy of communication and information as well as contributions to clinical diagnosis. These reactions recognized that reliably discriminating report statements, or consensual statements providing relevant data, increased report adequacy and augmented the usefulness of reports for clear, useful decisions regarding referral and subsequent interventions. These decisions affected patient management, supported clinical diagnoses, provided valid predictions of home care placements, and encouraged recommendations leading to improved behavioral outcomes of counseling.

Recently, Finn and Tonsager (1992) advised that the extent of client benefit from the contents of psychological reports or their predictive validity required demonstration, a conclusion consistent with this history of surveys, research studies, and research indicating that considerable improvement in the contents of reports is required before consumers can be routinely expected to benefit from assessment services.

Assessment Feedback Research

The research history of assessment interpretation has separate components including 42 false feedback, six honest feedback, and 4 mixed studies (Dana, 1982, chap. 10). The false feedback studies, although methodologically sound, were without apparent clinical relevance and were ethically suspect because the deception research strategy used with college student participants has potentially affected any subsequent exposure to honest feedback in clinical assessment settings.

The earliest honest feedback study (Comer, 1965) compared MMPI feedback with no feedback prior to counseling and the student clients accepted interpretations as helpful in establishing relationships and as useful formats for discussion. The Comer (1965) study antedated the development of a college course in oneself (Comer, 1974) that was a popular perennial vehicle for discussion of personal assessment information. This course became a model for other similar therapeutic assessment courses (e.g., Dana & Fitzgerald, 1976) as well as workshops designed for special groups including high school students, paraprofessionals, clinical and counseling undergraduate and graduate students, divorced persons, and teachers of Native American children (for a review, see Dana 1984a). Students in subsequent honest feedback studies have preferred trait rather than medical descriptions and demonstrated increased reflection and/or enhanced communication reactions to accurate statements.

The honest feedback studies have suggested research methodologies to increase the utility of psychological reports, whereas the false feedback studies ultimately contributed to ethical assessment practice embodied in a credo emphasizing assessor accountability, phenomenological equality of assessor and client, and "giving away" assessment procedures through education (Dana, 1975). Four early approaches to sharing the assessment process and findings with clients were "contextual" (Fischer, 1986), "sharing oneself" (Craddick, 1975), "joint feedback" (Dana, Erdberg, &

Walsh, 1978; Erdberg, 1979), and "existential assessment" (Dana & Leech, 1974).

Existential assessment included feedback that shared assessment findings directly with the client, encouraged mutual discovery of the most credible and useful interpretations, but was apparently limited to use with clients who were able to assume responsibility for self-interpretation (Dana, 1984b). A subsequently developed service delivery paradigm incorporated levels of test information, emotional contingencies, and transfer of power to clients in the form of ownership for interpretations enabling full partnership during the entire assessment transaction (Dana, 1985). These models for sharing test interpretations presaged what is now known as therapeutic assessment I describe in chapter 4 (this volume). Therapeutic assessment is a collaborative relationship-engendering psychological evaluation resulting in positive diagnostic and therapeutic outcomes by combining powerful ingredients of assessment and therapy.

Psychological Report Preparation

Historically, psychological reports have been evaluated by an assessor's reputation for credibility and competence in the absence of consensual guidelines for evaluation and psychological reports of assessment findings. Training in report writing per se has been minimal and provided by limited practice in writing reports supplemented by critical readings of a small number of these student reports by their instructors. I vividly remember producing 150 Stanford Binet (Terman & Merrill, 1973) and Wechsler reports without any feedback from the instructor during a course in intelligence testing in 1949. There are few available research-generated suggestions for the contents of descriptive Rorschach reports (e.g., Dana, Bonge, & Stauffacher, 1981) or the TAT (Dana, 1996c, 1999a). An examination of contemporary assessment paradigms contains superb examples of reports on one Native American volunteer assessee using instruments germane to these different perspectives (Wiggins, 2003), reminiscent of Shneidman's (1951) presentation of TAT and Make-A-Picture Story Test (Shneidman, 1949) reports for one Veterans Administration patient.

Recommendations for writing reports contained in 16 published reactions to surveys of assessment findings (summarized in Dana, 1982, pp. 234–235) have been subsequently incorporated in formal models of report preparation (e.g., Hammond & Allen, 1953; Huber, 1961; Klopfer, 1960; Ownby, 1997; Tallent, 1993).

Ownby (1997) described hypothesis-oriented, domain-oriented, and test-oriented formats for assessment reports. *Hypothesis-oriented* reports provide assessment answers to referral questions. In these reports, following a reasons-for-referral section, subsequent paragraphs address specific concerns. Summary paragraphs describing overall client functioning conclude the report. Hypothesis-oriented reports are restricted in information and may omit information relevant for clinical diagnosis and subsequent treatment. *Domain-oriented* reports use selected headings organizing report contents to achieve a comprehensive and balanced discussion of strengths and weaknesses. A variety of different organizational formats are used for these reports, with or without headings, to provide a narrative describing abilities and personality functioning. These reports are sometimes considered to provide excessive information. Finally, a *test-oriented* format uses headings for each test or method used with the client. Although all three psychological report models may be useful with multicultural clients, the domain-oriented and test-oriented models are especially recommended. Domain-oriented reports will be more likely to have sufficient information to reduce bias. These reports are obligated to indicate limitations of each test for particular clients.

Test-oriented reports describing themselves are useful for graduate students prior to standard or multicultural assessment training. Feedback concerning these written reports provides an assessment experience as assessee and well as a means for personal evaluation of the adequacy of assessment-derived descriptions prepared by experienced assessors. For multicultural students, this report format provides an opportunity to discuss the limitations of cross-cultural equivalence for each test used. This is of special importance when the tests employed fail to provide a good fit between client and normative data due to acculturation status, use of English as a second language, or extreme differences in worldview and attitudes toward psychological tests as legitimate vehicles for personality and/or psychopathology description.

Regardless of the report format used, the clinician is obligated to understand the extent to which each test used is applicable to the client. Moreover, in addition, it is an ethical necessity to provide an explicit and informed statement concerning the adequacy, accuracy, and fairness of the test results for the particular client. The limitations, omissions, and failures of the 1992 American Psychological Association ethical code to protect multicultural clients did not relieve clinicians of their responsibilities to provide quality assessment services (Dana, 1994), although some of these deficiencies were addressed in the 2002 APA Ethics Code described in chapter 3 (this volume).

Although these arguments have not been made explicitly for multicultural clients, Klopfer (1960) emphasized accuracy, integration, individuality, clarity, and readability as essential elements of competent reports. Accuracy is necessary for fairness and attention to reduction of cultural bias. Integration requires a high level of cultural competence to know how personality is organized and psychopathology displayed within a particular cultural context. Emphasizing individuality minimizes stereotypy by an understanding of the normative expectations for behavior and the tolerated latitude for expression of specific behaviors, affects, cognitions, and symptomatologies. Clarity and readability are essential for consumers of reports, especially if these consumers have limited cultural knowledge. In addition to these essential elements of psychological reports, the personal style is important because it imposes the clinician's personality and outlook on statements describing clients (Huber, 1961).

My own personal style was illustrated by many reports included in an earlier assessment text (Dana, 1982), a report published by Klopfer (1983), and a recent TAT report (Dana, 2003a) as well as by some of the reports contained in this book. This style focuses on describing personality by selection, elaboration, and integration of several central themes in the test data. In so far as is feasible, descriptions of pathology should be in behavioral terms to facilitate sharing of reports with assessees who are the legitimate owners of these self-descriptions. My own reports frequently employ a somewhat literary style, described somewhat pejoratively by Tallent (1993). Nonetheless, I believe this style helps to convey a sensitive understanding of the person conveyed by descriptions perceived as vivid, genuine, and accurate to the extent of stimulating discussion that is mutually helpful for both assessor and assessee.

Training for Preparation of Reports

Although several early studies have attempted unsuccessfully to use interpretive statements abstracted from the contents of reports (e.g., Davenport, 1952), I have used this methodology for over 20 years (for descriptions, see Dana, 1982, 1998d; Dana et al., 2002). The general method requires 6 to 12 students and one or preferably several experienced criterion assessors to prepare four to six reports based on the same sets of psychological test data. Concepts are subsequently abstracted from each set of reports, and similar concepts are clustered. This process can be accomplished with substantial scorer reliability for concepts ($r = .95–.99$) and clustering of concepts ($r = .84–.99$; Dana & Krauter-Willcockson, 1980; Willcockson, Dana, & Rau, 1981). Concepts are compared across student reports and between the student reports and criterion reports. Concepts occurring two or more times are considered consensual; concepts occurring only once are unique. All concepts are evaluated as acceptable or unacceptable using an agree–disagree format by the assessees who contributed the data sets. Following several replications of this process, the unique concepts can be examined in student and criterion reports using assessee acceptance–rejection as a basis for distinguishing between skill (accepted unique concepts) and eisegesis (rejected unique concepts). Students generate greater numbers of unique concepts and employ an increasing number of consensual and unique concepts over time and with practice writing reports and receiving feedback from reports by peers, more experienced assessors, and assessees.

This methodology was applied in studies distinguishing different classes of concepts in Rorschach reports (Dana & Fouke, 1979) and used to examine the range of possible concepts in Rorschach reports (Dana et al., 1981). Concepts have been generated directly from assessment data and used to examine the validity of child Rorschach records (Dana & Back, 1983) and sentence completion interpretations (Turnbow & Dana, 1981). This training process has been adapted for multicultural assessment courses (Dana, Aguilar-Kitibutr, Diaz-Vivar, & Vetter, 2002).

A CHECKLIST FOR MULTICULTURAL ASSESSMENT REPORTS

I use an informal checklist (Table 1.3) to consider the adequacy, completeness, and relevance of contents in multicultural assessment reports and particularly in reports prepared by students. This checklist includes some formal report characteristics described earlier in this chapter and contains ingredients believed essential for a report on any person who is not of Euro-American origins because attention is focused on potential sources of bias, confounds, and interactions. It culminates in a summary statement of recommendations and limitations. Such a report incorporates cultural information resources and contents relevant to identity status or racial identity developmental issues because this information facilitates the selection of appropriate tests/methods and contributes to the preparation of *DSM–IV* cultural formulations and identification of culture-bound psychopathologies as well as to the development of conceptualizations relevant for culture-specific or identity-specific interventions (see chap. 4, Fig. 4.1, this volume). The examiner is responsible for identifying potential sources of instrument bias reported in the research literature or resulting from deficits in cultural knowledge or professional experience. The summary statement also includes recommendations for subsequent interventions or other activities stemming from the interpretive statements. Finally, I recognize a number of formal characteristics of a good report. These characteristics do not explicitly include separate report sections for each instrument, although instrument-specific report segments can facilitate the process of learning to prepare reports as described earlier in this chapter. This occurs because each instrument provides a definitive

TABLE 1.3
Psychological Report Ingredients for Multicultural Assessment

Ingredient	Description
1. Relationship	
Examiner behavior	Examiner behaviors enact good social etiquette and meet client expectations for professional relationship; requires culture-specific service delivery style
Outcome quality	Determines adequacy, sufficiency, consistency, usefulness, and reliability of client data
2. Cultural information	
Describe identity	Cultural/racial identity status/description, selection of subsequent instruments: standard (imposed etic) and/or emic (culture specific)
Understand culture	Required for DSM diagnosis (e.g., cultural formulation, culture-bound syndrome) or for problems in living (e.g., culture-specific and/or identity-specific conceptualizations)
3. Using test data and cultural information	
Interpretations	Citing test data and cultural information in reports to inform/document personality and psychopathology interpretations
Data/information usage	Adequacy for understanding client culture?, completeness/adequacy for describing personality issues?, adequacy for describing client DSM–IV psychopathology (e.g., cultural formulation, culture-bound syndrome) or problems in living (e.g., culture-specific and/or identity-specific conceptualizations)?
4. Recognizing/describing confounds and interactions	
Confounds	Culture personality, culture psychopathology, psychopathology-social class
Interactions	Culture-personality-psychopathology-social class
5. Summary statement of report adequacy	
Recommendations	For interventions (i.e., standard, combined, or culture specific)
Limitations	Of tests, methods, and/or assessor experience and cultural understanding.
6. Formal report characteristics	
Length	Statements of several paragraphs per section including background/behaviors, measures employed, cultural information from moderators, instruments, and summary
Style	User friendly: personal, informal style, primarily in behavioral language.
Organization	Instrument-specific subsections emphasize unique contributions and potential sources of bias followed by integrated summary statement of findings.
Readability	Everyday vocabulary: avoid jargon, use simple language, short descriptive sentences.

Note. DSM = Diagnostic and Statistical Manual of Mental Disorders; DSM–IV = DSM (4th ed.).

and relatively unique contribution to assessment (see chaps. 5, 6, 7, and 8, this volume), and clinical applications are premised on research literature that has been typically test/method specific.

Table 1.3 outlines a stepwise process premised on relationship quality and incorporating cultural information relevant for the interpretive statements contained in a psychological report and identified by number as ingredients. A psychological report for a multicultural client should be prepared from a representative and relatively complete data set that can provide sufficient information for accurate scoring and subsequent interpretation of scores. Adequate data can only be provided within the context of a trusting relationship (Number 1 checklist ingredient) that includes credible examiner behavior demonstrated in professional social etiquette throughout the entire assessment process. This data set must be examined subsequently by the examiner within a context of culture-specific knowledge adequate in breadth and depth for the particular assessment objectives (Number 2 checklist ingredient). Test data and cultural information resources are used in interpretation statements that specifically cite data descriptively relevant to personality and psychopathology (Number 3 checklist ingredient). The adequacy of these interpretations may be suggested by specific examiner questions evaluating report adequacy and completeness. Because examiner or instrument bias can dramatically affect the high-stakes nature of multicultural assessment, both potential confounds and interactions within a context of cultural knowledge should be considered (Number 4 checklist ingredient). Finally, a summary statement of report adequacy (Number 5 checklist ingredient) should contain both recommendations to the client for interventions and other relevant activities as well as a clear presentation of possible limitations of tests, methods, and examiner knowledge or experience. Finally, the report should be examined for formal characteristics including length, style, organization, and readability (Number 6 checklist ingredient) to ensure that the narrative employs everyday language that can be understood, examined, and evaluated easily by the client.

Cultural Differences
in Belief Systems

Chapter 1 (this volume) described standard and multicultural assessment and presented a psychological-psychometric context for multicultural assessment. This chapter provides an overview of cultural differences inherent in the self-presentations of multicultural clients that affect their responses to standard tests. An understanding of cultural differences embodied in worldview is necessary for the development of multicultural assessment competencies. Ethnic/racial group identities and individual cultural identities may be distinguished within worldviews. Group identity is an immutable life circumstance, whereas individual cultural identity or the cultural self is susceptible to modification by acculturation status and/or racial identity development. An examination of ethnic/racial group identities as well as individual identity embodied in the cultural self is essential for understanding the impact of several overarching belief systems on assessment instruments and service delivery.

I examine mind–body relationship (mind–body dualism vs. physical monism), values, spirituality/religion, health–illness, individualism–collectivism, and locus of control and locus of responsibility in this chapter. These belief systems illustrate the potential magnitude of differences between multicultural clients and their clinicians of predominantly Euro-American origins and, in addition, provide a framework for the kinds of new learning, information acquisition, and behavioral accommodations that contribute to interpretation of assessment data from multicultural clients.

WORLDVIEW

For many years, the overarching importance of worldview has been acknowledged as a framework encompassing the collective wisdom necessary for structuring reality and creating a meaningful context for life experiences that fosters survival and adaptation (e.g., Kearney, 1975). Figure 2.1 provides an elaboration of worldview derived from an earlier description for assessors (see Dana, 1993, p. 10). Group identity, or ethnicity/race, is separated from individual identity, or cultural self within a context delineating values and major beliefs in specific language contexts

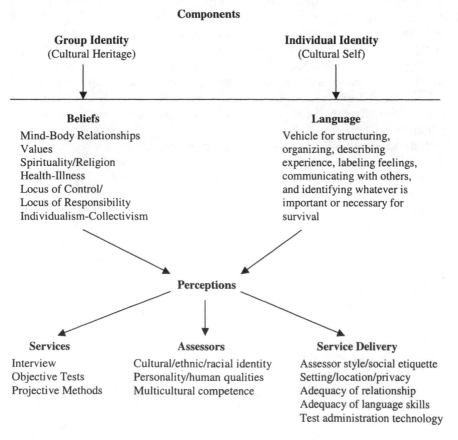

FIG. 2.1. Worldview components and perceptions of assessors and assessment services. *Note.* From *Multicultural Assessment Perspectives for Professional Psychology* (p. 10), by R. H. Dana, 1993, Boston: Allyn & Bacon. Copyright 1993 by Allyn & Bacon. Adapted with permission.

that structure the perceptions of service providers, services, and service delivery of five major cultural/racial groups in the United States. This somewhat artificial separation occurs because an individual cultural self is an adaptation constructed by the person's position within a culture of origin as well as by her or his acculturation status or racial identity status in the United States. Group identity, or ethnicity, evolves from history, cultural heritage, and a sense of location within a particular geographic environment.

The term *ethnicity* appeared during the early 1930s (Glazer & Moynihan, 1976) to describe prideful belongingness to a particular group or nation with a common cultural background (Betancourt & López, 1993). Ethnicity serves as a focus for group identity; the shared characteristics of group identity are called *culture*. Group identity is composed of values, beliefs, and language that structure, organize, and orchestrate expressions of emotions, cognitions, and behaviors, including those aggregations of symptoms described within each culture/society as psychopathologies. Both group and individual identities should be assessed for individuals due to the heterogeneity of each ethnic/racial/cultural population. Self-acknowledged group identity typically remains relatively constant over time, although individual cultural identity changes over time and by generation.

Individual identity is composed of personality and the cultural self. This self is the locus of a personal identity encoded into behaviors, emotions, and cognitions. Personal characteristics, life experiences, and socio-economic status (SES) contribute to dimensions of the self as well as to the variety of contents (including their organization, relative importance, extent of control) and boundaries of the cultural self (Dana, 1998b). Depending on whether or not a person is from an individualist or collectivist society, the contents of the self may include few or many other persons in designated relationships (e.g., family, extended family, significant others, and individuals in the immediate or larger community), the community as an entity. In addition, animals, plants, and natural and supernatural forces related to spiritual dimensions may occupy a significant and prominent position within the cultural self. The boundaries of this self may be rigid, exclusionary, or permeable and susceptible to expansion and dilation to become more inclusive. The composition of the cultural self varies in the number, kind, range, and importance accorded to various elements.

For example, the African American cultural self may include the individual as well as extended family, frequently with an informal network of other persons in addition. Originally, in Africa, there were linkages within the cultural self to ancestors, nature, a spirit world, and the universe; a residual of this cultural self is found in individual spirituality and in survival of an oral tradition providing interconnectedness among persons and continuity over time within churches. Traditional Native Americans and Alaska Natives have an internalized self that has fluid boundaries containing family, community, and tribal components with linkages to a spirit world and to natural worlds. Asian Americans, although affected by acculturation differences over time and across ethnic groups, have a cultural self with family preeminence over the individual that is expressed by priorities and obligations (e.g., filial piety). Hispanic/Latino Americans have an extended concept of cultural self that includes family (e.g., *la familia*) and for some persons also includes the natural and spirit worlds. Euro-Americans often have a sense of ethnicity that is poorly formed, acknowledged, or understood. The cultural self consists primarily of the individual, possessions, and power. A more extended cultural self for many Euro-American women also includes children. For an expanded discussion of identity and the cultural self for these groups, see Dana (1993, 1998b).

The cultural self-system is instrumental in determining response sets, acceptable topics for communication within the assessment context, as well as nonverbal behaviors. Unfortunately, there are no available measures explicitly delineating the cultural self, although there is a large literature on the self as well as a conspicuous number of self-concept measures for Euro-Americans (Wylie, 1989). Nonetheless, moderator measures of worldview and individualized and collectivist selves can provide information necessary for a description of the cultural self.

Consistent with an individualist self is an unquestioning belief in the necessity to use personal control artifacts of money, power, and recognition to achieve an orderly world and comfortable self-definition (Sampson, 1985). An individualized locus for the cultural self involves separation from others by rigid boundaries containing a private, goal oriented, and self-actualizing agenda. Self-evaluation occurs by reflected appraisal as validated by self-expression. This individualism is characteristic of many predominantly White persons in the United States, especially males and psychologists (Wallach & Wallach, 1983). However, it is important to note that many women display cooperative behaviors and admit their children as part of the self (Jensen, McGhie, & Jensen, 1991) and that there are also within-group differences in individualism that also occur among males in the United States (Lykes, 1985).

An interdependent or collectivist locus for the self is characterized by flexible boundaries for personhood that include others and stimulate awareness and activities designed to realize the goals and foster the well-being of others. Self-definition occurs as a consequence of relationships in specified contexts and a continuous adaptation of the self in the interests of harmony with others. Comparisons have been made between self-contained or individualist and ensembled or collectivist selves predicated

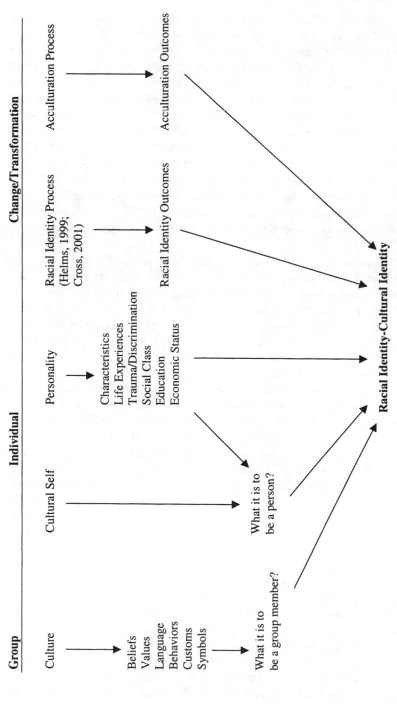

FIG. 2.2. Group, individual, and change/transformation sources of identity formation. *Note.* From *Understanding Cultural Identity in Intervention and Assessment* (p. 18), by R. H. Dana, 1998e, Thousand Oaks, CA: Sage. Copyright 1998 by Sage. Adapted with permission.

on interconnectedness among persons (Marcus & Kitayama, 1991; Sampson, 1988).

Figure 2.2 provides a second conceptualization of worldview components as related to identity formation among individuals. This conceptualization also separates group identity from individual identity and is focused on changes or transformations due to acculturation or development of racial identity. All ethnic minority groups in the United States have acknowledged cultural identity as essential for their self-definitions as individuals. In addition, many African Americans also affirm racial identity as well because "race matters" in the United States (Carter, 1995). Figure 2.2 illustrates both the complexity and change processes occurring in the development of individual cultural/racial identities. Figure 2.2 attempts to integrate group and individual identity components with the alternations occurring as a consequence of acculturation status or racial identity stage development.

A separation of group characteristics in this figure from the cultural self highlights a general problem for all assessors of multicultural clients. The comparative research literature typically has used group differences often derived from incomplete, partial, inexact, and asymmetrical group descriptions as a frame of reference for assessment of individuals. Using nomothetic information to answer idiographic questions has been described as the therapist's dilemma (Levine, Sandeen, & Murphy, 1992) and results in homogenizing all members of each ethnic/racial group by standard tests. A major task of this book is to emphasize the complexity of individual differences in cultural/racial identity. This complexity can only be addressed by assessment reports prepared with the explicit assumption that not only is culture central to personality psychopathology but that specific descriptions of the individual's cultural self or cultural identity are always necessary. Only in this manner can psychological reports achieve their primary purposes of accurate diagnosis, responsible recommendations for subsequent interventions, and provide coherent feedback for clients.

Implications for Assessors

Ibrahim (1985) was among the first psychologists to recognize that acceptance of mental health services by clients was dependent on a convergence, or reasonable overlap, between clinician and client worldviews. When worldviews clash, mental health services, including assessment, cannot be understood as meaningful, relevant to presenting circumstances, or potentially beneficial. A recent chapter by Ibrahim, Roysircar-Sodowsky, and Ohnishi (2001) concluded that "worldview interacts with all client variables and, consequently, must be addressed in the conceptualization of diagnosis, presenting problems, and treatment" (p. 429). The Ibrahim et al. (2001) chapter supplements an earlier review (Dana, 1993) by summarizing empirical studies on worldview and value orientations relevant to individual cultural identity and cultural self and includes recent findings on college students and professional persons from many additional countries as well as from a variety of ethnic groups in the United States. The international samples in these studies have included a number of African and Afro-Caribbean countries as well as persons from Brazil, Central America, China, Hong Kong, Japan, Singapore, and Taiwan.

Euro-American professional psychologists have minimized the magnitude of worldview differences and the effects of these differences on responses to their assessment tools and style of assessment practice. During the assessment process, an assessor must have in-depth background knowledge of a client's culture of origin as well as current acculturation status information to understand the cultural self. My assumption for clinical practice, illustrated in the development of culture specific intervention models for Asian American and Hispanic/Latino clients (Dana, 1998e) was to begin with as much knowledge concerning the culture of origin or group ethnic identity as can be acquired prior to assessing an individual's cultural identity. For African Americans who may be actively engaged in discovery, exploration, or consolidation of racial identity, cultural identity may be a secondary concern to be described and evaluated with available instruments.

Group and individual client identifications can affect every step in the assessment process. Misunderstandings of assessment objectives, directions, tools, and limitations interact with client feelings of acceptance or rejection of test materials; the assessor ultimately facilitates compliance or noncompliance with specific questions, tasks, and procedures. Client beliefs, values, and language fluency structure a cultural reality that determines perceptions of assessors, assessment services, and credible social etiquette that provides a comfortable structure for rapport during the entire process. Subsequent chapters illustrate the manner in which cultural issues impact the amount and quality of elicited data, the accuracy of subsequent interpretations, as well as the use of feedback, including contents and language, with the client and/or family members.

BELIEF SYSTEMS

Client systems of beliefs and values provide a structure for determining the limits and contents of appropriate and acceptable behaviors for both client and clinician. These systems articulate core differences between ethnic/racial groups that structure their attitudes toward personality assessment per se, invoke an immediate approach to particular tests/methods, and define acceptable topics for communication within an assessment context. These systems also predetermine some portion of the content of subsequent test responses including response sets as well as nonverbal behaviors. Moreover, they provide a context for development of a cultural self with boundaries, the relative importance of particular contents, an organizational structure, and qualitative consciousness dimensions.

Examples of psychological reports in subsequent chapters suggest that cultural belief system components are not only inseparable and interrelated but constitute essential and individualized ingredients of the cultural self. Although these systems have cultural specificity, they also overlap and are shared to an extent across non-Western societies. Acculturation results in alterations and modifications, especially when mainstream Euro-American and traditional beliefs and values are juxtaposed. Belief switching may often occur, particularly with Native Americans and Alaska Natives, to permit access and subsequent utilization of either mainstream or indigenous mental health services (e.g., Fuchs & Bashshur, 1975). Beliefs and values thus constitute relevant information that should be available to clinicians prior to selection and administration of imposed etic or emic tests.

Mind–Body Dualism

Mind–body dualism is part and parcel of an acquired Euro-American consciousness in which the development and internalization of a "critical observer" or "meta-self" (Kleinman, 1988) functions to interfere with a "total absorption in lived experiences" (p. 50). Euro-American mind–body dualism is responsible for a separation of events with presumed mental and physical origins (Lewis-Fernandez & Kleinman, 1994). As a consequence, in Lewis-Fernandez and Kleinman's (1994) words, "the dualistic professional model systematically misinterprets the nondualistic cultural experience of patients as reflecting lack of introspection . . . and forces a differentiation between psychological and somatic experiences where none exists" (p. 67). This distinction between mind and body permits *DSM* identification of psychopathologies consisting of organic disorders experienced with psychological distress or psychological problems presenting with somatic components.

Standard assessment instruments are also dualistic because they assume an internalized psychological locus for personal problems as exposed by symbolism in inkblot responses, direct representation without awareness in stories to TAT cards, or inferred from response choices in self-report instruments such as the MMPI/MMPI–2. Clients who do not share the mind–body dualism characteristic of mainstream American society often experience difficulty understanding an assessment rationale predicated on the existence and credibility of psychological problems and internalized sources of distress.

Groups with non-European origins, such as African Americans, have retained human potentials for a culturally conditioned consciousness that differs from so-called normal or Western consciousness. A culturally conditioned or altered consciousness is evidenced by sharply focused attention, an immediate and unreflective responsiveness to crisis, and enhanced openness to spiritual contents (Bell, 1982; McGee & Clark, 1974). The more limited accessibility of mind–body unity resulting from split consciousness "divested the Western self of the literalness of bodily metaphors for intimate personal distress as well as access to gods, ghosts, and ancestral spirits" (Dana, 1998e, p. 31). This rupture of human consciousness resulted in the development of a psychological metalanguage to provide cognitive distance from immediate experiences and a person-centered self with rigid boundaries that is prone to Western culture bound personality disorders.

Values

Values are beliefs referring to desirable goals/modes of conduct, transcending particular actions/situations, providing selection/evaluation standards, and occurring in hierarchies of relative importance (Schwartz & Bilsky, 1987). Problems of cross-cultural measurement, relations to individual and cultural levels of analysis, and national differences in value priorities have been carefully described and examined (Smith & Schwartz, 1997). Value dimensions have been examined generally using structured questionnaires except in studies of indigenous psychologies (Kim & Berry, 1993). The values orientations model (Kluckhohn, 1960; Kluckhohn & Strodtbeck, 1961) presents common human problems requiring differential solutions in five aspects of life: dimensions of human nature (good, evil, mixed), person–nature relations (subjugation to nature, harmony with nature, mastery over nature), time sense (past, present, future), activity (being, being in becoming, doing), and social relations (lineal, collateral, individualistic).

Carter (1991) summarized these cultural value orientations for various cultural/racial groups and found striking group differences and influences from social class, generation, gender, and psychological (including racial identity developmental status) as well as other demographic differences. Measurement of these value orientations may be accomplished using the Scale to Assess World Views (SAWV; Ibrahim & Kahn, 1987) as a moderator variable.

Spirituality

In cultures that reject mind–body dualism, belief systems pervasively interconnect and interrelate, mind, body, and spirit synergistically within a holistic perspective (Fukuyama & Sevig, 1999). These beliefs function as changing, fluxing "forces in motion" within the self that serve to modulate ingredients and attenuate resilience and permeability of the self boundary. Recent publications have been criticized for compartmentalizing spirituality and multiculturalism (Ponterotto & Sabnani, 1989); nonetheless, by adding passion, advocacy, and action in the interests of social justice to personal awareness, knowledge, and skills, spirituality can be integrated into multicultural competencies. These infusions of spirituality add dimensions of an enlarging humanity to the individual that includes the heart as well as the head and functions to actively repudiate the legacy of oppression. Standard assessment has been focused almost exclusively on detection of psychopathology rather than amplification of positive personality resources that evidence capacity for change, self-development, as well as an individualized and crescive humanity within a community context.

Constructs suggestive of positive personality resources examined carefully by many psychologists include resiliency, coping skills, defenses, integration, well-being, and sense of coherence, for examples. These separate personality resources are just beginning to be scrutinized as potential components of an overarching construct and examined with construct validation methodology (e.g., Viglione, 2002). Moreover, research in this area has been focused almost exclusively on predominantly White college students, although recent discussions of positive personality resources inherent in other cultural populations have emphasized spiritual resources (e.g., Lightsley & Christopher, 1997; McCubbin, Thompson, Thompson, & Fromer, 1998). To date there has been no appreciable impact of these research ideas on scoring and interpretation of standard assessment instruments probably as a consequence of the prevailing professional focus on psychopathology and clinical diagnosis rather than personality description.

In assessment data, spirituality may be evidenced by creativity, enhanced capacity for intimacy, detachment permitting intermittent holding on and letting go, as well as through love and compassion for other persons. These characteristics suggest that scoring categories for standard assessment instruments (e.g., Rorschach, TAT) are necessary to describe a healthy cultural self with capacity for change, growth, elaboration of internal components, and substantive enlargement within semipermeable boundaries. Standard tests often distort or pathologize such evidences of spirituality simply because many mainstream Americans of European origins have a cultural self that is devoid of these internal characteristics with boundaries that constitute relatively permanent and rigid containers for the person and his or her personal attributes. Unwarranted assumptions have been made that this restricted cultural self is universal as a result of congruence with many Euro-American personality theories and conformity with expectations for absence of *DSM* psychopathology. Test responses representing an enlarged self may appear infrequently in normative populations and occur as accompaniments of high ego development levels or as a consequence of cultural differences. These responses may be susceptible to interpretation as personality deficits or psychopathology indicators rather than potential resources indicative of strength and positive assets.

It should be noted that there are now at least seven instruments for assessing spirituality (Stanard, Sandhu, & Painter, 2000). Analysis of the contents of these instruments, however, suggests a prevailing Judeo-Christian perspective and an absence of cross-cultural relevance.

Health–Illness Beliefs

Causal beliefs for Euro-Americans include health as absence of illness and illness as disease with organic and psychological origins. Many other groups, however, believe that illness may be caused by curses, demons, gods, ghosts, punishment for sins, spirits, the supernatural, taboo violation, and witchcraft (Narikiyo & Kameoka, 1992). Because beliefs in causality and credible curative procedures are linked, it is essential to have knowledge of beliefs that are relevant to causes of distress or symptomatology. For example, a case history of a 16-year-old Taiwanese adolescent with bizarre behaviors described ghosts, fright, poor luck, retribution by ancestors, and sorcerer malice as possible causal agents that led to a variety of subsequent interventions (Harrell, 1991).

With increasing acculturation and bicultural or marginal identity status, individuals are often able to acknowledge personal problems and thereby accept assessment that is focused on Western causal explanations for distress. However, due to extreme within-group acculturation differences in all cultural/racial populations, it is imperative to identify and understand cultural orientation status prior to interpretation of standard assessment instruments. Only by careful attention to acculturation information can the clinician evaluate the extent to which traditional culture impacts the assessment data.

Some examples suggest expectations for causal beliefs in origins of distress among different cultural populations. Traditional sub-Saharan Africans believed that inseparable, interchangeable, physical or mental components of distress represented a loss of spiritual-societal commitment to harmony within a self that was composed of others, nature, the spirit world, and the universe (Dana, 1993, 1998e). Although this conception of health is no longer intact in the United States, some Africentric African Americans believe that restoration of individual harmony is a family concern and a community responsibility within culture-specific programs (Akutsu, Snowden & Organista, 1996). Standard assessment would not be acceptable to many of these individuals, particularly if proffered by White assessors, whereas the use of emic measures by African American professionals would have considerably more credibility (see Jones, 1996; Morris, 2000). Rural Southern Black members of fundamentalist religions believe fate and God have control over their health status (Berkuis, Cook, Holt, & Scott-Lennox, 1995) and may be motivated to seek help from folk healers or in alternative settings (Cheung & Snowden, 1990).

Native Americans and Alaska Natives conceive of health–illness as a continuous cycle of wellness–unwellness or harmony–disharmony within the mind, body, and spirit of a person (Dana, 1993, 1998e). Unwellness has natural origins in violations of sacred tribal taboos; unnatural origins include witchcraft. Wellness is fostered and sponsored by spirit helpers, protective objects, isolation of the self, healing rituals, medicine people, and employment of a natural support system.

Chinese, Chinese Americans, and other Asians construe mental illness as multifaceted and may accept moral, religious, physiological, psychological, social, and genetic explanations. For a Chinese example, yin–yang, a balance of force in nature, provides a systematized account of differences and changes (e.g., positive–negative, active–passive, strong–weak, light–dark, warm–cold, full–empty). Harmony in gender roles, psychosocial development, and psychological functioning is required for normalcy. A lack of harmony, or yin–yang imbalance, results in dysfunction or illness. Similarly, physiological excess of any kind, including exhaustion, is a precursor of illness. A lack of cultural experience historically in labeling, describing, and communicating affect has led to difficulties in expression of emotion. Correct and proper social behavior also required control and/ or denial of emotion, particularly in public settings, to avoid disrupting familial and social relations. Simultaneously, there was training in "listening" to the body, and transforming subjective discomfort into descriptions of internal bodily functions can result in somatization and reporting physical symptomatology (Saner-Yi & Saner-Yu, 1985).

Traditional Hispanics believe in a balance with God and harmony or tranquility with family, others, and the proprieties of the Catholic Church (Weclew, 1975), although folk beliefs may also remain relatively intact, particularly among recent Mexican American and Puerto Rican immigrants. For example, many Puerto Ricans believe that individuals are vulnerable to external influences from invasive spirits and the enmity of others, whereas minor and temporary sickness is attributed to nerves and represents disordered emotions embedded in one area of personal experience (Koss-Chioino, 1989). Similarly, an Afro-Cuban belief system ascribes disease to object intrusion as a consequence of magic, soul loss, spirit intrusion, and anger of specific gods (Sandoval, 1977). Most Hispanics believe that minor emotional problems are to be endured or solved without help from friends or relatives. Effective psychological assessment should recognize and describe self-control as well as avenues toward personal responsibility using personal strengths and personality resources.

Individualism–Collectivism

The separate constructs of individualism and collectivism have been carefully described, summarized, and researched as an individualism–collectivism dimension by Triandis (1995, 1990). In Triandis' (1995) words, "Tendencies toward individualism and collectivism exist within every individual and in every society. Most people start by being collectivists, attached to their families. They become detached from them in different degrees and learn to be detached from collectives in different situations" (p. xiii). Thus, individualism–collectivism is an ostensible universal or etic worldview dimension that always has culture specific or emic specification of considerable interest for assessors. The use of moderators to provide descriptive information was suggested by Triandis (1995) and is endorsed in chapter 5 (this volume) as an essential ingredient in cross-cultural assessment for this purpose.

Locus of Control and Locus of Responsibility

From Rotter's (1954) social learning theory, he developed the locus of control (LC) Scale (Rotter, 1966) to delineate two major psychological orientations describing control of reinforcements or outcomes either by the self or by others and unpredictably. Internal control (IC), or personal control as a consequence of behaviors or personal characteristics, was differentiated from external control (EC) and reliance instead on chance, luck, or fate. Rotter (1966) recognized the usefulness of his scale for conceptualization of social problems as well as recognition of individual feelings of powerlessness.

The LC Scale, however, does not systematically vary agents of action, consequences, outcomes, and situations (Munroe, 1979). Nonetheless, the LC scale has generated well over 4,000 studies (Marks, 1998) including documentation that the meanings of LC items differ among cultural groups as well as lower SES and other demographic variables. For examples, as African American racial identity increases and develops, so does IC (Martin & Hall, 1992). For Japanese Americans and other Asian Americans, IC increases by generation (Padilla, Wagatsuma, & Lindholm, 1985; Park & Harrison, 1995). EC often remains as "cultural fatalism" for Hispanics (Comas-Diaz, 1993), as "luck" for Chinese Americans (Wong & Piran, 1995), and "cosmic order" for Asian Indians (Kumar, 1986). Native Americans may have both external personal control and internal group or societal control (Trimble & Richardson, 1983).

Sue (1978) employed an individual system blame factor (Gurin, Gurin, Lao, & Beattie, 1969) to describe locus of responsibility (LR) and then plotted LC and LR graphically. The four quadrants of this graph were (a) IC and internal responsibility (IC–IR), (b) IC and external responsibility (IC–ER), (c) EC–ER, and (d) EC–IR. Each of these quadrants provided a cluster of beliefs related to individual efficacy. IC–IR persons are characterized by belief in personal power for active problem solving and responsibility for one's own actions. Multicultural EC–IR persons, however, may blame themselves and passively accept second-class social status. EC–ER persons blame the social system and feel powerless to initiate change. IC–ER persons believe they can endure and ultimately prevail when confronted by strong environmental pressures for failure.

Sue's (1978) conceptualization recognizes that counseling and psychotherapy practices in the United States are primarily derived from an IC–IR perspective, a commentary and criticism that also applies to assessment. Furthermore, the recommendation for use "as an aid to understanding possible psychological dynamics of a culturally different client" (Sue, 1978, p. 461) is relevant not only for selection of culturally appropriate interventions but suggests a need for empirical evidence with regard to matching specific cultural competencies with individuals in LC–LR quadrants.

Moreover, clinicians and clients often differ in their LC beliefs, and these differences at termination of therapy are associated with negative outcomes (Foon, 1985). Differences in these beliefs may also be relevant for outcomes of assessment services because providers of Euro-American origin typically believe that IC and IR, derived largely from Judeo-Christian teachings (Sampson, 2000), are desirable, beneficial, and assumed to be universal. Rotter (1966) cautioned practitioners to avoid assuming that IC and EC were positive and negative characteristics, respectively. However, professional psychologists have not altered their assumptions and continue to minimize cultural differences. As a consequence, more routine use of LC–LR moderator data is desirable, and assessment-relevant, research–derived LC-LR information would be helpful.

Moderator information on culture-specific LC and LR styles is thus obligatory for assessment practice. The Multidimensional Health Locus of Control instrument (Wallston, Wallston, & deVellis, 1978) separates control by powerful others and chance from IC and has been used with multicultural populations (e.g., Stein, Smith, & Wallston, 1984; Tait, De-Good, & Carron, 1982). Macaranas-Sittler (1986) developed an LR scale that can be employed with the Rotter (1966) LC Scale as moderators informing cultural formulations and identity conceptualizations for multicultural assessment and clinical diagnosis.

3

Assessment Bias
and Cultural Competence

Bias, at the most abstract level, is related to what Hall (1997) called "cultural malpractice," an increasing failure of professional psychology to be socially relevant. Institutionalized bias in professional psychology results from continued affirmation of a Eurocentric worldview expressed in research procedures minimizing the importance of cultural differences and treating culture as a distal rather than a proximal variable. Remediation for cultural/racial/ethnic bias must be systemic and occur initially in research demonstrations and standards. The availability of consensual research standards for major ethnic minority populations provides a formal means to reduce bias in present and future research (Council of National Psychological Associations for the Advancement of Ethnic Minority Interests [CNPAAEMI], 2000). The juxtaposition of bias and competence begins with descriptions of multicultural research technology for bias reduction. I describe several independent sets of existing research guidelines for multicultural populations in this chapter.

Recognizing bias in research and debate concerning the role of ethical codes as mandates for bias reduction preceded awareness that minimizing bias in professional training was an ethical responsibility. In professional psychology, an awareness of the pervasiveness of bias and advocacy for cultural awareness and cultural proficiency exists primarily but not exclusively in the area of counseling psychology. In a context of developing interventions for ethnic minority populations during the 1980s, this advocacy resulted in identification of constructs representing awareness, knowledge, and skill components of multicultural competence subsequently operationalized in a number of self-report instruments. A

49

continuing examination of these multicultural competence constructs and their derivative instruments is necessary as one approach to the design and evaluation of multicultural competency training in professional psychology. This training is designed to facilitate unqualified acceptance by students of culturally different persons. Competent multicultural assessment training is part and parcel of multicultural competency and includes the awareness, knowledge, and skill components.

In this chapter, I introduce and precede generic competency guidelines with a review of available multicultural assessment guidelines as preparation for a detailed procedural inventory and discussion of components believed to be essential for multicultural assessment practice described in chapter 4 (this volume).

CULTURAL MALPRACTICE

Cultural malpractice is a harsh term, but it serves to focus attention on historic and current inequities in psychological services available for multicultural populations. Many training programs omit multicultural assessment and intervention from serious consideration and thereby foster what Kazarian and Evans (1998) called "cultural negligence." Rather than elaborate these pejorative labels, I describe cultural competence deficits in professional psychology research as prefatory to constructive suggestions for remediation in research and assessment training.

Most professional psychologists have simply maintained the status quo by failure to seriously consider culture as central to research, training, and practice (Brown, 1997; Dana, 1998e; Strickland, 2000). For example, applied psychology journals as recently as 1993 through 1997 have failed to report ethnicity in published research studies or represented ethnicity inadequately (Case & Smith, 2000). Omission and distortion of ethnicity was further examined in articles appearing in three major clinical and counseling journals during a 30-year period (Beutler, Brown, Crothers, Booker, & Seabrook, 1996). Race and ethnicity (as well as sex, gender, age, and maturity) were used as demographic referents in the absence of empirical or conceptual clarity. Beutler et al. (1996) concluded by recommending that editorial standards require authors to acknowledge these terms as constructs requiring operational definitions and discussion of their measurement status during the research process and subsequent reporting of results. Nilsson et al. (2003) examined *Professional Psychology: Research and Practice* between 1990 and 2000 and found "a lack of focus on specific cultural groups" (p. 611) as well as a continuing omission of race/ethnicity demographics affecting the generalizability of these clinical studies. Munley et al. (2002) identified many of these omissions in empirical articles contained in American Psychological Association journals during 1999. Descriptions of personal identity dimensions of age, gender, education, geographic location, and race/ethnicity were generally reported. However, dimensions of citizenship, employment, income, language, marital status, military experience, occupation, physical disability, sexual orientation, social class, and religion were seldom reported. Incomplete descriptions limit understanding of research participants, leading to over-generalizations potentially affecting interpretations, conclusions, and applications of research findings. Another study of journal practices (DeLeon & VandenBos, 2000) found that 29% and 26.8% of *Professional Psychology: Research and Practice* articles during 1989 through 1995 and 1995 through 2000, respectively, were devoted to "training and education," whereas only 5.8% and 4.3%, respectively, had "ethnicity/diversity" content in spite of participation by ethnic minority psychologists on their editorial board (14.7%) and as ad hoc reviewers (8.4%).

Hall and Maramba (2003) described differences between the citation impact of empirical articles in international cross-cultural (Euro-American) and U.S. ethnic minority publications (non-Euro-American origins) published between 1993 and 1999. Cultural diversity was "virtually invisible" in first-tier journals due to a historic separation between these two areas of psychology as well as to conservative procedures employed by reviewers who have not conducted research on cross-cultural and ethnic minority issues. Given this history of research inadequacies and absence of relevant publication standards, it is not surprising that a majority of the preponderantly Euro-American professional psychologists surveyed in 1990 felt that their training inadequately prepared them to provide competent services for their multicultural clients (Allison, Crawford, Echemendia, Robinson, & Knepp, 1994; Allison, Echemendia, Crawford, & Robinson, 1996).

Multicultural Ethics and Current Ethical Codes

Ethical multicultural practice is predicated on awareness of many sources of potential bias in providing psychological services (Keitel, Kopala, & Adamson, 1995) as well as the necessity for understanding a client within a cultural context to improve the accuracy and usefulness of personality or psychopathology assessment (Pope & Vasquez, 1991). The 1973 Vail (Colorado) psychology training conference endorsed the development of cross-cultural counseling competence guidelines (Ivey & Leppaluoto, 1975). Reviewing this early history, Burn (1992) emphasized that training must acknowledge counselor worldview biases and inherent power differentials as potentially negative influences on client self-determination and cultural autonomy. The contrast between the abstract nature of ethical standards and their practical applications has been considered tantamount to a crisis within psychology (Pedersen & Marsella, 1982) that has not abated over time and is largely denied or ignored by a substantial portion of professional psychologists.

Historically, ethical codes (e.g., American Counseling Association, 1995; American Psychological Association, 1992) have favored a dominant culture perspective evidenced by incorporating implicit cultural biases including preference for individualism; avoidance of dual relationships; the importance of privacy; as well as positivist, empirical, and linear assumptions (Pedersen, 1997). Pedersen (2002) also believed that "ethical guidelines need to be interpreted in light of each situation and cultural context. Clients or counselors from different cultural backgrounds might follow the same ethical guidelines in identical situations by displaying different behaviors" (p. 13). The 1992 American Psychological Association code did not recognize an obligation for explicit assessment guidelines to develop cultural knowledge and skills relevant for multicultural practice (see Dana, 1994).

However, the new ethics code (American Psychological Association, 2002) represents a conservative revision and standards described as "fair" (Knapp & VandeCreek, 2003, p. 301). This code embraces several assessment subsections representing substantial changes that are relevant for multicultural practice. First, instruments of established reliability and validity for particular populations are now required. However, because these data frequently do not exist, or available data is flawed or incomplete, a discussion of test limitations is required in psychological reports. Second, test interpretation must also consider linguistic and cultural differences. For example, the adequacy of second-language skills can be assessed, although evaluation rarely occurs. Finally, adaptations of standard tests derived from cultural knowledge and clinical judgment are now recognized, although no consensually accepted, research-derived basis exists to date to provide standards for adaptations. In other words, although practice procedures are ultimately predicated on research-derived knowledge as a basis for standards, existing research is flawed and incomplete. Most of this research has been accomplished without sufficient understanding or application of the recent consensus on multicultural research standards (CNPAAEMI, 2000). The dilemma here is that the new American Psychological Association ethical code aspires to provide standards by recognizing the necessity for responsible adaptations of standard instruments and assessment procedures. Beutler, Crago, and Arizmendi (1986) defined clinical competency as adherence to procedures relevant to identified standards. Following this definition, the existence of multicultural research standards as well as the recent guidelines including assessment (American Psychological Association, 2003) reinforce and undergird the emerging consensus for multicultural assessment competency.

The chapters in this book devoted to standard tests—MMPI–2, Rorschach, and TAT—represent attempts to modify practice for multicultural populations using these standards tests including service delivery styles and interpretation procedures as a basis for eventual compliance with the documentation required to identify standards in Section 9.02b of the revised American Psychological Association (2002) ethical code.

The ethical standards of the American Psychological Association also reflect managed mental health care cost-cutting practices resulting in undertreatment; reduced quality/appropriateness of existing treatments; and increased risk for low income, limited education, ethnic minority, and non-English-speaking populations (La Roche & Turner, 2002). These populations increasingly experience reduced access and culturally insensitive treatments coupled with limited awareness of relevant and necessary treatment-relevant information that is also unavailable to providers. In the words of LaRoche and Turner (2002), "Future revisions of the ethics code might benefit from a statement about the historical context in which the ethical dilemmas . . . have emerged. By embedding these ethical conflicts within their socioeconomic and cultural contexts, the competing demands of individualism versus compassion might more easily be identified" (p. 196). Due to ignorance of the magnitude of differences among cultural perspectives and their complexity, practitioners may oversimplify ethical problems. Uncertainty then accompanies their decisions or actions due to "conflicting cultural values, unfamiliar behaviors and idioms, and role expectations that differ between themselves and their clients" (Ridley, Liddle, Hill, & Li, 2001). An oversimplification of cultural perspectives can thus also contribute to unintentional racism (Ridley, 1995).

As a remedy for deficiencies and omissions in ethical codes, Ridley et al. (2001) suggested that ethical decision making first requires knowledge of practitioners' ethical perspectives with subsequent individual self-identification of their own beliefs and learning to articulate these perspectives in professional settings. A prescriptive version of their model contains processes/methods for ethical consideration of cultural data, and resolution of cultural conflicts uses stages/steps of critical reflection and creative problem solving. Ethical decision making entry points are provided for avoiding a potential ethical problem and for an ethical problem that has already occurred. Case examples were included by Ridley et al. (2001) to illustrate application of their model.

BIAS REMEDIATION

Recognized sources of assessment bias (see Dana, 1998c, 1998e, 2000c, 2001b) were identified in Table 1.1. In this chapter, I introduce remediation strategies for these sources of bias by marshalling evidence for the continued presence of bias in frequent omission of cultural competence training, particularly in assessment courses, including assessor bias, deficient service delivery social etiquette, inadequate normative data, minimal cultural equivalence research evidence, and limited *DSM–IV* applicability to multicultural populations.

A major source of bias among assessors occurs as a consequence of inadequate training to provide services for multicultural client populations. Assessor bias may be observed in racism, prejudice, stereotyping, and ethnocentrism. Blatant racism or prejudice is rare among professional psychologists and usually is denied on confrontation. A recent example in my experience occurred when a White psychologist employed by an agency serving an 80% non-White client population used indirect, research-specific arguments to prevent use of cultural formulations for *DSM–IV* diagnoses with multicultural clients in a public agency, particularly Mexican Americans and other Latinos. At the time, this event was not recognized as racist in motivation, although later, several employees independently identified other discriminatory behaviors, and unrelated conflicts with management led to dismissal of the psychologist.

In mental health service delivery to Euro-Americans, a social etiquette modeled from medical practice is often impersonal, formal, and task oriented. Although this style may be uncomfortable for some individuals of Euro-American origins, it is unacceptable to many persons with other cultural origins. Students and professional assessors serving multicultural populations must learn culture-specific service delivery behaviors as well as credible usage of affect to foster sufficient task orientation for gathering reliable data from interviews and standard tests (see chap. 4, this volume, for details).

Standard tests have been constructed and norms have been developed and standardized primarily on middle-class, White persons of Euro-American origins. These tests have excluded, underrepresented, or failed to match persons of color on relevant demographic variables. Nonetheless, these imposed etic tests have been applied to all persons in the United States and exported worldwide as if they were genuine etics or universal in applications rather than Euro-American emics (Dana, 2000d). Cross-cultural equivalence of these tests in language (translation), constructs, and format is necessary and largely unknown, as indicated in chapter 1 (this volume) and as I describe in chapters 6, 7, 8 (this volume), and have been described elsewhere (Allen & Dana, 2004; Allen & Walsh, 2000).

The *DSM–IV* provides Euro-American symptoms, syndromes, and disorders also used as genuine etics. Preparing cultural formulations relies on use of cultural knowledge by assessors, supplemented whenever necessary by information derived from moderators and other available emic measures. Cultural formulations can lead to more accurate clinical diagnoses especially when accompanied by awareness of the high frequencies of culture-bound disorders (e.g., Zheng et al., 1997).

Sources of bias have been carefully and comprehensively addressed and documented in the recent surgeon general's report—*Mental Health: Culture, Race, and Ethnicity* (U.S. Department of Health and Human Services, 2001). The contents of this report were provided by well-published advocates (i.e., Steven Lopez, Spero Manson, Lonnie Snowden, Stanley Sue) from four major ethnic minority professional populations. A brief recounting and overview of the surgeon general's report appears in a special journal issue (Leong & Lau, 2001). These articles follow an earlier organizational framework for ethnic minority research (Rogler, Malgady, & Rodriguez, 1989) that delineated community problem emergence, help seeking and utilization, diagnosis and assessment services, psychotherapeutic services, and posttreatment adjustment. Readers should also be aware of the special issue of *Culture, Medicine, and Psychiatry*—"Culture in the Politics of Mental Health Research"—on the surgeon general's 2001 report (Delvecchio Good & Good, 2003). These public resources have documented the history of disparities and inequalities of mental health services to non-White populations. They also serve as eloquent testimony to the centrality of cultural issues in human strength and human distress and emphasize the necessity of self-awareness, knowledge, and skills in all cross-cultural contacts. Finally, O'Roark (2002) reminded us that cultural competency is predicated on assessment competency.

Multicultural Research

Published research has continued to consistently omit or minimize methodological considerations that clarify the nature and magnitude of cultural influence. Generality may be forfeited due to insufficient knowledge of research participants, particularly in group-comparison studies. Inappropriate matching results in invidious comparisons that serve primarily to reinforce stereotypes. Omission of acculturation status information reinforces false beliefs in the homogeneity of each cultural/racial group. External validity in ethnic minority research has been chronically underemphasized and this neglect also compromises the development of adequate group-specific research knowledge (S. Sue, 1999). Moreover, the frequency and magnitude of group differences have been minimized by use of the conventional null hypothesis. The statistical assumption of no difference has been accompanied by a research history of invidious group comparisons using White, middle-class persons as the standard with inadequate and incomplete descriptions of non-White participants. Neglect of these desiderata in published research has resulted in insufficient, inadequate, and misleading empirical knowledge concerning ethnic minorities that impairs the adequacy and credibility of available assessment services for these individuals.

Multicultural research studies have been particularly deficient in applying appropriate and available methodologies incorporating the consensual research desiderata for all ethnic minority research I describe later in this chapter. Discussions of these and other neglected research considerations have been made available by Cuellar (2000), Dana (2000d), Okazaki & Sue (1995, 2000), and Roysircar-Sodowsky & Kuo (2001). Attention to culture-specific research desiderata is now an absolute necessity, but commensurate recognition must also be given to the proper use of the entire range of existing research designs and statistical techniques (Allen & Dana, 2004). This technology requires examination, expansion, and supplementation for fairness and accuracy in all research with multicultural populations (e.g., Allen & Walsh, 2000).

Guidelines for Research in Ethnic Minority Communities (CNPAAEMI, 2000) were developed by the professional organizations for African American, Native American, Alaska Native, Asian American, and Latino psychologists. This compilation of standards for acceptable research with multicultural populations is a necessary precursor to development of a responsible, credible, and ethical body of empirical literature describing culturally competent psychological services including assessment. The consensual desiderata for cultural/racial group research include (a) a careful and detailed description of ethnicity/race/tribe, (b) recognition of the magnitude of within-group differences or heterogeneity, (c) necessity for always assessing and reporting acculturation status, (d) an understanding of the effects of oppression, (e) communication style and response sets, (f) an understanding of cultural worldview, and (g) the reporting of participant language status and fluency. Routine inclusion of these desiderata for dissemination of cultural knowledge in reports of research conducted with multicultural participants was recommended and should be included by editors in information provided to authors, particularly in those counseling psychology journals routinely publishing cross-cultural and multicultural studies

A Training Rationale

Cultural competence is predicated on developing frames of reference for understanding individual progress toward an ultimate objective of unqualified acceptance of culturally different persons. Two strikingly similar examples of developmental continua are ethnocentric-ethnorelativistic thinking (M. J. Bennett, 1986) and cultural incompetence–competence

(Cross, Bazron, Dennis, & Issacs, 1989; Issacs-Shockley, Cross, Bazrun, Dennis, & Benjamin, 1996).

M. J. Bennett (1986) presented a stage process moving from ethnocentrism or denial of differences (Stage 1) to an ultimate integration of ethnorelativism into one's own identity fostering an ability to evaluate cultural phenomena relative to a cultural context (Stage 6). Intermediate stages are reaction by defense or reactivity to threat by denigration of differences (Stage 2), minimization and trivialization of differences by acknowledgment and toleration (Stage 3), tacit intellectual acceptance of differences (Stage 4), and adaptation or modifications in worldview that render culturally appropriate behavior/thought/empathy automatic and habitualized as in bicultural or multicultural individuals (Stage 5). Presently, most students and many professional psychologists are at Stage 4, implying that both overt differences and underlying values and construction of reality are comprehensible and acceptable.

Issacs-Shockley et al. (1996) provided a 6-point scale ranging from cultural destructiveness (Point 1) or genocidal programs, policies, and behaviors, and culminating with advanced cultural competence or cultural proficiency (Point 6) or esteeming and valuing culture at all levels of research, training, and practice. The intervening points are cultural incapacity (Point 2), cultural blindness (Point 3), and cultural precompetence (Point 4). Cultural incapacity results from ignorance, fear, and discrimination. Cultural blindness embodies the belief that there are no racial, ethnic, or cultural differences among persons. The cultural precompetence level represents implied movement, recognition of weaknesses, and a predominance of good intentions. Criteria, detailed characteristics, and assessment instruments for this scale have been developed (see Cross, 1992, and Mason, 1989). In spite of the striking similarity between successive points in both cultural competence conceptualizations, no comparisons have occurred to date.

Several available generalized training methods are available to facilitate Stage 4 development in M. J. Bennett's (1986) ethnocentrism-ethnorelativism stages. Copeland (1983) identified consciousness raising, cognitive understanding, experiential-affective understanding, and skills training, whereas J. M. Bennett (1986) employed a variety of educational methods. Generalized training approaches have been used in some counseling psychology programs in which self-examination of student identity has also been facilitated. Immersion in another culture and development of language skills are strongly recommended for all assessors, although it is recognized that providing assessment services in a second language requires idiomatic fluency. An integration approach to training necessitates the presence of cultural contents in all required courses (Copeland, 1982).

Competent Multicultural Assessment Training

In this book I recommend that standard and multicultural assessment training occur in the same assessment training courses followed by supervised assessment practice, preferably by multicultural supervisors. Personal therapy for graduate students has become commonplace, endorsed, and facilitated in most programs, and this therapy could be used directly to provide a relevant multicultural experience. Many White students enter professional psychology programs with stereotypes and prejudices in addition to their personal histories of unearned and unexamined privilege as well as a conspicuous absence of personal experiences with discrimination (see Neville, Worthington, & Spanierman, 2001; Ponterotto, Casa, Suzuki, & Alexander, 2001, chap. 1–13; Robinson & Ginter, 1999). As a consequence, it is now mandatory for programs to provide training in bias reduction that includes careful examination and understanding of students' own cultural identities (see Dana, 1998e, chap. 4). As part of self-awareness training, self-exploration using didactic and experiential activities are recommended to help students understand how their own socialization processes affect development of values and attitudes and "how their personal biases about others influence their ways of being and operating in a wide range of interpersonal situations" (Constantine & Ladany, 2001, p. 491).

Training is also needed by students to reduce their negative emotional reactions to cultural contents in their courses (Jackson, 1999). For examples, cultural issues were abruptly extirpated from courses in one graduate program after the first class of predominantly Euro-American origin students complained to their program director about the added burden of learning about cultures in assessment courses. Students of predominantly multicultural origins during 2 previous years had endorsed this teaching model particularly because standard assessment and multicultural assessment training were offered in the same courses (see Dana, Aguilar-Kitibutr, Diaz-Vivar, & Vetter, 2002).

Native American and Alaska Native students, in addition, may also need desensitization of their negative attitudes toward assessment per se, either during assessment training (Allen, 2002) or in a separate course for assessment consumers preceded by a psychopathology course emphasizing culture within the same program. For example, the final exam of one Alaska Native student who completed my consumer oriented, multicultural assessment course contained this sentence—"I strongly feel that a course such as this one should be offered and required of all psychology graduate student programs so that, even though we are basically forced to use these outdated and culturally biased tests, students will at least be aware of how to administer them in a more accurate and effective manner."

Even in counseling psychology programs that embrace cultural issues, multicultural assessment has not received primary attention (Rogers, Hoffman, & Wade, 1998) in spite of advocacy for training in projective techniques (Clark, 1995). Nevertheless, assessment courses in some training programs (e.g., UCLA, Fielding Institute, University of Alaska–Fairbanks, University of La Verne) for varying periods of time clearly have focused on careful examination of multicultural issues in test selection, usage, and interpretation (Dana, 2002d).

MULTICULTURAL COUNSELING COMPETENCIES

The major approach to multicultural competence has been provided by models of multicultural counseling leading initially to identification of relevant training areas and subsequently providing a number of self-report measuring instruments. Three broad competency areas have included attitudes/beliefs, knowledge, and skills constructs (Sue, Arredondo, & McDavis, 1992; Sue et al., 1982). A transition to training was provided by operationalizing these competencies into explanatory statements (Arredondo et al., 1996). Several self-report instruments were then developed to measure the identified competency areas as tools for evaluating professional training (for review, see Ponterotto, Rieger, Barrett, & Sparks, 1994). Evaluation of cultural competence training outcomes as well as the efficacy of particular counseling programs using these instruments was proposed and recommended (Ponterotto, 1997). Although these three constructs were robust, the derived instruments differed both in the numbers of derived factors describing the original training areas (Constantine & Ladany, 2001) as well as in the magnitude of intercorrelations between the construct scales in different instruments.

Limitations of the available multicultural competence measures were addressed and further corroborated in a larger study with 1,244 mental health service providers to develop a composite, multicultural competency measure, the California Brief Multicultural Competence Scale (CBMCS; Gamst, Dana, Der-Karabetian, Aragon, et al., 2004a). In this study, 15 of 197 items contained in four of five extant multicultural competence measures correlated significantly with the Marlowe–Crowne Social Desirability Scale (SDS; Crowne & Marlowe, 1960) and were subsequently excluded from the abbreviated scale of items with adequate reliability. The resulting CBMCS has 21 items and four factors—Non-Ethnic Ability, Awareness of Cultural Barriers, Multicultural Knowledge, and Sensitivity to Consumers. The items comprising each of these factors provided content domains for development of staff training manuals in the areas delineated by these factors (Dana, 2002b, 2003b). These manuals permitted subsequent development of the Multicultural Competence Training Program (Arellano, Huff-Musgrove, & Morrow, 2003) for trainers and clinicians within one agency and endorsed by the California Department of Mental Health for piloting and statewide application. The effects of this training program will be evaluated to examine the effects of training and other clinician variables on treatment outcomes for ethnic minority client groups in a comprehensive mental health center research program.

This body of research using self-report measures has been criticized for potentially biased efficacy evaluations in the absence of a baseline for comparisons with a competence standard. The presence of culture-specific response sets, in addition, may measure anticipated behaviors and attitudes rather than their correlates. The perceived importance to multicultural clients of items contained in these instruments has only infrequently been examined by focus groups (Pope-Davis, Liu, Toporek, & Brittan-Powell, 2001). Moreover, the extent to which untrained persons may be unaware of their knowledge deficits is not known. However, there is empirical evidence that social desirability measured by the Marlowe-Crowne SDS is a frequent response set in multicultural competency measures contributing to what has been called "impression management" (Constantine & Ladany, 2001). Sodowsky, Kuo-Jackson, Richardson, and Corey (1998) corroborated this finding with a new social desirability scale.

As a consequence of these limitations, direct measures were developed to evaluate multicultural competencies that included portfolio evaluations, demographic and training program variables, multicultural case conceptualization skills, hypothesized linked constructs, and formalized input from supervisors and observers of counseling sessions (Ponterotto, Fuertes, & Chen, 2000). Constantine and Ladany (2001) also suggested dimensions for an alternative conceptualization of multicultural counseling competence including self-awareness, general knowledge, self-efficacy, understanding of unique client variables, an effective counseling working alliance, and multicultural counseling skills.

Hong, Garcia, and Soriano (2000) believed three of these constructs (omitting Non-Ethnic Ability) represent increasing levels of multicultural competence development that begins with Awareness of Cultural Barriers (Stage 1) and proceeds through Multicultural Knowledge (Stage 2) to Sensitivity to Consumers or skills (Stage 3). Awareness of oneself includes values and attitudes as well as negative emotions in the form of preconceptions, assumptions, biases, and stereotypes. Hong et al. recommended self-examination by students of their locus on a cultural competence continuum in addition to examining their own families and cultures of origin. Genograms can also be used for this exercise.

The second stage described by Hong et al. (2000), acquisition of multicultural knowledge, requires a continuing critical exploration of "theoretical, empirical, journalistic and popular literature sources" (Constantine & Ladany, 2001). Some information resources descriptive of the four major cultural/racial groups in the United States have been compiled for assessment practitioners (Dana, 1998b). A variety of book chapters have presented cultural information for each of the four major groups (e.g., Cuellar & Paniagua, 2000; Dana, 1993, 1998e; Locke, 1998; Paniagua, 1998; Sue & Sue, 1999).

Detailed information on families with a wide range of cultural origins is available in separate family therapy text chapters (e.g., McGoldrick, Giordano, & Pierce, 1996; McGoldrick, Pierce, & Giordano, 1982). These volumes include Native American, Alaska Native, African American, African American Muslim, Amish, Arab, Armenian, Asian, Asian American, Asian Indian, Black, Brazilian, British, Cambodian, Central American, Czech, Chinese, Cuban, Dutch, English, Filipino, French Canadian, German, Greek, Haitian, Hungarian, Indonesian, Iranian, Irish, Israeli, Italian, Jamaican, Japanese, Jewish, Soviet Jewish, Korean, Latino, Lebanese, Mexican, Nigerian, Norwegian, Polish, Portuguese, Puerto Rican, Russian, Scandinavian, Slavic, Slovak, Vietnamese, and West Indian. Both editions (McGoldrick et al., 1996, 1982) include different chapters on 12 of these groups. Family information resources are vital for cultural competence training because families provide the context for transmission of culture and ethnicity contained in belief systems and acceptable modes of interaction and adaptation (Preli & Bernard, 1993). Another very useful resource for professional psychologists, developed originally for nurses, follows a consistent outline to describe cultural/racial identity, communication, activities of daily living, food practices, symptom management, birth and death rituals, family relationships, spiritual/religious orientation, illness beliefs, and health practices in 24 groups (Lipson, Dibble, & Minarik, 1996). Cultural information, although an absolutely necessary prerequisite for practice, is simply a precursor to multicultural clinical competency.

The third-level skills can be addressed in practicum and internship training following courses that integument cultural issues. Hong et al. (2000) summarized these specific skills to include verbal and nonverbal communication, identifying and consulting traditional helpers, advocacy, accessing literature, and reflective skill for self-monitoring. Assessment-relevant skills are also included: test selection, administration, and interpretation for application to culture-specific clients; use of emic approaches; and identification and integration of cultural diagnostic issues leading to recognition of culture-bound syndromes.

GENERAL GUIDELINES
FOR PROFESSIONAL SERVICES

General guidelines emanate from professional organizations and individuals in professional psychology, health promotion and disease prevention, and nursing. These guidelines impact specific areas and contribute to an overall perspective on dimensions of cultural competence. An early formulation of general guidelines for providers of services to ethnic, linguistic, and culturally diverse populations was developed by the American Psychological Association Office of Ethnic Minority Affairs (American Psychological Association, 1993; Guzman, 1993). These guidelines include statements of practical consequences to illustrate nine general principles:

1. Required information for clients.
2. Relevance of client-specific research and practice issues.
3. Incorporation of ethnicity and culture "as significant parameters in understanding psychological processes" (American Psychological Association, 1993, p. 46).
4. Respect for family roles and community structure within culture.
5. Respect for the cultural significance of religious-spiritual beliefs and practices.
6. Conformity with language preferences or referral.
7. Recognition of adverse societal impact in assessment and interventions.
8. Work to eliminate bias, prejudice, and discrimination.
9. Need for documentation of relevant cultural and sociopolitical factors.

A second set of guidelines (Hays, 2001) synthesizes the contributions of both the American Psychological Association and Canadian Psychological Association and calls attention to specific cultural influences relevant for designated cultural groups. These guidelines provide a convenient mnemonic—ADDRESSING—for practitioners as well as an organizing framework for Hays' textbook. ADDRESSING refers to "age and generational influences, developmental and acquired disabilities, religion and spiritual orientation, ethnicity, socioeconomic status, sexual orientation, indigenous heritage, national origin, and gender. An entire section of three chapters devoted to "Culturally Responsive Assessment and Diagnosis" contains specific guidelines for working with interpreters, culturally related strengths and supports, obtaining accurate and important information in an assessment, questions for assessing mental status and intellectual functioning, and suggestions for making standardized tests more culturally responsive.

The ADDRESSING format is used to summarize relevant content concerning cultural influence in an example of a Tunisian American client containing *DSM–IV* Axis referents and data. This case example leads to key ideas for making a culturally responsive diagnosis. A new cultural Axis VI employs the ADDRESSING acronym to complete Axis IV, Psychosocial and Environmental Problems, followed by Axis III, General Medical Conditions. The client's problem conceptualization is then considered as a potential bridge to *DSM–IV* categories and to provide a transition to systemic thinking and possible relational disorders. Finally, caution is invoked regarding the diagnosis of personality disorders, and careful attention to choice of language is required to explicate the meaning of the diagnosis to the client.

A third set of general guidelines, emphasizing a health promotion and disease prevention perspective available in a Cultural Assessment Framework (Huff & Kline, 1999), describes five distinct levels, each containing assessment areas and specific questions. Level 1 is culture-specific demographics with the following areas: age and gender characteristics, social class and status, education and literacy, language and dialect, religious preferences, occupation and income, patterns of residence and living conditions, and acculturation and assimilation. Level 2 is epidemiological-environmental influences with areas for morbidity, mortality, disability rates, and environmental influences. Level 3 is general and specific cultural characteristics with the following areas: cultural/ethnic identity; cosmology; time orientation; perceptions of self and community; social norms, values, and customs; and communication patterns. Level 4 is general and specific health care beliefs and practices with the following areas: explanatory models, response to illness, Western health care and health promotion use, and health behavior practices. Level 5 is Western health care organization and service delivery variables with areas for cultural competence and sensitivity, organizational policy and mission, facilities and program preparation, and evaluation of culturally competent services.

The Huff and Kline (1999) book may be considered an alternative resource consistent with my objectives in this chapter in attempting to provide a format for articulating information components relevant to culturally competent description of clients. The careful attention to specific questions provide a resource for assessors who prefer to use an interview format for gathering the cultural information required for the preparation of *DSM–IV* cultural formulations.

These general guidelines served as precursors for the American Psychological Association (2003) guidelines on multicultural education, training, research, practice, and organizational change for psychologists. This

landmark document clarifies usage of major terms to legitimize a professional role for promoting racial equity and social justice with a focus on
the centrality of culture in the following specific guidelines:

1. Commitment to cultural awareness and knowledge of self and
   others.
2. Recognition of the importance of multicultural sensitivity
   embodied in responsiveness to cultural knowledge.
3. Education that employs multiculturalism and diversity constructs.
4. Ethical, culture-centered research.
5. Application of culturally appropriate skills in practice.
6. Support culturally informed organizational change processes in
   policy and practice.

It should be noted that American Psychological Association Guidelines 4
(research) and 5 (practice) specifically outline the assessment issues elaborated on in this book.

MULTICULTURAL ASSESSMENT GUIDELINES

More specific and germane standards for multicultural assessment and
associated responsibilities for providers were developed by the Association for Assessment in Counseling, a division of the American Counseling Association (Prediger, 1994). This compilation of 34 guidelines for
use of standard tests provides classification by assessment-related tasks
that included selection (i.e., content, norming, reliability, validity), administration and scoring, and use/interpretation of results. Each of these
guidelines indicate user responsibilities, specify the sources of documentation, and enumerate limitations of various standard educational and
psychological tests.

Geiger and Ponterotto (1995) suggested a framework for assessment
in multicultural counseling. This framework includes assessment of
client and family psychological mindedness (i.e., awareness of psychological constructs); attitudes toward helping and counseling; as well as
worldview, acculturation levels, and attitudes toward acculturation.
Eight examples describing Irish American, Italian American, Taiwanese,
Dominican Republic, Ghana, Ethiopia, and India clients illustrate these
components. Three features of this framework are noteworthy: (a) recognition that client and family may constitute a single unit for assessment
and intervention purposes; (b) emphasis on the importance of client and
family psychological mindedness; and (c) calling attention to attitudes
as well as specific behaviors, processes, and procedures congruent with

these attitudes. This framework is applicable to an interview format for gathering cultural information and one important moderator, the SAWV, is included (Ibrahim & Kahn, 1987).

A third set of procedural guidelines (Roysircar-Sodowsky & Kuo, 2001) contain

1. Rapport.
2. Facilitation of client understanding.
3. Preassessment acculturation evaluation.
4. Selection of appropriate measures.
5. Search for constructs of interest in selected measures.
6. Search for germane reliabilities.
7. Generation of hypotheses for further testing from measures lacking cross-cultural validation.
8. Use of translated measures with linguistic and construct equivalence.
9. Incorporation of information from observation of client's test-taking behavior.
10. Use of multiple methods of assessment.
11. Caution in using computerized reports due to omission of culture, ethnicity, and socioracial effects.
12. Caution in using computerized reports due to their negative emphasis omitting strengths.
13. Use of racial/ethnic consultants.
14. Extra-assessment information from literature.
15. Use of language that clients understand.

A fourth set of guidelines, the multicultural assessment procedure (MAP; Ridley, Li, & Hill, 1998), described as pragmatic, flexible, and cyclical to permit revised decisions, contains decision points, four progressive phases (i.e., identifying cultural data, interpreting cultural data, incorporating cultural data, and debiasing strategies) for assistance with a sound assessment decision. The MAP focus on ethnic and racial minority issues has been questioned as unclear and overly narrow regarding incorporation of specific social and psychological issues (Arbona, 1998). Nonetheless, Constantine (1998) suggested that involving clients directly in the assessment process can minimize errors in clinical judgment, although "the results of traditional psychological tests alone will (not) allow clinicians to gain a comprehensive picture of clients' psychological issues" (p. 924).

These caveats and recommendations are especially important because they direct assessors to search for nonstandard instruments measuring constructs that are either not included or not sufficiently validated in standard tests and to develop consulting relationships with racial/ethnic clinicians. The inclusion of psychometric issues relating to possible non-equivalence constructs, cross-cultural score interpretability, nonrepresentative samples as well as dubious selection criteria in available samples, and recognition of culture-specific response sets calls attention to research deficits.

Peroration

Both similar contents and unique ingredients are included in these sets of guidelines. The parameters of cross-cultural assessment are still not entirely understood or agreed on; nonetheless, the frequent failure of standard tests to yield relevant responses and scores can preclude preparation of psychological reports with coherent and client-acceptable contents. Test inadequacies and interpretation lacunae have created a necessity for additional information resources. Moreover, many multicultural clients do not believe that psychological constructs/traits and human problems are related. External stressors and physical manifestations of general health status are frequently more credible than perception of internal distress related to mental health. Similarly, if legitimate and nonstigmatic sources of help are believed to reside exclusively within the family, assessment procedures—especially tests—will be distrusted and devalued. As a consequence, task orientation is impaired, resulting in insufficient compliance to provide a set of test data representative of the client. Finally, whenever client health–illness beliefs are coupled with a physical monism explanation for mind–body relationships, any serious test-taking behaviors may be precluded beyond the courtesy and minimal attention used to signify respect for the assessor.

4

Multicultural Assessment Practice

As the preceding chapters make clear, the delivery of culturally competent assessment services requires careful attention to many issues. In this chapter, I develop an assessment practice model and lay out guidelines (Table 4.1) for the consideration of language skills, cultural competencies (attitudes, knowledge, and clinical and research skills), cultural and racial identity, standard and emic instruments, *DSM–IV* diagnosis (cultural formulations), test-specific interpretation recommendations, reports, and feedback of assessment findings.

I have deliberately not labeled this compilation in Table 4.1 as standards because they lack the necessary systematic research documentation and consensus among assessors to qualify as standards. My intention is simply to detail a coherent set of desiderata providing an interim basis for culturally sensitive assessment practice with multicultural populations until comprehensive, consensual standards are available for professional psychologists. This application integrates ingredients that have already been accepted or are novel in the sense of their initial presentation in this book. As such, these ingredients provide an overarching framework for ethical assessment practice with multicultural populations by professional psychologists.

These suggestions both antedate and accompany an engagement with assessment tests/methods and their guidelines for applications with multicultural clients. A unique component herein is inclusion of the MAIP model. A history of models for culturally competent counseling is available (Ponterotto et al., 2000), although the appearance of clinically derived frameworks for multicultural assessment and cultural identity are of

TABLE 4.1

Ingredients for Ethical Multicultural Assessment Practice

Ingredient	Function	Source
1. MAIP practice model	Overall conception of culturally relevant issues	Dana, 2000b
2. Client–clinician language skills	Early evaluation of communication adequacy of persons and tests	Malgady & Zayas, 2001; Arnold & Matus, 2000
3. Cultural competency	Specification of ingredients necessary for training	Sue et al., 1982
A. Attitudes, knowledge, skills	Distillation of multicultural competence measures	Dana, 2003c; Gamst et al., 2004a
B. Clinician self-appraisal/self-understanding	Knowledge of own cultural/racial identity	Dana, 1998a, 2004; Kurasaki, 1999
C. Multicultural research standards	Consensual basis for credible, ethical research	CNPAAEMI, 2000
D. Service delivery etiquette	Culture-specific prerequisites: rapport/relationship necessary for compliance with directions	Sue & Zane, 1987
4. Cultural/racial identity	Determine adequacy of standard tests for client	Cuellar, 2000
A. Cultural identity evaluation	Conceptualization and proposed measurement of cultural self	Dana, 1998b
B. Racial identity evaluation	Conceptualization and measurement of developmental status	Cross & Vandiver, 2001; Helms, 1990
5. Use of standard and/or emic instruments	Relevance of test construction, standardization, and norms for specific multicultural populations	Dana, 2000c, 2000d; Roysircar-Sodowsky & Kuo, 2001
6. *DSM–IV* diagnoses	Cultural formulations	Mezzich, Kleinman, Fabrega, & Parron, 1996; Paniagua, 2000
7. Need for interpretation guidelines	Increase applicability of standard tests for multicultural populations	APA, 2003
8. Assessment reports	Primary vehicles for communication	Pope, 1992
9. Feedback of results	Therapeutic feedback to client entity	Dana, 1982, 1993; Finn, 1996c

Note. MAIP = Multicultural Assessment-Intervention Process; *DSM–IV = Diagnostic and Statistical Manual of Mental Disorders* (4th ed.).

relatively recent origins (Aponte & Barnes, 1999; Ponterotto, Gretchen, & Chauhan, 2001; Ridley et al., 2001). MAIP is consistent with Malgady's (1996, 2000) recommendation to reverse the null hypothesis by assuming that culture impacts significantly on each step in the assessment intervention process until there is sufficient research-derived information to demonstrate otherwise.

Ponterotto, Gretchen, et al. (2001) described idiographic assessment frameworks including the MAIP identified as Dana's six-step cultural assessment model. Paniagua (1998) cited MAIP as a precursor to checklist ingredients including Number 2 (use native or preferred language), Number 6 (culture-specific service delivery style), Number 7 (cultural identity evaluation), Number 8 (use culture-specific instruments), and Number 12 (culture-specific strategy for feedback of assessment findings). Morris (2000) recommended a hybrid model for African Americans combining the MAIP, a generic model, with racial identity development stages (Helms, 1990) because the more generalized MAIP did not include a specific Afri-centric focus. Figure 4.1 contains these recommendations accompanied by salient references; descriptions of the ingredients follow in this chapter.

MAIP PRACTICE MODEL

Originally presented as a stepwise flow chart describing the assessment process (Dana, 1993, p. 218), MAIP was revised to incorporate areas of service delivery, clinical diagnosis, culturally relevant and appropriate interventions, as well as a research and practice applications in a community mental health center (Dana, 1997a, 1998a, 2000a, 2001a, 2001c, 2001d, 2002a; Dana, Aragon, et al., 2002). This model has choice points designating when relevant questions can be asked that inform the process, increase reliability of *DSM–IV* diagnoses using cultural formulations, advocate use of identity-specific or culture-specific conceptualizations for non-*DSM* problems in living, and ultimately suggest and clarify the cultural nature and composition of intervention components.

The choice points indicated by questions (1–7) in Figure 4.1 acknowledge and illustrate that considerations of culture are proximal rather than distal in multicultural assessment. At the onset, there is explicit recognition that universally applicable assessment instruments and procedures, although desired by many professional psychologists, are not yet available as an exclusive, acceptable, and mandated technology (MAIP Question 1; see Dana, 2003a). At present, the employment of tests and methods requires not only a culturally acceptable service delivery style and information from test or interview moderators to identify a client's acculturation status or racial identity status (Question 2). For traditional clients, a clinical diagnosis

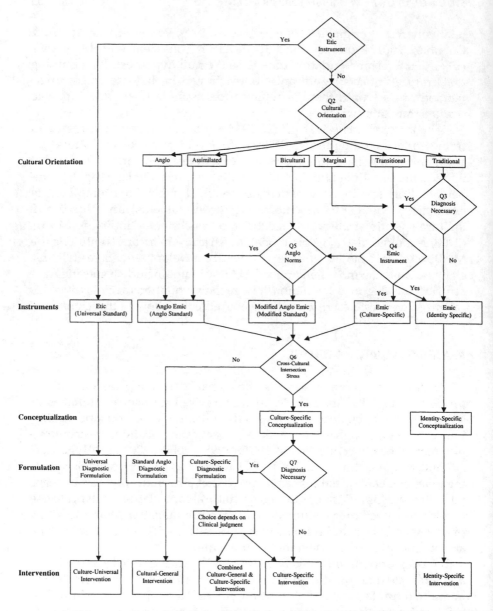

FIG. 4.1. Multicultural assessment-intervention process model. *Note.*
From *Handbook of Cross-Cultural and Multicultural Personality Assessment*
(p. 7), by R. H. Dana, 2000a, Mahwah, NJ: Lawrence Erlbaum Associates,
Inc. Copyright 2000 by Lawrence Erlbaum Associates, Inc. Adapted with
permission.

may not accurately describe behavior within a cultural context (Question 3), although a subsequent identity description may lead to an identity-specific conceptualization requiring an identity-specific intervention for nonpathological problems. Acculturation or racial identity status information also provides information on the applicability or inapplicability of standard test norms. Whenever standard test norms are inapplicable, the feasibility of employing culture-specific tests or emics, if available, should be considered (Question 4). However, these emic tests are primarily available at present only for African Americans (Jones, 1996). Acculturation or racial identity status information can also indicate when Euro-American norms are relevant as well as suggesting the necessity for alterations in conventional usage or interpretation (Question 5). Nonetheless, the use of standard tests, with or without corrections, cannot be used for evaluation of distress/anguish due to a history of cross-cultural interaction stressors resulting from discrimination and a history of oppression. Such stressors, whenever present, should be incorporated into the diagnostic assessment process (Question 6) by development and use of a culture-specific conceptualization. This additional information may still suggest the necessity for a cultural formulation to provide a *DSM–IV* clinical diagnosis or diagnosis of a culture-bound disorder (Question 7). A cultural formulation may also indicate the presence of specific stressors as the major ingredient of presenting problems that require a culture-specific intervention.

Note that MAIP Question 6 specifically includes attention to oppression effects on persons of color in all assessment practice. Although these effects have been omnipresent, acknowledgement and examination by professional psychologists is relatively recent (e.g., Clark, Anderson, Clark, & Williams, 1999; D'Andrea & Daniels, 2001; Neville et al., 2001; Utsey, Bolden, & Brown, 2001). All of these authors have delineated and documented physical, psychological, and quality of life effects of oppression and discrimination as well as the unwitting and continuing impact of White privilege and color blind racial attitudes on all persons of color. The labeling of selected oppression effects as posttraumatic stress disorder has also increased awareness (Marsella, Friedman, Gerrity, & Scurfield, 1996), although pathologization of these effects may focus remediation efforts exclusively toward the individual rather than encompassing the racism that provides precursor conditions as well as reinforcers of individual distress. Comas-Diaz and Jacobsen (2001) suggested the term "ethnocultural allodynia" to describe a nonpathological variant requiring somewhat different culture-specific interventions. Other responses to oppression appear in the form of overt expressions of anger, generalized apathy, and intellectual detachment (Malgady, Rogler, & Cortes, 1996). These effects may not be pathological in the sense of existing *DSM–IV* categories or currently included in the glossary of culture-bound disorders but nonetheless can contribute to an exacerbation of personal distress. Such distress may lead to blatant *DSM–IV* diagnostic inaccuracies in the same manner as the process of developing racial identity can spuriously elevate MMPI/MMPI–2 clinical scales (Whatley et al., 2003). Assessors now have direct responsibility not only for understanding the manifold effects of oppression on their clients of color in addition to careful reexamination and reappraisal of their assessment procedures, instruments, and interpretation strategies.

CLIENT-CLINICIAN LANGUAGE SKILLS, INTERPRETERS, AND TEST TRANSLATIONS

Unbiased assessment requires an early evaluation of the communication adequacy of clinicians and information concerning their tests and methods. Accurate communication between clinician and client can avoid or minimize the distortion, misunderstanding, miscommunication, blatant misdiagnosis, or diagnostic bias due to underemphasis or overemphasis on symptoms as well as stereotypy and/or caricature resulting in loss of significant information (Malgady & Zayas, 2001). Communication adequacy is defined by the properties, characteristics, and vocabularies of the language used by the clinician as well as by the level of verbal competence displayed by the client as a product of education, social class, and occupation.

As a consequence, clinicians should recognize that both English language and first- or native-language fluencies of clients should be ascertained during a preliminary assessment, especially for bilinguals (e.g., Altarriba & Santiago-Rivera, 1994; Carbonell, 2000; Lambert, 1955), that also emphasizes development of information on the clients' language dominance, preferred language, and acculturation status (Malgady, Rogler, & Costantino, 1987). Whenever feasible, the client's language preference should be honored in service delivery. Similarly, it is of equivalent importance to ascertain the language skills of clinicians in a standard fashion. Perdomo (2000) recommended the Bilingual Verbal Ability test for this purpose; self-assessment using the Woodcock–Munoz Language Survey (Woodcock & Muñoz-Sandoval, 1993) has also been suggested (Delgado, Guerrero, Goggin, & Ellis, 1999). As acculturation progresses and English language skills augment, client self-presentation becomes increasingly bicultural and bilingual, leading to frequent language switching necessitated by the expression of specific cognitive content and emotions.

Malgady and Zayas (2001) reviewed some consequences of limited English proficiency among Hispanic clients. Perceived uncooperativeness may be due to a negative, self-effacing attitude, with disturbances of speech and motor patterns resulting from stress induced by speaking a second or nondominant language. Similarly, flattened affect may be interpreted as withdrawal or inappropriate emotionality, whereas inaccurate and diminished self-presentation is frequently construed as low intelligence and poor self-esteem.

Clients who present problems and symptoms in their first languages typically provide this information within culture-specific health–illness belief systems and in accord with implicit rules for expression of these contents in interviews or tests. The language context thus can influence responses to tests that may or may not be misinterpreted as pathology but always provide some distortion, stereotypy, or a caricatured understanding of the individual. For example, Tiemann (2001) examined Rorschach and TAT records administered to bicultural Spanish–English bilinguals. Protocols were administered in a repeated measures design. Rorschach measures of affect and self-perception did not vary by language. However, English protocols scored higher on measures of cognitive complexity. In addition, there was a positive correlation on English protocols between measures of emotional expression (C, CF) and acculturation to Anglo norms. Level of acculturation was related to freedom of expression to the extent that differences by language in Rorschach protocols affected key CS variables and EB style. Higher acculturation levels increased C and CF, whereas FC and Sum C' were unaffected, leading to the conclusion that separate norms were mandatory. Rorschach norms were found to vary significantly from published norms (Exner, 1993). Content analysis of stories in Spanish and English to Card 2 differed in levels of emotional engagement, creativity, focus on details, and implied approaches to conflict.

Foreign students and visitors, sojourners, and immigrant clients in the process of learning English as a second language or with no English skills whatsoever may require assistance in communication to receive adequate assessment services. Such assistance occurs optimally and preferably in the form of a bilingual, bicultural clinician, but often a translator or use of translated tests is necessary. However, translators/interpreters who are not bicultural/bilingual clinicians require considerable training (Acosta & Cristo, 1981). Training, however, is costly and must be extensive to be effective. Moreover, the employment of translators sacrifices the possibility of using language as a service modality, although training helps to avoid breaching confidentiality and can reduce common errors of omission, additions, simplification of content, and distortion as well as errors (Altarriba & Santiago-Rivera, 1994).

Translations of standard tests developed in the United States for use in other countries are ubiquitous. Nonetheless, a recent review (Leong & Lau, 2001) suggested that translation into some non-Indo-European languages has proven inordinately difficult or infeasible and that even adequate translation per se can not assure construct equivalence. Moreover, Leong and Lau found that original factor structures may not generalize to Asian Americans, and even with adequate reliability indexes, discriminant validity may not be achieved.

Application of translated tests can occur by simply using literal translations, adapting parts of instruments, or construction of entirely new tests (Van de Vijver & Hambleton, 1996). However, consistency with Malgady's (1996) reversal of the null hypothesis requires assuming that bias is present in any translation unless cultural equivalence has been demonstrated. Translations should be accomplished using systematic methods and procedures (e.g., for guidelines, see Butcher, 1996a, chap. 2, for MMPI–2 translation steps; Brislin, Lonner, & Thorndike, 1973; Geisinger, 1994) including field testing of translations with the new client population (Nichols, Padilla, & Gomez-Maqueo, 2000). These translation procedures assure linguistic equivalence or comparability in meaning of test items (Helms, 1992), although items and scales must also demonstrate similar distributions between original and target groups (Drasgow & Hulin, 1987).

Competent translation, however, does not address the presumed equivalence of constructs measured in a target cultural or national context that differs from the setting in which the test originated. Construct equivalence demonstrations are mandatory for tests of psychopathology and personality developed in the United States because cross-cultural validity is assumed to be universal. Without such demonstrations, these tests are simply etic measures of specific symptoms or traits improperly employed as pseudo etics or imposed etics rather than genuine etics. When construct validation actually occurs to demonstrate construct equivalence, replication of factor analytic dimensions is typical (Ben-Porath, 1990), although this methodology alone has been described as insufficient to provide unequivocal demonstrations (Irvine & Carroll, 1980). Thus, cross-cultural and multicultural applicability of standard tests remains unproven in spite of available translations in the absence of construct validation research within each population for which adequate translation has occurred.

The construction and application of emic or culture-specific tests recommended by Van de Vijver and Hambleton (1996) has been accomplished using emic–etic models by operationalizing etics within emic contexts (Davidson, Jaccard, Triandis, Morales, & Diaz-Guerrero, 1976) as well as by construct identification, measurement, and subsequent cross-cultural comparisons (Hui & Triandis, 1989). In the area of personality measurement, the State-Trait personality inventories for Anxiety and Anger (Spielberger, Moscoso, & Brunner, 2004) are robust across cultures, methods, and populations with norms by culture and language.

The Revised NEO Personality Inventory (NEO–PI–R; Costa & McCrae, 1992) exemplar of the Five-factor model is another noteworthy example.

However, the five Chinese NEO–PI–R factors differed from the original factors; only one was comparable, and it was infeasible to import the original explanations for factors (Yang & Bond, 1990). In addition to cross-cultural differences in numbers and/or interpretation of factors, the predictability of relevant behaviors diminished without inclusion of an emic measure of traditionality in collectivist cultures (Triandis & Suh, 2002).

Differing cultural realities remind us

> That distortion and caricature are inherent in pseudo-etic instruments exported as genuine etics. . . . (these) instruments simply have been unable to deal competently with conceptual and item equivalence as a result of limitations in applications of existing methodologies, failure to make use of newer methodologies, and satisfaction with easy methodological solutions to complex issues of cross-cultural validity." (Dana, 2001b, p. 456)

CULTURAL COMPETENCY

Specification of Ingredients Necessary for Training

Consensus does not exist at the present time among professional psychologists concerning identification of the relevant contents of cultural knowledge embodied in beliefs, values, behaviors, the cultural self, cultural/racial identity, and social class structures. Psychologists do not know how much knowledge or what kinds of knowledge are desirable or mandatory for multicultural assessment purposes, nor have we discovered the most effective formats for communication, teaching, and training students to become knowledgeable assessors. The self-report multicultural competency measures were originally conceptualized to identify relevant and necessary areas for training students and practitioners. However, as a result of applying these measures, it is clear that clinicians may have specific deficits in one or more of these areas, rendering them uncomfortable with multicultural clients and leading them to question their ability to provide beneficial services. This discomfort increases with the magnitude of differences between clinician and client worldviews. As a consequence, for predominantly Euro-American clinicians, a hierarchy of perceived discomfort and difficulty suggested by survey findings goes from African American to Hispanic American, to Asian American, to Native American, and to Alaska Native (see Allison et al., 1996). Imparting this knowledge to students in assessment training has been described for several programs (e.g., Dana, 2002c), but research comparing different approaches used in graduate programs has not been undertaken (e.g., Copeland, 1982, 1983; LaFromboise & Foster, 1992).

One approach to reconciliation of the dilemma presented by a number of different multicultural competency measures is to reduce the numbers of items in these measures to a relatively smaller number and to employ these items to identify relevant training domains. This has been done by constructing the CBMCS (Gamst, Dana, Der-Karabetian, Aragon, et al., 2004). The 21-item CBMCS has been used as a resource for developing empirically derived, open-ended training manuals. These manuals have been designed to permit incorporation of new knowledge and different presentation styles to facilitate employment by a variety of trainers (Dana, 2002b, 2003b) endorsed for piloting and statewide application by the California State Department of Mental Health (for summary, see Dana, in press-a).

Understanding the histories, beliefs, and behavioral expressions composing different cultural perspectives is needed to achieve responsible and ethical assessment outcomes. Knowledge, or what has been called cultural literacy, is absolutely necessary for assessors. However, neglect of experiential-phenomenological understanding in pursuit of this knowledge can lead to stereotyping clients by identifying them exclusively with their cultures rather than as culturally identified individuals with varying admixtures of dimensions, contents, and boundary characteristics of a cultural self, a distinction made earlier in Fig. 2.2 (chap. 2, this volume).

It is thus necessary to equalize the importance of the assessor's head and heart to achieve a better balance between cognitive knowledge per se and attributes of the heart such as curiosity, naivete, and respect (Dyche & Zayas, 1995). These personality ingredients can lead to awareness of clinician–client power differentials as well as suggesting the use of acculturation narratives as vehicles for therapy and their role in acquisition of cultural knowledge by the clinician. This process-oriented approach is similar to a recommended therapeutic stance of teaching and learning about culture from Native American and Alaska Native clients (Mail, McKay, & Katz, 1989). It should be remembered, however, that typically, assessors strongly favor a comfort level provided either by low inference, nomothetic, normative or high inference, idiographic, and humanistic ideologies/models resulting in preferences for objective tests or projective methods.

Clinician Self-Appraisal, Self-Awareness, and Self-Understanding

The awareness dimension of cultural competency, or beliefs and attitudes, includes self-awareness of one's own cultural heritage as well as emotional reactions to other ethnic groups (Hong et al., 2000). The development of cultural competency is related to one's own personal history of developing knowledge of who one is and who others are or cultural identity issues inherent in understanding the self and others. Two helpful frameworks for identifying personal progress, as I described in chapter 3 (this volume), are a cultural competence continuum (Cross et al., 1989) and ethnorelativistic thinking (J. M. Bennett, 1986).

First-person accounts of experienced oppression and development of self-awareness are available largely from non-White psychologists who have documented the development of their racial/cultural identities (Ponterotto, Casas, Suzuki, & Alexander, 2001; Robinson & Ginter, 1999). Kohatsu and Richardson (1996) described a variety of White identity models including the Helms (1990) model, for example. Applications of these models for training clinicians, particularly White clinicians, exist primarily in counseling psychology programs (e.g., see Ponterotto, 1998).

Helms (1990) described two phases—disengagement from White racism and development toward a nonracist White identity, each containing three stages. Disengagement contains contact or superficial awareness of being White with evaluation of others from a standpoint of unquestioned White privilege followed by disintegration in which the inherent moral dilemma provokes guilt and anxiety that can lead either to reintegration of racism or a transition to Phase 2 during which a positive White identity is redefined. A pseudo-independent stage invokes trial and error behavioral applications in cross-cultural relationships that, if successful, result it immersion–emersion with attempts to acquire accurate information to reconstruct worldview. Finally, during autonomy, there is active seeking for diversity and focus on reducing oppression.

It is suggested that White students and practitioners who have not already done some systematic self-exploration apply the Helms (1990) model or another of the available models reviewed in Dana (1998e) to their own life experiences. For example, my own development of self-awareness and awareness of others can be highlighted by significant events relevant to the Helms (1990) model for White racial identity (see professional autobiography, Dana, 2004).

> During my earliest years, contact for me consisted of love and care from two women, a Black Jamaican and later a Polish immigrant, surrogates for a working mother. As the Depression worsened, family poverty soon found us living in an urban slum where my culturally diverse childhood companions provided continued contact experiences. Although we moved away from the inner city, my closest friends continued to be of diverse origins.
>
> My mother's parents were Eastern-European immigrants who came to the United States alone as teenagers, probably from areas of Lithuania and Romania or Russia. Her parents were nominally Jewish, but her education was in Catholic schools, and she attributed her success as a newspaper columnist, fund-raiser, and publicity director to denial of family religious

origins. She impressed on me the necessity for similar denial, an early source of grievous discomfort. Her marriage and later remarriage to gentiles and her avowed atheism partially alienated her from her two brothers and other family members. My gentle and always loving father—scion of an upper-class New England Episcopalian family, country gentleman, and premier amateur athlete of his generation—was unable to earn a living following the loss of the family international import–export business in World War I. Because she was unwilling to continue supporting him financially, mother divorced him for "desertion," and the three of us returned home from the courthouse. My father left us several months later to live with his sister. Mother subsequently remarried a respected public official whose racist tirades were directly responsible for my leaving home at 15. Visits home for many years were infrequent because my friends continued to be unwelcome during my stepfather's lifetime.

Contact during these early and adolescent years did not result by any immediate moral dilemma but simply in an attenuated transition toward personal identity complicated by a different time schedule for accepting both components of my heritage. I failed to recognize my own White privilege or to internalize an understanding of the impact of oppression on others. After returning from military service to my White elitist college, I saw a bulletin board notice of a summer interracial project in Washington, DC. For the first time in my 20 years of contact, during nonviolent summer sit-downs in Washington, DC restaurants sponsored by the Quaker Fellowship of Reconciliation and the Congress of Racial Equality, I shared experiences of discrimination and violence. The prolonged contact phase was replaced by direct experience in immersion–emersion as part and parcel of sharing daily lives and the personal consequences of oppression experienced by non-Whites.

During this Washington summer of the pseudo-independent stage, my academic mentors were joined by Bayard Rustin whose advocacy, charisma, and social conscience propelled me belatedly into a psychology major instead of languages and poetry in the naive belief that here was a sanctuary that would honor and accept my social ideals. I discovered immediately in graduate school from Black students in sociology and education that it only required one racist psychology professor to make program completion infeasible for them. Nonetheless, I still denied the implications of White privilege from within the secure confines of an exclusively White, male, graduate program, and over the ensuing years, a disintegration of identity occurred. In retrospect, during this extended time period, extrusions from earlier understandings appeared in existential, humanistic conceptual and ideological publications coupled with a spate of training manuals for self-assessment and self-understanding completely dissociated from the empirical research that facilitated my academic advancement. However, at no time was I able to confront the moral dilemma that what I chose to do by way of research largely ignored personal convictions and my own human development despite the earlier summer experiences and subsequent graduate school training in anthropology and sociology.

A return to the immersion–emersion stage was delayed until I reexperienced the consequences of oppression on Native American reservations under the aegis of a former student, Rodger Hornby. During the last 25 years, the moral implications of what I do as a professional psychologist have become figure rather than ground with rewards in relationships, acceptance by others, self-acceptance, new learning, and personal satisfaction. I would not aggrandize any of this time as constituting Helms' (1990) autonomy phase, although I have attempted to apply my professional skills toward understanding service barriers and bias with an advocacy stance to address the psychological oppression inherent in current applications of research methodology, assessment instruments, assessment training, and psychological interventions.

Multicultural Research Standards

Criteria for reviewing research studies in the form of systematic, consensual, and published multicultural research standards were available in January 2000 (CNPAAEMI, 2000). These guidelines were provided by four national ethnic minority psychological associations and contained recommendations for corrections of bias.

Prior to the availability of these research standards, no consensual research criteria for multicultural assessment or intervention practice existed despite the presence of isolated papers that have implicitly recognized the necessity for multicultural research standards. Several of these new research caveats received careful and critical discussion because they represented examples of flagrant departures from conventional research practices in science (e.g., adequate descriptions of ethnicity, recognition of the magnitude of within-group differences, and the necessity for including an analysis of response sets directly affecting assessment findings). These isolated research caveats and examples, however, did not stem directly from systematic, consensual knowledge concerning the practice of psychological science.

Note that assessing and reporting acculturation status is neither an acceptable part of assessment procedures at present nor did the American Psychological Association's 1992 ethical code suggest that this information was necessary. In fact, the Ethics Committee was on record as rejecting this suggestion (Dana, 1994, 1998e, pp. 41–46; S. E. Jones, personal communication, December 2, 1994). Nonetheless, there is abundant information that understanding acculturation status is directly relevant to the ethical use of standard assessment tests with multicultural clients. The question of whether or not a test should indeed be used with a particular multicultural client has typically not even been asked because of the implicit assumption that standard tests are universal in application. Similarly, there is now a growing conviction that oppression effects must always be examined in assessment of multicultural clients. Although the evidence for these effects in health and mental health status is no longer controversial, there was no explicit recognition of this in either the American Psychological Association's 1992 or 2002 ethics code.

In spite of the presence of consensual standards for research on multicultural populations, these standards are only beginning to influence professional psychology research and practice (except in counseling psychology in which application has already occurred) because they represent an enlarged and somewhat altered appreciation of psychological science may be applied to human beings. Euro-American assumptions concerning the efficacy of research methodologies and the selection, composition, and application of these methods for construction, interpretation, and validation of psychological tests continues to reflect a narrow definition of science. However, the burgeoning presence of a multicultural society in the United States during this millennium is accompanied by a dramatic alteration in the legitimate functions of science toward advocacy for equity in mental health research and services to the entire population (e.g., see Ponterotto, Casas, et al., 2001).

Service Delivery Etiquette

Culture-specific communication styles result in attitudes that affect the assessor–client relationship, immediacy of compliance, and ultimately the entire response process and interpretation procedures. These attitudes impact directly on responsiveness in objective tests by encouraging the use of response sets. Credible social etiquette by assessors is mandatory to provide a climate of rapport necessary for the compliance required to focus the attention of multicultural clients on assessment materials sufficiently to elicit data sets that are adequate for reliable interpretation.

Social etiquette in multicultural client–clinician relationships was described in general terms as "credible" and "giving" (Sue & Zane, 1987). In assessment practice, the service delivery must always be culture specific. This implies an explicit recognition that clients have diverse rules for credibility of services and know the kinds of contents and behaviors constituting "gifts" for them. Euro-American professional psychologists generally emphasize behavior and words within a formal structure emphasizing distance, noninvolvement, and impersonality as primary tools for an objective understanding of their clients.

Nonetheless, nonverbal communication and informality also can contribute to credibility of services. Nonverbal communication in the form of timing, pitch, and emphasis as well as facial expressions and body language of clients often signals compliance or noncompliance in assessment tasks (Herring, 1990; Keating, 1994). Although some emotional expressions such as fear, anger, disgust, sadness, enjoyment, and contempt are believed by authorities to be universal (Ekman, 1993: Matsumoto, 1992), the research methods underlying this conclusion have been criticized (Russell, 1991, 1994). The exact meanings of emotions and their display rules are markedly influenced social factors including the context in which emotional expressions occur (Josephs, 1955; Kleinberg, 1938; Lutz & White, 1986).

Multicultural clients focus on nonverbal behaviors because racism is subtle; composed of implicit attitudes, often unconscious or deliberately omitted from verbalizations; and an insurgent, intrusive bias that can override the job focused, good intentions of clinicians. Persons of color who have been wounded repeatedly by discriminatory interpersonal behaviors are exquisitely sensitive to the attitudes of clinicians. This is particularly true of African Americans who have strong Africentric identifications. These individuals demand that their clinicians of Euro-American origins respond well to "sizing up and checking out," described following, and many of these individuals prefer clinicians who are also persons of color, particularly when responsiveness to this demand is not forthcoming.

In simplistic terms, some rules for relationships by group can be described. However, extreme within-group variability as well as differences in acculturation or racial identity status means that many individuals in each group will understand and respond positively to a classical Euro-American service delivery stance. Some of these persons feel they must passively accept both mainstream and culture-specific styles to receive services, an attitude that includes an element of learned helplessness.

African Americans. An understanding of mainstream and emic service delivery styles is characteristic of African Americans who have struggled and persevered for decades to receive poor quality services from Euro-American clinicians (Dana, 2002c). Although most African Americans clearly understand the Euro-American professional service delivery style, services conveying the humanity and cultural understanding of service providers are preferred.

A social etiquette that conveys these meanings has been described as sizing up and checking out (Gibbs, 1985); microstages of this process include appraisal (Stage 1), investigative (Stage 2), partial identification (Stage 3), loyalty and personal regard (Stage 4), and engagement (Stage 5). In Stage 1, clients may be aloof, guarded, reserved, and superficial while awaiting signs of personal authenticity. Stage 2 includes client challenges of the qualifications, values, beliefs, and understandings, particularly of oppression. Stage 3 results from a degree of client comfort and emphasizes subsequent overtures designed to establish a more personal relationship. Stage 4 only occurs if the clinician's responsiveness is sensitive, flexible, and nondefensive. Stage 5 permits assessment (or treatment) to begin with client involvement, cooperation, and motivation. This process does not necessarily occur with all African American clients; it is more likely to be enacted by clients actively engaged in the process of developing racial identity who may have preferences for an African American clinician as well.

A second approach by Parham (2001) stems from an Africentric conceptualization of healing in which the skills involved in connecting, facilitating awareness, and setting goals are described using videotaped transactions. The process of connecting—analogous to a preassessment conversation—is initiated by asking the client to participate in a ritual demonstration, "What do you need to know about me?" This gives the counselor/assessor an opportunity to be with the client by exhibiting "congruent realness" using self-disclosure. Parham's humanistic approach to the relationship was designed to unify theory and practice within one culture-specific intervention.

Native Americans and Alaska Natives.   These clients also understand and can accept two disparate styles of service delivery—traditional and mainstream. However, there is preference for an absolute informality that makes no distinction between professional interactions and other social interactions. In some community settings, the granting of permission by a relative or friend signals that the nonnative clinician is trustworthy as a healer (Albert & Bill, 1990). When the assessor is a stranger, "common basing," recommended by Hornby (1993), provides an opportunity for self-disclosing chitchat concerning mutual acquaintances, shared understandings, and topics of mutual interest including local issues and concerns or tribal history. This process is deemed of greater value than getting "down to business" by immediately conducting an interview or administering tests because common basing encourages trust by communicating respect for the Indian self as well as for all living forms (Matheson, 1986).

As suggested elsewhere, "Trust will not materialize from a simple application of provider presence or good intentions, regardless of relationship skills. Trust develops slowly, if at all, with an outsider in the shadow of genocide, and is based on a longstanding social relationship and a positive provider reputation in the Indian community" (Dana, 1998e, p. 137). Moreover, social etiquette is always local and requires knowledge of tribal nonverbal communication and ultimately an appreciation and awareness of the client's native language and belief system. Finally, I emphasize that only a very few Euro-Americans can cultivate a credible social etiquette and professional skills that convey acceptance and understanding of how the Native American and Alaska Native worldview dimensions impact and permeate credible assessment (Dana, 2000b).

Hispanics/Latinos. It is not surprising that a comfortable and acceptable service delivery style for Latinos also contains elements similar to those ascribed to their folk healers. There are client expectations for hope, faith, and confidence within a complex network of social relationships between practitioners and their clients (Vega, 1982). An anticipated cultural script includes use of the client's first language, demonstrable cultural knowledge, and high frequencies of affiliative/affectional behaviors or *simpatía* (Triandis, Marin, Lisansky, & Betancourt, 1984). This script is conveyed by respect (*respeto*), personal, informal, individualized attention (*personalismo*), and chatting to create a warm personal atmosphere (*platicando*; see Dana, 1998e, Table 8.1, p. 189).

The following quotation illustrates differences between Euro-American and Mexican service delivery styles used for administration of an intelligence test:

> The American tester was detached and, to the Mexican observer, cold. The American child was absorbed, challenged, and involved with the tasks. He/she gave to most of the observers the impression of competing with the tester. The noise level and commotion were minimal. The Mexican tester was vehement and expressive—to the American observers, overly warm. The Mexican child was responsive and involved in the interpersonal relation; it seemed that he/she wanted to please the tester with good answers to the tests. The noise level and commotion seemed high to the American observers. (Diaz-Guerrero & Diaz-Loving, 1990, p. 491)

Asian Americans. These clients conform to role relations dictated by age, expertise, and gender and characterized by credibility and gift giving (Sue & Zane, 1987). Credibility is dependent on ascribed status (i.e., an older man) and achieved status (i.e., formal training and expertise, power, confidence, and skills displayed by educational background, personal credentials, willingness to engage in multiple roles, work experience) used to provide evidences of credibility (Lee, 1982). Lack of achieved status maybe responsible for failure of a client to appear for a return appointment (Sue, 1993). An opportunity for gift giving can only occur if credibility is present. Gift giving symbolizes a connection between whatever has been accomplished during an assessment contact and some perceived alleviation of immediate anxiety/distress by "a gesture of caring" (Sue, 1993, p. 284).

The entire service delivery process is also expected to be logical and structured (Atkinson, Maruyama, & Matsui, 1978) but nonetheless, must conform to an appropriate and acceptable style embedded in body language and linguistic forms that differ for clients from each Asian group. For example, Japanese clients practice very different social rituals to structure relationships for insiders (family and/or close friends) and outsiders (strangers; see Dana, 1998e, chap. 7, especially Table 7.2). Chinese clients may engage in an invitational discourse emerging and reinforcing their cultural identity even when using the English language (Mao, 1992). Given the extraordinary importance of the nuances of proper service delivery social etiquette, it is not surprising that Asian and Asian American clients have the highest dropout rates in many mental health settings. For additional discussion of the depth and quality of required cultural knowledge and the service delivery difficulties confronted by Euro-American clinicians with these clients, see Dana (2001a).

Peroration. The importance of an acceptable service delivery style cannot be overemphasized. Whenever the social etiquette is discordant with client expectations, attention, interest, and subsequent task orientation may falter and affect the entire response process and subsequent interpretation of assessment data. Unfortunately, there is no empirical evidence concerning the effects of differences in service delivery style on performance. However, it is reasonable to conclude that intelligence test scores may be decreased and Rorschach or TAT productivity diminished as a consequence of examiner behaviors that are either unanticipated by clients and/or perceived as aversive, demeaning, or discriminatory. This is a complex issue, and there have been demonstrations that test performances can be altered or enhanced on intelligence tests as well as on individually administered projective methods by the behaviors of the assessor (e.g., Back & Dana, 1977, 1980; Dana, Dana, & Comer, 1972).

CULTURAL/RACIAL IDENTITY

It is assumed that "one's culture is a major, if not the major, factor contributing to individual differences in behavior" (Lonner & Adamopoulos, 1997, p. 52). This assumption gains credibility as a practical outcome of Malgady's (1996, 2000) reversal of the cultural null hypothesis. Culture exerts both direct and indirect effects on thought and behavior in the form of mediator and moderator variables (Cuellar, 2000). Mediators account for a relation between culture and personality psychopathology by impacting both predictor and criterion. These relations may be too complex for assessment practice applications and more amenable to investigation in research designs using appropriate statistical techniques. Moderator variables, however, exert influence by providing directional control and indicating the strength of a relation between culture as a predictor and personality psychopathology constructs as criterion variables. In assessment service delivery, culture can serve as a moderator, either in the form of tests applied prior to the formal assessment process or by test items embedded in an interview.

Information is available from moderators for many purposes depending on the objectives of the assessment process. First, acculturation information in the form of cultural orientation status must be determined during a preassessment task. Second, this acculturation status information is necessary to decide whether standard tests can be administered and interpreted without modifications in the interpretive process or conventional standards. Whenever standard tests have inapplicable norms, "corrections" are mandatory to increase the validity of test interpretations. If standard tests are clearly not applicable or of unknown applicability, for example, for refugees, immigrants, transients, or non-English speakers, then emic tests constructed and normed for the particular client population are necessary and required whenever available. Third, information from moderators and emic tests can be used to describe the cultural self. Fourth, this description of the self is useful for culture-specific and identity-specific conceptualizations whenever a clinical diagnosis is not required. Fifth, if a *DSM–IV* diagnosis is required, then all accumulated cultural information will be used to answer questions contained in the outline for a cultural formulation.

The use of moderator variables can increase control over the assessment process with multicultural individuals by permitting an estimate of the magnitude of cultural variance in responses to standard tests. If cultural variance is high due to a traditional cultural orientation, then extreme caution is required in the interpretation of responses to these tests. Knowledge of cultural orientation status thus serves to predict the manner in which the test situation per se is construed, the nature and magnitude of culture-specific response sets, and the potential impact on the numbers, kind, and quality of responses. I describe a variety of moderator variables for evaluation of acculturation status and racial identity.

Cultural Identity Evaluation

Acculturation status refers to a rough categorization used to locate a person in the process of cultural change as a result of personal, sustained, and continuous contact with a host culture (Dana, 1992a). Acculturation is concerned with changes in an individual accompanying group-level acculturation (Berry & Kim, 1988). Berry and Kim (1988) described physical, biological, and cultural changes as well as reactivity in the form of acculturative stress that can affect mental health. Attitudes toward modes of acculturation were also described in relation to two questions, the value of maintaining cultural identity and the value of maintaining relationships to other groups. "Yes" responses to these questions results in integration, "no" responses result in assimilation or marginalization, respectively, and maintenance of cultural identity in the absence of relationships to other groups leads to separation. These terms were slightly altered in the MAIP practice model (Figure 4.1; i.e., integration to bicultural, assimilation to Anglo, and separated to traditional), and a transitional category for Native Americans and Alaska Natives was added to identify bilinguals who questioned traditionalism and religion without fully accepting dominant culture values (see LaFromboise, Trimble, & Mohatt, 1990).

Depending on the kinds of information desired and the purposes of assessment, my personal preference for selection of moderators includes an acculturation status measure, whenever available, supplemented by one or more emic instruments providing culture-specific information. Acculturation information is not only necessary to provide answers to MAIP Questions 3, 4, and 5 but also to test hypotheses relevant to *DSM–IV* diagnoses and describe the cultural self.

For example, there has been some consensus in the literature that biculturalism may optimize mental health, whereas marginalization is frequently associated with at-risk mental health status (for review, see Romero, 2000). Romero suggested that a multidimensional and orthogonal conceptualization of culture permitted an examination of the cultural self consistent with biculturality in the United States as part of a multicultural world. The cultural self is composed of values (collectivistic and individualistic), ethnic identity, acculturation status, and social context.

Reviews of available instruments for acculturation measurement (i.e., Cuellar, 2000; Dana, 1993; Kim & Abreu, 2001; Lai & Sodowsky, 1996; Zane & Mak, 2003) are necessary resources for selection of instruments applicable to particular multicultural clients for specific assessment purposes. My intent in this chapter is to provide an overview with descriptions of exemplar instruments representing basic tools for each group. Chapter 5 (this volume) contains examples of how these moderators are used in assessment batteries and reports, and in subsequent chapters, I present group-specific examples of assessment data sets and reports including additional moderators.

African Americans. Both cultural and racial identity can assume importance, although racial identity measurement has been a priority. Cultural identity is composed of traditional elements of religious beliefs/ practices; family structure/practices; socialization; traditional foods; preferences for music, arts, television, games, activities; interracial attitudes; superstitions; and health beliefs/practices and can be measured by the African American Acculturation Scale (AAAS; Landrine & Klonoff, 1994). This scale facilitates research on acculturation status and moderators to reduce bias in comparative studies as well as to demonstrate that African Americans possess a distinctive culture.

Native Americans and Alaska Natives. Two alternative moderators are now available and recommended. Brown (1982) developed a four-generational format to describe acculturation using case history/interview and behavioral criteria for family/self, social, spiritual, and training/education preferences (see Dana, 1993, chap. 7, Table 7–6). This format in chart form by generation or level can be used as part of an interview and is generally nonintrusive. A test alternative, primarily for college educated individuals, the Northern Plains Bicultural Immersion (NPBI) Scale (Allen, 1998) was developed to assess behaviors associated with traditional and Anglo cultural orientations. Preliminary samples have yielded a four-factor structure with dimensions for traditional and Anglo cultural practices, English, and tribal language usage. These factors guided selection of items for the four subscales. These subscales were combined into major dimensions for American Indian Cultural Immersion (AICI) and European American Cultural Immersion scales (EACI). A circumplex bicultural immersion model resulted from use of AICI and EACI as axes with high and low dimensions forming four combinations including AICI, EACI, bicultural immersion defined by high scores on both dimensions, and diffusion defined by low scores on both dimensions.

Hispanics/Latinos. For Hispanics/Latinos, interest in measurement was provided by a delineation of acculturation including language proficiency/preference; culture-specific traditions, customs, and identifications; value orientations; and SES (Olmedo, 1979). This interest led to an initial review of 13 instruments designed for Latinos (Dana, 1993) followed by a selected review (Dana, 1996a). The ARSMA/ARSMA–II (Cuellar et al., 1995; Cuellar, Harris, & Jasso, 1980) served as progenitor and model for the evaluation of acculturation status. The 30-item ARSMA–II is a multidimensional, two-axis, four-quadrant scale used to derive bicultural typologies representing the major cultural orientations in MAIP. Acculturation scores were available for the first five generations, and mean scores for Anglo and Mexican orientations and frequencies of cultural orientations and their subtypes were included. A software program for scoring and a computer-generated report is also available (Cuellar, 1994). Although ARSMA/ARSMA–II is the most widely used instrument for Hispanics, separate instruments for Puerto Ricans, the Psychological Acculturation Scale (PAS; Tropp, Erkut, Garcia Coll, Alarcon, & Vazquez Garcia, 1999), and Cubans, the Bicultural Involvement Questionnaire (BIQ; Szapocznik, Kurtines, & Fernandez, 1980), are available. In addition, a brief, primarily research instrument has been used with Mexican Americans and Central Americans, the Hispanic Assessment Scale (HAS; Marin, Sabogal, VanOss Marin, Otero-Sabagal, & Perez-Sable, 1987).

Asian Americans. The sheer number of different Asian cultures, religions, and countries of national origin have necessitated the development of culture-specific identity and/or identity formulations as precursors for acculturation instruments (for reviews, see Ibrahim, Ohnishi, & Sandhu, 1997; Roysircar-Sodowsky, Kwan, & Pannu, 1995; Roysircar-Sodowsky & Maestas, 2000). Culturally informed assessment of Asian Americans has also been fostered by reviews of unique emic dimensions of personality psychopathology and the development of culture-specific assessment models (Okazaki, 1998, 2000).

Unidimensional and bidimensional culture-specific instruments for evaluation of acculturation status are available for Chinese (Tsai, Ying, & Lee, 2000), Filipinos (Filipino American Aculturation Scale [FAAS]; Advincula, 1999), Hmong (Rick & Forward, 1992), Koreans (Kim & Berry, 1985), Japanese (Meredith, Wenger, Liu, Harada, & Kahn, 2000), Southeast Asians (Anderson et al., 1993), and Vietnamese (Celano & Tyler, 1990). Detailed information on many of these instruments is available in other sources (Dana, 1993; Kwan, 1999; Roysircar-Sodowsky & Maestas, 2000); reviews of standard tests used with Asian Americans are also available (Okazaki & Sue, 1995, 2000).

A pan-Asian acculturation measure, the Suinn–Lew Asian Self-Identity Acculturation Scale (SL–ASIA; Suinn, Rickard-Figueroa, Lew, & Vigil, 1987), a unidimensional pan-Asian instrument, was developed by modifying ARSMA. SL–ASIA is useful for identifying acculturation status in research studies and merited use as an assessment moderator prior to the development of acculturation status measures for separate Asian American cultural groups (Abe-Kim, Okazaki, & Goto, 2001).

Emic measures providing culture-specific information include the Social Interactions Scale (SIS) translated for the Chinese American Psychiatric Epidemiological Study (Kwang, Chen, Kurasaki, Mak, & Takeuchi, 2000). A multidimensional identity perspective for Chinese immigrants is available from the Internal–External Ethnic Identity (Int–Ext Id) measure that examines interrelations of these identity aspects as well as saliency of ethnicity, fear of loss of face, and cultural stress (Kwan, 2000; Kwan & Sodowsky, 1997). This theory-driven, comprehensive measure provides information on ethnic identity types with factors describing ethnic friendship/affiliation, emotional expression, food orientation, and family collectivism.

Pan-Asian instruments focus on dimensions shared by Asians from diverse cultural and national backgrounds including individualism–collectivism, acculturative stress, ethnic identity, family conflicts, and values. The Individualism–Collectivism Scale (INDCOL; Hui, 1988), developed from extensively researched constructs (Triandis, 1990, 1995), taps what is believed to be a universal dimension of personality. INDCOL has subscales for spouse, parent, kin, neighbor, friend, and coworker, and a short form is available (Hui & Yee, 1994).

Other pan-Asian instruments include the Asian Values Scale (AVS) that provides a total score embracing six factor clusters plus additional items (Kim, Atkinson & Yang, 1999). The Asian American Family Conflicts Scale (FCS; Lee, Choe, Kim, & Ngo, 2000) was constructed for Asians of diverse national origins, primarily first- and second-generation college students. The Asian American Cultural Experience Survey (AACES; Sasao, 1994) provides additional multidimensional perspectives on cognition, behavior, affect, language and communication, cultural knowledge and practice, social interaction, social network, and support components (Tang & Fouad, 1999). The Cultural Adjustment Difficulties Checklist (CADC; Sodowsky & Lai, 1997), an acculturative distress measure, includes factors of distress and intercultural competence. The Sense of Coherence (SOC) measure, originally developed in Israel by Antonovsky (1984), has been translated for Southeast Asians-Vietnamese, Cambodian, Laotian, Hmong, and Chinese-Vietnamese (Ying, Akutsu, Zhang, & Huang, 1997). SOC examines the extent to which a person believes that the world is comprehensible, manageable, and meaningful.

Racial Identity Evaluation

Racial identity is a complex, multifaceted concept that includes unidimensional measures of identity formation, cultural connectedness, and multicultural experiences as well as multidimensional measures (Burlew, Bellow, & Lovett, 2000). Racial identity measures have been widely used in research and can be applied in assessment practice, particularly whenever culture-specific or identity-specific interventions are needed. Measures of multicultural experiences, especially perceived racism, racist events, acculturative stress, and cultural mistrust, are also available.

Racial identity measures based on the Nigrescence model of Black consciousness development have been initially represented by stages in the Racial Identity Attitude Scale (RIAS; Parham & Helms, 1981) and the Developmental Inventory of Black Consciousness (DIB–C; Milliones, 1980). The RIAS and the DIB–C used different labels for the same stages and also differed in the stages represented in the instruments. More recently, the Nigrescence model was expanded into a comprehensive theory with six of eight Black identity exemplars operationalized by a new Black racial identity measure, the Cross Racial Identity Scale (CRIS; Cross & Vandiver, 2001). This more sophisticated theory embraces the self-structure with a differentiation of personal and group identity, identity socialization, and adult identity conversions, recycling, and functions.

USE OF STANDARD
AND/OR EMIC INSTRUMENTS

Standard instruments should be used whenever there is an absence of acculturation status, racial identity status, or demographic information indicating profound differences in worldview. Although it would have been preferable to include racial identity and acculturation status moderator information, Meyer (2002, Table 1) provided adequate demographic and Rorschach variable information to suggest the strong likelihood that no additional CS differences would occur subsequently between his Euro-American and non-Euro-American hospital patients in spite of their group differences in diagnoses. Careful selection of research participants by detailed demographic description, recommended in the multicultural research standards, can be a legitimate substitute for more specific worldview information. Nonetheless, in evaluating individual clients or patients, demographic information alone cannot substitute for moderator-derived information because of the high-stakes consequences of erroneous diagnosis as well as subsequent employment of nonrelevant therapies or other interventions.

The use of available emic or culture-specific assessment instruments becomes necessary whenever information from acculturation/racial identity status indicates that standard instruments should not be relied on due to lack of translation into client first language; acculturation/racial identity status; presenting problems of oppression, discrimination, or identity; as well as client preferences for specific instruments.

DSM–IV DIAGNOSES

DSM–IV diagnoses for all traditional clients and some marginal or bicultural clients as well can lack accuracy and constitute bias in the absence of a cultural formulation. A cultural formulation provides evidence for whether or not a clinical diagnosis is required. If a clinical diagnosis is not relevant, this formulation can then permit, enable, and inform a culture-specific or identity-specific conceptualization leading to an appropriate nonpsychiatric intervention. A necessary clinical diagnosis may be based on accurate identification of a culture-bound disorder either present in the *DSM–IV* glossary or available in other sources (e.g., Hughes & Wintrob, 1995; Paniagua, 2000; Simons & Hughes, 1985) and also call attention to the need for subsequent combined mainstream and culture-specific interventions or identity-specific interventions.

INTERPRETATION RECOMMENDATIONS

Most psychologists consider psychology an etic or universal science. Standard tests are conceptual and methodological derivatives of this science. The adequacy of test theory, test construction, available reliability and validity research, as well as published test norms provide the basis for ethical and responsible professional assessment practice using standard tests for all clients. Nonetheless, these tests were constructed primarily for Euro-Americans and as discussed in chapter 1 (this volume) are imposed etics. Many users of these tests assumed their pan-cultural, pan-national, or universal status not only as products of an etic science but because the tests were predicated on the pervasive and largely unquestioned belief in minimal differences among cultural/racial groups. As a result, multicultural clients were either excluded from normative data or, if included, were not representative of their ethnic/racial group for a variety of reasons including SES as well as acculturation and racial identity status.

DSM–IV is also an emic or culture-specific system misconstrued as a universally applicable or imposed etic diagnostic nomenclature. The standard tests providing *DSM–IV* clinical diagnoses, as indicated previously, are also imposed etics. Thus constitutes a dilemma directly affecting the welfare of multicultural mental health clients. Two attempted resolutions of this dilemma available to assessors are denial of the centrality of culture or incorporation of a multicultural perspective.

First, many assessors remain in denial of the consequences of using biased instruments for multicultural populations as a result of their training and familiarity with research that advocates universal applicability of standard tests. This denial was fostered by a history of research using ethnicity as a demographic variable distal to the personality processes underlying potential cultural differences in test scores or interpretation. Whenever ethnicity is used as a demographic variable in the absence of measured acculturation status, the dimensions responsible for cultural differences or lack of such differences are compromised and may fail to be adequately explored.

Second, assessors are now subjected to a professional critique concerning the scientific status and effectiveness of the Rorschach, MMPI–2, TAT, and other instruments for assessment of personality and mental illness (e.g., Lilienfeld et al., 2001; Wood, Garb, Lilienfeld, & Nezworski, 2002). The instruments in question have enjoyed widespread and continuous use in the United States and internationally for more than 50 years on the basis of increasingly sophisticated research demonstrations of validity comparable to medical tests (e.g., Meyer et al., 2001). In spite of inaccuracy and hyperbole, these assaults threaten assessor livelihood from within the profession even as managed care constitutes an external threat to the continued responsible usage of standard tests. Managed care stipulates parsimony in the form of narrow assessment objectives, an immediate focus on clinical diagnosis, severe limitations on the numbers/kinds of assessment instruments employed, and drastic reduction in compensated time for assessment (Camara et al., 2000).

As a consequence, psychologist assessors now experience feelings of increased vulnerability concerning their hard-won status as legitimate scientists. An omission of historical and cultural research contexts and an acceptance of these tests as etic instruments also contributes to less responsible interpretation of findings from standard tests and methods. Selective, partial, and confused awareness of methodological multicultural research issues as well as a burgeoning multicultural assessment literature (Allen & Dana, 2004) provides a message for assessors that they must simultaneously and immediately become better scientists and culturally competent as well.

Although psychologist assessors might accept new tests conceptualized, constructed, normed, and validated for multicultural persons, with the notable exception of the TEMAS (Costantino et al., 1988), there is a paucity of relevant new tests. As an immediate and partial substitute for new tests, revised interpretations of standard tests for some clients in each ethnic group are necessary to incorporate evidence using information derived from moderator variables, validation evidence, extratest cultural information, and other research information from methodologically sound studies. Assessors with cultural and methodological awareness now can augment their interpretations of standard tests by using moderators, selected revisions, or a variety of corrections for multicultural populations to compensate for bias (e.g., Dana, 1995, 2000c). However, in the absence of a methodologically adequate research edifice addressing the relevance of specific test/method interpretations for multicultural clients, a majority of assessors continue to be trained to interpret standard tests as if these standard measures were indeed bona fide etics rather than imposed etics.

A cultural competence option, however, is not without controversy. For example, I have been accused of fostering an inadequate emic approach to science and "an overly limited and methodologically-bound characterization of the field" (Butcher, 2001, p. 622) that essentially abandons mainstream professional psychology standards for research and clinical practice, particularly as applied to corrections on the MMPI/MMPI-2 (e.g., Velasquez et al., 1996). This view of cross-cultural test application considers that "careful translation is perhaps the most crucial aspect of assuring that a psychological test adapts effectively across a different language and culture" (Butcher, 2001, pp. 621–622). This statement presumed tests constructed in the United States measure the same human characteristics everywhere and that local or national demonstrations of construct equivalence and method equivalence are difficult to accomplish and essentially gratuitous.

Although competent translations of all tests are indeed necessary, translations by themselves are insufficient to provide a credible basis for cross-cultural or multicultural test applications because constructs describing personality and psychopathology in the United States may provide only fragmentary, incomplete, and irrelevant information in other cultures. Constructs are embedded in linguistic terms expressing particular culture-specific beliefs and shared historic understandings about human nature. Thus, constructs originating in the United States may have completely different behavioral, cognitive, and emotional ingredients in other countries or may be unrecognized or have other identifications in some countries (for depression as an example, see Brandt & Boucher, 1986).

ASSESSMENT REPORTS

Assessment reports are products or outcomes of a process that employs both interview and test data that is codified and systematized by low-inference scoring procedures and transmuted as a result of both low- and high-inference interpretation into the primary written vehicles for communication to clients and about clients. In chapter 1 (this volume), I described an early history of research on the communication adequacy of psychological reports, I noted a number of how-to-do books describing the mechanics of using test data in various formats for different communication purposes, and I described report formats for multicultural assessees. For the immediate present, in the absence of demonstrated cross-cultural equivalence, an argument can be made for reports that first examine the findings from each standard test administered separately, noting the limitations of each test for the particular assessee, and proceeding to a cautious summary across tests. Although preparation of test-specific reports is contrary to the established practice of preparing domain-oriented reports, I prefer test-oriented reports for test data generated by graduate students as part of their assessment training or with multicultural assessees for demonstration purposes using therapeutic feedback. In other settings, domain-oriented reports may be preferable, although these reports may be more susceptible to bias due to limited equivalence research findings for particular tests. Attention to the Table 1.3 (chap. 1, this volume) checklist is especially necessary to provide accountability safeguards in preparing domain-specific reports describing multicultural persons.

FEEDBACK OF ASSESSMENT RESULTS

Klopfer asserted that assessment "feedback is not only ethically necessary and humanly desirable, it is also clinically valuable" (1983, p. 516). Pope (1992) described 10 essential aspects of feedback to clients "(a) feedback as process; (b) clarification of tasks and roles; (c) responding effectively to a crisis; (d) informed consent and informed refusal; (e) framing the feedback; (f) acknowledging fallibility; (g) counter transference and the misuse of feedback; (h) records, documentation, and follow-up; (i) looking toward the future; and (j) assessing and understanding important reactions" (p. 268). With some elaboration and tailoring, these aspects are relevant for multicultural clients.

A feedback rationale that has been designed primarily for Euro-Americans emphasizes information relevant to specific assessment objectives in a context of empathy, support, and reassurance leading to client ownership of findings and ability to empower a transformation of the new knowledge into a self-efficacy resource (Dana, 1974, 1982, 1985). Such feedback can be therapeutic when it "stems from an affective bond with the . . . provider and mutual understanding of the patient's subjective reality" and "provided in a relaxed, affiliative manner by a warm, giving caregiver" (Dana, 1985, p. 600). This feedback rationale is supported by research findings that self-healing occurs under conditions of relaxation and positive emotions (Schwartz, 1984).

There is strong resemblance of this feedback model to the "salutogenesis" definition of psychological health operationalized in the SOC measure (Antonovsky, 1984) by meaningfulness as motivation, manageability as adequacy of personal coping resources, and comprehensibility as the cognitive sense that clear information permits predictable behaviors. These components correspond to desire for feedback, availability of resources necessary to utilize feedback, and the adequacy of the feedback communication process. Acknowledging a presumed and tentative etic status of the SOC construct and its components (see Ying et al., 1997), then culture-specific protocols of client meaningfulness translated into motivation for assessment and feedback can establish the climate prior to the onset of the assessment process. A test-referenced basis in adequate personal resource data to describe manageability is also helpful. For examples, Asians generally expect life to be harder than do Euro-Americans and therefore may be relatively passive in accepting a level of inner turmoil and hardship without feeling any necessity to label distress or a perceived need for any changes to assist their personal coping efforts. Hispanics may also tolerate greater unlabeled internal distress for reasons that necessitate sustained coping coupled with containment of negative affect by fatalism and self-reassurance of external support. Finally, comprehensibility requires that the language employed to convey assessment findings is shaped and conditioned by cultural knowledge. For example, the client may not experience any internalized responsibility for personal circumstances and thus may neither welcome nor understand increased power as an individual to alter life circumstances. Other persons, including family members, extended family individuals, indigenous healers, and so forth, may possess the inherent power the client denies, lacks, or is unwilling to mobilize. If this is the case, these other persons—or the client entity—must share in the feedback process to render it comprehensible and a potential basis for intervention of any kind.

Acceptance and consensual use of the therapeutic assessment feedback model by psychologists has been predicated on empirical documentations of MMPI–2 efficacy (e.g., Finn & Tonsager, 1992; Newman & Greenway, 1997), as well as by demonstrations of usefulness with the Rorschach and other projective methods (Finn, 1996a) with a variety of client populations and different diagnoses. In addition, advocacy for therapeutic assessment practice, competent teaching (Finn, 1996b, 1998), and managed care utilization (Finn & Martin, 1997) has provided a context for sustained professional attention to the empirical evidence.

An introduction to therapeutic assessment for multicultural populations begins with the question, "How much of what we know about feedback and therapeutic assessment feedback is applicable cross-culturally?" This question can be discussed using Pope's (1992) format of essential feedback aspects including the context of culturally credible relationship ingredients, client response sets as impediments, tangible and intangible elements susceptible to cultural interpretation, cultural beliefs and assessor/therapist obligations, and an assessor obligation to facilitate and ensure client understanding of feedback contents.

First, the manner of developing the collaborative relationship must be emotionally acceptable and culturally credible (see Ingredient 3D, service delivery etiquette in Table 4.1). The affect must conform to the client's anticipated interpersonal style, whereas the structure, pace, and contents of service delivery should conform to cognitive beliefs including health–illness beliefs and contents permissible in a same- or cross-gender professional relationship.

Second, in providing therapeutic feedback of assessment findings, the presence of culture-specific response sets can dilute or even nullify the entire process. Acquiescence to findings can occur because some Hispanic clients do not want to be disrespectful to the assessor or appear ungrateful or critical. Fear of loss of face during assessment can be a major impediment to a collaborative feedback process with Asians and Asian Americans because it leads to denial and minimization of test findings, especially contents that are critical or suggestive of disturbance. For example, empirically identified components of loss of face or threat to loss of social integrity include hiding mistakes, avoiding criticism, withholding complaints, forgetting embarrassing events, and generally adhering to social norms (Zane, 1993). Some potential limitations of the feedback process can be acknowledged and offset by using moderators for information pertinent to acculturation status, responses sets, and additional cultural information. Thus, feedback may have positive or negative consequences (Smith, 1978). Negative consequences occur whenever an unacceptable style or language is used (e.g., impersonal, infused with jargon, laden with psychiatric descriptions of pathology, etc.). This is particularly important with culturally diverse persons who often make different assumptions concerning the usefulness of assessment per se or experience different constraints about the kinds of personal contents they are willing to share in professional settings.

Third, tangible and intangible elements of feedback as a process will be defined, anticipated, and responded to differently as a result of style, affect, tempo, behaviors, language usage, as well as the extent to which such intangibles as respect, empathy, cultural understanding, beliefs, and values are exposed by the assessor. As a consequence, Pope's (1992) feedback essentials, tailored for specific cultural credibility and acceptability, are relevant for multicultural clients.

Fourth, the relatedness of cultural beliefs to assessment tasks and roles asks the question, "What are the mutual prerogatives and responsibilities of client and assessor for participation in tasks that may be defined similarly or differently by both parties?" Not only is clarity imperative, but discussion of mutual understandings is mandatory. As Pope (1992) indicated, "When roles or tasks are neglected, are improvised as the testing proceeds, or are viewed differently by those involved, problems result" (p. 268). One problem concerns a mutual understanding of informed consent. Informed consent can include refusal of feedback as a necessary option. For example, in ignorance, I once made the profound error of not juxtaposing these options at the onset only to discover that a Sikh-American neither wanted nor appreciated the feedback because it was incidental to her intensely positive experience and process of exposing her cultural identity for her own use in planning her immediate future (for assessment report, see Dana, 2003a). Although she cursorily acknowledged, accepted, and, I believe, understood the validity of interpretations, it was of no importance or utility to her that she actually received these findings.

Finally, and related to the clarity of client options in receiving feedback, Pope (1992) also emphasized the assessor's obligation to be certain the client has in fact understood the written and/or oral communication of test findings. Professional judgment is required, but this judgment must be tempered and informed by sufficient cultural knowledge. Pope's (1992) words are essential here to convey the magnitude of obligation: "Using scrupulous care to conduct this assessment of the client's understanding of and reactions to the feedback is no less important than using adequate care in administering the standardized psychological tests; test administration and feedback are equally important, fundamental aspects of the assessment process" (p. 271).

How the assessor frames the feedback in language and content is related not only to acceptance or rejection of feedback per se but to subsequent client choices as well as decisions that others might make for the client. In other words, assessment of individuals who are culturally different from the assessor is always a high-stakes situation for clients due to increased potential for destructive consequences. In this regard, as Pope (1992) emphasized, "Clinicians conducting assessments . . . are vulnerable to a variety of personal, intense, irrational, sometimes unconscious reactions to the individuals to whom they provide services. . . . Such personal reactions . . . can influence, distort, and subvert the feedback process" (p. 270).

In "looking toward the future," Pope (1992) referred to unanticipated low probability consequences that deny the accuracy of inferences from assessment data and he cited custody hearings, disability evaluations, and worker compensation claims. To this list I would add discrimination and other infringements on civil rights as a result of cultural/racial bias or inadequate understanding of how culture influences the entire assessment process and outcomes to these unanticipated events.

II

Multicultural Interpretation

Multicultural Interpretation: Orientation and Information Resources

This chapter initially sets the stage for applying standard tests/methods with multicultural assessees by considering several questions. How these questions are answered by assessors provides a general framework of expectations for assessee performances on standard tests, the potential usefulness of conventional normative interpretation, and the desirability of mobilizing additional information to minimize cultural bias.

I describe in detail moderator variables, or information sources for cultural and racial identity information, following their introduction in chapter 4 (this volume) as proximal sources for cultural information and acculturation status documentation. Four examples of specific moderator usage with selected multicultural assessees include rationales for usage, effects of this information on interpretation of standard tests/methods, and the infusion of cultural information in psychological reports.

ORIENTATION QUESTIONS

Three questions are used to minimize stereotypy or caricature, evaluate anticipated cooperation, and suggest the extent of assessee follow-through with the assessment process. These questions are employed to separate general knowledge concerning a particular ethnic/racial group from information describing an individual with a specific group membership (see Fig. 2.1, chap. 2, this volume) and to provide a framework for examination of the potential usefulness of moderator information.

The first question, "What is the reason for this assessment?" recognizes that test-taking attitudes can dramatically affect the response process. These attitudes are often culture specific and for immigrants can mirror the attitude toward psychological evaluation per se, the relation between individuals and the government in the country of origin, or expectations for positive or negative reactions from the mental health system or their representatives. Is the assessee volunteering for assessment to gain information relevant for plans or decisions subject to personal control and implementation? Or is the assessment an involuntary referral for clinical diagnosis or a possible prelude to hospitalization? Is the setting for assessment medical, legal, or academic? The answer to this question is relevant to anticipated cooperativeness, adequacy of data samples, validity of inferences, and responsiveness to feedback of results.

A second step involves an examination of the difference between group identity and individual cultural identity. This step is necessary because assessors are prone to minimize within-group differences. The general question asked is, "How typical or representative of the culture is the assessee?" Typicality refers to characteristics related to acculturation status, social class and/or social roles, and educational level. These dimensions of potential within-group differences include traditional beliefs concerning health–illness, mind–body relationship, and LC/LR but do not necessarily encompass, for example, individualism–collectiveness preferences that may inhere independently of demographic variables. Standard tests employ different constructs and construct definitions and elicit different response styles that may be directly measurable or need to be inferred. The development of a context for interpreting each standard instrument entails these general questions as well as instrument-specific steps (see chaps. 6, 7, and 8, this volume) describing a coherent process for compiling data and leading to descriptive inferences relevant to assessee participation in assessment.

A third step is informed by the question, "What is the cultural orientation status of the assessee?" Additional information, often using moderator data, is necessary to describe acculturation status and/or to provide information relevant to understanding the cultural self in this chapter. It is mandatory to examine acculturation status for all assessees who are sojourners, recent immigrants, or of first and second generation in the United States. Third generation individuals, especially of non-European origins, may also need to be examined for acculturation status, especially if the family uses a language other than English in the home.

Cultural orientation status information is used to decide whether or not standard tests or tests constructed for a particular ethnic/racial group are applicable for a particular assessee. If group-specific or emic tests are not available, and standard tests must be employed instead, increased caution in interpreting psychopathology is necessary.

Another major issue affirming the desirability of using all three standard tests (perhaps the reason underlying their high frequencies of usage for over half a century) is that these instruments differ in the kinds of information provided. Whenever one or more of these instruments are inapplicable on the basis of acculturation information, it is important to consider whether or not a substitute emic measure can fulfill a role comparable with the standard instrument it is intended to replace.

These questions of purpose, typicality, and cultural orientation assume complex interrelations. An analogy to research matching mental health clients and their clinicians is relevant (e.g., Gamst et al., 2002; Gamst, Dana, Der-Karabetian, & Kramer, 2000, 2001, 2004b). This literature has shown an attenuated relation between ethnic match and cultural responsiveness due to the presence of approximately a dozen covariates. Figure 2.2 (chap. 2, this volume) presented the group–individual identity blend in values, beliefs, and language that structure an assessee's perception of assessors, the service delivery process, and specific assessment services. This figure also illustrated some variables covarying with ethnicity and emphasizing the extreme magnitude of within-group differences. Thus, it is important not to oversimplify the potential importance of interactions among ingredients comprising the makeup, gender, cultural humanity, and individuality of a particular assessee when confronted with the test stimuli and gender, cultural humanity, and professional skills of the assessor.

As an additional recognition of complexity, "identity maps" (Dana, 2003b) adapted from the perceptual schema model (Ridley, Mendoza, Kanitz, Angermeier, & Zenk, 1994) are employed in multicultural training to help clinicians appreciate the relevance and interactions of cultural information for the elderly or disabled, men and women (gender), heterosexual or homosexual (sexual orientation), and those from impoverished socioeconomic backgrounds. Identity maps illustrate the potentially complex interaction of figure and ground characteristics present in individual assessment data.

CULTURAL/RACIAL IDENTITY INFORMATION RESOURCES

The MAIP model initially encouraged use of this information solely for purposes of describing acculturation status. This usage supported and facilitated decisions to rely on or eschew standard tests for some multicultural assessees, particularly individuals who are traditional or marginal in cultural orientation status. However, it soon became apparent that more adequate and comprehensive descriptions of the cultural self were necessary to infuse and nourish the assessment process by additional sources of culturally relevant information.

The availability of additional cultural information encourages awareness and understanding of the magnitude of cultural differences between mainstream Americans of European origins and those of non-European origins, particularly recent immigrants or sojourners, and others who have lived in cultural enclaves and/or have retained language skills, religious practices, and culturally distinct customs and values. Moderators include culture-specific variables that directly provide acculturation status and other culturally relevant information as well as measures of response sets and/or response styles (Kleinman, 1977). General response sets/styles originated in the psychometrics of test construction in the United States (e.g., social desirability, acquiescence, deviation) as validity indicators and are culture-specific interpretations now recognized. Culture-specific response sets/styles were developed explicitly to evaluate culture-specific interpersonal dynamics such as Loss of Face (LOF) in Asian cultures. I introduced response sets and response styles in chapter 1 (this volume) and instrument-specific elaboration in chapters 6, 7, and 8 (this volume).

To my knowledge, there are no available instructional resources to demonstrate how these findings can be integrated into assessment reports and communicated to assessees (see Dana, 1998b). Many professional assessors, particularly Euro-Americans, have been reluctant to incorporate these variables into their assessment batteries perhaps because cultural information continues to be perceived as embodied in general descriptions of individuals rather than in delineation of specific behaviors. This section describes the range of these information resources I have used in demonstration assessments and for teaching purposes. Using some or many of these instruments to gather cultural information is dependent on the assessor's familiarity and depth of experience with a particular culture.

As a cautionary note, many of these instruments have research origins exclusively, and their applications for clinical assessment purposes may be difficult because of limited, dated, or problematic psychometric data on test construction, reliability, and validity as well as omission from these research reports of relevant details concerning administration, scoring, and interpretation. Moreover, early moderators provided only modest increments of information because they were either brief instruments facilitating research screening or monolevel measures describing only the extent to which an original culture had been retained. When used as part of an interview, however, a monolevel format may be more acceptable for some traditional persons, particularly Native American and

Alaska Native persons and others who experience the metric employed in many standard paper-and-pencil tests as uncomfortable or irrelevant. Distrust and skepticism concerning use of additional tests can also result in preference for an oral process as the primary vehicle used for developing a relationship that includes information acquisition and exchange. Psychologists, however, may be more comfortable with tests because of minimal interviewing training and experience or because of the belief that test data is more accurate and reliable than interview information. Bilevel acculturation measures have now largely replaced monolevel acculturation status instruments due to the perceived necessity for an independent or orthogonal evaluation of the extent to which values and behaviors of the host culture have been incorporated.

Finally, the issue of how much additional time is required for inclusion of moderators in an assessment battery is important because managed care providers report severe reductions in compensated time for assessment services. For example, a 1993 survey reported that over 5 hr were necessary for administration, scoring, and interpretation of the Rorschach, TAT, and MMPI–2 (Ball, Archer, & Imhof, 1994), although an average time expenditure of less than 2 compensated hours was reported for assessments using these same instruments (Camara et al., 2000). These comparative figures do not include usage of any additional tests to provide cultural information. The amount of time required for administration, scoring, and interpretation of these instruments has not been examined in any survey. Nonetheless, it is reasonable to assume that at least 30 min may be necessary for administration, scoring, interpretation, and write-up of several brief measures. Moreover, an increasing demand for culturally competent assessment includes an ethical responsibility to be aware of new acculturation status measures and research applications of other potentially relevant information resources.

I have belabored this discussion because many assessors are not yet sufficiently integrated into a multicultural society on the basis of their daily life experiences, relationships, and opportunities for acquisition of relevant cultural information. Until societal changes mandate, encourage, and support cultural learning throughout the life span, moderators can provide potentially corrective information for pathology bias, reduction of stereotyping, and more adequate understanding of individual humanity.

AN INVENTORY OF MEASURES

This chapter began with a description and summary of instruments for cultural and racial identity evaluation in assessment demonstrations and clinical practice. Many of these moderators were described in chapter 4

TABLE 5.1
Selected Culture-Specific and Culture-General Measures

African Americans
  African American Acculturation Scale (AAAS)
  Developmental Inventory of Black Consciousness (DIB–C)
  Cross Racial Identity Scale (CRIS)
  Racial Identity Attitude Scale (RIAS)

Native Americans and Alaska Natives
  Four Generation Acculturation Format (Brown, 1982)
  Northern Plains Bicultural Immersion Scale (NPBI)

Asian Americans
  Asian American Cultural Experience Survey (AACES)
  Asian Values Scale (AVS)
  Suinn–Lew Self-Identity Acculturation Scale (SL–ASIA)
  Cultural Adjustment Difficulties Checklist (CADC)
  Ethnic Identity Scale (EIS)*
  Filipino American Acculturation Scale (FAAS)
  Family Conflicts Scale (FCS)
  Individualism–Collectivism Scale (INDCOL)
  Internal–External Ethnic Identity (Int–Ext Id)
  Loss of Face (LOF)
  Social Interactions Scale (SIS)

Hispanic Americans
  Acculturation Rating Scale for Mexican Americans (ARSMA/ARSMA–II)
  Bicultural Involvement Questionnaire (BIQ)
  Hispanic Assessment Scale (HAS)
  Psychological Acculturation Scale (PAS)

All Cultural Groups
  Multigroup Ethnic Identity Measure (MEIM)*
  Scale to Assess World Views (SAWV)
  Sense of Coherence (SOC)
  Twenty Statement Test/Who-Am-I? (TST)*

Note. See descriptions in chapter 4 (this volume). An asterisk (*) identifies measures examined primarily in this and later chapters.

(this volume); others, identified by asterisks, I introduce and discuss primarily in this chapter. This summary of instruments (Table 5.1) by cultural/racial groups requires an extended introductory commentary.

For African Americans, the distinction between measures of cultural identity (AAAS) and racial identity (RIAS, DIB–C, CRIS) is of major importance because measurement of cultural identity has importance particularly for individuals seeking interventions to explore identity-relevant issues (see Dana, 1998e, chap. 5). However, a description of racial identity is mandatory for accurate *DSM–IV* diagnoses due to the potential confound between the behavioral and cognitive effects of racial identity development and symptoms of psychopathology. MMPI/MMPI-2 research evidence of this confound is available for other major groups (e.g., Hoffmann et al., 1985; Montgomery & Orozco, 1985; Sue et al., 1996), and belatedly for African Americans (e.g., Whatley et al., 2003).

For Native Americans and Alaska Natives, acculturation status information is always necessary to avoid misuse of standard tests (Allen, 1998). As suggested earlier, however, a majority of these individuals are uncomfortable with standard tests and paper-and-pencil moderator instruments. As a consequence, the NPBI should be used primarily for college-educated individuals with their consent because these students will be familiar with the test format and accustomed to testing as part and parcel of their educational experience. By contrast, Brown's (1982) questions are acceptable for almost all native persons within an interview context. Acculturation status estimates for native persons in urban and rural colleges have been derived from the NPBI measure (Allen, 1998). These percentage estimates for rural and urban colleges, respectively, are Traditional (45/25), Bicultural (2/24), Marginal (54/17), and Assimilated (3/33). Other college studies (Byron, 1995; Johnson & Lashley, 1989), using different methods, also reported relatively few assimilated individuals and similar percentages of Traditionals and Biculturals. However, 65% of the national, noncollege sample were of Marginal acculturation status (French, 1989). These estimates are included to suggest that the numbers of traditional native persons remains higher than for immigrant groups after many generations even in college populations due to less willingness to acculturate and large urban–rural differences in acculturation status.

For Asian Americans, the SL–ASIA is available for use with all Asians. Culture-specific instruments for seven distinct national populations are cited in chapter 4 (this volume). However, professional psychologists in the United States generally lack sufficient cultural knowledge to prepare *DSM–IV* cultural formulations for Asians and Asian Americans (see Dana, 2001a, 2002a) or identity culture-bound syndromes (Paniagua, 2000). The variety of emic measures described in chapter 4 (SIS, Int–ExtId) and pan-Asian measures (AACES, AVS, CADC, FCS, INDCOL) suggest that information resources provided by moderators are essential for description of the cultural selves of Asians and Asian Americans as well as to improve diagnostic reliability and accuracy. The development of cultural response set measures for Asian populations to date includes the LOF (Zane & Yeh, 2002). East Asian Taiwanese and Japanese students tend to use midpoint ratings for self-report items, whereas North American students employ more extreme values (Chen, Lee, & Stevenson, 1995).

The ARSMA and ARSMA–II acculturation status measures provide evidence for a pathology-culture confound that limits the diagnostic validity of MMPI/MMPI-2 for traditional Hispanic Americans. These ARSMA and ARSMA–II findings may reflect extreme responding as a cultural response set. For example, traditional and less educated Hispanics prefer extreme responses and agreement with self-report items, or acquiescence, in contrast with non-Hispanic Whites, and these differences are reduced with increasing acculturation differences (Marin, Gamba, & Marin, 1992). Socially desirable responding also occurs more frequently among lower SES individuals and with age among traditional Mexican Americans and Mexicans (Ross & Mirowsky, 1984). A variety of other moderators were developed in addition to ARSMA/ARSMA–II primarily as sources of information on the cultural self (see Cuellar, 2000; Dana, 1993, chap. 7; Dana, 1996a; Roysircar-Sodowsky & Maestas, 2000). In chapter 4 (this volume), I introduced only the major acculturation measures for Hispanics, including Mexican Americans (ARSMA/ARSMA–II), Mexican Americans and Central Americans (HAS), Cuban Americans (BIQ), and Puerto Ricans (PAS). Use of these moderators can facilitate the preparation of cultural formulations or descriptions of the cultural self in preparation for culture-specific interventions. Finally, several more moderators are potentially useful with all multicultural groups.

The Twenty Statements Test (TST; Kuhn & McPartland, 1954) is my most frequently used measure and serves as a benign beginning for an assessment process that may conclude with the potentially stressful Rorschach. The TST, also referred to as the Who-Are-You? or Who-Am-I? (WAY), was originally applied with different religious denominations and later internationally with Hong King, Swedish, and Ethiopian students (Watkins, Yau, Dahlin, & Wondimu, 1997).

I use the original directions contained in both of the previously mentioned articles:

> There are twenty numbered blanks on the page below. Please write twenty answers to the simple question "Who Am I?" in the blanks. Just give twenty different answers to this question. Answer as if you were giving the answers to yourself, not to somebody else. Write the answers in the order that they occur to you. Don't worry about logic or "importance." Go along fairly fast, for time is limited. (p. 69)

In developing the TST, Kuhn and McPartland (1954) used content analysis to distinguish between consensual and subconsensual references. *Consensual* references were more frequent and referred to "groups and classes whose limits and conditions of membership are matters of common knowledge" (Kuhn & McPartland, 1954, p. 69) such as "engineering student," "woman," "daughter," "Muslim," or "Peruvian." *Subconsensual* referred to "groups, classes, attributes, traits, or any other matter which would require interpretation by the respondent" (Kuhn & McPartland, 1954, pp. 69–70) such as "happy," "interesting," and so forth, without positional references or with reference to consensual classes using ambiguous modifiers. Assignment of responses to these categories was highly reliable in Kuhn and McPartland's study and subsequent studies as well. The Midwestern, college student respondents provided all of their consensual referents before including any subconsensual descriptors.

The TST has been used in literally hundreds of earlier studies, although Wylie (1974) was disappointed that construct validity could not be demonstrated from existing scoring systems for inferring self-conceptions and omitted it from her second review (Wylie, 1989). In their review of cross-cultural TST use, Watkins et al. (1997) expressed concern that 20 responses were too many for non-Western participants. Nonetheless, cross-cultural differences were found in many studies, especially between Asian collectivist societies and individualist Western societies. In Asian societies, trait attributions were infrequent, and there were fewer abstract and more specific and social responses (Rhee, Uleman, Lee, & Roman, 1995). Japanese participants used fewer abstract, psychological attributes (Cousins, 1989). It is important to be aware that East Asians are less likely to provide behavioral referents including traits, dispositions, or other internal states simply because of a more holistic conception of a person in a social context (Choi, Nisbett, & Norenzayan, 1999). Furthermore, as a consequence of neither focusing on nor labeling internal processes, individuals may fail to identify the importance/salience of their negative feelings.

The SAWV, described in chapter 2 (this volume), provides information on five value orientations affected by cultural origins, acculturation status, and generation in the United States. SOC, described in chapter 4 (this volume), differentiates characteristics of robustness and beliefs in positive outcomes in coping with problems-in-living as a consequence of self-efficacy, fate, denial, or optimism among other sources of temporary relief. I use the SOC whenever there is evidence of distress that I suspect merely suggests a high cultural tolerance for symptoms coupled with denial of disturbance. The Multigroup Ethnic Identity Measure (MEIM; Phinney, 1992; Ponterotto, Gretchen, Utsey, Stracuzzi, & Saya, 2003) was designed to tap common identity elements in a variety of cultural groups within a multicultural society. The MEIM examines identity achievement including attitudes and behaviors relevant for ethnic identity exploration by means of ethnic identity and other-group orientation components.

EXAMPLES

The following examples illustrate moderator usage informing major standard assessment instruments for foreign and American students from a number of cultural groups. These assessments include both clinical referrals and demonstrations. A minimum of $50 was paid to each demonstration participant, and written and oral feedback was available to the extent desired by each assessee. I typically select demonstration assessees from students whom I have observed over a period of time as employees in a research setting. This process reduces the likelihood that the assessment process or feedback will result in a referral for treatment.

Selected moderators emphasize frequently or routinely used measures and others applicable primarily to particular assessees: a Korean-American "volunteer" multicultural student who knew that I was learning cross-cultural assessment by administrating demonstration batteries and providing feedback in report format, a Japanese student referred by her counselor for therapeutic assessment; and a Vietnamese American student and a Sikh American student participated in demonstration assessments.

Korean American

This example illustrates the TST, a moderator that I use routinely in all assessments. Additional moderators are also used to provide descriptive cultural information. In this example, separate sections of the completed report provide minimal background information and describe behavior during assessment, the moderators, and interpretation of one projective method, the TAT. My intention in these examples is to describe the cross-cultural and multicultural assessment process used to train myself to gather and interpret data that is relevant to credible psychological report contents using a therapeutic assessment format. I begin each assessment process with a brief interview placing the assessee in a context of family and culture and incorporating relevant behavioral notes in this description. In this initial example, the introductory paragraph in a report prepared for the assessee follows:

> A 22-year-old married Korean-American college student volunteered for this assessment demonstration. Her mother was born in Korea and her father is of mixed European heritage: her parents were divorced when she was 5 years old and she grew up with her mother and younger sister. Her relationship with her mother is strained and communication has been difficult. She believes mother prefers her sister who is more Korean in physical appearance. She describes herself as "Korean at home; American elsewhere," but in the past she has not experienced acceptance as sufficiently Korean by her kin or fully American by peers and classmates due to ignorance of customs and behaviors she was expected to know.

Her TST responses appear in the following completions:

1. woman; 2. Korean-American; 3. strong inside; 4. intelligent; 5. good listener & speaker; 6. sister; 7. daughter; 8. wife, niece, & granddaughter;

9. writer; 10. prepared; 11. student; 12. student of life; 13. lover of plants; 14. friend to be counted on; 15. good daughter; 16. all these things and more I have not yet to discover; 17. caring; 18. person with a big mouth who talks too much; 19. person with a large self-conscious; 20. someone with a cool (Korean) middle name which I am proud of.

Following the TST administration, I select several moderators not only to have information on acculturation status but to provide a larger sample of relevant cultural contents as well. I use an acculturation status instrument constructed for the specific culture whenever it is available; otherwise I use instruments that are generic, for example, for East Asian cultures. An 80-item monolevel Korean Canadian acculturation scale in an unpublished thesis was not used due to length and need for further research (see Kim & Berry, 1985). In this demonstration assessment, I employed the INDCOL (Hui, 1988), the SL–ASIA (Suinn et al., 1987), the SAWV (Ibrahim & Kahn, 1987), and the LOF (Zane & Yeh, 2002). The following descriptive paragraph on these moderators was prepared for the report:

> INDCOL suggests a primarily collectivist identity with spouse, parents, kin, and coworkers, but more individualism is expressed with neighbors and friends. On SL–ASIA, you are bicultural but Asia-oriented. On the TST, six of your responses were culture-specific in a context of trying to make a good self-presentation. The SAWV indicated culture-specific preferences for harmony with nature and collateral-mutual relationships in a context with Anglo time and mixed values otherwise. LOF was at the mean for Asians suggesting a strong concern with maintaining outward appearances, particularly with strangers.

Twenty-one TAT cards were subsequently administered with card 3BM included because of perception equally by men and women as a male or female figure. In examining the stories for cultural contents (see chap. 8, this volume, for details), I attend to the percentage of stories that include cultural themes (11/21 or 52.5%) and then to the relevance of contents. The general interpretation rationale follows Tomkins (1947) by considering his dimensions as a framework for sensitization to the potential information presented. The format developed by Stein (1955) is useful for abstracting stories and subsequently cluster and organize themes by card stimulus values, described in an earlier text (Dana, 1982). Prior to TAT interpretation, I familiarize myself with the assessee's culture or review what I know about that culture in the context of assessment data (see Dana, 1998b, 1999a). This patently high-inference interpretation uses cultural knowledge as content within a more or less formalized interpretive structure. Because I am aware of the twin pitfalls of eisegesis (or personalization) and the potential inadequacies of idiographic approaches (as opposed to nomothetically based interpretation), I always test the accuracy of interpretations by sharing findings with assessees and carefully discussing their reactions to the statements contained in reports. The outcome of this process is a revision of report contents either formally by rewriting the report or informally discussing alterations in content, meaning, and intensity to accurately reflect the feedback process. The TAT portion of this report follows:

> Your TAT presents a picture of a mixture of Korean and American contents. The Korean content comes out clearly in the stories to six cards (1, 3BM, 11, 12, 15, 19) to reflect values of unquestioning duty/obligation to family wishes, particularly for achievement, the necessity to remove shoes at home, the importance of "good heart" as a measure of human worth, recognition of customs surrounding death and funeral offerings, and residues of belief in appeasement of dragons and the presence of ghosts as guardian spirits. At a secondary level, Korean attitudes are probably present in social class concerns (2, 5, 13), age distinctions (12F), and a shared family togetherness that constitutes happiness (16).
>
> This surface presentation is of two ways of life in uneasy juxtaposition with an unsureness concerning your Korean side because you lack full knowledge of the culture and lack fluency in the language. Similarly, the American side of you is mired in daily struggles to achieve through education, to strengthen your American side in marriage, and to work toward an ideal life with economic security, middle-class status, and an intact family that shares joys to embody happiness. However, this struggle is difficult. Fatigue and discouragement, and even occasional inertia are present as a byproduct of incessant work, determination to succeed, and your desire to maintain a cheerful, pleasant, cooperative surface appearance that may belie or contradict inner experience.
>
> This struggle is difficult because beneath the easy social extraversion, the consideration for others, the wry sense of humor, and the outpouring of positive emotional responsiveness to your world there is anxiety, anger, and fears of disrupting the fabric of your social milieu that cannot be ordinarily exposed or expressed. This internal maelstrom dissipates energy, creates fatigue, and is coupled with internalized self-doubt and self-criticism. This internal struggle appears to stem from not feeling sufficiently connected to other persons, probably originating in your fears that you were not completely accepted by your mother.
>
> In your TAT stories there is a lack of engagement with many pictures, a search for picture details to provide structure in lieu of creating stories that recount a reciprocal interplay of feelings and actions among persons. This attention to picture cues provides stories that obliterate the potential for interpersonal discomfort or distress in human relationships in cards that usually "pull" for conflict, problem-expression, and problem-solving in social contexts (4, 6GF, 7GF, 9GF, 13, 18GF). As a consequence, the quality and intensity of human relationships is reduced and human interactions are bland and copasetic, at least on the surface. To be sure, there is consideration

for others (13MF), even devotion to providing adequately and responsibly caring for family members (14), comfort in human relatedness (10), and matter-of-fact disruption of a relationship (18GF), but responsiveness to others is muted, particularly with respect to your capacity for relatedness and the desirability of greater mutual contact with others. Life has become focused on hard work to better yourself, fulfill family obligations, move up in the social class structure, and eventually achieving your ideal family togetherness and happiness rather than on a day-to-day fulfillment of your strong needs for intimacy, acceptance by significant others, and increased perdurability of your own feelings of self-worth and intactness.

Much of the distress you experience is situational in nature as a result of the pressures, hassles, anxieties, and fatigue of daily living. You have ample resources to manage these stressors. However, due to a relationship with your mother that lacks closeness or comfort on a daily basis and your underlying anxieties concerning how you can put together your two identities—Korean and American—to provide a unique combination of strengths, some of the energy required to resolved the daily problems in living is not available to you. This energy is buried in feelings experienced as anxiety, self-doubt, unanswered questions, and despair. These feelings are constantly stirred up by the unrequited relationship with your mother. I would suggest that your most important personal business lies in gaining knowledge of your Korean cultural origins, particularly the language, while simultaneously trying to bridge your mother's distance and emotional unavailability. You may be able to enlist your sister, or other relatives, to gain mother's attention to this process within yourself and to understand how important it is for you. If this cannot be accomplished, or if mother is unable to hear and attend to your concerns, I believe you could be aided by a Korean-American counselor who could work with you to understand your identity issues and how these issues have been made more salient and poignant as a result of the relationship with your mother.

Japanese

A 27-year-old Japanese college student referred by her counselor for therapeutic assessment was administered the SL–ASIA and INDCOL followed by 12 TAT cards (1, 2, 3BM, 7GF, 11, 12M, 13MF, 19, 16 plus 5, 12F, 10). The joint-feedback technique (Dana et al., 1978) was used as a format for discussion of assessment findings with the client and her counselor.

Constructed and normed for Asian American college students, SL–ASIA was used qualitatively. The Ethnic Identity Scale (EIS; Meredith, 1967) that distinguishes among three generations of Hawaiian and mainland Japanese Americans was not used because information on acculturation status did not appear relevant for the counseling process. INDCOL was used because it provides subscale information on behavior in six roles; her responses were examined, but formal scoring was not done due to the research origins of the instrument. The following content was prepared from notes using the original words put into better sentence format:

> On the SL–ASIA she is clearly Asian identified with extreme scores on 17 items. Japanese was her first and only language for 18 years and she reads and writes Japanese better than English. The fit of her responses is good with Asians, especially for food preferences and some values. On 3 items, she identified as Asian American and bicultural. On 7 items, however, she was non-Asian identified. The English language and English movies are preferred; Americans are preferred associates/friends and her fit with American values is good. On INDCOL she showed a fierce independence, especially on Spouse and Parent subscales, in time management, work, and decisions in areas of occupation, religion, friends, and music tastes. With any potential spouse, she would have a joint bank account and exercise freedom in planning time use. With parents, she has a stand-off and does not share personal information. Their willingness to help is acknowledged, although she does not ask their advice.

I include her stories to three TAT cards (4, 12F, 16) to represent culture-specific content and I follow them first by a conceptualization of the interpretation procedures and then by the report:

> 4. This man and a woman are having relationship for years. She's working at the bar so they met at this bar. When they met, he was tired so actually he was hopeless. He has tiny, little bit money, maybe ten bucks. Hanging around. She fell in love with him at first sight. Knew his past: fired, not have money. She had empathy—took him to her house. He started to stay with her but he (long pause) first couple of months looking for job but couldn't find it. Area not so many businesses—he had habit—alcohol—turned to be very hostile/angry. No business firm wants to hire him. He loves having sex with her, sleeping, eating, but doesn't work. She forgives him whatever he does. She loves him so she cannot leave him even though he is not useful. So their relationship will last four more years.

> 12F. (Long pause) This picture reminds me of—We have two faces—one is the face we have in public which we call "face"; the other one is invisible face but it is also your face. I feel that she had a concern about something—family matters—actually she's a second wife—even the family matters is kind of a second-hand program. She appears being concerned about this matter, but, in fact, she doesn't care about this matter. She looks—she seems that she treats the matter as interesting thing even though she is family member. She pretends she is mother or wife; in reality she makes a distance between rest of family members and is just an observer. Also I think she cannot understand others' feelings—others' sad feelings.

> 16. I imagine a flower—just a lot of flowers—pink, purple, pastel color flower—(Don't know be story or not) I feel good when I see flowers. Even

though flower's life is short, couple of days, dry out, ugly. When fresh, blooming, so beautiful, natural. I like beauty of flowers. I want to have flowers around all year, makes me feel good. Even pictures of flowers make me feel good. Flowers quiet/beautiful. (Almost soliloquy, musing tinged with sadness, with story put aside) Woman better be quiet, not speak one word more. Existence like flower not like definition of woman—woman useless. Not use for woman, natural flower is different.

When coupled with moderator information, these stories provide examples of conflict between yearnings for independence and inherent dependency. As a woman, she feels essentially useless, fragile, and time limited, an ornament victimized by men and forced into conventional socialized roles dichotomizing her feelings and behaviors. Doi (1973) articulated a historic Japanese construction of dependency occurring from the bond between children and mother/family described by the noun *amae,* to depend and presume on another's dependency (Doi, 1990). *Amae,* as expressed in the verb form *amaeru,* to snuggle up and be enveloped in indulgent love, has a complementarity of acceptance of another's *amaeru* as *amayakasu,* and both have active and passive connotations (Fujii, Fukushima, & Yamamoto, 1993). *Amae* produced extraordinarily intense family relationships continuing throughout life in attachments to family and society. I have described *amae/amareu* elsewhere (Dana, 1998e, Figure 7.2 and pp. 157–159) as distinct components of a cycle of the health–illness relation. These components are self-checked by how relationships are structured with different situational and behavioral standards. Enactments, as inner expressions, differ with family and/or close friends and outer expressions with strangers. These internalized affects permit spontaneous exposure of socially interdependent feelings, whereas externalized behaviors enable a temporary restraint, under conditions of threat, followed by currying favor. Distress or symptomatology and ultimately psychopathology are exposed by inability to *amaeru,* improper use of *amae,* or situational inability to make correct inferences from others' behavior (Doi, 1973, 1990).

For this young woman, there has been a loss of *amae* manifest in acculturation issues, a sense of being alone, lack of social support from her Japanese peers, and fear of the consequences of close relationships with men leading to muted expression of feelings and desire for protection from exploitation and abuse. In spite of cultural bias against psychological explanations, the counseling process has permitted her to receive support, learn self-esteem, exercise some power to control her own life, express real feelings, and eschew dependent–subservient, male–female relationships. A personal redefinition of *amae* can provide a new start enabling her to continue and complete her education and to avoid dependency by increasing self-sufficiency. The following report provides an example of how to present this information in therapeutic assessment format:

Your stories to these TAT cards, with few exceptions, were atypical for American college students. Your major themes expressed conflicts concerning acculturation experiences in the United States as well as feelings about yourself in your search for sufficient inner strength to enable an intimate, loving, enduring relationship with a man. You require inner strength, genuine feelings in close relationships, and self-confidence in order to express these feelings, be yourself, and not role-play with other persons. The last story you told (Card 10) exposed concern that it is not easy to establish a love that is shared, mutual, and non-exploitative. In your own words, "they make sure (in) loving someone, they are being loved."

Acculturation has been a challenge for you and sometimes painful because there are no clear rules for use of *amae* in intimate and casual relationships in the United States. Sometimes you are uncertain of understanding others because people are often spontaneous and expose many kinds of meaning by their words and actions. Nonetheless, you have intense needs for social support, for a secure context in which to live and learn.

I suspect that part of this struggle is due to conflict over expressing *amae*. *Amae* is part of you, but often involved role-playing in the past that muted your own feelings and wishes for more direct expression. You said that you felt alone even in Japan and this sense of being alone is also present here.

In many TAT stories that might have a variety of themes, you describe a close male–female or husband–wife relationship. However, except in Cards 5 and 10, this relationship is always exploitative, painful, and unequal. Men are perceived as untrustworthy, sexually and financially exploitative, and may even be abusive, at least emotionally if not physically. The women in these stories lack the self-confidence to speak out, to express real feelings, and prevent exploitation. I suspect that you either witnessed such as relationship or may have been involved yourself in a similar dilemma. There is fear that by speaking out, by expressing negative feelings, especially anger, the relationship would be terminated thereby depriving you of a vital source of *amae*. Moreover, part of the painful dilemma of being a woman for you is secret sadness—an inevitability of circumstances or fate—that women should be of transient beauty, essentially useless, and above all silent (Card 16). Men may also lose by having unequal relationships without honest communication; they die (Card 13), are killed (Card 6GF), but they have less to lose because they are seen as controlling power in relationships. With apparent impunity, they can have affairs, travel on "business," or terminate the relationship. As a result, it is the wife who suffers most from deception and inability to react with timely strength (Card 4). And if the wife reacts with passion or impulsivity, she also loses (Card 6GF) and cannot escape punishment.

Also in Card 6, I felt I was depicted as the "detective" (also "firefighter/policeman") who "asks many questions" and can potentially at least, "reveal the truth" about you. But the "truth," I believe, is something you already know and have taken constructive steps to act upon by entering counseling.

In your stories, you describe father, but there is no mention of mother even in the three additional cards I administered. The father you describe is often absent (as are husbands, too), but provides "gifts" in the form of presents and a tutor to express his "love." In Card 12M, the father can be kind to a son and grieves and is very sorry that his son is gone (drowned). This is conjecture, but I wonder if your father did not hope to have sons, or a son, instead of two daughters? Or can this be a wish on your part to have been a son for him?

Since an intimate, honest, abiding relationship with a man is elusive and difficult to achieve, you must have something else. This "something else" can either contribute to the ability to protect yourself in an intimate relationship, and/or become a substitute for such a relationship. This "something else" includes a new start here, the educational opportunity and process, self-confidence and greater self-esteem. All of these ingredients provide power to assume control of your own life. And, I believe, it is your awareness of these needs that have led you into a counseling relationship that, in addition, provides a supportive context in which to gain understanding and nourish your intentions to have a happier life.

Vietnamese American

In this example, Vanessa, the 22-year-old undergraduate student emigrated from a farming community when she was 5 for a year in a Thai refugee camp before coming to the United States with her parents and younger brothers. Because it was my initial assessment with a Vietnamese, a variety of moderators were used in the following order: TST, SL–ASIA, AVS, INDCOL, SAWV, and SOC. Three standard instruments were administered: (Rorschach Inkblot Method (RIM), TAT, MMPI–2, and the Incomplete Sentences Blank (ISB; Rotter, 1950). Two sections of the report—moderators and personality evaluation—are included to illustrate the impact of these moderators on interpretation:

Vanessa is more Asian than bicultural (SL–ASIA score 2.1), although she is bilingual and equally comfortable with Asians and non-Asians. However, her identity is exclusively Vietnamese rather than pan-Asian. On the SAVW, she is profoundly but realistically optimistic, Oriented primarily toward the future, invested in collateral-mutual relationships, engaged in actively participating in life while pursuing a future consonant with her values which are largely but not exclusively traditional (SAWV). Family is of overarching importance to her, but complete conformity is not mandatory (AVS). However, it is essential that she must consider family reputation as a primary guide to her behavior and bring no shame or disgrace to the family. In this regard, achievement and filial piety are absolutely essential. However, she can envision some sources of trust, dependence, and help outside the family and has confidence in her own sources of strength. There is personal integrity and consistency in her collectivist values (INDCOL). Her SOC score indicated extremely high resistance resources (+2 sigma).

Vanessa presents herself as a friendly, outgoing, demure, gentle, non-aggressive, nice, pleasant, obedient, self-respecting person who is culturally Vietnamese and behaviorally American. Her Vietnamese self attends to culturally determined perspectives that include nature, warm–cold evaluations, and everyday events, particularly within a family context. Her response to the TAT, ISB, and WAY were innocuous, descriptive, and designed to be non-revealing of internal events or personal contents.

On TAT Card 8GF she was "posing" for me, tired but obedient and complacent. On Rorschach Card II her only human movement response was a face-to-face situation of patient, matter-of-fact involvement with another person while Card IV was seen as a "really, really old tree" with someone looking up at it, perhaps symbolizing potential respect and veneration of older males.

These Rorschach responses suggest that assessment was a special situation for her and she wanted to please me by participation but had some culturally determined reservations concerning the content she was permitted to include. Further evidence was found in MMPI–2 responses that suggest the limits of this apparent conformity. For example, during a post-test interview, items admitting fits, faints, and dizziness, and urges to shock others were simply denied while the two items admitting shoplifting/thefts were responded to with equivocation and embarrassment.

On the MMPI–2, both the F and Sc scales were elevated (61, 60), with Persecutory Ideas (Pa 1, 75), and Bizarre Mentation (BIZ, 73). A discussion of these items indicated that her family was talking about her, trying to influence, punishing her without cause, making her obey, and giving her discussion about her life. She acknowledged often feeling that things are not real, or are only seen by her, and that she has had visions, particularly of the future. She also acknowledged health worries and many physical symptoms including upset stomach, tingling body parts, neck pain, and muscle weakness. She also recognized herself as being high strung with many fears and worries, brooding, frequent anger and crying, poor sleep, and night fears. Her Ego Strength (ES) score was very low (31). The scores for F, SC, BIZ, and Pa 1 can be understood within a cultural context, although these scores also reflect the presence of extreme family pressure for obedience.

The TAT affirms the presence and intensity of family conflict but also evidences an extreme contextualization of her life within the family matrix. In fact, the dimensions of her present life include family and work/school pressures as well as recourse to nature for balance and recuperation. The natural world per se (Card 16) provides insufficient and transient relief from family responsibilities and stressors.

The Rorschach suggests a magnitude of distress in the absence of sufficient coping skills to raise a question of suicide potential, but it would be a mistake to interpret these signs on the basis of non-Asian normative data. Coping skills among Southeast Asians are related to external resources such as family strength and religious convictions (Catholicism) and internal resources of optimism, high perseverance, denial of conflict, denial of internalized distress, and implicit reliance on normatively acceptable physical symptoms and fatigue to bind the circumstances of daily life into an acceptable burden. Here there appears to be an inflexible extraversion that permits continuous immersion in the surface of daily life including a pervasive task orientation and an acceptance—albeit almost fatalistic—of family prerogative and dominance that may be questioned but never overtly flouted. Vanessa believes that daily life is an unremitting struggle that must be endured with prevailing optimism, good humor and good behaviors toward others as well as a consistent focus on the future. Her emotional are normatively intact and her body also normatively protests the burdens of stress and distress in her life in culturally acceptable terms.

Sikh American

This 23-year-old student, Diana, was of striking and exotic appearance. She was dressed entirely in red and displayed a shoulder tattoo. Her long black hair was streaked with green and held with a silver barrette, and a silver turquoise ring on the first finger of her left hand was complemented by dark red nails. She was selected because my cultural knowledge of Sikh history, religion, and culture was limited and superficial. Because there were neither moderators nor psychological literature for this population, several pan-Asian and generic moderators were used: MEIM, INDCOL, SL–ASIA, and SAWV. Excerpts from the TAT report are quoted here and the entire report is available elsewhere (Dana, 2003a, pp. 139–140):

> Her appearance made a statement of freedom for self-expression, of individuality, and a self-assured conviction and pride in who she is—a Seikh who is also an American. (Dana, 2003, p. 139)

> She is typically at the midpoint between traditional and European American acculturated (SL–ASIA, MEIM). On INDCOL, she is very independent, but simultaneously loyal and closely identified with reciprocal obligations to parents/kin in contrast with European American women. She shares information with parents/kin but not decision-making and receives social support from her friends who may be involved in decisions. Her SAWV worldview is unique in presenting an absence of the culturally imposed extremes typical for many ethnic groups. Human nature is seen as good, evil, and both good and evil. Human relationships are flexible and can be collateral, individualistic, or hierarchal. She appreciates the power of nature and is much less comfortable with the typical Western belief in controlling nature. She is especially attuned to life in the Present and future while maintaining significant contact with the past. Her activity orientation is both doing and feeling, equally and simultaneously, within a context of becoming. (Dana, 2003, pp. 139–140)

> The two major cultural themes (in the TAT)—internality and self-sufficiency—are intertwined and constitute the major focus for her interest, energy, and

activities. This internalized focus for experience among Sikhs has enabled their survival on the basis of group identity during three hundred years of pressure for assimilation from Mughals, British colonizers, and a repressive Hindu government. This experienced consciousness of a separate identity is at once mystical, ecstatic (in the sense of loving admiration), and unifying. The ability to find peace, sustenance, and unbounded energy and strength within herself permits her to live each day with a passionate intensity. She is not "a rebel without a cause" (described in TAT Card 4), but is her own cause. She flaunts her difference, her individuality, her uniqueness by becoming the "exotic parrot" in her Rorschach. Her exterior is a militant fabric that allows her to be present but not necessarily involved (as in not wishing to be studied here but permitting it to happen) and to hide a depth in which self-containment, self-mastery, autonomy, and special strength accompany clearly articulated and closely held beliefs and loyalties. (Dana, 2003, p. 140)

6

Rorschach and the Rorschach Comprehensive System

Rorschach (1921/1942) believed that his inkblot method was a pareidolia or mirror in which optic stimuli activated latent kinesthetic images that could be projected onto the inkblots and perceived as responses (for discussion, see Dana, 1982, pp. 25–26; Ellenberger, 1954). Rorschach synthesized his conceptualization of human personality—*Erlebnistypus* or Experience-Balance (EB)—from the major theorists of his era and designed his inkblot experiment as a resource for collecting data relevant for diagnosis of psychopathology and personality description. A scoring system for each inkblot response designated (locations), utilized inherent inkblot characteristics (determinants), and described whatever was perceived (contents) in a consensual format for using these response components. A profile, or psychogram, summarized the contributions of determinants for describing individual personality and hypothesizing interrelations among determinants representing constructs subordinated to EB as the master, unifying, and overarching construct.

This original scoring format was preserved over time in the context of additional scoring variables. Low-inference interpretation was emphasized and supplemented by very cautious use of high-inference interpretation elaborating contents, symbols, and formal scoring. A number of amplified scoring systems with normative data and interpretive schemas representing conceptual orientations and emic (national–local) perspectives were devised to elaborate, refine, and apply the original inkblot method. Succeeding generations of assiduous inkblot applications have provided information on various assessment objectives, psychometric methodologies, and measurement theories.

Exner's ambition to endow the Rorschach with a common language and method permitting standardized administration, scoring, and interpretation in training, practice, and research has been largely fulfilled. Exner (1969) initially examined the existing scores developed by Rorschach and augmented in five disparate systems. Development of the CS (Exner, 1974) resulted in refinement of these scores, the addition of new scores and indexes, and augmentation of reliabilities, validities, and utilities. Content scores were elaborated and incorporated, computer applications were recognized and endorsed, and the interpretive frame of reference was supplemented by a number of major conceptualizations. Despite recent intraprofessional allegations that the Rorschach is poor science, a landmark meta-analysis (Meyer et al., 2001) reaffirmed credibility and ensured continued popularity and future promise of the method nationally and internationally.

Following a brief historical resume that includes special attributes and cross-cultural usage, in this chapter, I suggest how normative data and response components can be used for CS interpretation with cross-cultural and multicultural assessees. I describe an interpretation strategy for these populations within a context of general guidelines and contemporary research evidence.

SPECIAL ATTRIBUTES
AND UNIQUE RELEVANCE

Rorschach developed the ambiguous and nonverbal inkblot stimuli and introduced EB within an interpretive framework of constructs for interpreting inkblot responses. EB permitted simultaneous monitoring of stability and change in human personality within a single instrument by describing the styles of creative introversion and reproductive extraversion. These ostensibly universal psychological functions composed an active, unconscious nucleus of personality continuously affected and modulated by day-to-day experiences within the context of an enduring steady state. Exner (1978) recognized these core personality functions by coping styles and capacity for control employing the "four square" designation of EB, EA, eb, and ea applied in some protocols. Introversiveness, or responsiveness to inner experience, was defined by free and transitory immersion in kinesthetic phenomena as a stimulus for self-awareness. Introverted persons were credited with greater individualized intelligence, creative ability, inner life, stable motility, and awkwardness (Rorschach, 1942). Extratension, or affective responsiveness to external stimulation, was inferred from use of the colored portions of inkblots. These persons lived in the world external to themselves with stereotyped intelligence, labile affect, greater reality adaptability, interpersonal skills, and restless mobility.

EB coping styles are measurable by the numbers of Movement and Color responses. Rorschach delineated five Swiss EB types representing more Movement than Color (introversive), more Color than Movement (extratensive), equal amounts of Movement and Color (ambiequal), no Color or Movement (coarctation/high Lambda style), and abundant Movement and Color (dilated). Each of these types exposed and delineated an experiential process for accommodating to a perceived world utilizing available resources represented by the array of scoring variables. EB, as a master construct instrumental for perception and organization of experience, provided substance and credibility to the belief in the universality of the Rorschach inkblot method (RIM), a term subsequently employed by Weiner (1994) for descriptive precision and accuracy.

EB cognition and affect were measured using Movement and chromatic Color Determinant scores. Form (F) represented rationality, control, repression, and constraint over unbridled emotionality. Human Movement (M) was differentiated as active and passive as well as flexor and extensor. Pure chromatic Color (C) indicated unmodulated impulsiveness either moderated to an extent by secondary Form (CF) suggesting affective lability or predominant Form (FC) representing a capacity for rapport/adaptation. Chiaroscuro reactions, based on distinctions among inkblot surface shading, depth, and texture, were analogous with Movement, Form, and Color responses (Boehm, 1977). Rorschach considered these light–dark nuances of separate shadings, including Vista, as secondary to Form. Exner (1974), following his predecessors, maintained these earlier distinctions. Shading, or variations in ink saturation (FY, YF, Y) was associated with unpleasant emotional experiences and helplessness during stress. Texture, or light–dark variation (FT, TF, T) represented need for emotional contact. Vista, or depth or three dimensionality (FV, VF, V), was recognized as ruminative introspection. Form visualization, or adherence to blot shape, was described as "normal" or "good" (F+) and "less clear" or impaired (F–). Good form was composed of common responses, described by Andronikof-Sanglade (2000) as "just tolerably adequate, quite evident, and easily seen" (p. 337) and unique or perfectly fitting superior Form responses, occurring once in 100 protocols, and designated as Orig +. The percentage of good Form (F + %) was calculated in the basis of frequency. Responses perceived by one in three persons, originally labeled as "vulgar" or "banal" and later as Populars (P) were tabulated.

Response locations described portions of blots used in responses including Whole (W), large Details (D), and unusual or small Details (Dd) and White Space (S). Large details could be expanded into Whole responses (DW) or interpreted in place of a Whole response (Do). Sequences of location responses for each card were delineated as Apperceptive Types. Content designations for Humans/Human details (H/Hd), Animals (A/ Ad), Objects (Obj), and other categories were introduced. A% was calculated from the numbers of A + Ad responses.

Assessment of strengths, or personality assets, as well as liabilities, or pathology-induced limitations, were feasible using the RIM. Exner (2003) described applications for problem solving, stress tolerance, and coping styles. Lerner (1995) advocated equal attention to adaptive capacities and psychopathological signs or diagnostic labels. Weiner (1998) suggested that understanding self-perception and interpersonal orientation was aided by thematic imagery and the "most compelling themes are those that are repetitive, dramatic, original, and spontaneous" (p. 194). Openness and adaptability can be examined in creative, novel, and complex responses (e.g., Franklin & Cornell, 1997). Identification of some healthy aspects of functioning including optimism, creativity, playfulness, and transitional relatedness remain relatively neglected (Handler & Potash, 1999).

CROSS-CULTURAL USAGE

Rorschach (1921/1942) originally described cultural differences in EB between Swiss Bernese and Appenzeller canton residents. These cultural differences were related to kinds and frequencies of psychopathologies as well as specific symptoms. Rorschach (1921/1942) claimed that "the experience type should be very different in various peoples and races" (p. 96). Lindzey (1954) noted these preliminary data on group cultural differences and recognized the Rorschach potential for cross-cultural transportability. A large number of early reviews described emic Rorschach applications frequently employing a Euro-American psychoanalytic framework for interpretation. Universality of the method was assumed for "primitive"/ "indigenous" groups and characterizations of individuals in societies impacted by modernization (e.g., Abel, 1948, 1973; Adcock & Ritchie, 1958; Barnow, 1963; Hallowell, 1941, 1945; Henry, 1941; Kaplan & Lawless, 1965; Lantz, 1948) and acculturation effects (e.g., Boyer et al., 1989; Boyer, Klopfer, R. Boyer, Brawer, & Kawai, 1965; Kaplan, 1955, Linton, 1940). Rorschach's faith that his method was useful for diagnosing schizophrenia and describing personality in cultural settings using a variety of theoretical-conceptual formulations has been affirmed and perpetuated.

Weiner (2004) assumed that the RIM is a culture-free method (e.g., "the dimensions of personality are universal phenomena . . . reflected in the same structural data," p. 351) and suitable for multicultural and international applications because culture "gives context to personality functioning but it does not determine its basic structure and dynamics" (Weiner, 1996, pp. 1–2). Weiner (2004) believed that the RIM can be administered in the native or second language of both clinician and assessee. Culture contributes thematic imagery and symbolic meaning of RIM contents, and clinician familiarity with a particular culture is mandatory for adequate interpretation. Weiner (2004) recommended employing culture specific normative standards based on population norms including P responses, common or Unusual responses, and Form responses. Culture-specific norms can then be used to calibrate Rorschach criteria for inferring personality characteristics.

Ritzler (2004) evaluated the Rorschach as "a major, culture-free assessment method that is likely to yield similar results across a wide range of cultures" (p. 581). Ritzler (2004) believed that "In only a few circumstances does the Rorschach seem sensitive to cultural differences" (p. 581) and further described the necessity to include moderators for acculturation, culture, modernism, and race within an enlarged context including the Rorschach, apperception tests, and figure drawings. Dana (1993) and Frank (1993) also have recommended an examination of moderator variables. Frank (1992, 1993) recognized that group norms potentially could provide Rorschach descriptions of differences in the United States, although the within-group heterogeneity militates against the practical usefulness of this information

The term "culture-free" implies endorsement of standard RIM interpretation for worldwide applications on the basis of U.S. CS normative data. This belief fostered the additional assumption that cross-cultural human similarities are greater than the differences in life as well as Rorschach data and thereby contribute to the contemporary "insensitivity" to cultural issues by fostering the continued investigation of these issues as distal rather than proximal variables. At the present time, there is not sufficient research evidence for these assumptions because the range and applications of research methodologies now available with the Rorschach remain incomplete and unsystematic (see Allen & Dana, 2004). The multicultural assessment resources I review here are necessary for interpretation until consensual interpretive procedures for Rorschach CS applications with multicultural and cross-cultural populations have been developed and are available as practice standards.

I provide a brief, general discussion of normative data resources that precedes information on how these resources can be applied in multicultural assessment practice. I use information concerning expectations for cultural differences in normative standards to suggest consecutive interpretive steps illustrating how conventional interpretation is affected by cultural knowledge.

TABLE 6.1
RIM Variables in North American CS Norms Occurring With Lower
and Higher Frequencies in Selected International Populations

Population	Lower Frequency	Higher Frequency
Finland (adults)	D, H, Zd, P	W, Dd, S, m, Y, V, DEPI, CDI, Fr + rF
France (children)	M, FM, T, H	C', Id, A, Bt, Na, Ls, CDI, DEPI, SCZI
Japan (children)	W, FQ	R, D, Dd, S, DQ
Portugal (adults)	W, P, M, Fc, T	Dd, S, V, Y, Lambda, DEPI, Fr + rF
Portugal (children)	W, T, EgoC	D, V
Spain (adults)	T, P, COP, SumC, Afr	Dd, S, Y, MOR, CDI, Lambda, Fr + rF
Venezuela (adults)	T, FC, P, COP	Dd, Lambda, Fr + rF

Note. RIM = Rorschach Inkblot Method; CS = Comprehensive System.

NORMATIVE DATA RESOURCES

Cross-Cultural Differences in Normative Data

National Rorschach CS norms are available for Portugal (Pires, 2000), and norms for Klopfer-based scores (Klopfer & Kelley, 1960) were developed earlier in Finland (Mattlar, 1986). CS normative data from other countries were contained in samples primarily from normal populations of adults and children. Differences between U.S. CS norms and consistent and well documented international data samples from Japan, Vietnam, Europe (e.g., Belgium, Denmark, Finland, France, Italy, Spain, Portugal), and South America (e.g., Argentina, Chile, Mexico, Venezuela) have been presented in two symposia (Erdberg & Shaffer, 1999; Shaffer & Erdberg, 2001). These differences occur for Locations (e.g., W%, Dd, S), Determinants (e.g., M, FM, m, C', Y, V), Content areas (e.g., Cl, Fi, Ls, A%), Special Scores (e.g., MOR, DV2, COP), and other ratios and summary data (e.g., Lambda, Fr + rF, Afr, SCZI, DEPI, CDI) and include both higher and lower frequencies occurring consistently or idiosyncratically in these five categories across countries (Behn, 1997; see Table 6.1). C.-E. Mattlar (personal communication, June 20, 2004) noted that the U.S. CS samples were less representative and enjoyed better health status than the general U.S. population (Exner, 2002; Exner, 2003, pp. 210–214). By contrast, the international normal samples may have represented their national populations less selectively, but these samples were also healthier than outpatients.

The findings in the preceding symposia (Erdberg & Shaffer, 1999; Shaffer & Erdberg, 2001) may be understood using several possible interpretations: "(1) a real difference in personality or psychopathology attributes, (2) nonequivalence of the measure or its metric properties, or (3) a shift that has occurred across cultures in the underlying construct tapped by the measure and its associated nomological network" (Allen & Dana, 2004, p. 195). At present, in the absence of an adequate research basis for differentiating among these explanations, the presence of consistent cultural differences in many CS variables provides a rationale for continuing to use these data as a primary information resource for interpretation.

Using National Normative Data

The meaning of observed differences between norms on existing CS variables in the United States and between these norms and international norms and/or normative samples remains unresolved and a source of disagreement and controversy. The multicultural and cross-cultural samples that have been used in these comparisons are nonsystematic in origins and composition and typically lack adequate descriptions of ethnic and cultural characteristics required by available methodological guidelines (e.g., CNPAAEMI, 2000; Okazaki & Sue, 1995), although this deficiency is addressed by additional descriptive information to be published in a *Journal of Personality Assessment* supplement including 22 samples with 6 U.S. and 16 international samples (T. W. Shaffer, personal communication, July 4, 2004).

For example, the existing scores for 14 CS variables in 32 U.S. studies were described as inaccurate and flawed because nonpatients appeared psychiatrically disordered (Wood, Nezworski, Garb, & Lilienfeld, 2001a). These allegations were countered by recognizing that samples, scoring rules, and test administration skills differed, and CS data sets including additional scores were required (Meyer, 2001). Subsequently, an adult data set containing 69 CS variables in data sets from eight countries (Erdberg & Shaffer, 1999) provided statistically significant differences averaging a .4 *SD* (Meyer, 2001). These differences were interpreted as not clinically significant and representative of recent cultural and demographic shifts in the U.S. population, although when this data set was subsequently reanalyzed (Wood, Nezworski, Garb, & Lilienfeld, 2001b), clinically significant differences of .8 *SD* were obtained for selected variables.

These data samples demonstrate restrictions in the variety and number of determinants because Europeans, for example, differ in their willingness to analyze or justify their own perceptions and are unaware and/or indifferent to elaborating what is obvious to them (Andronikof-Sanglade, 2000). This explanation suggests differing general attitudes or overarching response sets in addition to more personal predispositions or response styles. Response sets and/or response styles provide a major source of distraction during interpretation because so many CS variables are affected. A summary of these effects follows:

Many Europeans ... inhibit their responsivity and personalize their RCS (CS) responses as a consequence of differing dynamic processes and reasons. These Europeans are more homogeneous in education, income, and middle-class status than samples with other national origins. Many of these persons prize their distinctive national and cultural idiosyncratic differences from one another as exposed by creativity, eccentricity, intellectual sophistication, and a refined and traditional sense of social etiquette. (Dana, 2000c, p. 111)

Response sets/styles are also relevant for African Americans and other cultural populations in the United States. In a review of 16 U.S. studies, Frank (1992) attributed the lower R in these African American samples to a response style: reluctance to self-disclose. Meyer (2002) argued that the social dynamics of an earlier era were responsible for Frank's (1992) findings, although oppression is known to have intergenerational behavioral consequences particularly among African Americans espousing an Africentric ideology. During development and implementing an international CS research agenda, applications of North American interpretive standards in Europe and elsewhere must be done with caution using clear and discrete interpretive steps incorporating recognition of cultural differences and simultaneously maximizing reliability of inferences.

Whether or not national norms and/or normative data samples are necessary and useful for multicultural interpretation cannot readily be resolved in a climate that accepts the universal applicability of RIM and separate CS scores/variables by fiat. Resolution of this dilemma is feasible only by acknowledging that the cross-cultural construct validation status of CS variables has not been adequately investigated and by providing culture-specific empirical demonstrations of construct equivalencies.

The importance of doing this research is underscored by the high-stakes nature of long-term decision making using tests for diagnosis, selection, certification, and accountability with minority populations (Padilla, 2001). At present, applications of U.S. norms with international Rorschach assessees or foreign nationals in North America should be undertaken with extreme caution. It is also apparent that CS normative data examples will change over time and will be affected by decreasing traditionality coupled with augmenting modernization, continuing urbanization, changing demographics, and generational shifts in expectations and priorities, particularly within a climate of increasing globalization. Globalization implies increasing biculturality by maintaining traditional cultural values and superimposing English as a universal second language with adoption of more uniform behavioral standards for intercultural communication with increased informational resources via the Internet and personal mobility to facilitate multicultural contact and experience (Dana, 2003a).

Ephraim (2000a) also addressed the question of how to employ available national norms and/or normative data for CS interpretation with multicultural and immigrant populations in the U.S. Ephraim (2000a) suggested comparing CS norms with minority-based norms using dual normative profiles and examining the interpretive significance of discrepancies. Unfortunately, minority-based norms are not available at present, and even if available in the future, such norms would obscure within-group differences and omit acculturation status. However, norms and normative data from many international populations are currently available for comparative inspection and can foster restraint in literal CS interpretation by suggesting interpretive limitations of particular CS variables.

A more direct application of dual normative data can be provided by acculturation status information already available from moderators. Use of this information is now an ethical necessity for decisions concerning the applicability of the MMPI/MMPI–2 with multicultural individuals (Dana, 2000c). This normative application with the RIM would require concurrent administration of acculturation status measures recommended in chapter 5 (this volume) to provide informed judgments of high, moderate, or low potential for culture-psychopathology confounds as a consequence of standard interpretation using U.S. CS norms. This application would identify those individuals for whom existing CS normative data may be suspect or inapplicable (i.e., for many traditional and some marginal or bicultural individuals). Although acculturation status norms for standard tests do not exist at present, ethical assessment in a multicultural society requires development of new normative resources to facilitate responsible CS interpretation rather than investment in developing separate norms for each ethnic minority population.

Many authors have favored using national normative tables as well as renewed efforts to establish construct equivalencies (e.g., Behn, 1997; Dana, 2000c; Ephraim, 2000a; Pires, 2000; Vinet, 2000). National norms can substitute for the U.S. CS norms in their countries of origin. These data can serve to reestablish empirical cutoff points, although abundant empirical data is required. Vinet (2000) suggested the usefulness of tables for Location, Popular responses, Form Quality, and Z defining high and low values for variables on the basis of local normative data for patients and nonpatients.

Mattlar (2004) concurred with Weiner (2004) in accepting the RIM as a genuine etic due to the presence of similar distributions for many structural variables and discouraged the development of national norms as unnecessary and labor intensive. Mattlar (2004) believed that natural/cultural reference values derived from culture-specific expectations are required to calibrate Rorschach Workshop CS norms for some variables (Mattlar, Forsander, & Maki, 1997). In Mattlar et al. (1997), these reference values are distinguished from culture-specific norms per se, and their subjective origins are emphasized in a historical review including Finnish data. Despite access to availability of cultural information for many European countries, the specific information required for establishing these expectancy values for each country has not been sufficiently described and quantified to date. For competent international CS applications, it is now necessary to understand how societies orchestrate, prioritize, and individualize their social and economic resources to permit less than a total demand on individuals simply for survival rather than supporting an engagement with more idiosyncratic activities contributing to quality of life.

In support of Mattlar's (2004) recommendation, Daroglou and Viglione (2002) and Daroglou (2003) have examined specific cultural expectations for CS variables using a Greek reference sample for comparison with a matched Euro-American sample stratified by gender, urban–rural residence, marital status, and SES. Daroglou applied cultural expectations to an examination of interrelatedness among Greek social values, familial, and societal roles. Daroglou found significant differences on Good and Poor Human Representations (GHR/PHR) and T after controlling for productivity, motivation, and deviance (e.g., R, F%, PTI). The finding that Greeks have superior interpersonal relationships with greater interconnectedness than Americans (i.e., in the presence of greater social anxiety and less dependency but without any special need for closeness) is consistent with an understanding of cultural differences within a context of changes in Greek values by generation and a shift toward individualism. These cultural differences include a culture-specific view and delineation of interpersonal events and realistic impressions of others. Calibration for productivity and corrections for overpathologizing (e.g., Viglione, 2002) suggests the usefulness of GHR with Greeks and provides an empirical example of normative cultural expectations affecting CS interpretations.

UNDERSTANDING CULTURAL DIFFERENCES AMONG CS VARIABLES

The abundant evidence for culture-general and culture-specific differences in CS variables occurs within an assessment climate of skepticism and disinterest regarding utilization of these information resources to develop a rationale and procedures for multicultural interpretation. In the following discussion, I review a number of explanations for these consistent differences between CS variables in North American and international normative data. These explanations include national differences in construct descriptions, component definitions, and national base rates for psychopathological conditions contained in epidemiological studies. I review selected CS variables here beginning with Locations, including

P responses, followed by the master construct, EB, and proceeding to various Determinants (M, C, T, F/FQ) representing specific constructs and finally to Contents.

LOCATIONS

Exner (1993) carefully identified W, D, Dd, and S card areas in working tables. For example, his Table A for Card I includes 7 D and 13 Dd and two DdS responses, including FQ categories for Ordinary (o), Unusual (u), and Minus (–), plus Populars and Z values. Table B illustrates FQ+ responses by card, whereas Table C provides Organization (Z) values by card. Table D includes best-weighted Z Sum prediction when Zf is known. Ordinary and Minus FQ accuracy coding provides reasonably good correspondence with locations of more and less than 2% of 7,500 U.S. adults (Weiner, 1999, 2003). This coding affects Form Level summary scores (i.e., F + %, X + %, Xu%), and cultural differences in these summary scores and P can be misleading. Weiner (1999) recommended recoding using culture-specific expectations prior to interpretation and the coding of FQ– and X – % are presumably unaffected by culture because "the boundaries between realistic and unrealistic perception are universal and not culture bound" (p. 49).

The information in Exner's (1993) tables can be compared and contrasted with information provided by Vaz (1997) based on 17,600 Brazilian responses contained in 850 protocols from Porto Alegre and the contiguous Rio Grande do Sul area. Separate tables for several indigenous groups are included. Although his approach was influenced by a wide variety of European resources as well as a number of Brazilian Rorschach scoring and interpretive systems and Rorschach societies, Vaz began with reliance on Klopfer (1941) location categories, whereas Exner (1993) employed Beck's D score (Beck, 1950). As a consequence, there are many differences in location categorizations and identification of Popular responses and content specifics.

Populars (P) and Originals (O)

Popular responses represent an assessee's ability to perceive and identify reality in a manner consistent with many persons in their reference group. Exner's (1993) U.S. CS database provides 13 Popular (P) responses occurring in approximately one third of 7,500 nonpatient and schizophrenic adult protocols, although other authors have also suggested responses occurring once in four, five, or six records. The highest frequency P responses to Cards III, VI, and VIII appear in 89%, 87%, and 94% of nonpatient records, respectively, whereas others appear in at least 40% of protocols in a 12 country international sample collected for the Rorschach Research Foundation. Nonpatient adults average 6.69 P responses.

Exner (1993) cited Spanish and Finnish examples of failure to produce P responses to Cards II, IX, and X, noting that some high frequency CS P responses were conventionally perceived, universally distinctive forms (e.g., III, VI, VIII), although the specific responses varied over time. Unfortunately, Spanish authors including Miralles Sangro (1997) relied only on identification of nine CS P responses in Spanish data and apparently did not report unique responses occurring with the same frequencies. Recent international normative studies (e.g., Shaffer & Erdberg, 2001) have reported the numbers of P responses but have omitted the card designations for these responses and failed to include descriptions of other responses in these studies meeting the frequency criterion for CS P responses.

Weiner (1999) suggested "Populars require recoding based on culture-specific expectations before they can be interpreted according to usual standards as measures of conventionality in perception" (p. 53). The employment of normative data to derive P response standards was recommended for each culturally distinct group by Bleuler and Bleuler as early as 1935. Mattlar, Carlsson, and Forsander (1993) noted that P has been defined using frequencies of 14% to 33% by other Rorschachs. Agreement among experts in different countries on P is about 66%, and there are also unique, country-specific P responses (e.g., Card II, Elves in Finland; Mattlar & Fried, 1993). Mattlar (2004) cited Oberholzer's claim that there are nine universal-international P responses (see responses to Cards I, III, V, VI, VIII, and IX).

CS P responses are calculated in all foreign studies, but I have been unable to discover independent frequency data for culture specific and culture general P responses except in early studies. For example, Hallowell (1945) described the 25 most frequent Ojibwas responses and suggested differentiating group-specific or unique, common, and universal P responses. Using Hallowell's (1945) classification, Bourguignon and Westerkamm Nett (1955) described the most frequent responses in an adult Haitian sample. These Haitian responses were subsequently compared with responses from Joseph and Murray's (1951) Chamorros, Hallowell's (1945) Ojibwas, as well as universal Popular responses. Four of these P responses suggested by Klopfer and Kelley (1941) occurred in all groups (i.e., I and V "winged creatures," VIII "quadrapeds," and III "two human figures"), whereas common P occurred in two groups, and four non-Klopfer P responses occurred uniquely in one group. Piotrowski (1957) also observed that P responses varied across cultures.

In spite of these early Rorschach P studies, there has been insufficient systematic research designating and reporting non-Exner P responses in cultural populations. Similarly, the frequencies of tabulated response contents are neither tabulated nor reported in published sources. A recent dissertation (Gowri, 1999), however, cited agreements and departures from CS P responses in early Rorschach studies from Algeria, Congo, China, Finland, Greece, India, and Iran using a tabularized format labeling frequent P as well as CS P not seen in these samples.

Information by cultural group on responses designated as universal, common, and unique would be helpful for interpretation, and these data are available primarily in foreign non-CS texts. For example, as described earlier, Vaz (1997) reported not only different blot locations for responses, but he also obtained different frequencies for Determinant and Content categories. Gowri (1999) employed judges with specific cultural knowledge to rate responses for cultural saturation using his Rating Scale for Culture. Respondents from the same culture as the responses to be rated provided higher ratings, suggesting the facilitative role of intimate cultural knowledge in identifying cultural contents appearing in frequent, infrequent, and pathological responses. Asian Americans produced highly complex, culturally saturated responses, although their relatively nonculturally saturated responses were less complex than Euro-American responses. This is an important finding because it suggests that identification of culturally saturated responses is necessary to augment interpretation by emphasizing the contents of highly relevant, personalized responding. These complex, well integrated, culturally saturated responses are especially prevalent with English language proficiency and bicultural acculturation status. In another example, Dana (2003a) reported a similar usage of TAT themes that were identified, tallied, and described as cultural contents that provided the most salient data for a personality evaluation of a Sikh American.

ERLEBNISTYPUS (EB)

EB, a blend of behavioral and attitudinal components, provides a projective method alternative to the statistical apportioning of variances from observational or objective test data. EB has been underutilized for cross-cultural CS interpretation. An independent and parallel development of Rorschach's EB and Jung's Introversion–Extraversion Attitudinal Types has concealed their similarity (Bash, 1955; McCully, 1971), obscured potential relationships between EB and Jungian psychological functions of feeling–thought and sensation–intuition (Mindess, 1955), and led to non-Jungian major reviews (Hertz, 1943; Molish, 1967; Singer, 1960).

Nonetheless, a Rorschach–Jungian context confronts the paradox of monitoring stability and change simultaneously, and the use of a separate score, Experience Actual (EA; Exner, 1974), summates all EB components and exposes preferred avenues of dealing with experience, either ideational–contemplative or emotional–expressive (Weiner, 2003). EA changes as a consequence of successful treatment that ostensibly provides an enhanced organization of personality resources.

Cross-cultural interpretation can be facilitated by utilization of documented differences between normative EB data in the United States and Europe. Rorschach's original EB coping styles were supplemented by U.S. CS norms describing a preponderance of Extratensives (44%) with somewhat fewer Introversives (36%) and relatively fewer Ambitents (20%). Weiner (1998) noted the flexibility and efficacy of "a clearly defined but not pervasive introversive or extratensive EB style" (p. 149). Ambitents, however, were contrasted as inconsistent and unpredictable, with uncertain self-images due to conflict between head and heart and frequently were developmentally challenged young persons aged 5 to 14 and increasingly maladaptive as outpatients or hospitalized depressive adults.

By contrast, however, a representative Portuguese normative sample (Pires, 2000) provided comparative Extratensive, Introversive, and Ambitent proportions of 22%, 28%, and 50%, respectively. Coping style differences from the 41 CS variables for Portuguese Ambitent respondents were of greater magnitude than in the United States and included lower R, W, Sum C', Sum Y, EA, es, DEPI, Blends, Xu%, Fi, and high Lambda, T, and CDI. If U.S. interpretive standards were applied in Portugal, half of this normal population would be described as seriously disturbed and compromised in their ability to function adequately in daily life. There were also significant differences across these EB styles for a majority of CS variables in Portugal (i.e., R, W, M, FM + m, CF, WSumC, Sum C', Sum Y, es, EA, Lambda, Ego index, a [total active], p [total passive], Blends, Color shading blends, P, Pure H, all H contents, FD, P, Xu%, A, Bl, Fi, COP, and AG). The extent and magnitude of these differences has invited consistent criticism, alternative explanations, and suggestions for research.

Weiner's (2003, pp. 158–159) interpretation of Ambitents as potentially pathological is contrasted by inferences from normative data in Belgium, France, Norway, and Spain, reviewed by Andronikof-Sanglade (2000), which concurred substantially with Pires' (2000) norms. Kalla et al. (2004) also found percentages of Ambitent psychotic patients in Finland and Spain comparable to Pires' normal Ambitents. All of these samples have displayed decreased productivity with less M and less C in a context of blatant coping style differences suggesting fewer organized resources leading to simplified information processing and cognitive mediation. Nonetheless, the structure and adequacy of the social milieu in collectivist or less individualistic societies may permit many Ambitents to function with lower EA values without recourse to severe psychopathology (Vinet, 2000).

DETERMINANTS

Human Movement (M)

Human Movement has been represented by more construct-driven research than other CS variables (see Allen & Dana, 2004). Nonetheless, the construct status of M remains only weakly delineated. An empirically derived description of M constructs for North Americans (Dana, 1982, pp. 197–203) included delay, time sense, intelligence, creativity, fantasy, and interpersonal relations that provide a capacity for humanization or personhood. These potentials for behavior, which have been described in over 100 early studies, are a product of socialization resulting in capacity for delay, focused attention, and withholding action. Delay fosters development of a personal and consensual time sense defining past, present, and future. Learned and practiced intellectual defenses contribute to adjustment within a social context using anxiety, conflict, directional controls, and a sense of identity. Tangible behavioral outcomes of these potentials constitute social interests providing a basis for caring for and about other persons. Investing feelings in other persons contribute to relationships with depth, stability, and meaning. Two distinct M factors load on intelligence test variables or a different context of Determinants that distinguish between kinesthetic and visual dynamics (Arnheim, 1951). The context of other variables within which M is embedded determines an emphasis on introversiveness or external stimulation.

This review suggests that M is represented as a collocation of at least six North American emic constructs with behavioral manifestations occurring as a consequence of socialization primarily between 1930 and 1970. M may have somewhat different construct elements in other countries due to characteristic or unique socialization processes as well as changes over time resulting from increasing modernization and homogenization within the European community.

Color (FC, CF, C)

Color usage has been reported in several ways including the Form-Color Ratio (FC: CF + C), WsumC used in EB and EA with Cn excluded, and as Sum Color (FC + CF + C) with varying figures in different U.S. normative samples. Color usage in international normative samples typically diverges downward from U.S. norms for WSumC and Sum Color (Shaffer & Erdberg, 2001).

Behn (1997) found large numbers of individuals in the international samples with a preponderance of less Form-dominated Color. The ratio is hypothesized to refer to modulation of affective displays. FC relates to greater modulation of affect and CF + C to less. Whenever FC is at least one point more or twice that of CF + C and C = 0, an assessee is assumed to control or modulate emotional discharge in a conventional manner. Above this level, more stringent control is likely to be exerted. A reversal of the expected Color ratio is found in Spain, Portugal, and Venezuela. In the United States, this reversal occurs only in children under age 12, in patient groups (Exner, 1993, p. 493), and among Hispanics (Costantino, Flanagan, & Malgady, 1995). These differences can influence EB and EA. Consistent differences in data generated in various sociocultural settings suggests that interpretation in the absence of local norms can lead to miscommunication concerning the nature and meaning of affective control. Different configurations of personality variables can have adaptive advantages and disadvantages within different environments.

Form/Form Quality (F/FQ)

Form and Form-Quality, or "goodness of fit," are pertinent to reality appraisal by orientation to reality, perceptual distortion, as well as adaptive ability and necessary for consideration of mediation capacities (Behn, 1997). Form-related variables, X – %, Xu%, X + %, P, F + %, FQx+, SCHIZ, M–, and S–, reported in nine international normative samples, differed from U.S. CS norms, although all samples did not display the same differences. The range and quality of these discrepancies suggests that reality appraisal is essentially a process beginning early in life and consolidated between ages 5 and 7 by seeing the world with sufficient consensual accuracy to be socially correct and congruent with significant others without invoking perceptual absolutes. Several authors have noted that cultures differ in how much conformity in terms of veridicality of reality perception is required and how much latitude for individualism is permitted.

Cross-cultural comparisons are inevitably loaded in favor of an implicit criterion culture (e.g., Exner's 1993 U.S. CS normative standards); hence, significant departures in scores and other variables occurring in normative samples from well functioning persons may be erroneously construed as psychopathological. As a consequence, good Form judgments may not necessarily or inevitably generalize beyond a given cultural context. Weiner (2003) indicated that "The boundaries between realistic and unrealistic perception are universal and not culture bound" (p. 53). Whether or not this is a valid statement may be debatable. These boundaries do not appear to be fixed or absolute, but remain permeable under certain cultural circumstances in the ideational processes of shamans and other powerful but respected nonpsychotic deviants (Dana, 2000b). Nonetheless, because cultural differences obtain in the frequencies of X + % and

Xu% based on FQo and FQu definitions of good correspondence between blot location and object by 2% of U.S. nonpsychotic adults, respectively, recoding on the basis of culture-specific expectations may be necessary prior to interpreting perceptual conventionality.

Andronikof-Sanglade (2000) examined the European and U.S. definitions of Form Quality to understand the subsequent interpretation of X + % as reality testing. Rorschach and other Europeans believed that resemblance between the objective shape of the blot and the shape as identified by the assessee was the defining characteristic. In the United States, however, there was a shift from Form accuracy to conventionality of shape and ultimately to conventionality of vocabulary. Thus, CS X + % measured assessee distance from the "average American language use and reference world" (Andronikof-Sanglade, 2000, p. 338), and this definition implied that cross-cultural language and environmental differences are measured.

Exner (2003) changed the focus for appropriate use of Form by two new CS variables, XA% and WDA%, used together to describe mediational activities yielding situationally appropriate behaviors. XA% includes the proportion of all responses with a good Form (Sum of FQ+, FQo, FQu/R), whereas WDA% employs only those responses to W and D locations (Sum W + D of FQ+, FQo, FQu/Sum W + D; Exner, 2000). These values should be similar, although WDA% generally will have the higher value due to responses to obvious blot areas. Interpretation depends on the values for each variable as well as the magnitude of difference between the values. X − %, X + %, and Xu% continue to be scored. Using XA% augments the predictive validity of SCZI, whereas WDA% detects perceptual-mediational difficulties.

Texture

As noted earlier in this chapter, Exner (1974) differentiated between responding to light and dark as Pure Shading, Shading as dimensionality, and Shading as Texture or Tactile sensation. Pure Shading (FY, YF, Y) and Shading as dimensionality (FV, VF, V) have been less noteworthy in cross-cultural reports. However, high Lambda (defensiveness), low Afr and C (low affective involvement) and Y responses (feelings of dysphoria linked to passivity and anxiety) were obtained in Latin American countries where power differentials between assessor and assessee lead to respectful behaviors masking internalized distress (Vinet, 2000). In Vinet's (2000) words, "the subject will be attentive to the examiner's needs by trying to avoid a difficult situation for the assessor" (p. 360).

Weiner (1998, 2003) has reported increasing T, Tactile sensation, in children from age 5 to 8 when the adult mean of one was approximated and remained stable thereafter for 89% of nonpatients with at least one T, whereas 11% provided T-less protocols. From these data, Weiner (20003) inferred that "the presence of T provides a good indication of adaptive capacity to anticipate and establish close, intimate, and mutually supportive relationships with other persons. Generally speaking, people who give T responses are likely not only to enjoy but need, want, and reach out for physical and/or emotional closeness to others" (Weiner, 2003, p. 173). T-less records indicated less comfort with people characterized by distant, detached relationships and perceived intrusiveness of others. Psychopathology was accompanied by increasing percentages of T-less protocols in inpatient depressives (57%), outpatients (64%), inpatient schizophrenics (70%), and character disorders (72%; Weiner, 2003).

However, T findings contrast with U.S expectations in most countries with the exception of Finland. In Portugal (Pires, 2000), T was .68 and was even closer to zero in Spain and Latin America. Andronikof-Sanglade (2000) reported T was seldom found in Europe but whenever expressed, more than one T response was generally found and interpreted as a frustrated craving for closeness. From a perspective of Spanish normative data (Fuster, 1993), one T suggested a need for therapy. North American norms were seen as reflecting Puritan influences and deprivation of interpersonal tactile contact by physical touching between mother and child, brothers, friends of the same or opposite sex, or casual acquaintances except under conditions of socially stigmatized relationships including homosexuality, adultery, incest, and promiscuity. In contact cultures, there is frequent physical touching, hugging, and kissing in infancy and childhood within a socialization process resulting in emotional closeness that is uninterrupted and sustained throughout life. In contrast, U.S. children, socialized in a noncontact culture, by age 8 learn to restrain their natural needs for physical and emotional contact and express the special need for physical closeness by their T responses. Vinet (2000) noted that CS Texture responses retain their interpretive meaning in contact cultures, although T values require different cutoff scores in each country predicated on empirical research.

CONTENT

My initial awareness of culture-specific Rorschach content differences occurred initially in a 1951 study of Chinese graduate students using Cards II, IV, and VIII (Dana, 1959a). Personalized response contents resulted from self-defined role taking during testing that may have reduced fearfulness (e.g., jokers in circus, playing a game, prisoners handcuffed together). Nature (8%), decorations (7%), and patterns (5%), in addition to "silk worm"

(20%), provided cultural contents including at least one P in each card from each participant. The Dana (1959a) study illustrated that tabularized, national, normative content expectations facilitate understanding the locus of an individual assessee within a complex cultural matrix.

Weiner (2004) recognized the salience or potential interpretive importance of thematic imagery and symbolic meaning of response Contents. Andronikof-Sanglade (2000) contrasted content categories of 6- and 7-year-old French and American children. The French children had less H, (H), and Fd with more A, Na, and Bt responses. These French children were closer to the natural and physical worlds and less identified with adult humans suggesting differences in socialization experiences and expectations. Moreover, these Content findings were reported in a context of Determinants suggesting greater inhibition and less self-centeredness than their American counterparts.

Gowri (1999) described a method for evaluating culturally saturated responses. In addition to recognizing culturally derived response Contents, understanding the meaning of these responses within the culture is necessary. Raters from the same cultural group gave higher culture saturation ratings to these responses, suggesting the importance of cultural knowledge for identification of these responses. The Rorschach inquiry may need to focus on elaboration of these responses, particularly whenever components of the cultural self are represented that may be infrequent or missing in contemporary North American society. Cultural responses should be tallied and percentages used to suggest the importance of specific cultural issues. Culture-specific P responses also occur, although they may be difficult to identify without available frequency data on Content categories similar to published expectations for Finland (Mattlar et al., 1993).

A CROSS-CULTURAL/MULTICULTURAL INTERPRETIVE STRATEGY

Weiner (1999, 2003) identified structural CS variables relevant for attending to experience, using ideation, modulating affect, managing stress, viewing oneself, and relating to others. Weiner (1999, 2003) noted the correspondence between these six areas and seven clusters of CS variables (i.e., information processing, cognitive mediation, ideation, control and stress tolerance, affective features, self-perception, interpersonal perception) and one array of variables (situation-related stress). These areas of interpretive significance identify activities in which good and poor functioning can be anticipated, and adjustment difficulties or psychological disorders can be examined within a context describing the goodness of fit of various psychotherapeutic interventions. Weiner (2003) tabularized (see Table 3.1, p. 63) specific interpretive steps identified by CS variables in each of these areas. Weiner (2003) also acknowledged the potential invalidity of records with fewer than 14 responses, although briefer records that do not contain, for example, high Lambda, many P responses, and D locations coupled with a narrow range of Content, questionable X + %, few Blends, and scant verbiage may provide a modicum of reliable information (see Brickman & Lerner, 1992).

Employment of this interpretive paradigm with multicultural assessees is predicated on transformations across steps beginning with consistent administration and recording procedures, proceeding to scoring of responses, and consensual inferences represented by increasing increments of abstraction in weighted scores, summarizing variables, and indexes. However, for these assessees, reliable transformations are more difficult. Data processing of response components requires infusing information from test behavior and assessee mood consistent with assessment objectives and the service delivery setting. Although reliability of coding CS variables is consistent and adequate, Weiner's (1999, 2003) steps progress from low-inference protocol scoring to higher inference interpretation requiring increments of assessor judgment, clinical skill, and experience. Reliability is generally known to decrease across the four levels of the inference process: Level 1, scores; Level 2, inferences from scores; Level 3, psychological report language; and Level 4, diagnostic statements or predictions (see Dana, 1982, chap. 5). Application of the RIM with multicultural assessees requires usage of both low- and high-inference interpretation. Level 1 scorer reliability for CS variables displays little variability in the United States (Meyer et al., 2002), but international studies have not generally been examined for possible differences in cross-national coding procedures (Allen & Dana, 2004). Nor has there been comparable attention to Level 2 reliability of cross-cultural inferences or interpretations from CS variables. High-inference interpretation provides greater risk for cross-cultural/multicultural assessees due to the high-stakes nature of assessment decisions for populations inadequately represented by normative data. For these populations, the easy recourse to U.S. normative standards can increase the risk of inappropriate clinical diagnoses by inattention to cultural differences. These differences pertain to health–illness beliefs, public thresholds for awareness of dysfunction, and assessor ignorance of specific cultural resources reducing the necessity for hospitalization or other interventions.

Weiner (1998, 2003) recognized the potential inadequacy of available norms with regard to age, gender, and cultural background but cautioned against lumping of diverse groups and also recommended attending to the possible relevance of group differences in personality characteristics for adjustment status by using both normative data and conceptual guidelines. In addition, cultural differences should be evaluated with reference to the construct validation status of CS determinants, the impact of culture on language (including service delivery and understanding of responses), and accuracy of response coding.

Assessors learn Weiner's CS procedures (1999, 2003) primarily with assessees from their own familiar cultural and social milieu who expose problems relevant to their training, experience, and health–illness beliefs. Assessors continue to rely on these procedural outcomes of their training with assessees who are culturally dissimilar to themselves. For these assessees, however, it is often necessary to modify their expectations for behaviors and Rorschach performances on the basis of specific cultural knowledge that is not readily acquired in formal academic or professional settings. Multicultural assessment competence requires not only a reexamination of the credibility and limitations of prior professional training for new populations of professional interest but also demands a formidable investment in new learning about the lives, values, experiences, and worldviews of others who may be markedly dissimilar to themselves.

The following series of recommended interpretive steps may appear admittedly less coherent, precise, and comfortable because they do not emerge from comparable foundations in empirical research and clinical experience. Nonetheless, these steps provide a modus operandi for employing the RIM cautiously with multicultural assessees. These steps are predicated on the importance and potential relevance of consistent international discrepancies from U.S. CS norms for appreciation of cultural differences in information processing, cognitive mediation, affects, and interpersonal perceptions.

Recommended Interpretive Steps

Step 1. Culturally competent Rorschach CS interpretation begins with attention to the orientation questions discussed in chapter 5 (this volume) referring to assessment purposes, cultural typicality, and cultural orientation status. These questions call attention to the assessee's prehistory with mental health services and authority figures, highlight potential discrepancies between the assessee's group identity and individual cultural identity, and structure the relevance of an inquiry into acculturation status. These considerations may occur before initial contact with the assessee and suggest the nature of the preparation required to conduct the administration and interpretation of the Rorschach. Anticipation of cooperativeness, potential adequacy of Rorschach data, validity of inferences, and responsiveness to feedback provide important cues relevant to the role of the Rorschach experience in the assessment process.

Step 2. Assessor cultural competence refers specifically to understanding an assessee's culture that may include language skill as well as experiential and cognitive knowledge. This step requires an awareness of how to locate and review information resources, particularly for unfamiliar cultures, and how to acquire information on acculturation status and other moderators using emic instruments and/or interview data. The step requires assessor self-scrutiny regarding competence to conduct the Rorschach portion of the evaluation.

Step 3. Knowledge of culture-specific social etiquette is mandatory for sufficient rapport and task orientation for acquisition of a protocol of adequate length, clarity, and detail for reliable coding and subsequent interpretation. This step necessitates blending behaviors and affect in a manner acceptable and comfortable for the assessee. These three initial steps provide ingredients for a data set that adequately represents the assessee for an assessor who feels sufficiently knowledgeable to be responsible for high-stakes interpretation. The next five steps abstract and apply essential information contained in this chapter to the CS protocol of a particular assessee.

Step 4. Interpretation is predicated on comparisons of available normative data for the assessee population of interest with U.S. CS normative data. Table 6.1 provides examples of expectations for lower and higher frequencies of selected CS variables in several countries. Anticipated scores differences for these variables should be linked with cultural expectations for their interpretation. Whenever this data does not consist of national norms (e.g., Portugal), the size, representativeness, and relevance of available data sets must be considered. Where there is no available national data relevant to immigrants, refugees, or sojourners (e.g., Afghanistan, Ethiopia, Fiji, for examples), the assessor's specific cultural knowledge coupled with extreme caution is necessary. Where there is no available local data (e.g., Ecuador), regional data from Venezuela, for example, can provide limited reference information within a generalized interpretive context for Latin Americans (Ephraim, 1996; Vinet, 2000).

Step 5. An examination of coping styles requires normative data specifying the relative percentages of Introversive, Extratensive, Ambitent, and Avoidant individuals within a context of significance levels for relationships between these scores and other CS variables (Exner, 2003). Descriptive summaries of the cultural meaning of these percentages are useful for understanding the adequacy of these resources for good and poor functioning within the cultural milieu. Coping styles are essentially behavioral, and EB types provide a vehicle for their examination. These

TABLE 6.2
Suggested Interpretive Procedures with Cross-Cultural and Multicultural CS Data

Step	Description
Orientation questions	Assessee assessment expectations? Assessee typicality? Assessee cultural orientation status?
Assessor cultural competence	Assessor awareness/understanding of assessee cultural origins: Is more information necessary? Adequacy of available emic information resources? Are test/interview moderators needed to gather specific acculturation status information and/or to decide whether or not standard tests are applicable to assessee?
Service delivery	Assessor use of proper and credible social etiquette: Adequacy of trust, task orientation, responsiveness?
Normative data	Adequacy of available normative data for cultural origins and acculturation status? Which CS scores—if any—may be affected for this assessee? If acculturation status is bicultural, marginal, or at least third generation, are any interpretation corrections required?
Coping styles	EB and test-taking attitudes: Impact on entire response process (R and use of determinants). Apply Pires model for clustering CS variables associated with these styles as described in other national normative data resources
Determinants	Culture-specific expectations for determinants: M, C, T, F? Organize CS data by Weiner stepwise requirements for information processing, cognitive mediation, affect, and interpersonal perception noting Ephraim caveats. How do culture-specific determinant interpretations relate to CS variables within each cluster? Examine goodness-of-fit between standard cluster interpretations versus specific cultural meaning of cluster and required components in each cluster
Cultural saturation	Expectations for cross-cultural content differences (Cl, Fi, Ls, A%); differentiate between culture-specific and idiosyncratic, personalized, and/or psychopathological contents
Pathology	Cultural expectations: Health–illness beliefs; *DSM* differences from local symptoms and base rates; culture-bound syndromes
Report validity	How likely is CS interpretation to be valid? Review by client entity feedback in context of potential cultural response sets; peer review by professionals representing assessee cultures

Note. CS = Comprehensive System; *DSM = Diagnostic and Statistical Manual of Mental Disorders.*

specific styles, applied to Rorschach interpretation, should be distinguished from general attitudes, described as response sets that have been investigated primarily with paper-and-pencil tests such as the MMPI.

Step 6. Determinants provide a major normative data source for culture-specific expectations. These expectations are associated with some major components in steps identified by Weiner (2003) in seven clusters and the situation-related stress array of CS variables. In a context with other variables, these specific Determinants—M, C, T, F—contribute to salient cross-cultural inferences in four areas summarizing Weiner's (2003) seven clusters (Ephraim, 2000a) including simplified information processing (% Pure F, Lambda), more subjective and less conventional cognitive mediation (fewer P, fewer FQ, lower X + %) in international studies, and less socialized affect evidenced by much lower FC means in a context of fewer responses involving two or more objects with COP among Iberian Americans.

Step 7. Cultural saturation addresses Content as a function of cultural context. These expectations can only be properly addressed on the basis of frequency tables for Content categories. Assessor immersion in the culture and familiarity with an assessee's first language will foster more accurate and complete identification of cultural Contents and appreciation of the relevance of particular Content categories for personality issues and psychopathology.

Step 8. Cultural expectations for recognizing and diagnosing psychopathology are dependent first on explicit knowledge in three areas: (a) health–illness beliefs and culture-specific symptoms and syndromes, (b) base rates for psychopathologies, and (c) culture-bound syndromes in cultures of origin.

Health–illness beliefs vary within the range permissible within the culture of origin and are affected by an assessee's demographic position, acculturation status, and generation of family residence in the United States. It is of special importance to recognize that the frequencies of culture-bound disorders, even among persons with several generations of U.S. residence, are considerably higher than generally believed. These culture-bound disorders must always be ruled out for traditional and marginal individuals, refugees and sojourners, and even for bicultural persons. The use of the RIM is not sufficient alone for diagnosis but must be used with other tests/methods. The assessor's test experience must be coupled with practice providing *DSM–IV* cultural formulations for individuals from a variety of cultures.

Peer review by professionals from relevant ethnic/cultural groups is recommended and may be mandatory for accurate diagnoses. For example, I would need peer review for cultural formulations with Asians in spite of some familiarity with specific diagnostic issues (e.g., Dana, 2001a, 2002a) as well as for all Africans and many Blacks with non-Hispanic Caribbean origins. I would feel somewhat greater comfort preparing cultural formulations with most Latinos (Dana, 1998d), African Americans (Dana, 2002c), and Native Americans and Alaska Natives (Dana, 2000b).

The CS is frequently employed for *DSM–IV* diagnosis, and knowledge of national base rates representing different nosological systems can be helpful for preparation of accurate diagnostic statements. Using the depression construct as an example, research has identified both presence and absence of this construct in different countries. Where the construct exists, the components may be few or many, and there are wide differences in these components by countries. *DSM–IV* depression criteria frequently provide an inexact fit with a particular culture, but the base rates for depression also vary by country and are dependent on the construct definition and the diagnostic system in use. For example, Finns and Portuguese exhibit very high prevalence rates for depression. The CS Depression Index (DEPI) also has very high percentages in other countries (i.e., Argentina, Belgium, Chile, Denmark, Japan, and Spain), ranging from 17% to 57% by contrast with 5% in U.S. CS data. Thus, although an elevated DEPI may signal distress, the meaning of this distress is complex and related to specific societal definitions, demands, and resources.

The goodness of fit between CS data and culture-bound syndromes has not been explicitly investigated. Nonetheless, these syndromes occur with greater than anticipated frequencies in multicultural populations in the United States. Understanding the symptomatology of these syndromes is necessary for preparation of cultural formulations.

Step 9. All multicultural assessment reports should contain a clear statement concerning (a) adequacy of the standard (derived etic) test/ method and other (emic) instruments and (b) the anticipated validity of inferences derived from each instrument for an assessee representing a given culture and acculturation status. This statement is predicated on the completeness and adequacy of available information on the assessee's culture and the kind, extent, and depth of the assessor's knowledge and experience with individuals who acknowledge group affiliation and/or cultural identity. If the assessor feels uncomfortable concerning the validity of the test data or accuracy of the completed report, the desirability of peer review should be noted and acted on whenever feasible.

Minnesota Multiphasic
Personality Inventory

Beginning with a brief description of test construction and development, this chapter examines MMPI relevance for psychological assessment as a unique information source with special attributes. These attributes—trait measurement, psychometric status, and conspicuous role in research and contemporary assessment science—resulted in more consistent and frequent usage over time than other measures of psychopathology or personality. Despite limitations as an emic or imposed etic instrument that potentially affects multicultural populations in the United States and cross-cultural applications internationally, the development, research, and utilization of scales, normative data, and standard interpretation procedures provide a reasonable basis for adaptations to increase applicability to these populations. I follow a review of the controversy concerning the nature of legitimate adaptations for multicultural and international usage by examining test adaptations contributing to a framework for interpretation with an expanded range of assessees. Orientation questions anticipate the extent to which standard interpretation may be credible, and I follow these by interpretation guidelines containing procedural steps.

MMPI CONSTRUCTION, DEVELOPMENT, AND INTERPRETATION

The MMPI is a self-report test constructed during the 1930s for differential diagnosis of psychiatric disorders in the medical patient hospital population (Hathaway & McKinley, 1943). A large pool of selected descriptive items provided clinical and validity scales in a 566-item inventory. An empirical test construction procedure, the criterion keying method, contrasted responses to these items by normal, White, rural, hospital visitors from psychiatric inpatients representing various diagnostic subgroups. The original test had limited ability to predict specific psychiatric diagnoses. Empirical correlates of scales and combinations of scores with clinically relevant behaviors, traits, and symptoms were soon demonstrated. As a means for dispensing with the original Kraeplinian scale labels, combinations of scale scores were described as code types with scales designated by code numbers. Actuarial research applications led to MMPI interpretations predicated on use of empirical scale correlates and code types derived from large-scale studies.

A revision, the MMPI–2, followed an examination of an experimental version and ultimately yielded a more representative standardization sample, refurbished unacceptable items, and omitted sexist language (Hathaway & McKinley, 1989). Furthermore, a more readable instrument was designed to facilitate the translation process, and new itinerant normative data preceded the development of international norms (Butcher, Lim, & Nezami, 1998). Although essentially unaltered in numbers of items and in the contents of clinical, F, and K scales, the 567-item MMPI–2 contained several new validity and content scales.

These MMPI versions were developed from an exclusively psychological vision of assessment science spanning a wide variety of potentially relevant behaviors employing simple linguistic and response requirements and providing a large item pool amenable to review and revision. Low-inference interpretation substantiated by research demonstrating validity and clinical utility for specific measurement objectives has been substantially achieved and documented by well over 10,000 studies to provide a major assessment tool for normative populations within the United States (Butcher, 1987).

SPECIAL ATTRIBUTES

In this section, I examine the role of the MMPI as a unique information resource with psychometric status for measuring traits/constructs describing psychopathology and personality within contemporary assessment science.

Unique Information Resource

There has been convincing documentation that qualitatively different types of information are obtained from the MMPI–2 and the Rorschach. Meyer (1997) examined 11 characteristics differentiating the self-report method

TABLE 7.1
Meyer (1997) Self-Assessment MMPI and Performance-Based
RIM Distinctions

Distinction	Self-Report	RIM
Expectations	Well defined	Minimally defined
Stimuli	Familiar	Novel
Response options	Narrow range	Wide range
Task	Consider self, characteristic traits in self-presentation decisions in T-F format	Formulate perceptions, select responses, respond to inquiry
Administration/scoring	Clerical	Requires judgment
Benchmark	Assumes similar decisions by assessees on traits	Assessor provides classification
Context	Alone	Assessee with assessor
Personal characteristics	In vitro description	In vivo demonstration
Raw data	Dependent on conscious awareness, complexity of self-presentation	Dependent on engagement with task, ability to articulate perceptions and their determinants
Disimulation/impression management	Affects reported symptoms	Affects task engagement
Preferred tool for	Information regarding specific overt symptoms, events, experiences	Assessing personality predilections absent or present in overt behavior or consciousness

Note. MMPI = Minnesota Multiphasic Personality Inventory; RIM = Rorschach Inkblot Method. Adapted with permission by Gregory Meyer.

from the Rorschach and described their responsiveness to unique sources of influence and bias (Table 7.1). Unequivocal and consistent directions for group administration, employment of standard scoring procedures, and low-inference interpretive considerations contrast with the relative ambiguity of RIM and TAT stimuli with their theoretically derived interpretive rationales, more difficult development of reliable scoring variables, and controversial descriptive status as tests. The MMPI–2 and RIM differ in the nature of the tasks imposed on assessees and also by their utilization of responses styles contributing systematic sources of positive and negative error by inflating or deflating obtained scores (Meyer, 1997).

Psychometric Status

MMPI/MMPI–2 reviews have cited obsolete diagnostic criteria, simultaneous psychopathology and personality measurement objectives, absence of a consistent measurement model or an explicit theory-driven rationale, as well as structural problems of measurement as a result of increasing psychometric sophistication over time (Eysenck & Eysenck, 1982; Helmes & Redden, 1993; Holden, 2000). However, the MMPI/MMPI–2 success may be partially attributable to measuring general psychopathology independently of *DSM* while simultaneously measuring personality traits linked relevantly but not necessarily unambiguously with specific psychopathological conditions. More sophisticated developmentally, MMPI-derived psychometric instruments are now available (e.g., Basic Personality Inventory [Jackson, 1997], Holden Psychological Screening Inventory [Holden, 1996]), but to date they have neither replaced nor supplemented the MMPI/MMPI–2.

The absence of an explicit theoretical rationale, deliberate in MMPI construction, remains a legitimate approach within the domain of a parsimonious, test-specific assessment science. Nonetheless, structural problems of measurement (e.g., modest internal consistency reliabilities for basic standard clinical and content scales) may represent assets, although the appreciable clinical scale intercorrelations provide a genuine psychometric limitation. For example, MMPI–2 internal consistency and test–retest, 7-day median reliabilities range from .34 to .91 for basic, content, and supplementary scales (Butcher et al., 1989). Some scale intercorrelations exceed .80 due to item overlap and item redundancy. Similarly, failure to employ a construct validation paradigm, especially methods for evaluating convergent and discriminant validity, renders the MMPI/MMPI–2 vulnerable to overreliance on translations for linguistic equivalence and concomitant neglect of construct and metric equivalence.

Trait Measurement

Traits are contemporary survivors of earlier concerns by psychologists with various terms providing recognition of biological origins for universal human characteristics modified by habitual use in particular environments. Murray (1938) differentiated between manifest and latent needs, or motives, and general traits. Allport (1937) considered traits as predispositions to respond consistently by uniting functionally equivalent adaptive and expressive behaviors and suggesting the necessity for a taxonomy of trait terms by an alphabetical listing of unabridged dictionary personality-relevant terms (Allport & Odbert, 1936). Cattell (1943) reduced this list to bipolar clusters modified by reference to personological literature followed by an empirical reduction process and factor analytic identification of major dimensions. The search for parsimonious representation continued during the 1980s with a taxonomy describing the range, scope, and universality of individual personality differences within the structure of a Five-factor approach (McCrae & Costa, 1985, 1997). Big Five models have been compared with competing models of personality and criticized as "experimenter-imposed variable sets" that exclude important characteristics and fail to capture all the variance in human personality (John, 1990, p. 27).

Traits in concert with cognitions and motives now provide a generally accepted paradigm for quantitative assessment of the basic building blocks of personality. Personality traits and motives are associated with social environmental influences, whereas temperament is associated with a biological basis of behavior (Berry, Poortinga, Segall, & Dasen, 2002), although McCrae (2000) considered personality traits "as stable, pervasive, biologically based characteristics" (p. 11) providing "enduring individual differences in overt styles of thinking, feeling, and acting" (p. 12). It may be ultimately feasible in principle to develop a comprehensive natural language of personality description employing a set of traits covering all major areas of individual human behavior, but this has not been unequivocally accomplished to date.

Measuring traits as psychological characteristics of persons has been criticized as originating in perceivers' cognitve constructions or inherent in behavioral responses to situations. Nonetheless, the measurement of traits in tests as tools of psychological theory is part and parcel of a constructive realism (Loevinger, 1957; Messick, 1981) with historic origins in Allport, Cattell, and Eysenck (Harkness, 2002). From this perspective, traits exist in their own right as relatively enduring behavioral dispositions with underlying psychological structures as part and parcel of a scaffolding of scientific enterprise exposed by theory and substantiated in measurement.

However, the MMPI–2 does not emerge from theory to satisfactorily encompass these trait psychology parameters. As a consequence, the relevance of measuring traits as constructs must be demonstrated by research documenting the efficacy of adaptations for multicultural and cross-cultural MMPI–2 applications. Despite consensual appreciation and acceptance of trait measurement in the United States by the assessment establishment, the nature, composition, and cross-cultural identification of traits, constructs, and symptoms internationally has not been unequivocally demonstrated for the MMPI–2. MMPI–2 practitioners generally accept their test as a genuine etic applicable whenever competent translations are available. Nonetheless, description as an imposed etic more accurately reflects the contemporary research status because this test measures traits represented by items descriptive of behaviors relevant to psychopathology and personality construct domains understood in the United States. The MMPI–2 is used to measure symptoms, traits, and psychopathology in multicultural U.S. populations, although the research basis for these applications is incomplete without explicit attention to acculturation status and other adaptations. Non-Western cultures are characterized by a collective emphasis and interdependent construals of personality rather than by individualism and independence. Psychopathological states in these populations are defined by symptoms and disorders consonant with their understanding of socially acceptable behaviors.

Church (2000) suggested that an integrated cultural trait psychology provides one resolution for these measurement limitations and recommended an extension of methodologies already employed in Western psychology. Church (2000) listed the following sources of empirical evidence: "(a) replicable personality structure; (b) criterion validity; (c) replicable and interpretable cultural differences in personality traits; (d) temporal and cross-situational consistency of trait-relevant behavior; (e) interjudge agreement in personality ratings; and (f) heritability of culture-relevant traits" (p. 654). Church also noted that culture-specific traits may exist. Demonstrating cross-cultural replicability of trait dimensions in Western inventories (e.g., NEO–PI–R) does not imply that these instruments "carve up the personality domain in the same manner (and) existing instruments do to some degree 'impose' their structure in new cultural contexts" (Church, 2000, p. 655), and searching first for indigenous dimensions is recommended. Church also noted that lexical approaches are limited to identification of "global higher-order dimensions" (p. 656) and may omit encoding some personality aspects in natural language. Moreover, the NEO–PI–R and MMPI–2 differ in their degree of identification with trait psychology research criteria directing the search for a taxonomy and stemming from explicit theoretical origins. Thus, the manner of identifying items to represent traits, constructs, and symptoms is critical for development of an integrated cultural trait psychology.

Contemporary Assessment Science

The nature and dimensions of a contemporary assessment science began with the importation of scientific measurement principles from Europe applicable to methodologies for developing universal laws relevant to prediction and control of human behavior within biological and environmental characteristics. Psychometric psychology provided empirical rules for constructing tests to measure traits. Psychologists, however, differed in how they understood the nature and purposes of these rules and assumptions pertinent to a human science. Kimble (1984) developed the 12 Epistemic Differential scales to articulate these differences in values, knowledge sources, and methods among psychologists. Early MMPI, Rorschach, and TAT psychologists occupied very different positions in their preferences for objective tests or projective methods. MMPI adherents have defended and propagated their empiricism (e.g., Meehl, 1945).

At present, there is only limited preference and acceptance of an exclusively empirically driven process relevant to a test-defined version of assessment science as opposed to overarching conceptualizations of personality psychopathology defining the nature, procedures, and process of psychological assessment. For example, Rorschachers have worked assiduously toward legitimization of a test perspective but ultimately opted for method status, whereas TAT psychologist advocates have remained faithful to a more humanized, open-ended, interactive, and egalitarian perspective. MMPI/MMPI–2 proponents adhere to a more limited, test-oriented, conventional science perspective.

Matarrazo (1990) distinguished between tests and psychological assessment. Tests are low-inference, normative instruments; psychological assessment provides opportunity for both low- and high-inference integration. A test focus necessitates increasing psychometric sophistication applied to test construction and validation for a variety of measurement purposes. Training for psychological assessment competence should include applications of specific assessment technologies within a context of clinical and consultation skills. This differentiation signals a new era in the continuing development of an international assessment science and suggests an impending unification of the historically dichotomized, competitive, and internecine definitions of science.

Contemporary assessment science, as I described in chapter 1 (this volume), recognizes several salient influences on psychological assessment of psychopathology and personality. This science is incomplete without recognition of the necessity to expand standard assessment to encompass multicultural assessment to address assessment needs in the new millennium. A contemporary assessment science will be shaped by new parameters including public policy, globalization, human rights advocacy, and research sophistication affecting the empirical mechanics of knowledge acquisition and adaptation of tests.

MMPI–2 DESCRIPTION

MMPI–2 description within this chapter includes validity indicators; standard clinical, content, and supplemental scales; as well as normative data used for actuarial and clinical interpretation. With these materials, I follow the presentation format contained in Friedman, Lewak, Nichols, and Webb (2001) and provide MMPI–2 standard interpretation background for the cross-cultural/multicultural interpretation guidelines contained in this chapter.

Validity Scales

Friedman et al. (2001) described measures of profile validity as a frame of reference for clinical interpretation as well as to provide an index of self-description accuracy and additional psychological descriptors. D. S. Nichols (personal communication, July 25, 2004) employs a clustering of validity scales and a sequence beginning with scales evaluating completeness of self-reporting and proceeding to unfavorable self-description and malingering as well as favorable self-description including self-deception and impression management.

Consistency refers to "Cannot Say" (?) or unanswered items. More than 30 cannot say items requires discussion with the assessee and subsequent reexamination and completion of these items. Consistency also includes variable response inconsistency (VRIN) and true response inconsistency (TRIN). VRIN identifies inconsistent responses to items that are either similar or opposite in content, and TRIN identifies the frequency of yea-saying or nay-saying demonstrating acquiescence or defensiveness, respectively.

Self-unfavorableness/malingering includes the Infrequency scale (F), the F-Back (FB), F – K, Infrequency-Psychopathology or F(p), and the Dissimulation scale (Ds). The F scale suggests divergences in attitudes, experiences, and thoughts from a normal population for a variety of reasons including conscious or inadvertent dissimulation of psychopathology to be contextualized by inspection of the clinical scales. The FB scale identifies decrements in concentration or motivation over time in the test situation. The F-FB Index suggests serious depression when FB is higher than F, although an FB of 15 to 19, 8+ greater than F, indicates FB invalidity. The Dissimulation index (F – K), when strongly negative, merits consideration for positive defensive reactions to distress in the presence of moderate F and K scores. When VRIN is employed with elevated F or FB, severe psychopathology may be differentiated from random/careless responding or magnification of symptoms.

The Self-Favorable scales include impression management represented by the Correction scale (K), the Superlative scale (S), and the Socioeconomic Status scale (Ss), whereas the Lie scale (L), the Positive Malingering scale (Mp), and the Social Desirability scale (Sd) represent Self-Deception scales. The K scale was designed to detect test-taking attitudes of defensiveness and guardedness and to compensate for these attitudes by augmenting scores on Scales 1, 4, 7, 8, and 9 for adult inpatients. K-scale interpretation can be supplemented by the Mp scale, used in the Caldwell Report to differentiate "intentional self-favorable responding versus upper SES and self-deception" (described by Friedman et al., 2001, p. 204). K-scale interpretation, supplemented by the Ds scale, detects self-unfavorable overreporting as a result of panic or conscious effort. The Lie scale (L) suggests naïve attempts to appear virtuous, conservative, conscientious, and moral. The Superlative scale (S) supplements the L, K, and Mp scales by identifying favorable self-descriptions composed of subscales for Beliefs in Human Goodness, Serenity, Contentment With Life, Patience and

Denial of Irritability and Anger, and Denial of Moral Flaws. Butcher and Han (1995) suggested that moderate S scores describe positive mental health, although elevations exaggerate claims of inordinate adjustment. High S responders report greater self-control and fewer clinical problems, manifest symptoms, and negative personality features than MMPI–2 normal standardization participants.

These validity resources document assessee endorsement of items describing bizarre and painful personal experiences, favorable or unfavorable self-descriptions, and consistency or inconsistency in responding. Friedman et al. (2001) suggested cutoff scores on these scales for relevant interpretations and provided examples of the effects of random, true, and false response patterns on validity indicators and the clinical scales for men and women. Friedman et al. also delineated four basic and frequent validity configurations by age and educational level with suggestions for report language.

Standard Clinical Scales and Derivatives

The MMPI–2 standard clinical scales retained their original MMPI descriptive labels, but the following scale numbers in parentheses are generally used (Welsh, 1948): Hypochondriasis (1), Depression (2), Hysteria (3), Psychopathic Deviate (4), Masculinity–Femininity (5), Paranoia (6), Psychasthenia (7), Schizophrenia (8), Mania (9), and Social Introversion (0).

The 28 Harris and Lingoes (1955, 1968) subscales for clinical Scales 2, 3, 4, 6, 8, and 9 designate apparently homogeneous item clusters reflecting a single trait and/or attribute. These subscales are generally of less stability than their parent scales and are scored whenever clinical Scale T scores are between 60 and 80, although scores of 65 are generally interpreted. The Subtle–Obvious (S–O) subscales for Scales 2, 3, 4, 6, and 9 were derived from White adult samples (Wiener, 1948) and are used to suggest test-taking attitudes. Elevated S and O scores suggest response sets for faking bad by overreporting or faking good by underreporting of problems; summing their differences across clinical scales can be employed as a measure of test-taking attitudes (Friedman et al., 2001). However, the original S–O scales may not describe subtlety in African Americans because endorsed items are perceived more favorably by Whites corresponding with differing perceptions of items reflecting psychopathology on Scales F and 9 (Herkov, Gordon, Gynther, & Greer, 1994).

Content and Supplemental Scales

There are Content scales for Anxiety (ANX), Fears (FRS), Obsessiveness (OBS), Depression (DEP), Health Concerns (HEA), Bizarre Mentation

(BIZ), Anger (ANG), Cynicism (CYN), Antisocial Practices (ASP), Type A (TPA), Low Self-Esteem (LSE), Social Discomfort (SOD), Family Problems (FAM), Work Interference (WRK), and Negative Treatment Indicators (TRT; Butcher, Graham, Williams, & Ben-Porath, 1990).

Supplemental scales, described in Friedman et al. (2001), include Addiction Acknowledgment (AAS), Addiction Potential (APS), Alcoholism (MAC–R), College Maladjustment (Mt), Control (Cn), Ego Strength (Es), Dependency (Dy), Dominance (Do), Manifest Anxiety (MAS), Marital Distress Scale (MDS), Over-Controlled Hostility (O–H), Posttraumatic Stress Disorder scales (PK/PS), Prejudice (Pr), Social Dominance (Do), Social Responsibility (Re), Social Status (St), Welsh Anxiety (A), and Welsh Repression (R). A large number of supplemental scales are available, and assessors should select those scales with sound research histories that are applicable to their assessment objectives and relevant for their clinical populations.

Normative Data

The new MMPI–2 normative data included 2,600 male and female adults, aged 18 to 84, who were paid volunteers from seven states, excluding much of the South and Texas. A separate 1992, 478-item MMPI–Adolescents (MMPI–A; Archer, 1997) version provides normative data for youths from 14 to 18.

Ethnicity was underrepresented in the MMPI–2 norms for Asian American, Hispanics, and Native Americans and Alaska Natives and may be exacerbated by exclusion of lower SES ethnic minority public sector clients. Additional relevant changes from the original MMPI included raising the reading level from sixth to eighth grade.

Education level and occupational status were extremely different from census figures for "some college education" and "professional job status": 70.4% versus 40.8% and 33.1% versus 15.6%, respectively (Zalewski & Greene, 1996). These differences were investigated in an SES *Manual Supplement* (Dahlstom & Tellegen, 1993) reporting estimates concerning the influences of age, gender, occupational level, and race on basic validity and clinical scales. Note that these demographic differences probably have lesser effects on profiles than personality differences (Friedman et al., 2001). Nonetheless, educational level overrepresentation, the largest component of variance, increases scores on L, F, 1, 7, 8, and 0 and reduces K. This Manual Supplement also included a five-level breakdown of education level in separate tables for men and women illustrating the magnitude of effects on validity and clinical scales. Clients in public sector agencies and hospitals may also have a poor fit with MMPI–2 norms due to low SES (Caldwell, 1991; Duckworth, 1991); these clients also include high percentages of ethnic minority populations. For example, disability-benefit applicants with less than an 11-year mean educational level have dramatically F elevated linear T scores (Rothke et al., 1994), which can be substantially reduced by plotting the raw scores on both MMPI and MMPI–2 profile sheets for comparison. Friedman et al. (2001) emphasized, "When testing a low SES individual, the reader is advised to be aware that the positive skew in the MMPI–2 normative sample toward upper SES inflates the impression of psychopathology" (p. 24). The adoption of uniform rather that linear T scores was designed to render the percentile values of Scales 1 through 4 and 6 through 9 more similar across these scales and between men and women while it minimizes differences from the original linear T scores. Despite these overestimates, the MMPI–2 scale norms may accurately represent 1993 educational level census estimates of the U.S. population (Schinka & LaLone, 1997).

A review comparing the original MMPI adult norms with 21 studies (Pancoast & Archer, 1989) found consistent differences and indications of bias. Newer response patterns accurately reflecting the general U.S. population are necessary because continuing evaluation of psychiatric patients is predicated on norms producing codetypes across more than 40 years of empirical literature. There is also MMPI–2 college normative data on 515 male and 797 female college students from three state universities in Ohio, Minnesota, and North Carolina and the U.S. Naval Academy containing approximately 15% non-White ethnic minorities omitting only designated Hispanics (Butcher, Graham, Dahlstrom, & Bowman, 1990). Comparisons between this college data and the MMPI–2 normative sample yielded college elevations on Scales 6 (Pt), 7 (Sc), and 8 (Ma) of approximately ½ SD that reflected between-sample age differences. These norms are important because MMPI–2 college student samples from Argentina, China, Japan, Korea, Mexico, Thailand, and Puerto Rico, and Asian Americans as well as a Greek MMPI–A sample are available for comparison (Butcher, 1996a).

Interpretation

The modified Welsh (1948) code identifies the highest clinical Scale T score value by number as the first number in the code with two or more scales with identical scores recorded in ordinal sequence from left (1) to right (0). The relative elevations of all scales in the profile are identified by T-score values and corresponding symbols (Butcher et al., 1989). A shorthand method is used to describe the record rather than the entire code in which codetypes, codes, and code patterns are differentiated (Dahlstrom, 1992). Codes designate the highest single scale (high-point code), the highest two scales (two-point code), or the highest three scales (three-point code). Codetypes label grouping of several different code patterns into a more general set. Nichols (2001) advised that MMPI–2 norms differ from MMPI norms to the extent that approximately one half of profile patterns (codetypes) disagree. As a solution, Nichols recommended double profiling, which had also been endorsed earlier (Caldwell, 1997; Humphrey & Dahlstrom, 1995).

CROSS-CULTURAL/MULTICULTURAL USAGE

Adequacy of Contemporary Research Basis for Practice

Nichols et al. (2000) expressed concern over "the current lag in the production of data to establish the empirical correlates of MMPI–2 scales and profile patterns, even among Euro-Americans. . . . Until such data become available, MMPI–2 clinicians serving non-Euro-American patients, whether such patients are within or outside the United States, will be plying a difficult and risky trade in rather dim light. . . . Increased illumination will require hard work and there is much of it to do" (p. 264).

In this section, I highlight core cross-cultural methodological issues relevant to a rationale for developing MMPI–2 interpretation guidelines. Chapter 1 (this volume) test-method bias should be reviewed at this time as an introduction to cross-cultural/multicultural MMPI–2 practice. Several major issues, central to culturally responsible research with the MMPI–2, were contained in an article outlining current Rorschach research needs and recommendations (Allen & Dana, 2004, p. 193). Table 7.2 describes the MMPI–2 relevance of these issues: (a) linguistic equivalence; (b) normative data resources, including MMPI–2 U.S. existing norms and proposed acculturation status and racial identity status norms; (c) construct validation research, and (d) predictor bias.

In addition, setting/instructional set equivalence has not been systematically examined for self-report measures including the MMPI–2, although self-report instruments involve written instructions and associated instructional sets providing difficulties not only for unacculturated non-Westerners but also for Western counselors who complete multicultural competence inventories (Pope-Davis et al., 2001).

Butcher and Han (1996) also delineated methodologies in addition to translations relevant for demonstrations of equivalence and examination of assumed universality and suggested that "without evidence of equivalence at several different levels, no observed cross-cultural differences can be reliably interpreted (p. 44). More recently, Butcher, Derksen, Sloore, and Sirigatti (2003) recommended content validity, factorial validity, and predictive validity as necessary for demonstrating that translations "measure the same constructs in the same ways in the new culture as it does in

TABLE 7.2
Core Cross-Cultural MMPI–2 Methodological Issues

Issue	Description	MMPI–2 Relevance
Linguistic equivalence	Language translations using standard procedures addressing ethnic/regional differences in English usage	150+ translations with back translation; use in 22+ and more than 46 countries; limited field testing
Standard norms	Cross-national/cross-ethnic normative MMPI–2 comparisons infeasible whenever ethnicity is used as a demographic variable	Preferable to employ comparisons only to screen for group differences; instead, focus on culturally embedded variables responsible for observed score differences; can interpret these differences as equivalence, nonequivalence, or valid measure of underlying cultural difference
Identity norms	Identify assessee cultural orientation/racial identity status	Identity statuses describe heterogeneity of group membership; new norms can minimize pathologizing traditional or racially identified persons
Construct equivalence	Cross-cultural construct validation research demonstrating construct equivalence for ethnic minorities and international cultural groups	Violations of assumptions (e.g., normality, homoscedasticity); CFA, DIF, and IRT analyses and linear structural modeling evidence needed for problems with scale score error distributions
Predictor bias	Identify potential bias from basic validity theory perspective (i.e., differential validity for score in predicting criterion variable for ethnic group member)	Detect slope and intercept bias in psychopathology/personality (implicit assumption of construct equivalence)

Note. MMPI–2 = Minnesota Multiphasic Personality Inventory–2; CFA = Confirmatory Factor Analysis; DIF = Differential Item Functioning; IRT = Item Response Theory.

the culture of origin" (p. 822). There is now essential agreement between these independent efforts to delineate the research foundations necessary for multicultural and cross-cultural applications of standard instruments (Allen & Dana, 2004; Butcher, Cheung, & Lim, 2003; Butcher, Derksen, et al., 2003; Butcher & Han, 1996), although the importance of this research has been minimized historically.

In the next section, I begin by summarizing the relevancy of each Table 7.2 issue within a context of differences between currently sanctioned adaptations and additional adaptations recommended in this chapter for ethical multicultural and cross-cultural MMPI–2 practice.

Linguistic Equivalence

Linguistic equivalence, using systematic and consensual translations procedures, provides a necessary but incomplete demonstration of equivalence. Translation has been described in terms of adjustments using modifications described as formal (lexical-grammatical language requirements), transitional (reshaping item contents without radical changes), and radical (construction of new items with an equivalent meaning) (Mizra, 1976). Butcher (1996b) focused on linguistic equivalence using a careful seven-step procedure including translation, back translation, and subsequent comparisons by bilinguals (Steps 1, 2, 3), followed by field comparisons for equivalency to test acceptability of the translated instrument (Step 4), subsequently demonstrating the adequacy of American norms (Step 5), and the development of new norms with a representative normal sample of 1,000 containing 500 men and 500 women (Step 6), and finally ongoing research assessing cultural validity (Step 7).

Linguistic equivalents of the MMPI–2, using Steps 1 through 3, were established and reported for 18 languages including Spanish versions for Argentina, Chile, Mexico, Nicaragua, Puerto Rico, and Spain (Butcher, 1996b). By 1998, translations were available in 22 languages with ongoing developmental projects in Afrikaans, Croatian, German, Rumanian, and Portuguese (Butcher et al., 1998). Step 4 has not been routinely employed; Nichols et al. (2000) indicated "an ethnographic component of field testing in which bilingual investigators conduct interviews with a heterogeneous group of monolingual informants may be essential to establish that the stimulus values of the items in the target language are equivalent to those of the same items in the original language" (p. 251). Steps 5 through 7 are simply unrealized research possibilities.

Normative Data Resources

The standard MMPI–2 norms described earlier underrepresent ethnicity, overrepresent higher educational levels and professional job status, and pathologize normals to the extent of requiring downward adjustment of clinical scale cutoff scores. These limitations suggest caution whenever these norms are employed with ethnic minorities, particularly those individuals with minimal education, inadequate reading skills, and lower social class occupational status. Nonetheless, procedures for exercising caution have generally depended on the cultural knowledge, wisdom, and experience of assessors rather than exemplified by explicit steps in the interpretation procedure.

Published translation information and normative data is available on MMPI–2 adaptations for Asia and Southeast Asia (Japan, Korea, China,

Thailand, Vietnam, Hmong, and Asian Americans), Latin America and Spain (Argentina, Chile, Mexico, Nicaragua, Puerto Rico, Spain), Europe (Belgium: Flemish/Dutch, France, Greece, Iceland, Italy, Norway, Russia), and Middle East and East (Arabic language, Israel, Persia, Turkey; Butcher et al., 1998). These adaptations contain normative data from nine countries and Puerto Rico providing opportunities for comparison of item differences from true responses in U.S. data. Butcher, Derkson, et al. (2003) reported use of the English language version in the United Kingdom. In Poland, Denmark, Sweden, Croatia, Latvia, Lithuania, and Bosnia-Hercegovina there are translations, or translations are currently in process. Butcher, Nezami, and Exner (1998) indicated that scores in Norway and Iceland were too close to U.S. norms to justify national norms. Butcher, Derkson, et al. (2003) also suggested using American norms as itinerant norms with subsequent "rigorous evaluation to determine if norms need to be developed for the new populations" (p. 822). Although scores from Belgium, France, Holland, and Mexico were close to U.S. scores and within the *SEM*, separate national norms were developed to facilitate acceptance in these countries, whereas normative data is available in Germany.

Helmes and Reddon (1993) described MMPI normative bias (see also Pancoast & Archer, 1989) due to consistent elevations for normal men and women on Scales K, Hy, Mf, Ma, and Pa and suggested "the adequacy of the MMPI normative group poses serious problems when conclusions are drawn concerning profiles that are based on comparisons with the original normative groups, in that such conclusions may attribute pathology to groups or individuals that are normal by other standards" (p. 460). The use of uniform T scores for MMPI–2 clinical scales reduced scale elevations by approximately 5 points with a cutoff score of 65. Although elevations for normals on Scales Hy, Pa, and Ma were affected by differences in MMPI and MMPI–2 normative samples, uniform T scores fail to address potential difficulties with the MMPI research basis that has been generalized as applicable to the MMPI–2 without new validation data.

MMPI–2 conventional usage of 5 T score point differences was derived from approximately 0.5 SDs above the mean used for comparison purposes within the U.S. The 5 T score point difference may be considered a convention (J. Allen, personal communication, June 14, 2004) because the fact of group similarity or difference is not relevant to the question of construct equivalence (Weiner, 2000), and reliability associated measurement error appears considerably greater in magnitude than 5 points. For example, recent simulation research (Munley et al., 2004) suggested that 10 T-score points may be required for profile stability predicated on use of test–retest correlations.

Clinical scale reliability estimates and *SEM* data (see chap. 1, this volume) are required for comparison of U.S. MMPI–2 normative data profiles with normative data resources developed internationally. Butcher et al. (1989, Table D1) reported reliabilities for men ranging from .67 to .92, whereas reliabilities for women were from .58 to .91. To estimate the range of reasonable limits within which "true" scores would fall, ±1 *SEM* refers to 68% of cases, and ±3 *SEM* accounts for 99.7% of cases. Thus, using the MMPI–2 manual *SEM* figures, the range of probable error for reliabilities approximating .80 is ±4.47 × 6 or approximately 25 points!

Butcher et al. (1998) recommended use of U.S. normative data whenever comparative scale scores in other countries are within the *SEM*s reported in the United States. The MMPI–2 manual refers to *SEM* figures but does not explicitly calculate ranges of score for each clinical scale commensurate with 1, 2, or 3 *SEM* above and below obtained scores or indicate how accurately the range should be calculated within which the true score is likely to lie. Using 1 *SEM* ± an obtained score as the criterion for a true score range suggests that a 5-point difference does not constitute a significant difference between scores on any clinical scale. Using 3 *SEM*, or 25 points, including 99% of cases, effectively obliterates the basis for individual prediction predicated on group norms with this test in the United States! Based on research experience with the MMPI and MMPI–2, this conclusion is not tenable. However, this logic may be extended one step further to cross-cultural comparisons of clinical scales. Because assessors lack convincing construct equivalence demonstrations for each scale, the conventional 5-point difference probably does not represent a significant difference between scores on a given clinical scale in two different cultural settings. This statement should not be misconstrued as disregarding the elevations on these scales. Instead, I prefer to consider tentatively any difference in scale scores as potentially significant and examine other confirming or disconfirming evidence within the MMPI/MMPI–2 array of scores and externally from other data.

The employment of high-point codes requires not only profile similarity but is also affected by *SEM* figures used to calculate reliabilities of differences (*SEdiff*), described in chapter 1 (this volume), between pairs of clinical and validity scales. When this is accomplished using *SEM* figures, 8 points represents the minimum scale difference required for interpretable differences between scale scores due to overlapping items and chance errors. An example of item redundancy compromising discriminant validity is that 20 of 32 Hs items are also contained in Hy (Holden, 2000). Helmes and Reddon (1993) provided a convenient table (Table 3, p. 458) summarizing the numbers of overlapping items on validity and clinical scales.

MMPI–2 normative data should be used cautiously within the United States for ethnic minority individuals inadequately represented by these norms. Acculturation status information contained in the assessment data may be used to ascertain whether the normative data should be employed with a given individual. For traditional persons, refugees, sojourners, and others who are relatively unacculturated, using national norms from countries of origin, if available, is preferable. For sojourner assessees from outside of the United States, national norms should be used whenever available, and otherwise, itinerant norms should be employed cautiously. Such usage necessitates careful comparison of individual demographics, comparing information from orientation questions with the parameters of the available normative data.

Construct Validation

These are a number of construct validation paradigms relevant for the MMPI/MMPI–2 (Dana, 1993), although many have been infrequently applied; and these methods were considered costly, time consuming, and impractical (Butcher, 1996a). Nichols et al. (2000) noted that extratest criterion measures must equal or exceed the reliability and validity of the MMPI–2 for resulting correlates to be stable and generalizable. In an exemplar study with the Spanish MMPI–2 in the United States (Fantoni-Salvador & Rogers, 1997), the external measure, the Diagnostic Interview Schedule, (Robins, Helzer, Croughan, & Ratcliff, 1981), provided only modest MMPI–2 sensitivity and specificity rates with four major diagnostic categories—major depression, schizophrenia, anxiety disorders, and alcohol dependence. Clinical scale elevations and codetypes did not effect the number of symptoms experienced by these patients.

Butcher and Han (1996) recommended employment of factor similarity indexes, factor score correlations, and confirmatory factor analysis instead of the multitrait-multimethod approach despite their limitations for cross-cultural equivalence research (Allen & Dana, 2004). Noting that Butcher and Han (1996) cited only two studies employing their recommended methods, Nichols et al. (2000) suggested that cross-cultural validation of a translated test is essentially flawed due to capturing only overlapping symptoms in the absence of research demonstrating equivalency of psychiatric nosology. It can no longer be assumed without adequate documentation that symptoms and nosological groupings are universal and consistent across cultures.

Predictor Bias

Predictor bias occurs when there is differential validity for a test score in the prediction of a criterion variable for ethnic minority individuals (Allen & Dana, 2004). Evidence for underprediction of African American psychopathology was provided by slope and intercept bias in the MMPI–2 (Arbisi, Ben-Porath, & McNulty, 2002). Unmeasured differences in cultural identity processes, such as acculturation status, potentially provide an important third variable in predictor bias studies now including only limited sample descriptions. Moreover, as Cuellar (2000) noted, culture can function as a mediator variable influencing a predictor and criterion as well as a moderator variable affecting direction and strength of the predictor–criterion relationship. Predictor validity studies are difficult to interpret, leave important questions unanswered, and need to be addressed by direct tests of cross-cultural construct validity and equivalence of the interpretations of data from test variables.

TEST ADAPTATIONS: SANCTIONED AND DISPUTED

Test adaptations are relevant to ethical concerns and scientific limitations by emphasizing caution in employing standard interpretations with assessees who differ from normative populations. Butcher et al. (1998) sanctioned and endorsed only what they described as "appropriate test adaptations" (p. 189). These adaptations include facilitating translations by deleting objectionable items, eliminating cultural-specific items, and minimizing complex words or phrasing in MMPI–2 construction as well as by development and application of construct validation methods described earlier. Nonetheless, translation alone is insufficient for responsible multicultural and international applications of standard assessment instruments as long as there is a dearth of relevant and adequate documentations of method adequacy and construct equivalence research.

During the interim, while more adequate research foundations for multicultural assessment practice are being developed, nonsanctioned and other alterations are necessary to avoid questionably ethical and even discriminatory test applications. The objective of these alterations is to increase reliability so far as feasible for populations either not represented or underrepresented in available U.S. norms. Sanctioned adaptations have not included shortened administrations, factor scale profiles, the mini–mult, and short forms as reasonable substitutes (Dahlstrom, 1980) due to disputed equivalence. The legitimacy of specific test adaptations for Hispanics in the United States (Dana, 1995) was criticized because they "can introduce error into prediction by actually masking important differences ... (without) ... empirically-based formulas for integrating such data into the scoring and interpretation of Hispanics profiles" (Velasquez et al., 1996, p. 6). Unsanctioned adaptations include extratest considerations of service delivery social etiquette; use of moderator variables as sources of cultural information; simultaneous usage of dual MMPI and MMPI–2 profiles; as well as careful consideration of internal data requiring inspection of items by gender and in elevated, high-point, and "special" or culture-specific scales. Employing culture-specific scales has apparently not occurred despite their potential availability (e.g., Butcher, 1996a, Appendix D; Gomez-Maqueo & Reyes-Lagunes, 1994; Nichols et al., 2000).

Velasquez et al. (2000) expressed a valid concern with my earlier suggestions for unsanctioned MMPI/MMPI–2 adaptations or "special corrections . . . without providing a clear discussion of how one should go about making such corrections" (p. 401) and misunderstood my belief that these interpretation adjustments are helpful during the interim while necessary and relevant equivalence research is designed and implemented. The following guidelines suggest how interpretation bias can be addressed by using specific steps to increase reliability of interpretation with multicultural populations, including Hispanics.

INTERPRETATION GUIDELINES

These guidelines are designed to reduce interpretation bias (see Dana, 2000c), labeled by Church (2001) and described as resulting "from any combination of construct, method, or item bias" (p. 981). Table 7.3 summarizes interpretation guidelines including high-inference, extratest additions and low-inference internal adaptations. This interpretive approach proceeds from MMPI–2 items to scale scores and other item configurations. Hypotheses generated from these sources of low-inference data lead to confirmation of interpretive inferences using other information resources including other tests/methods, employment of moderator, interview contents, and behaviors.

Orientation Questions

These three questions are applicable in different ways to each instrument. The first question, reason for assessment, suggests the degree of assessor concern with examining validity indicators and especially the need for employment of culture-specific response sets or at least the awareness that such response sets may be operative. Use of the MMPI–2 with persons from cultures espousing disbelief in the credibility of mental health services can provide motivation for not taking the test seriously. The second question, cultural typicality of assessee, refers to the applicability of available normative data. Atypical, inadequately represented, U.S. multicultural assessees may be lower class, poorly educated and unskilled, or acculturating refugees of traditional or marginal cultural orientation status. By contrast, sojourners with international origins may be well educated, middle class, proficient in English, and either monocultural or bicultural

TABLE 7.3
MMPI/MMPI–2 Interpretation Guidelines

Guideline	Data Source	Description
Orientation questions[a]	Demographics	Reason for assessment? Cultural typicality of assessee? Need cultural orientation status?
Service delivery[a]	Social etiquette	Interview/instruments; four major groups + other groups
Acculturation status[a]	Moderator instruments	Examine profile credibility for multicultural assessees
Normative data[b]	MMPI + MMPI–2: Ethnicity adjustments	Examine validity, clinical, and supplemental scales regardless of magnitude of differences from normative expectations; double profile; compare with available national normative data; check *SEdiff* for comparisons between validity and clinical scale elevations prior to consideration of high point codetypes
Response sets[b]	Validity indicators	Use standard scale/profile validity indicators plus attention to culture-specific sets/styles[b] identified by existing scales and potential scales
Items[b]	All elevated scales	Identify potentially culture-specific items in elevated scales and examine these items with assessees
Clinical scales[b]		Examine all elevated clinical scales for possible psychopathology confound; employ extratest cultural knowledge for examining available, potentially universal scale-specific hypotheses for Hy, D, Pd, Pa, Pt, and Ma
Special scales[b]	Culture-specific scales	MEX example + potential for men/women from Chile, China, France, Japan, Korea, Mexico, Netherlands, Nicaragua, Puerto Rico, Spain

Note. MMPI = Minnesota Multiphasic Personality Inventory; *SEdiff* = reliability of differences.
[a]Extratest addition. [b]Internal adaptations.

in cultural orientation. The third question, cultural orientation status, is always pertinent for multiculturals in the United States, and assessment of cultural orientation is obligatory. However, although traditionality may be assumed for many foreign nationals/sojourners, their English proficiency and biculturality must be considered for relevancy of U.S. and national norms.

Service Delivery

In chapter 4 (this volume), I summarized some of the culture-specific ingredients for assessment service delivery behaviors. Appropriate social etiquette facilitates acquisition of valid test data even with standard printed directions on the MMPI–2 booklet. Every assessor contact with an assessee must credibly meet expectations for a professional encounter. Although it is notoriously easy from a U.S. perspective to overlook, minimize, or neglect specific culture rules for courteous behaviors, other cultures generally have strict and clearly articulated behaviors communicating respect and mutual interpersonal obligations for a variety of social and professional situations.

Acculturation/Racial Identity Status

In Chapter 4, I described moderator instruments for assessing acculturation/racial identity status and reviewed empirical studies of MMPI/MMPI–2 pathologization resulting from traditional cultural orientation status. Normal individuals from four major ethnic minorities in the United States have clinical scale elevations suggestive of psychopathology. Velasquez et al. (1996) initially did not accept this research evidence and said that "while it is still not fully clear how acculturation impacts MMPI–2 performance of Hispanics, as evidenced by inconclusive results in studies with the original MMPI, it is nonetheless a critical factor in assessment of Hispanics" (p. 15). More recently, Velasquez et al. (1997) reconsidered my earlier stance (Dana, 1996a, 1996b) and modified their conclusion by indicating that "it is evident from research with other psychometric instruments that acculturation must be considered when evaluating this population" (p. 114). Nonetheless, assessors have not routinely evaluated acculturation status using independent and available moderators as adjuncts to MMPI–2 practice.

Normative Data

Multicultural and cross-cultural interpretation has been historically compromised as a result of psychometric instrument limitations, normative bias, and absence of credible demonstrations of construct equivalence.

Multicultural assessment has accepted 5-point plus differences between the mean validity and clinical scale scores of ethnic minority/cross-cultural groups and normative U.S. data as evidence of significant cultural differences. However, Butcher (2000) noted that the meaning of very similar scores (i.e., within the 5-point convention) may vary between these groups. Cuellar (2000) suggested that moderating these scores may be necessary for understanding potential differences in meaning. Double profiling (i.e., MMPI plus MMPI–2 profiles) may provide additional evidence in this regard for ethnic minority populations within the United States (Caldwell, 1997; Handel & Ben-Porath, 2000), but double profiling alone without revising the expectation for T-score criterion differences and employing acculturation status information for multicultural U.S. citizens is insufficient.

Reliance on U.S. norms within the conventional 5-point range for similarity, although a convenient artifice, is no longer warranted for multicultural and cross-cultural MMPI–2 applications in the absence of demonstrated construct equivalence. Conservative profile interpretation for these populations hypothesizes the existence of a genuine difference (see Malgady, 1996, 2000) regardless of the magnitude of mean score differences and suggests the necessity for an examination of internal MMPI–2 adaptations including response sets, items, scale scores, and special scales for possible cultural salience. With multicultural assessees, conservative interpretation is preferable to conventional interpretation because cultural differences are assumed to exist until demonstrated otherwise by empirical research.

Response Set/Style

Careful examination of the full array of conventional MMPI–2 response sets/styles affecting validity indicators described earlier in this chapter provides a first step toward profile interpretation because cultural knowledge and understanding are employed during this process. This scrutiny leads to consideration of additional culture-specific response sets not already incorporated into conventional interpretation. However, "a number of factors . . . can confound cross-cultural comparisons of personality variables, including . . . cultural differences in response biases, self-presentation, and social judgments" (Grimm & Church, 1999, p. 415), although these potential confounds may be culture specific, and their relatively small effects do not necessarily change conclusions concerning personality constructs. However, response set and personality style (in addition to demographics) can be misleading and/or pathologizing for ethnic minority individuals, at least for Asian American students (Abe & Zane, 1990). For example, these culture-specific response sets/styles include social desirability, private and public self-consciousness, and self-monitoring (i.e., other directedness, pleasing others, conforming to social situations, masking one's true feelings, acting, and extraversion). Asian American and White American differences in levels of psychological adjustment may be confounded with ethnic differences in cultural and demographic variables such as generation level. Inadvertent underpathologization, recognized by López and Hernandez (1986), can also occur due to minimization of problems considered cultural in nature because ethnic differences in psychological adjustment and personal style occur independently.

Items

Identifying items contributing to elevated scale scores followed by discussion concerning how the assessee understood these items can suggest item-comprehension difficulties as well as possible intrusion of relevant cultural beliefs. Similarly, Cannot Say items may reflect cultural content leading to indecision and nonanswering. Critical item lists, although potentially useful, have not been validated for use with multicultural populations. Preparation of a list of endorsed critical items for subsequent discussion with an assessee is recommended.

Scale Elevations

Scale elevations in MMPI/MMPI–2 records of multicultural assessees require careful examination of alternative hypotheses prior to accepting the presence of psychopathology. Scales may be elevated for a variety of other reasons. First, using adult norms with adolescents can yield spurious elevations due to differences in item interpretations (Archer, 1987). Second, an inflated impression of psychopathology may occur in lower SES assessees due to the positive SES skew in the normative sample discussed earlier. Third, inflated scale elevations suggestive of psychopathology also occur as a by-product of traditional cultural or racial status reviewed in chapter 5 (this volume).

MMPI scale elevations for ethnic minorities were first identified for African Americans in Scales F, 4, 8, and 9 (Dahlstrom & Gynther, 1986), described as less than one half SD on Scales L, F, 8, and 9 for men and 5 and 9 for women in a meta-analysis (Hall, Bansal, & Lopez, 1999), whereas Greene (1987) noted a preponderance of no mean difference findings. Ethnic or racial background, employed as a demographic or proxy variable, obscured underlying psychological variables leading to lack of specificity in the independent or predictor variable in these studies.

By contrast, research has identified elevated MMPI/MMPI–2 scales as a function of acculturation or racial identity status. For example, earlier research findings of elevations in Scales F, 4, 6, 8, and 9 were compared with RIAS–B scores for African American college students. Scales 4, 8, and 9 were significantly related to racial identity stages at a level comparable with recent MMPI–2 predictor studies (Whatley et al., 2003). MMPI–2 elevations occurred on Scales F, Hy, D, Pd, Pa, Sc, and Si in low acculturated, or traditional, Asian American college students (Sue et al, 1996, Table 10–2, p. 213). Traditional Mexican Americans obtained significantly different MMPI scores on 10 of 13 scales and higher scores on F, Pt, Sc, and Ma (Montgomery & Orozco, 1985). Hospitalized traditional Native Americans and Alaska Natives, regardless of tribe or specific psychopathology, had similar profile elevations with significant elevations on Scales F, Pd, and Sc (Pollack & Shore, 1980), whereas Plains Indians had significantly higher elevations on Scales F, 4, and 8 (Hoffmann et al., 1985). These findings suggest caution in assuming that clinical scale elevations are indicative of psychopathology without examining scale items and other sources of potential confounding.

In addition, elevated scales may have personal or cultural meanings for assessees that have not been examined for cross-cultural MMPI–2 interpretation. However, pending this research, the hypothesized and ostensibly universal meanings of scale elevations can be examined using knowledge of different cultural developmental perspectives juxtaposed with a rationale for scale interpretation. Predicated on a review of Caldwell's unpublished papers, Erdberg (1979) described specific antecedent conditioning events leading to distinctive and homogeneous styles of personality operation appearing as elevations on clinical Scales Hs, D, Pd, Pa, Sc, and Ma. For Hs (with a secondary Hy elevation), the early conditioning event is catastrophic and associated with unending, unbearable pain and ultimately death. Sensitization to health concerns and shutting down sensory functions are adaptive compromises. For D, the event is loss experienced as irretrievable and overwhelming. Adaptation requires limited engagement with the present and future to forestall further trauma and loss. For Pt, the event is disruptive and unpredictable. Constant apprehensiveness decreases the likelihood of reoccurrence of unanticipated events. With concomitant increase in K, fear is more focused; with decreased K, the fear is more diffuse. For Pd, the event is rejection by parents and numbness to reduce stress. Threatened interpersonal contact produces anticipatory emotional arousal and consequent shutting down of readiness for relationship. For Pa, concern with aversive inroads on intactness and autonomy leads to preparatory vigilant sensitization accompanied by abrasive behavior and misreading interpersonal cues. For Sc, inferable from subscale scores, the disregard by the person (mother) primarily responsible for survival leads to absolute withdrawal and shutting down of information processing for protection. For Ma, the event is akin to a partial deprivation schedule with reinforcement according to parental needs. Acceleration of responsiveness, a future focus with restricted attention in the present, provides an overanticipation of future rewards for incessant activity.

Special Scales

Nichols et al. (2000) described the potential usefulness of a special scale, MEX (Gomez-Maqueo & Reyes-Lagunes, 1994), for examining possible MMPI–2 cross-cultural biases for Mexican college students. A scale was composed of item responses from the MMPI–2 for Mexicans with proportional endorsement rates over 25% for men and women when compared with U.S. restandardization sample items. The resulting 29-item scale was correlated with selected MMPI–2 scales and corrected for age differences between samples. In the words of Nichols et al. (2000):

> The MMPI–2 scale correlates of MEX are generally of modest magnitude but are highly patterned. Among the standard validity and clinical scales, Mania correlates positively (Ma; .20); Depression (D; –.22), Hysteria (Hy; –.21), Paranoia (Pa; –.23, and Social Introversion (Si; –.19) are correlated inversely with MEX. The remaining standard scales are all negatively correlated with MEX, with K at –.10. These trends are clarified among the Harris and Lingoes (1968) and Si (Ben-Porath, Hostetler, Butcher, & Graham, 1989) subscales in which a positive correlation for Ma1(.30) is found along with negative correlations for D1 (–.20), Hy2 (–.20), Pa3 (–.28), Sc2 (–.21), SC4 (–.18), and Si2 (–.27).
>
> These correlates are consistent with a view of MEX as reflecting qualities of buoyancy, optimism, cheerfulness, and gregariousness, along with skepticism about the motives of others. This pattern of correlates is largely replicated among the MMPI–2 content and content component (Ben-Porath & Sherwood, 1993) scales, with positive correlations with MEX for Cynicism (CYN, .29; CYN1, .32), Antisocial Practices (ASP, .35; ASP1, .39), and Type A Personality (TPA, .27; TPA2, .26), and a negative correlation with Social Discomfort (SOD, –.19; SOD1, –.24). These correlations extend the inferences given earlier in the direction of a skeptical and expedient view of rules, regulations, and authority and a capacity for vindictive responses to being wronged.
>
> Correlations between MEX and a variety of supplemental scales follow the pattern established previously, with negative values for Welsh's R (–.28), and Social Responsibility (Re; –.21) and positive values for MAC–R (.18), Hostility (HO, .27), Aggression (AGG; .32), and Positive Emotionality/Extraversion (PEE; .37). These correlates would appear to emphasize a mobilized and largely positive emotionality, social disinhibition, and a relaxed attitude toward duty while reiterating themes of reluctance to take others at face value and a readiness to retaliate for injuries suffered from others. (pp. 257–258)

Nichols et al. (2000) recognized the source of these inferences resides in a Euro-American understanding of MMPI scale correlates and they provided additional discussion emphasizing the necessity for understanding Latino test-taking attitudes as well as their relatively lower threshold for reporting symptoms on questionnaires. Thus, the assessor needs sufficient cultural sophistication to avoid stereotyping an assessee. This interpretive exemplar of a special, culture-specific scale is used to call attention to the availability of items for similar scales in normative samples from Chile, China, France, Japan, Korea, Netherlands, Nicaragua, Puerto Rico, and Spain (Butcher, 1996a).

A special scale should be examined initially for the percentage of true item responses for comparison with information from the orientation questions. A small number of endorsed items describe an atypical assessee in terms of normative data. Inspection of these items qualitatively yields potentially culturally relevant information for comparison with supportive and/or contradictory evidence from within MMPI–2 data resources as well as externally from all assessment ingredients employed as a frame of reference. The model, as employed by Nichols et al. (2000), provides a quantitative guide to what becomes a qualitative procedure in assessment practice. Note that the MMPI–2 scales selected for comparison purposes is dictated not only by the endorsed special scale items but also by the elevations on the selected scales. This process requires a clear knowledge of what each scale represents as well as its empirical correlates and is facilitated by sufficient cultural knowledge concerning the potential cultural relevance of each MMPI–2 scale.

Codetypes

Codetypes were deliberately omitted from Table 7.3 because of reliability issues and cultural differences in symptomatology, *DSM* clinical disorders, and culture-bound syndromes. Not only are these problems for multicultural assessment interpretation, but as the level of abstraction increases from items and scale clusters of items, reliabilities dramatically decrease when codetypes involving two or more clinical scales are interpreted. Codetypes usage is primarily dependent on research that has not been replicated for multicultural populations. I would only proceed to codytype interpretation when assessee similarity to U.S. norms is high and unmistakable (i.e., third generation, middle class, college education, monolingual English speaker).

Thematic Apperception Test

Earlier book chapters and papers have suggested a rationale for cross-cultural and multicultural assessment practices using the TAT with adult and adolescent populations (e.g., Dana, 1986, 1996c, 1997b, 1998d, 1998f, 1999a, 2000e). However, these contributions did not offer a detailed modus operandi for practical applications of the TAT with these populations.

This chapter contains a systematic framework for high-inference TAT interpretation with safeguards for reliability of inferences from TAT story contents. The story contents used in this interpretive framework were derived primarily from enduring stimulus characteristics of the original Murray (1943) TAT cards. These consistent procedures include guidelines for comparisons of story contents with historic normative expectations that are legitimized to some extent by cross-generational and cross-cultural findings predicated on these same early resources (Avila-Espada, 1986, 2000). I summarize data from application of these guidelines in a checklist format that organizes information relevant for preparation of reports.

This rationale and procedural contents remains incomplete, and supplementation is required using additional low-inference scores. The development and validation of new scores is imperative because the ultimate survival of the TAT as a legitimate assessment instrument for these non-Euro-American populations requires objective scores and eventually a consensual scoring system. The high-inference interpretation procedures I present in this chapter, even with increments in reliability of interpretation (Dana, 1970; Dana, 1982, chap. 7), require a body of validation research and normative data for new objective scores (Dana, 1962). A combination of low- and high-inference interpretation can provide an impetus for consensual TAT practice similar to the accomplishment of the CS for the Rorschach.

Components of a process contributing to ethical assessment consistent with the eventual development of acceptable standards for multicultural TAT practice include (a) historic resume and context, (b) special attributes and unique relevance, (c) prerequisites for interpretation, (d) interpretation format and procedural guidelines for increasing reliability of inferences, (e) presentation of a detailed example applying these guidelines to a cross-cultural TAT data set, and (f) addressing limitations of these contemporary interpretation procedures.

HISTORIC RESUME
AND CROSS-CULTURAL USAGE

The TAT was originally designed to measure the need and press components in a comprehensive personalogical theory, part of an intensive study of normalcy by Murray (1938). This theory assumed coexistence of physiological and psychological processes or needs within a directional context of unconscious motivation and psychoanalytically derived levels of personality and mediated by determinism as well as influences of outside forces or presses. The needs or motives were inferred from behavior or TAT fantasy; presses contributed the objective and subjective demand characteristics of externals. The different kinds of needs and their interrelations and modes of functioning interacted with presses to form a thema, although presses have not received comparable empirical attention.

The present set of TAT cards was developed from a variety of sources and revisions over a decade (Morgan, 2002) and were originally published in 1943 (Murray, 1943) by the Harvard University Press for use in the United States. In Argentina, during 2001, I discovered a Mexico City-Madrid-Buenos Aires printing of the TAT cards. This printing contains major differences in shading, facial expressions, and clarity of object definitions on a number of cards including 3BM, 4, 6GF, 11, and 19. Herzberg (2000) noted stimulus distortions and apparent perceptual discrepancies in Brazil from usual content expectations in the United States. There may be unknown effects of these different printings on clinical interpretation and comparative cross-cultural TAT research.

Few students in the United States now learn to apply TAT normative scores, which has been described by Vane (1981) and Teglasi (1993), or receive substantial guidance from empirical research during assessment training because the TAT has been used as a "projective interview" (Rossini & Moretti, 1997). However, if high-inference TAT interpretation continues in the absence of available low-inference objective scoring, preferably in scoring system format, the TAT may gradually be supplanted by other picture-story tests using redrawn Murray cards or cards designed and normed for specific multicultural populations such as TEMAS (Costantino et al., 1988).

In Spain, the complete set of Murray cards and objective scores developed in the United States were used to establish an integrative analysis system to provide a standardized scoring system with population norms legitimizing the TAT as a test for clinical assessment purposes (Avila-Espada, 2000). In addition to two new variables derived from empirical data, formal variables (i.e., reaction time, total time, word count) and thematic analysis variables (i.e., themes, outcomes) were designed to represent the stimulus values of the TAT cards. These variables came primarily from studies in the 1950s by Dana, Eron, Fine, McClelland, Murstein, and Rosenzweig; the recent Spanish norms for thematic data and stimulus values variables do not differ from U.S. norms during the 1950s! Two new sets of Murray cards, administered in their original order with Card 16 added optionally, included 1, 2, 3BM, 4, 6BM, 7BM, 8BM, 10, 13, 14, 15, 18BM for men, and cards 1, 2, 3GF, 4, 6GF, 7GF, 8GF, 9GF, 10, 13, 17GF, and 18GF for women. The verbal instructions included the components recommended by Dana (1955) with a 5-minute time limit per story, verbatim notes, recording, and a query for understanding the directions. Additions relevant for interpretation of the integrative analysis system were garnered from European TAT publications.

SPECIAL ATTRIBUTES
AND UNIQUE RELEVANCE

The TAT contains a number of special attributes and dimensions relevant to assessment of multicultural populations: (a) free association in storytelling, (b) cards and administration, (c) directions, (d) story literality/veridicality, (e) limitations due to Euro-American interpretation resources and assumptions, and (f) unavailable consensual scoring procedures.

Free Association in Storytelling

Storytelling is essentially a free-association process; story contents and meanings can be understood as manifestations of subjective culture (Howard, 1991). TAT stories represent storytelling in contexts with picture stimuli with histories of eliciting a variety of normative and personalized contents. TAT interpretation of these stories is dependent on capturing this free-association process by verbatim, recording to ensure exact reproduction of everything communicated by an assessee's words and concurrent behaviors. In addition to the sequence of exact words, recording should include the tempo and style of presentation because distortions and disturbances in free association can suggest personal relevance of the contents.

Cards and Administration

The TAT contains 20 cards designed for administration in a standard, numerical order by gender, although most assessors employ a smaller number of cards in no consistent order. Murray (1943) administered the first 10 cards depicting literal, everyday scenes during a one-hour session. A second hour was used for cards 11 through 20 that were "more unusual, dramatic, and bizarre" (Murray, 1943, p. 2). Assessors have only infrequently used all 20 cards because of time restrictions. Although various short forms have been employed historically, I prefer a short form consisting of Cards 2; 3BM; 4; 6BM/GF; 7BM/GF containing a person alone with someone of the opposite gender and with mother, father, and family; and supplemented by several additional cards including 11, 16, and 19 (Dana, 1956). I prefer to employ all cards whenever time permits and administer short-form cards in their original numerical order, although Murstein (1963) is probably correct that card stimulus properties are more important than order effects. Because assessors lack empirical studies concerning stimulus effects with multicultural assessees, all 20 cards should be employed to increase the reliability of inferences whenever feasible.

Directions

Many different sets of directions have been used for the TAT beginning with Murray's (1943) emphasis on imagination, intelligence, and fantasy, perhaps an appropriate introduction and challenge for Harvard students but less reassuring and even intimidating for others. Murray (1943) directions with some modification were used in many early studies, but these directions have failed to communicate that the TAT is a "guided opportunity for the subject to reveal a conception of Self and Other" (Peterson, 1990, p. 192). Standard administration directions for the TAT are necessary for reliable scoring and consistent interpretation procedures. Only verbatim oral or written directions can provide consistent administration procedures analogous to what Exner provided for the Rorschach CS. Since my first administrations of the TAT in the 1940s, I have enjoined students to use the following seven-part directions (e.g., Dana, 1959b, 1982). "I am going to show you some pictures, one at a time. I want you to make up a story about each. Tell what has led up to the scene, describe what is happening at the moment, what the characters are feeling and thinking, and what may happen in the future. Then give an outcome."

Story Literality/Veridicality

There is considerable latitude for voluntary control by inclusion or exclusion of specific contents and affect expression in TAT stories. Assessees can exercise control by excluding/omitting, selecting, or minimizing specific story characteristics and contents either deliberately or involuntarily by introducing false needs or withholding true needs (Holmes, 1974). Control may be augmented by education, sophistication, or motivation to be non-revealing. Whenever control is inadvertent, however, defensive styles of projection sensitization, primarily for men, and repression, primarily for women, can affect story contents (Heilbrun, 1977). Projection sensitization results in longer stories containing more feeling and thinking (Lefcourt, 1966), attribution of unfavorable traits to characters, and expression of needs congruent with overt behaviors. Repression leads to avoidance of threatening contents and neutral stories (Normal, 1969).

Zubin (1950) distinguished between projective methods by proposing a classification of inwardly accessible and outwardly reportable contents or parameters of awareness versus communicability. The TAT omits voluntarily suppressed but inwardly accessible contents. In other words, the TAT can reveal conscious content that an assessee is willing to reveal as well as symbolized contents that may be communicated without awareness, although other contents can be deliberately and successfully concealed (Tomkins, 1947).

However, when to accept story contents as literal and veridical autobiographical information and when to minimize personal relevance provides one of the major difficulties in high-inference TAT interpretation. Lindzey (1961) referred to this dilemma as consequence of the "imperfect" relation between fantasy and behavior. Although lapses in free association may indicate personal relevance, there are no consensual rules for translating these lapses into relevant inferences. Nonetheless, assessees tend to identify with TAT characters more like themselves; these stories are more likely to be literal in contents. Similarly, absence of indicators of remoteness of distance from the storyteller, such as congruence in time and geography, may be associated with more literal storytelling. Children generally describe family members accurately in stories. Finally, cards of medium ambiguity provide more revealing personality data at least for college students primarily of Euro-American origins (Kenny & Bijou, 1953)—as Murray believed was true for Cards 1 through 10—with greater numbers of emotional words (Ullmann, 1957), and verbalizations going beyond card description contained more credible contents (Prola, 1972). In addition to these findings for medium ambiguity cards, there are notable exceptions for interpretation of the most ambiguous Cards 11, 16, and 19 using specific card expectations or hypotheses discussed later.

Limitations Due to Euro-American Interpretation Resources and Assumptions

Interpretation of TAT stories by psychologists in the United States has been primarily a culture-specific or emic enterprise. Personality is assumed to reside largely within the person with relevant and largely unconscious contents symbolized in fantasy productions that may be reconstituted using projective methods. These psychoanalytic assumptions require some modification for cross-cultural interpretation. For example, personality may be visible more readily in social interactions within parameters of acceptability–rejection determined by beliefs within the culture of origin. There are explicit social norms for recognition or denial of internalized distress as well as for behaviors, emotions, or symptoms that are recognized as culturally legitimate expressions of distress. The distinction between levels of consciousness may differ by preoccupation with either awareness or denial of the importance and relevance of internalized experience for everyday life.

Several historic assumptions (Lindzey, 1952) have described TAT limitations and advantages and are relevant for contemporary interpretations of storytelling: (a) various TAT characters can represent the assessee; (b) all stories do not have equal interpretive significance; (c) introduced characters may or may not have real-life counterparts; (d) selected story events can recapitulate either past or current life events, either experienced or observed, especially in recurrent themes; (e) indirect or symbolic expression of personal characteristics may or may not evidence conscious dispositions or behaviors; and (f) group membership and cultural determinants appear in story contents. These assumptions articulate what assesses can do with a storytelling task, but interpretation must be augmented by including stimulus values of cards, selection of cards, directions for the storytelling task, and recommended interpretation prerequisites and guidelines for processing story contents.

The usefulness of the cross-cultural TAT interpretation presented in this chapter depends on the magnitude of several major differences between multicultural assessees and Euro-Americans that can suggest whether or not the above fundamentals and assumptions are applicable to an individual from a particular culture. These overarching differences include first-language family (Indo-European or non-Indo-European). The first-language family determines how fantasy and behavior coexist and are interrelated; TAT stories reflect this relation by selection and representation of coping skills as well as the means–ends intellectual operations for making decisions and solving problems. Indo-European languages afford a modicum of consistency in thought processes as well as opportunities for common cultural learning experiences within similar social class and educational parameters. Second, religions provide a common basis for values, meaning, and behaviors enacted in religious construals of individual lives, and the origins of the TAT suggest that usefulness at present may be limited to Judeo-Christian religions. Third, the relative importance of self and other, exemplified by the individualism–collectivism dimension, emphasizes major differences between the cultural selves of Euro-Americans and individuals from many other cultures. The cultural self contains diverse contents and boundaries of variable permeability organized in a manner to describe the relative importance of self and others as well as the presence and psychological contributions by natural and supernatural phenomena including spirits and ancestors. Fourth, there are extreme cross-cultural differences in the balance between reliance on internal and external sources of personal knowledge represented by LC and LR dimensions (Sue, 1978). An understanding of these sources of personal knowledge provides information on how the cultural roles of the self are understood, valued, and objectified. To the extent that these major sources differences are present in a particular assessee, there is necessity to go beyond the limitations of this Western interpretive lexicon for the TAT and to be extremely cautious in inferring not only psychopathology but personality attributes and characteristics as well. As I suggest in the final section of this chapter, there is need to develop and validate additional scores germane to psychological processes inherent in cultures with different language families, religions, cultural self and/or cultural roles, and sources of personal knowledge.

Consensual Scoring

The TAT was initially introduced with a scoring system predicated on personality theories. Several need scores from Murray's (1938) need-press system, available in scoring manual format, have been used in numerous research studies, although an early review indicated scant clinical applicability (Dana, 1968b). There are now 14 empirically supported available scores for nonclinical personality research (Smith, Atkinson, McClelland, & Veroff, 1992).

Many additional objective scores and scoring systems were developed for research and clinical purposes in the United States between 1940 and 1960, although no system achieved consensus among assessment practitioners However, training was soon available only for scores providing normative expectations by Arnold, Dana, Eron, McClelland, Atkinson, and Murstein (Vane, 1981). In addition, Teglasi (1993, 2001) has described the utility of some of these objective scores for research and clinical purposes. In this endeavor, Teglasi (1993, 2001) has succeeded in sustaining continuity of professional awareness that these objective scores were available for assessment training. More recently, Ephraim (2000b) demonstrated cross-cultural usage of a number of scores representing 10 presumably etic or universal Murray instrumental needs occurring in different forms regardless of the cultural context and applied within an etic–emic framework for personality assessment research. These themes are contained in normative emic data from different countries and for U.S. subpopulations (Ephraim, Sochting, & Marcia, 1997).

PREREQUISITES FOR INTERPRETATION

Preliminary Questions

To minimize stereotypy or caricature, I begin with three questions to help separate general knowledge about a particular culture/ethnic group from information descriptive of an individual assessee with a specific group membership.

These questions pertain to purpose, acculturation status, and typicality have different referential contexts when applied to the TAT. The first question—"What is the reason for this assessment?"—recognizes that test-taking attitudes can dramatically affect the response process. Test-taking attitudes are often culture specific and for immigrants can mirror either the attitude toward psychological evaluation per se, the relation between the individual and the government in the country of origin, or expectations of positive or negative reactions from the mental health system or their representatives. Is the assessee volunteering for assessment to gain information relevant for plans and decisions subject to personal control, or is the assessment an involuntary referral for clinical diagnosis or hospitalizaton? Is the setting for assessment medical, legal, or academic?

Storytelling is typically a relatively nonintrusive experience, and the contents of stories will often relate directly or indirectly to the purpose of assessment. For example, fear of negative evaluation or punishment by an authority figure or similar expectations in same or cross-gender relationships can be documented by frequency counts of various kinds. Objective scores, when available, can increase the reliability of these data and thus contribute to interpretation validity.

A second step is initiated by the question "What is the cultural orientation status of the assessee?" Acculturation status documentation should not rely on the TAT for cross-cultural assessees. Instead, the TAT stories are sources of cultural contents that help to describe the presence and importance of cultural issues. In other words, TAT stories inform the already established cultural orientation status; adequate interpretation of cultural material in stories requires detailed knowledge of the culture. For multicultural assessees, however, moderator data independent of the TAT may be necessary to describe acculturation status and to provide information relevant to understanding of the cultural self. It is mandatory to examine acculturation status for all assessees who are sojourners, recent immigrants, or first and second generation in the United States. Third-generation individuals, especially of non-Euro-American origins, may also need to be examined for acculturation status, especially if the family uses a non-English language at home.

A third step involves an examination of the difference between group identity and individual cultural identity illustrated by Fig. 2.1 (chap. 2, this volume) that indicates some of the variables that covary with ethnicity and emphasizes the extreme nature and magnitude of within-group differences. This step is required because assessors are prone to minimize within-group differences. The general question asked is "How typical or representative of the culture is the assessee?" Typicality refers to characteristics related to acculturation status, social class and/or social roles, and educational level. These dimensions of potential within-group differences include traditional health–illness, mind–body relation, and LC/LR beliefs but do not necessarily encompass, for example, individualism–collectivism preferences that may inhere independently of demographic variables.

Important information concerning typicality, however, can emerge from analysis of TAT stories, although there is no substantive normative data for direct comparisons. The available normative data for the TAT that includes themes and emotional tone was collected in the 1950s and is representative of college student populations in the United States. I have reservations concerning the adequacy or accuracy of this data even for college students at the present time. I am also intrigued that Avila-Espada (2000) found no differences over time or cross-culturally in his normative data. Nonetheless, normative data present and summarize stimulus characteristics of the TAT cards. Because these issues are unresolved, I urge students to familiarize themselves with Holt's (1978) normative guide to the use of the TAT cards and my chapter reviewing the use of normative data for TAT interpretation (Dana, 1982, pp. 379–414).

GUIDELINES

The following interpretive guidelines can reduce error to some extent prior to the availability of low-inference scoring categories, the development of comprehensive emic and etic–emic scoring systems, and culturally relevant normative data. Several major steps are described and discussed: (a) an adequate sample of stories including representation of medium- and high-ambiguity cards, (b) standard administration, (c) story abstracting procedures and organization of abstracted contents, (d) comparisons with normative expectations, and (e) analysis of congruence–incongruence between stimulus values and story contents.

Sample of TAT Cards/Stories

Use of the word *adequate* for sampling TAT cards is misleading because, as suggested earlier, use of the entire set increases reliability of interpretations. Having reiterated this caveat, when time restrictions require fewer cards, I recommend using the basic set of Cards 2, 3BM, 4, 6BM/GF, and 7BM/GF to represent basic interpersonal relationships plus Cards 11, 19, and 16 and supplemented by as many additional cards as feasible with 16 as the last card.

Administration

After the 7-part directions, all TAT stories are recorded verbatim. When the spontaneous stories are completed, assessors may use a few appropriate questions to elicit more information, to provide elaboration of the story, or to follow any cues that seem clinically relevant. The assessor should always note by a question mark (?) the points at which questions have been asked, especially the first question. If no outcome has been provided in the spontaneous story, the assessor should question the assessee to determine if an outcome is available. Although I generally do not use an inquiry following each story or the entire set of stories, many assessors find this practice adds useful content and information.

Story Abstracting Procedures and Organization of Abstracted Contents

Abstracting TAT stories in a consistent manner is necessary for subsequent analyses that result from frequency counts generated from these abstracts. I use a structural approach similar to Stein's (1948) but notably less psychoanalytic, which provides a convenient database, increases reliability of interpretation, has some empirical support, and helps to reduce eisegesis, the Achilles heel of high-inference interpretation described elsewhere (Dana, 1966). Students need practice in abstracting TAT stories for comparison with abstracts prepared from the same sets of stories by more experienced assessors. These criterion sets, used as external criteria, should have preestablished levels of agreement for reliability expectations.

Personal meaning is suggested by lapses in the flow of storytelling by interruptions, disruptions, deflections, or alterations and additions in story contents that should be noted including uneven pacing, pauses, ambiguities, misplaced concreteness or abstractions, as well as story and mood varia-tions across cards (for examples, see Dana, 1982, chap. 15). Lapses in the storytelling process help an assessor distinguish content that be interpreted literally as part and parcel of an assessee's personality or experience from content that is nonpersonal, nonrevealing, or embellishment.

How is a story abstracted? Abstracts should summarize potentially in-terpretive content in each story and include content cues for identification with characters and plots, structural cues serving as red flags for personal relevance and literal acceptability, and descriptive labels for thematic con-tents. Several readings of each story are necessary during the abstracting process. The purpose of the abstract is to distil the amount of story content and to identify potentially relevant hypotheses for examination by com-parisons with the contents of other stories.

Subsequent frequency counts of abstracted story contents or themes are based on the premise that the total number of cards can provide a rough estimate of available assessee energy (Tomkins, 1947). How this energy resource is expended may be estimated by the percentage of relevant cards containing designated story contents. With multicultural assessees in the United States, this figure suggests the importance, relevance, and meaningfulness of cultural contents and provides information on accul-turation status. A second tally is used to estimate the percentage of total energy usage to deal with specific problems and conflicts. I do this by using frequencies of themes obtained from story abstracts with additional descriptive information as the primary source of data for interpretation. This practice individualizes the process and permits considerable latitude in the kinds of contents identified and selected for abstraction.

As an alternative, assessors who have been trained with a need system may wish to use Murray's (1938) approach for labeling needs and infer-ring their strength using a 5-point scale, using frequency counts, and not-ing degree of elaboration. A number of Murray (1938) needs have credible research histories for this purpose including Achievement (Ach) in Cards 2, 4, 8, 14, and 17; Affiliation (Aff) in Cards 4, 8, 9, 10, and 17; Aggres-sion (Agg) in Cards 3, 4, 15, and 18; Autonomy (Au) in Cards 2 and 11; Dominance (Dom) in Cards 2, 4, and 17; and Nurture (Nur) in Cards 2 and 4 (Campus, 1976). Some of these needs have MMPI equivalents and the Edwards Personal Preference Schedule (1954) may be used for an inde-pendent estimate of need strength.

Comparisons of Abstracted Story Contents With Normative Expectations

As a basis for comparisons with normative expectations, college norms have been used in the United States for nearly 50 years. These normative resources include typical–atypical themes and emotional tone (Eron, 1950, 1953; Eron, Terry, & Callahan, 1950) and are in tabularized form from these original resources (Dana, 1982, pp. 144–147). The details of these norms are outdated, and assessors should be cautious in literal applications. A partial solution focuses on the more central and enduring stimulus values of the TAT cards to provide more generic and abbreviated guidelines, omitting details of the thematic content and including specific card hypotheses or major stimulus values identified in the TAT research history (Dana, 1982, Table XLI, pp. 381–383). In adopting this configuration of potential card stimulus characteristics, I have been encouraged by Avila-Espada's (2000) complementary Spanish findings using Murray (1943) cards with scores derived from these stimulus values. Card numbers are used to identify the following stimulus demand characteristics:

1 = achievement, family dynamics;
2 = independence–dependence, family relationships, family roles;
3BM, 3GF = central value;
4 = balance of power in heterosexual relationship;
5 = mother–adolescent child relationship;
6BM = mother–son relationship;
6GF = father–daughter relationship;
7BM = father–son relationship;
7GF = mother–daughter relationship;
8BM = father–son relationship;
8GF = fantasy;
9BM = social attitudes;
9GF = sibling relationship;
10 = quality of heterosexual relationship, intimacy;
11 = symbolization of current problem;
12M = attitudes toward receiving help;
13MF = heterosexual relationship;
14 = fantasy, achievement, depression;
15 = depression;
16 = ideal life satisfaction and/or symbolized current problem or conflict;
17BM = achievement, narcissism;
17GF = depression, suicide;
18BM = locus of control;
18GF = attitudes toward mother;
19 = family dynamics; and
20 = alienation/fantasy (Dana, 1986, 1996c).

Misidentification of card stimuli (for Harvard University Press printing only):

1 = violin broken/damaged, child's physical features—for example, blind;

3BM = gun as scissors, omitted;

4 = poster as person, omitted;

7GF = doll as baby, omitted;

8BM = rifle, omitted; and

11 = omission of monster/dragon, people as animals (Dana, 1982).

The preceding information is applied within general expectations for relations between card stimulus values and ensuing story contents. TAT pictures generally result in sad stories with unhappy outcomes. More specifically, the expectation is that blatant pictures evoke blatant stories, and neutral pictures elicit neutral stories. Thus, a discrepancy between expectations and elicited stories provides evidence for a literal interpretation of personal relevance. The cards themselves may be considered as either neutral or blatant in the sense of stimulating strong emotions (Dana, 1982, pp. 383–384). Discrepancies in card-by-card expectations for story contents are hypothesized as potentially suggesting omission, denial, or expression of content that is personally relevant. Neutral cards include 1, 2, 5, 7BM/GF, 8BM/GF, 9BM/GF, 10, 14, 16, 17BM, and 20. Blatant cards include 3BM/GF, 4, 6BM/GF, 11, 12M/F, 13, 15, 17GF, 18BM/GF, and 19.

Conflict strength may be estimated by tallying similar conflicts in different cards for comparison with the total numbers of cards to index the amount of energy expended by each conflict. For many assessees, this may be all that is necessary to adequately describe conflict strength. For some assessees, however, conflicts that are dissimilar across cards may occur frequently, leading to a possible interpretation of poor functioning and anxiety (Piotrowski, 1950). Tallies of similar conflicts in different cards and dissimilar conflict across cards should be done to examine data for this potential interpretation.

AN EXAMPLE OF STORIES, INTERPRETATION, AND REPORT

Stories

This data set is from a 36-year-old Argentine woman who is married with one 3-year-old child. She is of Spanish, Lebanese-Syrian, French, and Native Indian descent who is college educated with some training toward

Licensura in Psychology; yoga instructor and translator (English); and with 10 years of psychoanalysis (Laconian).

The TAT stories are presented together with their abstracts:

Card	Story	Abstract
1	A kid, a violin, of course. He's sitting at a table. Sheet of music Now what happens? (wants clarity on directions) Does it because he is sent to a teacher to learn how to Play the violin. Family wants a musician in the family. He is distressed because family is having a reunion—Gather together—asked to play the violin for all of them. He hates that. Sat there because he had to practice. Can't Make up his mind when to start training because he is not Willing to. He won't practice but he will have to play all the same. He will not do excellent performance but he will do his best. All Aunties and girl cousins will kiss him and he will say OK its already over. Afterwards everyone will have tea. He will be relaxed or relieved from the experience.	Initial hesitancy—wants to perform exactly as requested. Atypical story suggests personal relevance. Middle-class origins. Family expectations include social pressure for conformity. Large extended family. Stubborn as child. Ach not primary. Independence may be primary. Family rebel. Note: tea time 4–8 PM cultural tradition. Compromise with relief after performing
2	Well, people in country. Reminds me of a very old Argentine movies—40s or 50s. Don't look certainly happy (LP). Girl has a plain family—no outstanding situations. Probably make both ends meet with no urgency. Don't suffer. She's got some books probably going to town. Simple family—not illiterate—least plain—likes reading—going to library—can't buy books—take books back. Nothing particular happen to her in a short time. Will do the necessary to improve and whatever she wants—which is not the same as the woman leaning back on tree—not show any expectations.	Family scene contradicts C1?—distance from self by device of old movie? Marginal middle class status? Ambition in excess of family; fears mediocrity. Note possible identification with upper class elitist ideal?
3BM	What is this? (rhetorical). Trying to identify—first impression. Person is sort of . . . can't decide . . . woman crying or dozed off—probably waiting for someone who is not going to come back—her husband—have an argument—not the first one. He left home. What will happen? Be there until she wakes up. Put blame on him—doesn't mean	Requires time: be upset or deny personal story. She decides: husband leaves, but insight—she is to blame. Worn out suggests chronic marital issues, but must stay in relationship. Pessimism, lack of

he is One to blame. She looks like a worn out person. She won't find easily another person to share her life with. She's not prepared for that. She doesn't look like optimistic person—way she leans face downward—Not sort of energetic person—won't be easy to find activity that entertains her.

energy for change. Needs entertainment—Bored?

4   Here I see a couple. May be are on a picnic. Woman is very pretty. He is handsome. She probably attracts every man's attention— even if she wants to or not. Probably Appeared another man. Guy felt jealous—She is trying to avoid argument or row. Boy friend is madly jealous. Trying to persuade him to give up because they were having a very nice time. She will have to talk with him . . . make him understand that he can trust her because she loves him very much and can't help being pretty and attracting the attention of other men.

Conventional story. Sees self as attractive (flirtatious?), man macho—culturally expected. Discord. Woman tries to placate man with Unstated outcome.

5   Well, here//decide if door is inside or front door. Face of Woman not very enthusiastic. Might be a neighbor, friend of woman living in house. Friend ill the whole week. Neighbor Decided to visit her. Nobody answered door. She knew ill Person was inside house. Knew where extra key was hidden—opened the door—respectfully—she was worried—did not want owner to think she was snooping around. Opening the door—not see anybody. Nobody at home. Worried. Fears her friend had been probably taken to hospital. Will go back home. Left a note saying she was there and was worried and asking to be told what had happened.

Unusual story. Personal relevance. Display genuine caring/respect for others. Follows social rules. Takes responsibility for own acts.

6GF Reminds me of another movie. Not urgent. Very artificial what I see. They are in a house. Man is scaring the woman. Taken by surprise.Wasn't waiting for the man. Man let her know that. "You weren't waiting for me but I am here." There is conflict between them—but not a couple—involves sexuality—trying to go out with her. He will try to seduce her—Watching her may be saying threatening things. Wanting to know how

Unusual sexuality theme uses movie + 2 added distance indices. Usual surprise—fear. Very specific dialogue Conflict— verbal threat—argument requires external help from neighbor/police as if unable to help herself.

she will get out of problem. Argument
started. Next door neighbor who was near
the door heard them arguing. She called the
police—though something unpleasant was
happening. Woman in picture (does) not like
the man—widow—doesn't want to have a
relationship—even less with that man.

7GF   Can't identify what is in her hand. Probably   May be printing differ-
       a doll. Girl about to go out with friends or   ences. Middle-class. Strict
       Aunt. She's well dressed—not Teenager yet   mother. resentment short
       and the mother is telling her—has been a   lived.
       hundred Times—the same rules of behavior.
       Girl not looking at mother—looks sort of
       fed up with her advice. Waiting for the other
       people to ring the bell. She will probably
       enjoy the outing and when she comes back
       home she will have forgotten her mother was
       pestering her.

8GF   Young woman—looks very dreamy. She's   Ideal life situation. Action
       happy—probably in love. Received a letter   external to card. Perhaps
       from her fiancé—going to get married soon.   simply a wish for marital
       In letter he said he would be back from   happiness, propriety after
       a business trip in A couple of days. She's   preceding card.
       dreaming what she's going to do when She
       sees him and looking forward to that. When
       they meet they will speak about the wedding
       arrangements and he won't be leaving the
       town until they get married and she will
       accompany him—trip as a honeymoon.

9GF   Well, here the girl is behind the tree—was   Frequently sisters. Does
       reading. She heard someone running (can't   she have any sibs? Curios-
       identify)—near the coast or beach. Saw a   ity leads to action.
       girl. Girl running did not see her. Looks
       frantic. Not a very happy face. Girl reading—
       wondering what happened but she tried not
       be noticed. Stayed here to see if something
       else might happen. She will wait until there
       is a proper distance and will follow the girl to
       see what happened.

10   Here—a couple (joint story? 8GF con't).   8GF very important. Day-
       Fiancé—probably met—went out. Now in   dreams of good feelings
       ballroom and they are dancing. They are   toward man. Sexuality
       Enjoying one to be very close to the other . . . requires love to sanction a
       why their eyes are closed. Probably—they   socially OK relationship.

are going to go somewhere in car—don't
Know if going to make love in the car—40 to
50 years ago. Be a very romantic situation—if
they can, they are going to make love. If they
can't, they are going to wait.

11	What is this! Oh God, I can't understand. Landscape. Probably waterfall. Center—person/animal. Part of a bridge (can't fit)—fallen jeep—group of people crossed bridge—just in time—afterwards the bridge fell. Result in a movie. Showing for Impact on those who are watching the scene. Underneath hills or rocks . . . don't see—precipice—adds dramatic details.	3x delayed story. Description. Life is dangerous, risky. Movie provides distance from awareness of extent of risk in own life.
12F	Mother-in-law. Old hag doesn't belong to young lady's family. Ill-willed person with a very sarcastic gaze. Young Woman—sort of person gets this reaction. Sort of knows what she's doing—way she leads her life. Left house—lives in better place. Old lady says, "who does she think she is." Knows other woman's intentions, but she doesn't care.	Family discord. Use of "hag" plus descriptors may be literal/personal. Note upward mobility again. Social class difference between own family and husband's family? What are other woman's intentions toward her?
13	My goodness! Crime scene probably passional crime. Haven't seen each other for a long time. He's the one who came back—not normal couple of teenagers—came back—thought she would be thinking of him. She didn't show changes . . . made love—no, had sex. He found out she had been dating other men. She didn't take care of what she was saying . . . certain comments Slipped. He saw belongings from another man. Got mad. He strangled her. Did that out of madness because he was in love with her. He got dressed. Finally realized completely what he had done. He saw her lying there—started to cry—because he loved her desperately and because he's in danger. Setting is very depressing—matches with sort of life she led—or she lived.	Idiomatic English—"crime of passion" Sex-love distinction—she can make it but dire consequences. Macho male violence attributed to "madness" and "love." Guilt. Last sentence seems literal autobiographical.
14	Someone who has been in darkness all his life—young man—finally after struggling so much to find a way out, he could find his	darkess = depressive. Lives between despair and expectations?

way. He looks at the light as if he had discovered Something wonderful—even if I can't see his eyes. Darkness could mean depression or a very bad mood. Light represents Great, or at least pleasant expectations.

Struggle may refer to psychoanalysis. What has he discovered that nourishes hope?

15 Cemetery. My goodness! A living death. Man represents the soul of somebody who cannot rest in peace. He is wandering around the cemetery. Represented in an unpleasant way—did something wrong . . . something that might be punished. He can't See the brightness—next step to paradise or heaven. Everything is in darkness . . . shadows are mere impression. It will take a long time for that spirit to change the situation because it is a dark spirit.

Catholicism. Did something sinful/evil? "Dark spirit" may symbolize permanence of own "situation" and despair.

17GF Building-sun-water-bridge—might be a port—carrying heavy loads. Everyday situation, boss (capitas)—woman leaning on bridge—not trying to commit suicide, there because she wants to think about something that is worrying her. Sun is overcast; something in her life is overcast. Represented by the sun. Worried. Probably stay there until she can make out things. Nobody else will notice what she is undergoing because everyday life must go on. Loads may represent heavy load she may be carrying but is invisible to us.

Denial of depression or suicidal intent. Symbolism. "something" in her daily life is oppressive and preoccupying, but she does not want others to know ("invisible") or have her life disrupted as a result.

18GF What here? Two women. One is trying to strangle the other—hands around her neck, fingers tight, not caressing other. Very hard look in her eyes—face like petrified. She is in hatred. Probably relatives—might be sisters—not trying to hurt attacker—Arms at both sides of body—relative. Don't think attacker kill her—very angry—other one knows that—looking for not to be killed. Now waiting for the other to calm down.

Family conflict. Physical. Intense negative emotions. May identify primarily with victim but probably with both women . . . parts of self?

19 Here was snowing very hard because might continue. I see—house? Yes, windows covered with loads of snow but after the Storm is sunny. Blizzard three or four days. Sun finally came out—chimney—people

Usual story. External force vs internal hunger/lives in danger. No outcome— simply continued jeopardy.

inside waiting for blizzard to stop—very
worried—Not know if going to be able to
leave house. Short of food—planning how
to get to next town—20 or 30 kilometers
away—before another storm comes. Dark
shape—darkest tree bending because of
wind—grayish shapes are clouds. House at
foot of mountains—spots of green.

16   (Cruel of psychologists!) Not depressing   What does "cruel" mean?
     picture because it is white. Might have been   Pry, uncover, discover,
     black. Not obscure thoughts. I don't know.   challenge her ability. She
     White canvas—have to paint horse's head   does not respond with
     to give as present to a friend—background   anticipated symboliza-
     landscape which color—like horses very   tion of current problem,
     much. White/grayish horse very long   but neither does she
     mane—moved by wind—gentle look in   depict ideal life situation
     eyes. Without bridle in mouth—free horse,   perhaps because she can-
     landscape, spring flowers—bright and   not discern one Retreats
     darker green.   to free horse in nature
                                                        as best effort—benign,
                                                        idealized gift for friend.

Organizing and Summarizing Interpretive Data

A checklist for organizing TAT data initially questions whether or not these
guidelines for cross-cultural interpretation may be applied to the data set
with comfort or extreme caution. It is first necessary to complete the three
information items for similarity to standard emic assessees and the three
initial questions to suggest the ostensible usefulness of the interpretive
schema or invoke caution in examining hypotheses and subsequent inferences. Have a substantial N of cards been used for estimations of energy
utilization? Are the administration directions relatively consensual? Does
the free-association process offer any clues concerning the potential reliability of the data and extent of personal relevance of the contents?

Second, themes (or needs, if preferred) versus normative expectations
should be organized in several ways as typical–atypical; by frequencies
for various content categories; by parts of directions omitted, particularly
outcomes; and by misidentification/distortion of card stimuli. Third,
cultural contents should be noted by card numbers only for records
administered in the United States to provide information on acculturation status and outcome. Fourth, descriptive information for similar and
dissimilar conflicts by card should be listed; the total number/percent of
conflict stories should be noted. Separate tallies should occur for conflict
strength, or similar conflicts in different cards and conflict effects, or dis-

similar conflicts in different cards. Fifth, the relationship between picture stimuli (neutral and blatant) and the story content (neutral and blatant) should be noted.

Table 8.1 uses this checklist to summarize the TAT data for this assessee. She meets the criteria for a "standard emic assessee"; thus, the interpretive process is considered applicable and relevant. She also meets the condition of typicality in the initial questions. It is noted that the TAT cards were from the Buenos Aires printing, although there were no stimulus misinterpretations, and it was not necessary to use cultural contents in stories to estimate acculturation status. The seven-part directions were used, and free-association lapses were noted especially on those stories with salient personal content that may have been literal and self-descriptive. The story abstraction summaries provide the major data on conflict and energy usage for interpretive statements in the following report paragraphs and contain secondary information obtained from atypical themes and stimuli–story relations.

Report

These TAT stories contained several major themes that describe a precarious balance in your life. Family conflict (Cards 1, 2, 7GF, 12, 18GF) and marital conflict (3BM, 4) are found in seven stories consuming over 35% of your total energy. Reactivity to conflict appears as fear of men who may hurt her (6GF, 13), unresolved dangers (11, 19), depressive affect (3, 17GF), fears of mediocrity (2) and invisibility (2, 17GF), conviction of permanent effects of past wrongdoing and guilt (15), and fantasy solutions for immediate emotional needs (8GF, 10) in 10 stories account for over half of your energy.

More positive themes of sensitivity (3BM), responsibility and caring for others (5, 16), hope (14), and curiosity (9GF) occur in only five stories. You are driven by these positive forces to persevere on a day-to-day basis, to be successful in rebellion against the prospects of a dull, appropriate, mediocre life with acceptance of the traditionally compliant and dutiful role of a lower middle-class Argentine woman (Card 2 woman "without expectations" leaning against tree). Card 19 conspicuously omits a happy family or marital discord theme in spite of the opportunity offered by the picture. Thus, discord and reactivity in your major life situations consume much of the available energy, and attempts to provide balance erode even more energy. In 3BM, the woman is crying and dozing, waiting for her husband with sensitive awareness of her own responsibilities for marital discord and most important, "worn out" and experiencing neither optimism nor energy but merely despair.

In summary, the TAT stories suggest strong feelings of entrapment within your present life and a search for solace and respite in fantasy solutions that permit you to relive, reexperience, and atone for past mistakes and misdeeds. These fantasies may be your strongest current ally in maintaining family ties

TABLE 8.1
Completed Checklist for TAT Example

Assessee Identification: Argentine
  Indo-European language family? Yes
  Judeo-Christian religious heritage? Yes
  Self and other: Cultural self? Yes
  Balance of internal and external knowledge sources? Yes

Standard emic assessee? Yes

Initial questions
  Purpose: Demonstration
  Acculturation status: Not relevant
  Typicality? Yes

Guidelines
  TAT printing? Other
  N TAT cards? 19 Card 20 omitted
  Administration directions? Standard
  Cards with free association lapses? 1, 3BM, 5, 7GF, 10, 11, 13, 15, 16
  Story abstraction summaries
    1: family rebel; autonomy more important than achievement; family conflict
    2: social class/fear of mediocrity
    3BM: marital conflict; sensitivity; worn out, anergic, bored
    4: marital conflict; outcome of placation unstated
    5: respect/concern/caring for others; responsibility
    6GF: distance: fears unwanted male attention/sexuality
    7GF: family discord/strict mother
    8GF: fantasy-ideal; love and propriety
    9GF: curiosity leads to action
    10: (8GF con't) distance: daydream/good feeling for man; sex with love OK
    11: distance: life dangerous/risky; no outcome
    12F: family conflict-extreme; social class
    13: sex-love distinction; violence = madness + guilt
    14: "struggling" = psychoanalysis? Extreme mood swings; despair/expectation/hope
    15: (may continue from 14) did something wrong = punishment, guilt; permanent
        condition
    16: freedom only for a horse; horse as gift to someone else
    17GF: fear; denial of depression; daily oppression in daily life invisible to others
    18GF: family conflict—extreme/physical violence
    19: life is continuously dangerous; outcome unknown
  N stories with cultural contents? Not relevant
  N stories with conflicts? 12/19 (family = 5; marital/males = 4; self = 2; nature = 1)
  Misidentified stimuli? None
  Conflict effects? Not relevant
  Themes versus norms: N typical = 12; N atypical = 7 (5, 6, 8, 10, 12, 15, 18)
  Stimuli versus stories: neutral-neutral = 6; neutral-blatant = 3 (1, 5, 15); blatant-neutral =
    0; blatant-blatant = 10

Note. TAT = Thematic Apperception Test.

and responsibilities, work, education, and self-control. Several stories symbolize a caring responsiveness to persons, an inherent gentleness, and a love for animals coupled with a yearning for personal freedom. In spite of the precarious balance between stressors and reactivity that is simultaneously restorative and enervating, forward motion and mobility are maintained in daily living.

ADDRESSING LIMITATIONS OF INTERPRETIVE PROCEDURES

In this section, I suggest personality-psychopathology information provided by the TAT, review available objective scores, consider new measures of constructs, and indicate possibilities for a more comprehensive interpretive framework. As noted earlier, the interpretive framework contained in these guidelines is relevant for only a fraction of potential cross-cultural and multicultural individuals due to inherent limitations provided by the Euro-American emic origins of this interpretive approach. Applicability is restricted by language, religion, individualism–collectivism status as represented in the cultural self, and the relative relevance of internal and external sources of personal knowledge. These potential omissions refer to cognitive processes, the relationship of the individual to the group, the conception of the self and legitimate roles for the individual in interpersonal relationships, as well as utilization of knowledge resources for making decisions, coping with problems in living, as well as expression and mediation of psychological distress. These are some areas in which new low-inference scores would broaden the applicability of the interpretive framework as well as the guidelines contained in this chapter. In other words, an international conceptual frame of reference is now necessary for multicultural TAT interpretation.

The potential for information retrieval from interpretations of TAT stories has been examined historically using different methodologies at different points in time beginning with Shneidman (1951), who synthesized reports based on one set of stories by 16 experts and categorized frequencies of inclusion for specific contents. Hypotheses including ego strength, needs, sex-role development, content congruency with age-specific expectations, and defenses were subsequently derived from research (Dana, 1986). More recently, Teglasi (1993, 2001) has described methods to analyze stories for cognition, emotion, object relations, motivation, and self-regulation. Notable as candidates for supplementing the present multicultural TAT interpretation framework are Teglasi's (1993) descriptions of perceptual integration by congruence with picture stimuli, coordination of inner–outer elements of experience, and cognitive-experiential integration.

There remains a necessity for a potential conceptual aegis for these TAT interpretation guidelines. Antonovsky's (1987) construct of *saluto-genesis,* or the origins of health, embraces belief in personal efficacy and confidence that the internal and external environments are predictable with expectations for good outcomes apparent in self-esteem, trust, openness, and optimism. Dimensions of this construct—comprehensibility, manageability, and meaningfulness—may be universal in scope and acknowledged at present for understanding Southeast Asians psychological dysfunction (Ying et al., 1997). A second possible etic–emic rubric is present in Ephraim's (2000b) TAT psychocultural scoring system containing instrumental themes (i.e., achievement, control, cooperation-competition, competence, responsibility) and expressive themes (i.e., affiliation, appreciation, harmony, nurturance, pleasure). This system is predicated on an assumption that these basic thematic concerns in human relations are universal (De Vos & Vaughn, 1992).

III

Practice Examples

9

A Singaporean Assessee (MMPI–2)

Gerrian Wuts
Santa Anita Family Services, South Pasadena, CA

Singaporeans are readily presented with tests and assessments developed in other English speaking countries. Objective personality tests are commonly used in Singapore because Singaporeans are comfortable with self-report measures and may prefer these over detailed personal interviews. The MMPI was developed by Hathaway and McKinley (1943) and is now one of the most widely used personality inventories in the world (Butcher et al., 1989). The original MMPI was translated into more than 150 languages, and the MMPI–2 has been translated into 26 languages with more translations in progress (Butcher, 1996a). The MMPI is a robust clinical tool with well documented psychometric properties (Cheung & Song, 1989) used in more then 50 countries and widely accepted as an inventory to help with diagnosing psychopathology in clinical and forensic settings and for employee selection in professional settings. It has been used in Singapore since restandardization in 1989. Prior to 1989, the original MMPI was used in Singapore. Singaporean norms have not been available for either the MMPI or MMPI–2.

Translation issues are not relevant for English-speaking Singaporeans. A clearer exploration of cultural concerns using the MMPI–2 in Singapore as an imposed etic is thus feasible due to an absence of linguistic equivalence issues, especially the use of translations by bilingual translators for monolingual populations (Nichols et al., 2000). The term "imposed etic" was coined by Berry (1969) to use concepts (tests) provisionally in another culture until sufficient data is gathered to identify a true etic (cross-cultural concept). Etic approaches attempt to seek universal concepts and compare cultures without much consideration for meaning and interpretation of a concept in a targeted culture (Harris, 1976). Populations from other cultures were provided services on the basis of the belief that they are similar to Euro-Americans or will become similar over time (Dana, 1993).

Studying a culture from within, that is, the expression of symptoms in a culture, provides one with descriptive data that is informative but less easy to compare across populations or cultures. Hence, studies with the MMPI and MMPI–2 are generally imposed-etic studies whereby the MMPI is administered to a target population in the attempt to identify differences between the target population and the normative MMPI sample so that adjustments can be made in how to use the instrument, interpret findings, and develop norms for the targeted population.

SINGAPOREAN POPULATION

Singapore is a multiethnic country with Chinese, Malay, Indian, and Eurasian descendants. It is a small island, 659 square km (247 square miles) in South East Asia. In 1819, it was founded as a British Colony and remained under British rule until 1959. The native Singaporean population was ethnically Malay; in 1819, a total of 150 inhabitants lived in Singapore (Tsoi, 1985). Currently more than three and a quarter million people live in this city-state of which 76.8% are Chinese descendants, 13.9% Malay, 7.9% Indian, and 1.4% Eurasians or other ethnicities (Census, Singapore Department of Statistics, 2000). Although a multilingual environment, most Singaporeans born after 1965 have been educated in English, and the language of business is also English (Gopinathan, Pakir, Kam, Saravanan, 1998). In addition to English, every Singaporean takes language classes in their mother tongue (Mandarin, Malay, Tamil, and other Indian languages) and is expected to be proficient in their mother tongue. Entry to higher levels of education is dependent on their ability to read and write in their mother tongue. Furthermore, many Singaporean-Chinese are introduced to Chinese dialects that their family of origin grew up with; Singaporean-Indians may speak Hindi, Singhalese, Gujarati, or other Indian languages at home. Whereas the older generation of Singaporeans (first-generation or second-generation Singaporean) may still read newspapers in Mandarin, the younger generation (below age 40) prefers to read and write in English. The Singaporean population has a literacy rate of 93% (Census, 2000). Hence, Singaporeans have ready access to information that is generated in the English language and available in English speaking countries (America, England, or Australia) because translation is not required.

Mental Health

The first mental hospital in Singapore was developed in 1841, providing 30 beds (Tsoi, 1985). In 1928, a 1,030-bed facility was developed, and currently, this major hospital (Woodbridge) provides 2,500 beds. Moreover, there are private hospitals and general Hospitals (semigovernment, or subsidized) with inpatient and outpatient psychiatric facilities. In 1975, nearly 80% of the patients in Woodbridge Hospital were of Chinese decent, and of those, 61.8% were diagnosed as schizophrenic (Institute of Mental Health [IMH] annual report, 1998). In 1995, about 60% of new admissions to Woodbridge hospital were diagnosed as schizophrenic (IMH, 1998). Treatment involved electroconvulsive therapy and custodial care, and in the 1960s, psychotropic drugs, physical therapy, and outpatient treatment were included. Although an increase for mental health services has been noted in the private sector, the government hospitals have noted a leveling off of new clients seeking treatment. The government hospital may see more schizophrenics; the private settings tend to see more people with affective disorders (P. C. Ang, personal communication, July 14, 1997).

It is difficult to estimate the prevalence of neurotic syndromes (depression, anxiety, phobias). This syndrome may be similar to what in China would be classified as neurasthenia. Although the occurrence of mental illness is universal, the manifestation and interpretation of symptoms is culturally determined. Religion may be a factor in endorsing/acknowledging distress, and the presentation of somatic complaints is congruent with Buddhist teachings that unhappiness is a natural state (Obeyesekere, 1985). Although Singaporean physicians and psychiatrists are generally trained in England, they tend to diagnose similarly to American psychiatrists (Tsoi, 1985). The American classification system, the *DSM* (American Psychiatric Association, 1994) is more commonly used in Singapore than the International Classification of Diseases. Hence, diagnoses and classification of symptoms or syndromes cannot be separated from the cultural lens of the diagnostician, clinician, or researcher and his or her training and exposure to a culture. Singaporeans experiencing symptoms (somatic or emotional) tend to consult their private physicians prior to seeking help from mental health professionals. In addition, consultations with traditional healers (herbalists, acupuncturists, bomohs or spiritual healers) are still prevailing, especially among the first- and second-generation Singaporeans. Private as well as government hospitals tend to use diagnostic assessments and classification (personality assessments, *DSM–IV*) in addition to psychiatric evaluations or clinical interviews to aid in diagnoses and treatment planning.

MMPI–2 WITH CHINESE POPULATIONS

Studies with Chinese populations in Hong Kong and Taiwan have been conducted by Cheung and her team of researchers (Cheung, Song, & Zhang, 1996; Cheung, Leung, et al., 1996) who found that elevations in the upper 60s on Scale 2, 7, 8, and F were common among the nonclinical populations in the MMPI Chinese translation. The peaks on F, 2, 7, and 8 in the Cheung, Leung, et al. (1996) sample disappeared when the Chinese (People's Republic of China) norms were used as opposed to American norms with the cutoff score raised to 70 instead of 60. Comparison of Singaporean-Chinese and Chinese norms might be helpful, but the Chinese MMPI–2 norms have not been published (E. Shen, personal communication, July 9, 2002).

MMPI data on a Singaporean college sample was compared with Clark's 1954 U.S. college sample (Kadri, 1971), and the means and standard deviations in these two populations were very similar. Boey (1985) compared English-speaking Singaporeans with Chinese-speaking Singaporeans on the MMPI and conducted a test–retest study and found test–retest reliability over a period of two weeks to be .85 for the Chinese MMPI and .78 for the American MMPI. Detailed demographic information was not available. Neither Boey nor Kadri addressed MMPI construct validity. No Singaporean studies were conducted with the MMPI–2 prior to this authors' data collection in 1999. Although a fourth study was recently conducted by Y. L. Low (personal communication, July 8, 2002) comparing profiles of a general population sample with archival clinical data, Low found scale elevations on 70% of the MMPI–2 scales and subscales and concluded that Singaporean profiles were likely to be misinterpreted or pathologized.

MMPI–2 SINGAPOREAN PSYCHOMETRICS

This author collected data of a Singaporean population sample in 1999. These 207 volunteers from the general population and corporate settings included 67 men and 140 women aged 18 to 57 years ($M = 33.02$, $SD = 8.38$) with 88.9% of Chinese ethnicity compared to 76.8% (Census, 2000). Information on age, education, ethnic heritage, marital status, and profession was included to permit comparison with the MMPI–2 restandardization data. Psychometric equivalence of the MMPI–2 was evaluated by assessing construct validity using a principal component analysis (PCA). Subsequently, comparison of scales' elevations of the Singaporean sample

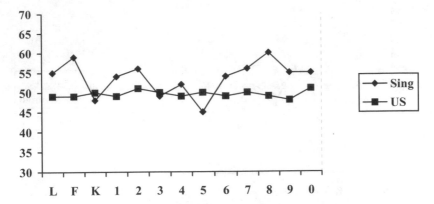

FIG. 9.1. MMPI–2 American restandardization norms versus Singaporean mean profile. MMPI–2 = Minnesota Multiphasic Personality Inventory–2.

(Wuts, 2002) compared to the U.S. restandardization data was conducted, and item endorsement frequencies were compared. Although linguistic or translation equivalence is not relevant with this English-speaking population, a glossary of 15 terms was provided to help respondents understand the English equivalents of American terms, for example, "standing in a queue" as opposed to "standing in line."

PCA on the three validity and 10 clinical scales provided the same four factors in the Singaporean (Wuts, 2002) and American sample (gender combined; Butcher et al., 1989). The factors are Social Introversion, Psychoticism, Neuroticism, and Masculinity/Femininity. Factor one was comprised of Scales 9, 2, 7, 8, 1, F, and –K, which was termed "Symptom Awareness." Factor two—Symptom Expression—was comprised of Scales 9, 8, 6, 4, 7, F, and –K. Factor three—Neurotic Expression—comprised Scales 1 and 3. Factor four—Traditional Role—was made up Masculinity/Femininity and –L. These four factors in the Singaporean sample took up slightly more of the total variance than the four factors in the U.S. restandardization data (78% compared to 72.7%; Butcher et al., 1989). Congruency of the four factors was identified using Spearman rankings of the communalities that contribute to each of the factors, resulting in a perfect correlation.

Scale means and standard deviations in the Singaporean sample were significantly elevated for nine of the 10 clinical scales (the exception is Scale 3, Hysteria) and two of the three validity scales (the exception is K). Elevations were as high as 10 T-score points (T = 60 compared to norm of T = 50) when comparing to the Singaporean profile for men and women to the American norm group (Fig. 9.1).

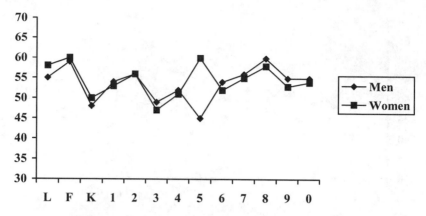

FIG. 9.2. MMPI–2 mean profiles for Singaporean men versus women. MMPI–2 = Minnesota Multiphasic Personality Inventory–2.

There were minimal gender differences between Singaporean men and women (see Fig. 9.2). The Singaporean general population would most likely be pathologized when American MMPI–2 norms are used with Singaporeans.

Item endorsement frequencies of the Singaporean population sample were compared with endorsement frequencies of the American restandardization population. Using a standard of 25% difference on a particular item, the Singaporean men and women responded very differently on 30 items. However, these differences cannot be interpreted as identifying more pathology because individual items can load in either a positive or negative direction on a particular MMPI–2 scale in addition to the item loading on various scales. For example, Item 215, "I brood a great deal," loads positively on the Depression scale and negatively on the Social Introversion scale. The 30 items provided in Tables 9.1 and 9.2 may be evaluated for their cultural interpretation with Singaporeans.

CASE STUDY

Several Singaporean women of the general population were asked to complete the MMPI–2 in July of 2002. Female Singaporeans were selected for the case discussion because construct validity was assessed based on a sample of 140 women as opposed to only 67 Singaporean men; hence, the statistical analysis conducted on the larger sample has more power. These female volunteers were compared to the Singaporean population data of 1999 (Wuts, 2002). The respondents were individuals from the Singaporean general population who did not identify themselves as suf-

TABLE 9.1
Items Answered True More Frequently by Singaporeans
Compared to American Norms

---

7. I like to read newspaper articles on crime
42. If people had not had it in for me, I would have been much more successful
46. I prefer to pass by school friends, or people I know but have not seen for a long time, unless they speak to me first
136. It makes me impatient to have people ask my advice or otherwise interrupt me when I am working on something important
170. I am afraid of losing my mind
193. In walking I am very careful to step over sidewalk cracks
212. I have at times stood in the way of people who were trying to do something, not because it amounted to much but because of the principle of the thing.
215. I brood a great deal
227. I don't blame people for trying to grab everything they can get in this world
241. It is safer to trust nobody
248. I do not blame a person for talking advantage of people who leave themselves open to it
254. Most people make friends because friends are likely to be useful to them
259. I am sure I am being talked about
283. The person who provides temptation by leaving valuable property unprotected is about as much to blame for its theft as the one who steals it
284. I think nearly anyone would tell a lie to keep out of trouble
305. I have certainly had more than my share of things to worry about
345. If given the chance I could do some things that would be of great benefit to the world

---

TABLE 9.2
Items Answered False More Frequently by Singaporeans
Compared to American Norms

---

29. At times I feel like swearing
88. I believe women ought to have as much sexual freedom as men.
107. My table manners are not quite as good at home as when I am out in company.
112. I like dramatics
118. I do not worry about catching diseases
183. I do not like everyone I know
189. I like to flirt
217. My relatives are nearly all in sympathy with me
232. Sometimes in elections I vote for people about whom I know very little
264. I have used alcohol excessively
278. I get all the sympathy I should
342. While in trains, busses, etc., I often talk to strangers
346. I have often met people who were supposed to be experts who were not better than I.

---

fering from emotional or mental health problems. The respondents were provided an interpretation generated by the researcher and the Caldwell Report, Scoring Services, 2002, using the same demographic information. The researcher used National Computers Systems (NCS) scoring keys and Psychological Assessment Resources (PAR) computer summary to generate her own report with a population for which no norms are available. Information on the interpretation source was eliminated to allow the respondents to read the interpretation without knowing how the report was generated. These respondents were asked to read two interpretations and respond to a few interview questions. The interview questions were the following:

1. Which interpretation describes you best?
2. Which interpretation do you prefer?
3. What do you identify with most in the interpretation?
4. What do you identify with least in the interpretation?
5. Would you like to comment on anything?

One woman was selected for discussion in this chapter because she fit the demographics better than the other female volunteers.

Case T

Ms. T, a 29-year-old Singaporean-Chinese woman who is married with one child works full-time as a clinic assistant in a private clinic. Ms. T is the older of two siblings, and her parents are first-generation Singaporeans in good health; she enjoys a close relationship with them. She completed 12 years of education, and although educated in English, she also speaks Mandarin at home. She was given the following two interpretations of her MMPI–2 profile, and compared to the Singaporean profile (see Fig. 9.3) with statements she strongly endorsed shown in bold type and underlined statements that were not accepted.

Caldwell Report[1]

Ms. T's profile indicates a moderate level of depression and anxiety, tension, worrying, difficulties in sleeping, and emotional overreactions to minor threats are suggested. She appears pessimistic, self-critical, and indecisive. Social discomfort is also suggested along with difficulties in expressing anger even indirectly. **She tests as mildly shy and socially inhibited and as uneven in her social skills with the opposite sex.** She may complain of lack of self-confidence and of difficulties in getting started on new tasks.

---

[1]From Caldwell Report, July 12, 2002.

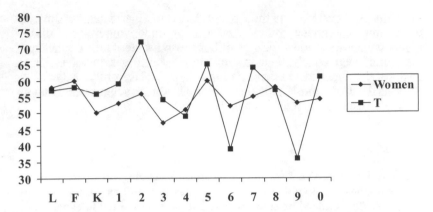

FIG. 9.3.   Mean profile of Singaporean women versus the case study of Ms. T.

The overall level of her day-to-day coping and immediate practical self-sufficiency tests as quite unevenly organized and as possibly disorganized in some areas. **The profile suggests a below average level of energy and activity and a generally slow pace.** Others may see her as somewhat lacking in general quickness and alertness. She would experience this as not having much "reserve energy." So that she has to pace herself carefully. A small sub-group of people with this pattern has psychotic disturbances that were poorly reflected in their profile. Including paranoid delusions and preoccupations about being unfairly treated. (This needs to be further evaluated in interview). Her pattern has often been associated with secondary somatic concerns, including tension symptoms, abdominal complaints, loss of appetite and overreactions to minor physical disturbances. Emotional reactions and fears would in part be focused on and thus expressed through her physical symptoms. She is apt to be apprehensive and pessimistic about her personal future and the limitations that her health may impose. Family attachments appear quite strong. She is apt to be conscientious and meticulous about her responsibilities if not unduly self-blaming over minor lapses and personal deficiencies. Her mild underlying self-dislike and the occasions when others are frustrated that she is not more emotionally responsive would interfere with the sustaining of close and warm relationships. Her interests and attitudes appear unusually masculine; esthetic sensitivities and abstract verbal pursuits would have little appeal to her.

Typical family backgrounds associated with this pattern have often involved emotional deprivations in childhood, such as the absence or death of a parent, rejecting attitudes by a parent, or family burdens so that she received less than a normal amount of love and affection. Although people like her learned conscientious roles in response to strict family expectations, some had personal habits or peculiarities that provoked teasing or other negative reactions from family members and unfavorable comparisons to "superior" siblings. Many of these people had stable marriages, but difficulties in emotional giving gradually built up an underlying sense of disappointment and occasional feelings of hopelessness. Hesitant to "challenge the world" aggressively, their incompletely resolved strivings has led to anxious, clinging, and self-depreciating behaviors. This profile is typically associated with diagnosis of depression, and in a small subgroup with paranoid trends and atypical delusional disorders.

Author's Report

Ms. T reports that she does not experience psychological distress, however, she does perceive that her physical health is not as good as that of her peers. She tends to be conservative and is less inclined to express her feelings openly, as she may readily feel misunderstood. She approaches life in a careful manner, taking into consideration what others may say about her. She is sensitive to what others think or say, and will allow their opinions to reinforce her self-criticism. Some of her physical symptoms may include stomach problems. As a result she may feel somewhat tired and does not feel she gets the rest that she needs to have. It is possible that she is suffering from a medical condition or ailment that preoccupies her and makes her concerned about the future. However, it is also possible that her stomach problems are symptoms of nervousness. Ms. T is inclined to worry and ruminate about things. She may find it difficult to make decisions and is probably concerned about what others will say or think about her. Ms. T is concerned about fitting in and does not want to draw attention to herself and tends to worry. Others in turn may become impatient with Ms. T. and want her to be more decisive and confident. Ms. T. is conscientious and inclined to work hard and takes her responsibilities seriously; she will try to get things done ahead of time. If she is unable to complete her tasks she is inclined to worry excessively. Ms. T. is overwhelmed with her worries and this affects her ability to work; she is less able to concentrate and feels easily tired. Ms. T is inclined to be self-critical and may feel less able in her work as she used to. She is concerned about her ability to concentrate and gets frustrated with herself. Her frustrations will not likely be expressed in overt or verbal manners but may lead to her worrying more and more about what she should have done instead. This could lead to her being unable to sleep because she worries and feels things will not change. **Ms. T acknowledges her tendency to worry and feel physically less fit.** However, she is not comfortable in talking about her feelings, and sees herself as she is ill at ease in her interactions with others. This results in Ms. T. having limited resources to cope with her distress and she struggles to cope with the duties of her day. **Ms. T is less likely to talk to others about her problems as she is more introverted and inclined to keep her feelings to herself.** However, this could further acerbate her worries as she may judge herself and become more negative, as oppose to checking her ideas and worries with others. While others can share their views and perspectives on a matter, Ms. T is inclined to be somewhat suspicious of those around her and inclined to see others as being less helpful. Her tendency to worry and become preoccupied with self-criticism will most likely contribute to her feelings of lethargy, tiredness, and depression. Ms. T. does not see herself as able to cope with her worries, as she has a low self-esteem and is apt to be critical of herself and her abilities. In addition, she is less inclined to ask others for help, as she is uncomfortable in her interactions and more inclined to keep to herself. Others may see her as somewhat of a loner and are less inclined to volunteer their opinions or support. It is not unlikely for people with a profile like Ms. T to feel they need to keep working hard as things will not change anyway. Ms. T's self-report resembles the profile of those who are depressed and struggling to cope with day-to-day problems. **However, it is possible that there is a physical component to Ms. T's lethargy and distress, which may require physical attention.**

Evaluation of Reports

Ms. T found the Caldwell report less readable and less accurate. The Caldwell Report uses the same set of standardized normalized norms for assessees in clinical settings or for personnel selection (personal communication, Janet, October 24, 2002). The report provided by the Caldwell Report may be more comprehensible for a professional psychologist rather than an assessee. She identified the author's report as overall more fitting with what she feels and experiences. Ms. T. shared that her parents are supportive and caring. She has a younger sister, and they get along well. Ms. T. was asked if she had a physical condition, and reported that she was diagnosed with hyperthyroidism in 1993; she is taking medication for this condition and often feels tired and lethargic. She denies depression and identified that she has physical symptoms due to her thyroid problem. In interviewing Ms. T, the author noted that she is somewhat shy and reserved. Although she will respond to questions, she is inclined to be less expressive if not asked a direct question. Ms. T's profile shows the elevation on Scale 2 that is commonly found among Singaporeans. The population prevalence rate for minor psychiatric morbidity (anxiety and depressive disorders) for all the Singaporean ethnicities averages to 16.6% (Fones, Kua, Ng, & Ko, 1998). The Singaporean-Chinese identified less psychological distress on the General Health Questionnaires compared to the other Singaporean ethnic groups (Malay Indians; Fones et al., 1998). Fones et al. concluded that Singaporean Chinese are likely to be less expressive of their psychological distress and thus less inclined to endorse items. However, Ms. T does not present with a typical profile, as she has a low 6 and may be somewhat naïve or overly trusting. In addition, she has a low score on Scale 9, which is less commonly seen among the Singaporean population; however, a low score on 9 is likely to be related to Ms. T's medical condition and her tendency to be reserved and withdrawn as she feels a lack of energy. Low scores on Scales 6 and 9 are indicative of introversive style and experience of interpersonal and social anxiety. Ms. T has a scale score of 72 on depression and elevations close to the clinical cut of T = 65. If she were an American, her elevation on Scale 2 would readily be interpreted as depression. However, Singaporeans tend to have elevations on Scales 2, 7, and 8 at the clinical cutoff and thus could readily be misdiagnosed as having pathology.

Examining clinical depression and symptoms in China, Kleinman (1986) found clinical depression was not reported in China before 1981. Neurasthenia was a more common diagnosis in Chinese psychiatric settings in which up to 80% of psychiatric outpatient clientele received the diagnosis neurasthenia before the 1980s (Zheng et al., 1997). However, the use of the diagnosis neurasthenia has decreased in recent years with prevalence rates of 5.5% to 6.3% in clinical settings (Zheng et al., 1997). Neurasthenia includes symptoms of fatigue or weakness accompanied by a variety of physical and psychological problems including poor concentration, memory loss, irritability, excitability, diffuse aches and pains, gastrointestinal problems, sleep disturbances, sexual dysfunction, and dizziness. Neurasthenia is not the same as depression but may be misdiagnosed as depression by professionals that are not familiar with the symptoms of neurasthenia. The most common psychiatric syndrome referred to the psychiatrist in Singapore is neurosis (Tsoi, 1985).

Although Ms. T's score on Scale 2 is more elevated, she also suffers from a hyperthyroidism that may have contributed to this elevation. Many of the items on Scales 2 and 7 identify physiological and somatic complaints. In addition, she has an elevated score on Scale 8 as well. Elevations on Scale 8 are more commonly found in non-Euro-American populations. With respect to item endorsement pattern, Ms. T endorsed 23 of the 30 items that are typically endorsed more true and more false by Singaporeans compared to Americans.

MMPI–2 APPLICATION IN SINGAPORE

The case report included here and discussed may not present the picture of a typical Singaporean, although it highlights the complexity of providing an MMPI–2 personality interpretation for a Singaporean. The issue is not so much how to obtain better descriptors of Singaporeans but more to look into developing a better understanding of using a test with populations that speak English but are not of the American culture (mainstream Euro-American heritage). Although Singaporeans have no difficulty responding to the MMPI–2, the interpretation provided may not fit the

Singaporean because interpretations need to be made in context of the Singaporean environment and lifestyle. Immersed in a Singaporean working environment and living in Singapore with a local family, the author's experience provided some understanding of the way in which Singaporeans express their distress (emotional or physical) and the difficulty this presents for diagnosis using *DSM* criteria or mental health descriptors for Singaporeans.

ASSESSMENT OF ETHNICALLY DIVERSE ENGLISH-PROFICIENT POPULATIONS

The following suggestions are made for assessment of Singaporeans (or an English-speaking population that is not native to the mainstream culture, i.e., first-generation immigrants in the United States or other populations for which no norms are available. The Singaporean population is very familiar with self-report assessments and questionnaires, but other ethnic groups may not be comfortable with this format for self-expression. Hence, prior to administering a questionnaire, the assessor needs to know if this population is accustomed to written self-reports. The following five steps provide guidance to help assessors with administration and interpretation:

1. Administration without modification (not translated).
2. Scoring using norms of American and other populations if available.
3. Interpretation from more than one source and verification of results with local mental health professionals.
4. Generate data for local clinic populations to provide a data bank for comparison of an individual to his or her cohort.
5. Review the report and discuss the results with client and/or relatives.

Administration

The MMPI–2 should be administered without modification. If the respondent is able to understand English, no translation is required. Bilingual or multilingual test takers should be given a choice in taking the test in either of the languages of proficiency, (or both) when these alternatives are available. However, taking the MMPI–2 in a translated language could lead to different response sets due to translation issues. In addition, a respondent may feel most proficient in English, but the profile may not fit that of the American normative sample.

Scoring

Although it is crucial to develop norms for every population, this is a lengthy process, and in the meantime, assessors can review normative data of other cultures. For example, when interpreting MMPI–2 profiles for Singaporeans, the means, standard deviations, and cutoff scores used with other Asian populations should be examined to develop an understanding of the differences between an Asian population's norms and those of the American population, especially when the norms for the target culture are not available. The target population (Singapore) is not necessarily equivalent to the norm group in other countries (China) but provides the assessor with a larger scope of different profiles and item-response sets for different cultures. When computerized scoring tools are used, it is important to obtain reports from more than one source (e.g., PAR, NCS, Caldwell Report) as opposed to one reporting agency because none of the reporting agencies has an adequate normative comparison group.

Interpretation and Verification

To interpret a report of a respondent that does not match the American norms and for whom no norms are available, the assessor after having decided to use the MMPI–2 will need to write a report through collating data from more than one source. In addition, the assessor may feel that he or she is not the best person to interpret and write the report. Considerable experience of the report writer in working with the target population is desirable but not sufficient. Discussion with local experts is encouraged even when the report writer is native to the culture. The perspective of other mental health professionals will aid in writing a profile and may prevent the report writer from falling prey to his or her own internalized biases and stereotypes.

Data Bank

Professionals in different countries may be working with specific ethnic populations and are encouraged to start generating a data bank of profiles that may facilitate developing norms of a specific subgroup. For example, collecting clinical profiles in a hospital setting is useful when providing comparisons among the hospital population. Collecting data of Japanese Americans (or a target population) that were born and raised in the United States can generate more appropriate norms so that other Japanese Americans (or identified target population) are compared to their own normative sample.

Profile Feedback

Giving profile feedback in writing and/or verbally can further help the assessor understand the population he or she works with. For example, discussing the profile with the respondent and his or her family may be desirable in certain populations. In working with the Singaporean culture, sharing the written report in a session was much appreciated by Singaporeans. It was observed that respondents who had received written and verbal feedback would talk about the report in several meetings. Hence, feedback can be received in many different ways and may not be a one-time event. Furthermore, the presence of family members may be culturally appropriate, as the involvement of family members with the individual varies greatly in different cultural subgroups.

FUTURE DIRECTIONS

Use of the MMPI–2 with Singaporeans (and other populations) will continue despite the lack of a normative comparison group. Although symptom expression varies among cultures and populations, endorsing a personality questionnaire is only one step in the process of generating a diagnosis. Additional test data as well as interview data needs to be obtained before a diagnosis can be made.

The case discussed in this chapter is a Singaporean woman from the general population. If Ms. T had been assessed using American norms without reviewing the profile for cultural differences and interpreting the profile with cultural awareness, she would have been pathologized, as was observed when Singaporean data was scored using American norms. The Caldwell Report interpreted Ms. T's profile as more pathological, requiring evaluation in the interview to assess for psychotic disturbance. A professional psychologist therefore should be familiar with the cultural nuances of the assessee and has to guard against misrepresentation or pathologizing of symptoms with assessees who are not mainstream Euro-Americans.

Taking into account that elevated MMPI–2 Depression scores are expected and culture specific rather than a pathological trait will help assessors interpret the Singaporean profiles. Nevertheless, this does not mean that any elevation on the Depression scale should be ignored. Although a cutoff score of 70 may be more applicable when assessing general population in Singaporean, further research with the clinical population is necessary before this adjustment can be made.

The author has observed that clinical populations in Singapore have elevated Depression scale scores, but these elevations may not be as significant as is observed in the American population. Hence, the non-depressed versus the depressed Singaporeans may differ less than 5 T-score points. In addition, the other MMPI–2 clinical scales will need to be evaluated for comparing clinical versus nonclinical populations, after which suggestions for adjusting clinical cutoff scores can be made.

It is recommended that prior to using the MMPI–2 with target populations in the United States or elsewhere, construct validity should be assessed and means and standard deviations compared between the target population and the American population, after which a comparison within the target population is conducted. Comparisons within the target populations should not be restricted to the general population but include studies with inpatient and outpatient clients as well as other groups such as personnel selection or forensic clients.

A Hispanic American Assessee (Spanish and English TAT/Rorschach CS Versions)

Johanna Tiemann
Private Practice, New York City

In this chapter, I offer some ideas that are intended to contribute to the development of culturally sensitive projective assessment for Hispanic bilinguals. After a brief iteration of what are thought to be key principles of Hispanic social tradition, I present and interpret Rorschach CS and TAT data[1] gathered from a fluent Spanish–English bilingual. I end the chapter with a report that synthesizes these Spanish and English data.

HISPANIC CULTURAL VALUES

The following points have been emphasized in the literature explicating Hispanic cultural values. First, the primary frame of reference for Hispanics is the family. A family may be comprised of lifelong friends, extended family, and godparents as well as the nuclear family (Ho, 1987). The high valuation of this unit is reflected by the insularity and self-sufficiency of the typical Hispanic family. The family is the main source of security, support, and identity. Members are expected to nurture relationships with one another, provide protection (Cohen, 1979), and to remain faithful to

---

[1]The data introduced here are from a study (Tiemann, 1999) exploring differences between English and Spanish Rorschach CS and TAT protocols given by bicultural, fluent Spanish and English speakers. Neither the translation of the Spanish protocol nor the English protocol use standard CS abbreviations.

tradition (see, e.g., Marin & Marin, 1991; Moncher, Holden, Schinke, & Palleja, 1990; Nyamathi & Vasquez, 1995; Sue & Sue, 1999).

The family structure is patriarchal with rigidly defined sex roles. Men aspire to the machismo ideal: to function well as sole provider for the family and to be courageous, autonomous, and diligent (Gloria & Peregoy, 1996). Women are expected to be submissive, nurturing, and self-sacrificing in their relationships with men.

Religion and spiritualism typically play a role in the lives of Hispanic people. The moralities of Christianity and Catholicism are embedded in cultural values; for example, sacrifice and charity are regarded as virtues, and victims of wrong-doing are expected to "turn the other cheek" (Acosta, 1984; Atkinson, Morten, & Sue, 1993; Sue & Sue, 1990). Spiritual systems revolve around dealings with good and evil spirits who can cure or create illness and control behavior (Delgado, 1978; Ho, 1987).

Other authors have described Hispanic cultures as collectivist (e.g., Hofstede, 1980; Triandis et al., 1984; Vinet, 2000), valuing conformity, cooperation, mutual respect, and sacrifice of one's own needs for the good of others. Although collectivism may suggest egalitarianism, in fact, rigid hierarchies exist in Hispanic cultures, and deference to more powerful members of society is expected. In this way, the society as a whole is a macrocosm of the typical Hispanic family unit.

Fuster (as cited in Vinet, 2000) identified the Hispanic culture as a "contact culture," that is, a culture in which physical contact is a natural part of social interaction. The expectation of contact is reflected in the use of interpersonal space; for example, Hispanic people may stand or sit closely by Anglo standards (Rosado, 1980). These cultures also support more emotional contact by encouraging open expression of affect.

These characteristics have vast implications for clinical work. In fact, some of these features apparently deter Hispanics from seeking help from mental health professionals altogether. The high value placed on personal relationships and respect for family members has been found to interfere with access to professional care (Abad, Ramos, & Boyce 1974; Carillo, 1982; Padilla, Ruiz, & Alvarez, 1989; Rosado, 1980). Disclosure of problems to those outside of the family unit is felt to bring shame on the family as a whole (Chilman, 1993; Espin, 1987; Falicov, 1982; Rosado, 1980).

Carbonell (2000) explained that a Hispanic person's compliant attitude toward authority figures may lead to miscommunication with clinicians. For example, the patient might agree to an appointment at the examiner's request. Failure to keep the appointment might not be a sign of noncompliance but the product of a reflexive act of accommodation of an authority figure's wishes that occurred when the arrangement was made.

Carbonell (2000) also commented on how fatalism, an aspect of Catholicism and the Hispanic spiritual systems, is fundamentally at odds with the values of Anglo culture. English speakers tend to see themselves as in control of their destinies, regarding responsibility as a virtue and irresponsibility as tantamount to sin. Hispanics may deny responsibility simply because to presume control over certain situations is to question the supreme power of God. Anglo clinicians may attribute poor judgment, irresponsibility, or passivity to a patient whose actions are actually a sign of deference to a higher power.

Moreover, Hispanics may ascribe emotional problems to spiritual entities or bad luck; therefore, the cure is logically found with the help of spiritual healers or the clergy. Illness is a matter of fate, and neither responsibility nor stigma is assigned to the patient. The Anglo perspective emphasizes the internal rather than the external nature of pathology, placing emotional illness in the secular domain of psychology and mental health professionals.

Carbonell (2000) also pointed out that an Anglo clinician may misdiagnose Hispanic patients who hold tenaciously to beliefs that seem irrational to the clinician. Although these beliefs may actually fall into the category of superstition from an Anglo perspective, they may be misconstrued as indications of pathology when first encountered. One example Carbonell gives—the belief that a black butterfly portends death—has particular relevance to Rorschach interpretation! Further, exaggeration, minimization, and embellishment of facts are all accepted modes of relating a narrative for Hispanics, whereas for Anglos, such behavior might be construed as deceptive or pathological.

In sum, the authors cited previously have discussed how difficult building trust may be with Hispanic patients. Gaining a patient's confidence may be especially difficult in an assessment situation in which time limits allow for building rapport but not an enduring relationship. However, a more trusting relationship can arise from the clinician's understanding of each individual's ecocultural context (Cuellar, 2000).

PROTOCOLS, DATA, SUMMARIES, AND INTERPRETIVE STATEMENTS

Because these data were gathered for research rather than for assessment purposes, neither background information nor behavioral observations were recorded. I do know that at the time of testing, our participant (referred to as "C"), was a 19-year-old woman who was born in the United States of native Colombian parents. Her first language was Spanish, but at the age of eight, she began to learn English in school. She stated, at the time of testing, that she was fluent in both languages but that she felt more comfortable speaking English than Spanish.

C's bicultural status was determined by administration of the Bidimensional Acculturation Scale (BAS; Marin & Gamba, 1996). At the time data collection for this research began, the BAS was considered to be the most current, reliable measure of acculturation for a variety of Hispanic populations (Marin & Gamba, 1996). The ARSMA–II, which was originally designed for Mexicans, had not yet been established as a reliable measure for other Hispanic groups. Furthermore, comparison of the two instrument's lengths and the complexity of their questions showed the BAS to be relatively short and simple. Given the time commitment involved in participation in the study, the brevity and simplicity of the BAS scale was extremely appealing.

C was in her first year of college and was working as a salesperson. She reported a household income of under $10,000 annually. She stated that she had once been in therapy but said that she was not currently in treatment. Her therapy, which lasted for less than three months, was conducted in English.

The first administrations of the Rorschach and TAT were performed in Spanish and the second in English. According to the administrator, C's English and Spanish appeared to be proficient, and no noticeable difficulties were perceived in her fluency in either language. The two administrations were done approximately three months apart.

The Spanish CS protocol was scored in Spanish in a collaborative effort between the translator, the administrator, and the coder. The English version was created through back translation.

Spanish Thematic Apperception Test Stories

Card 2. OK esta es una muchacha que tiene que pasar por una finca en camino a la escuela todos los días pero ella está enamorada del hombre que trabaja en la finca pero él está casado y en este momento ella pasa de allí y ve a la esposa del hombre que le gusta y se da cuenta que la esposa está embarazada. Ahora se está dando cuenta que ella es solo una niña y este hombre le pertenece a una mujer más madura. (¿Una conclusión?) Ella va a cambiar su manera de llegar a la escuela; va a coger el camino más largo para no ver más a este hombre y aceptar que a ella todavía le falta mucho tiempo para crecer y conocer a un hombre que en verdad sea solo para ella. (¿El hombre como se siente?) No se ha dado cuenta de todo lo que ha pasado pero su esposa sí lo sabía y por eso se paro ahí para que la niña la viera. (¿Algo más?) No.

Card 5. Esta Sra. es una viuda que se le murió el esposo recientemente y toda su familia está tratando de consolarla. Le ofrecían que ella se fuera a vivir con ellos, pero ella insistía que era una mujer fuerte y que podía vivir sola sin un hombre. Entonces ahora en este momento ella estaba durmiendo y de pronto al levantarse oyó un sonido en la cocina. Cuando ella

abrió la puerta de su alcoba se dio cuenta de que la luz de la sala estaba
prendida. Se quedó en silencio por un momento y comenzó a llorar de
miedo porque un ratero estaba en la casa. Entonces una planta que estaba
en la mesa se levantó sola y cayó encima del ratero. El fantasma del esposo
de la Sra. le había salvado la vida. Ella supo que nada más le iba a pasar
porque su esposo siempre iba a estar con ella.

Card 7GF.   Una niña rica que nunca sonreía. Le compraban vestidos
bonitos y le tenían una sirvienta y le leían cuentos y hasta que le com-
praron un perrito pero nada le hacía sonreír (long pause). Entonces un día
le hicieron un dibujo de ella sentada con su perro y su sirvienta y cuando
ella se dio cuenta de la cara seria que tenia en el dibujo se horrorizó y de-
cidió sonreír más para que todo el mundo supiera lo linda y rica que ella
era. La sirvienta detestaba a esa niña y hasta el perro no la dejaba tocarlo.
No sé que más decir.

Card 7BM.   El hombre joven era un hombre que detestaba su vida y
pensaba que tenía mala suerte con todo. Tenía mal trabajo, su esposa lo
engañaba y sus hijos lo detestaban. Entonces un día se miró en el espejo y
para su horror vio que su cara se estaba transformando en la de un viejo.
Se tocó su cara pero era él mismo y no una reflexión; era la de un hombre
anciano. El anciano le habló y le dijo "no seas menso" y que "todavía tienes
tu juventud. Deja a tu esposa y a esos niños que ni si quiera son tuyos y
vente a Cancún." El hombre le agradeció al anciano e hizo como él le dijo.
Pero todavía no estaba feliz. Consultó al espejo otra vez y le preguntó al
anciano que por qué todavía se sentía tan deprimido y el anciano le con-
testo, "esto no es un espejo. Yo soy el amante de tu esposa y ahora nosotros
estamos muy felices. De verdad eres un menso." Nada más.

Spanish Comprehensive System Protocol

Card	Response	Location	First Viewing	Inquiry
I	1.	W	Parece como . . . la cara de un gato	ERR S: Yo veo un gato porque aquí están las orejas (Dd34) y enton-ces tiene…y veo los ojos y la sonrisa de un gato E: ¿Dónde están los ojos? S: Los ojos están aquí (Dds30) y veo como una nariz chiquita (Dd27) como tiene un gato E: ¿Y la sonrisa? S: A sí la otra cosa . . . como se

				dice veo . . . como una bola de pelos en la boca (between 2 DdS29 areas). E: ¿Dónde esta la boca? S: Aquí y aquí está la bola de pelos E: ¿La bola está dónde? S: está aquí . . . E: ¿Como es que se parece a una bola de pelos? S: Hay un círculo en la boca y los gatos están siempre jugando con los pelos	
	2.	W		Yo veo como un gato bravo. (¿Algo más?) No, no más.	ERR S: Sí porque yo vi los ojos que hay en los dos lados para arriba . . . E: ¿Es el mismo gato de antes? S: Sí . . . no . . . sí, es el mismo gato de antes solo que lo vi bravo E: ¿Bravo? S: Sí bravo, violento E: ¿Por que violento? S: Porque cuando los gatos se ponen bravos empiezan a arañar.
II	3.	W		Dos personas con cabezas rojas (D2) y pies rojos (D3) que se tocan las manos . . . que están sentados. ¿Si veo otra cosa? (Si ves otra cosa me las dices) No, no veo otra cosa.	ERR S: (Nods head). Porque éstas son las cabezas . . . Parece como gallinas también si estos son los pies y estas las manos. E: ¿Los pies están dónde? S: Aquí E: ¿Todito? (referring to the whole blot) S: Sí. Están sentados y estos son los pies y están como jugando con las manos (demonstrates patty cake). E: ¿Parece como gallinas también? S: Sí, porque tienen como picos E: Los picos están dónde? S: Estos son los ojos, las bocas y esto es como un pico

				E: Las personas se parecen a gallinas? S: (Nods head)
III	4.	D1, D3, D7	(Picks up card) puedo (turns card) la cara de un animal con ojos rojos y una nariz grande . . . nada más.	ERR S: Sí, estos son los ojos aquí (D3) y parece como la cara de un dinosaurio y estos son los huecos (implies nostrils—white space above D8) de la nariz . . . E: ¿Dónde? S: Estos son E: ¿Y la nariz está dónde? S: Sí está parte de aquí (D7) E: ¿Y por qué se parecen a ojos rojos? S: Porque son chiquitos y los dinosaurios tienen los ojos chiquitos y por eso es E: ¿Y la cara? S: Todo entero es la cara y tiene como una sonrisa (D1) E: ¿Toda la lamina? S: No incluye está parte E: ¿Tiene una sonrisa? S: Sí, una sonrisa grande E: ¿La sonrisa, dónde esta? S: Todo esto aquí
IV	5.	W	Es como un oso acostado pero tiene una cola (D1) . . . nada más.	ERR S: Um . . . si pero yo quise decir no como oso . . . los animales que tienen las patas grandes (D6) es que se esconde en el bosque y que nadie lo ha visto y está como acostado porque la cabeza es pequeña (D3) y veo que la cabeza está lejos de mi. Porque se ve bien peludo y tiene los pies grandes E: ¿Me lo puedes describir como lo ves? S: Estos son los pies y está es la cabecita y esta es la cola grande y el está acostado boca arriba. Porque la cola es más clara entonces me parece que está con

				la boca arriba. Porque el color está claro yo veo que está de abajo entre . . .
V.	6.	W	Un murciélago.	ERR S: Sí porque tiene unas alas grandes (D4) y unas orejas grandes también (Dd31) y tiene los pies bien chiquitos.
	7.	W	También un conejo (D7) con un bosque atrás de el . . . nada más.	ERR S: O sí, si no un bosque como no… veo un conejo porque tiene orejas así también pero por los lados veo como plantas y arbolitos chiquitos (D4)… E: ¿Y el conejo dónde esta? S: Aquí con las orejas grandes y los pies chiquitos E: ¿Como te parece un bosque o plantas en la lamina? S: Porque cuando yo siempre he visto conejos están siempre [a luego de estos y frutas y algo][2]
VI	8.	W	Una alfombra de la piel de un oso	ERR S: Sí porque aquí veo las dos manos (Dd25) y es cuadrado como las alfombras que se ponen en la salas E: ¿Dónde está mirando? S: Completo. Está es como la cola (Dd27) . . . como se parece de un oso porque este es siempre el animal que se usa en las alfombras
	9.	D1	O una carretera	ERR S: Sí porque está parte de aquí parece como que los carros van de este lado y aquí de este lado E: Que parte estas mirando? S: Todo . . . el resto es tierra . . . es una carretera desolada porque esta parte no la apunte (top part) E: ¿Que hay en la lamina que te hace ver eso?

---

[2]Brackets are used to indicate two sections of the original transcript that were not legible. A "best guess" was made when translating these sections into English.

				S: Porque es una línea negra y hay una división blanca como en las calles (within D12)
	10.	W	O un animal boca abajo (D3) con una cola (Dd33).	ERR S: Sí casi como el oso pero que no está muerto E: ¿Me lo puedes describir como lo ves? S: Yo lo veo de un lado como durmiendo con la boca abajo E: ¿Pero como lo ves en la lamina? S: Estas son las manos y los pies y la cola pero como está boca abajo . . . está es la cabeza y a veces la tiene abajo.
VII	11.	W	Esto parece una . . . (struggles to think. Says to self "¿como se llama?") una rana disectada	ERR S: Veo una rana porque tiene la pierna doblada (D1) y la rana la tiene así para poder brincar y disectada porque está abierta . . . yo vi los brazos (D3) y las piernas y la cabeza no me fije mucho . . . E: ¿Y estas cerrando aquí para verlo? S: No es abierta esta disectada
	12.	D6	O un zipper abierto nada más	ERR S: Sí porque hay unas líneas chiquitas por todo esto entonces esto es como el broche y entonces está abierto como si alguien lo abrió fuerte E: ¿Porque fuerte? S: Porque está roto porque lo hicieron bruscamente porque parece roto porque está arrugado de un lado. La veo de un lado y a veces del otro (demonstrates by flipping hand back and forth).
VIII	13.	W	Un lobo (D1) mirando su reflejo en el agua (turns card all around)	ERR S: Sí, porque yo lo mire así de este lado y tiene un cuerpo grande y unas patitas chicas y está parado mirándose abajo y

				esto es como agua (D5) E: [¿Por qué tiene como unas liñas la agua que es?] S: Este aquí.
	14.v	W	O un corazón que está enfermo	ERR S: Sí . . . porque se ve como un corazón porque está rosado (D2) y la parte verde es como un cáncer (D5) o algo enfermo. E: ¿Estas mirando todo entero? S: Sí, todo.
	15.	D4, D5	O unas mon- tañas	ERR S: Sí esta aquí es la más alta de las demás; hay otras montañas pero son más pequeñas E: ¿Estas mirando toda la lamina? S: (Porque se parece) una montaña porque es como un triangulo y las líneas parecen como rocas
IX	16.	W	Como una máscara de carnaval	ERR S: Sí, porque tiene los colores de carnaval . . . los colores vivos . . . y me asustan un poquito porque en mi país donde tienen el carnaval me asustaban las pallas como de muchos colores E: ¿Pero una mascara? S: Sí porque las mascaras tienen la cara rara y las mascaras estaban acompañadas de mucho ruido (mucha música) y me asustaban. E: ¿Pero como lo ve en la lamina? S: Estos son los ojos (white on green near DdS23) y estos son los huecos (DdS23) para respirar y esta es la boca, esta línea aquí.
	17.v	D9, D8	Y el otro lado como humo (D9) que sale del agua (D8)	ERR S: Sí porque esta parte aquí azul es como mar y la parte rosada es como humo como cuando hay una explosivo

				E: ¿Toda la lamina? S: No, solamente la parte azul y la parte rosada
	18.	W	O un árbol rosado (D6) en el bosque . . . nada más	ERR S: Sí, porque la parte verde (D1) es como un árbol en el traje y esto es como un árbol y esto es un palo y esta parte (orange) es como la tierra.
X	19.	W	Como un grupo de diferentes animales . . . un gusano (D9) . . . un cangrejo . . . unos peces (D2), ranas (D10), y ratas (D8).	ERR S: Sí, el gusano es este aquí rosado y lo verdes también entonces y los cangrejos son estos azules y los marrones porque tienen muchas patitas. Peces están aquí chiquitos amarillos y azules porque tienen unos ojos grandes y parece que están nadando. Esto aquí verde parece como una rana brincando y estas (gray) son las ratas que están peleando. Parecen ratas porque tienen unas colas largas aquí.
	20.v	D2, D3, D10	Del otro lado como una cara colorada de un caballo que está bravo . . . no nada más entonces.	ERR S: Parece caballo porque estos son los ojos (D2) esto aquí . . . esto es la nariz (D3) y está bravo porque estas son las cejas (D10) porque forma como una "V" y da como una expresión de bravo. (not whole card)

Translation of Spanish Thematic Apperception Test Stories

Card 2. OK. This is a girl that has to go by a ranch on her way to school every day, but she is in love with the man that works on the ranch, but he is married and at this moment she goes by there and sees the wife of the man she likes and she realizes that the wife is pregnant. Now she is realizing that she is only a girl and this man belongs to a more mature woman. (A conclusion?) She is going to change the way she gets to school, she will take the longer path so as not to see this man anymore and accept that she still has a lot of time to grow and to meet a man that will truly be hers. (How does the man feel?) he does not realize everything that has happened but his wife did know and that is why she went and stood there so that the girl would see her. (Something else?) No.

Card 5. This woman is a widow whose husband died recently and all her family, trying to console her, offered that she go live with them, but she insisted that she was a strong woman and that she could live alone without a man. And then at this moment she was sleeping and suddenly she gets up and hears a sound in the kitchen. When she opened her room's door she realized that the living room light was on. She was silent for a moment and then started to cry from fear because a burglar was in the house. And then a plant that was on the table rose up on its own and fell on the burglar. The ghost of the woman's husband had saved her life. She knew that nothing else was going to happen to her because her husband was always going to be with her.

Card 7GF. A rich girl that never smiled. She . . . (they) bought her pretty dresses and she had a maid and she read stories to her and even bought her a little dog, but nothing made her smile. (long pause) And then one day they made a drawing of her sitting down with her dog and her maid, and when she noticed how serious her face was in the drawing, she was horrified and decided that she would smile more so that everyone would know how lovely and rich she was. The maid detested that girl and even the dog would not let her touch it.

Card 7BM. The young man was a man that hated his life and thought that he had bad luck with everything. He had a bad job, his wife cheated on him, and his children hated him. And so one day he looked in the mirror and to his horror saw that his face was transformed into that of an old man. He touched his face, but it was the same and not a reflection, it was that of an elderly man. The old man spoke to him and said "Don't be dumb," and that "you still have your youth. Leave your wife and those children who are not even yours and go to Cancun." The man thanked the old man and did as he had been told. But he was still not happy. He consulted the mirror again and asked the old man why he still felt so depressed and the old man answered "This is not a mirror. I am your wife's lover and now we are very happy." He was really stupid. Nothing else.

English Translation of Spanish Comprehensive System Protocol

Card	Response	Location	First Viewing	Inquiry
I	1.	W	It ll a cat . . . the face of a cat	S: I c a cat bc hr r the ears & so & it has . . . and I c the eyes & the smile of a cat

				E: whr r the eyes? S: The eyes r hr & I c a little nose like a cat has. E: & the smile? S: Oh yes the other thing . . . how to say it I c . . . like a ball of hair on the mouth E: whr is the mouth? S: hr & hr is the ball of hair E: whr is the ball? S: It is hr . . . E: How is it that I ll a ball of hair? S: It's a circle on the mouth & cats r always playing w/ hair
	2.	W	I c like an angry cat E: St else? S: No, nothing	S: Yes bc I saw the eyes that have the 2 sides upward E: Is it the same cat as before? S: Yes . . . no . . . yes it is the same cat as before only that I saw him as angry. E: Angry? S: Yes angry, violent. E: Why violent? S: Bc when cats get angry they get ready to scratch
II	3.	W	Two ppl w/red heads & red feet that touch their hands . . . that r sitting down. If I c other things? E: If u c other things tell them to me. S: No, I don't c other things	S: Bc these r the heads . . . they also ll chickens if these r the feet & these r the hands E: whr r the feet? S: Hr E: All of it? S: Yes they r sitting down & these r the feet & they r like playing patty cake E: They also ll chickens? S: Yes bc they have beaks E: whr r the beaks? S: These r the eyes, the mouths & these r like beaks E: The ppl ll chickens? S: (nods)
III	4.	Dd99	The face of an animal w/red eyes & a big	S: Yes these r the eyes hr & it ll the face of a dinosaur & these r the nostrils

				nose . . . noth-ing else	E: Whr S: These hr E: whr is the nose? S: ths part hr E: & why does it ll a red eye? S: Bc they r little & dinosaurs have little eyes & that is why E: & the face? S: The whole of it is the face & it has like a smile E: The whole blot? S: No, ths part E: It has a smile? S: Yes, a large smile E: The smile, whr is it? S: All ths hr
IV	5.	W		It is like a bear laying down but it has a tail . . . nothing more	S: Yes, but I meant to say not like a bear . . . the animals that have big feet they hide in the forest & no one has seen them & it is like laying down bc the head is small & I c that the head is far from me. Bc he looks very hairy & has big feet E: Can u describe for me how u c it? S: Ths r the feet & ths is the little head & ths is the big tail & he is laying down face up bc the big tail is clearer than it seems to me like it is face up. Bc the color is clear I c that it is from below
V	6.	W		A bat	S: Yes bc it has some big wings & big ears also & it has very little feet
	7.	W		Also a rab-bit w/a forest behind it. Nothing more	S: Oh yes, a forest of course. I c a rabbit bc it has ears like that but around the sides I c like plants & little trees E: whr is the rabbit? S: hr w/ the big ears & the little feet E: How does it ll a forest or plants? S: Bc when I have always seen

				rabbits they r after these fruits or st
	8.	W	A rug from the skin of a bear	S: Bc I c the 2 hands hr & it is square like the rugs that r put in living rooms E: The whole blot? S: All of it, ths is like the tail E: How does it ll a bear? S: Bc ths is always the animal that is used as a rug
	9.	D1	Or a highway	S: Bc ths part seems like the cars go on ths side & hr on ths side E: What part r u lking at? S: All of it, the rest is land. It is a desolate highway bc I did not point to ths part (top) E: What is in the blot that makes u c that? S: Bc it is a black line & thr is a white division like on streets
	10.	W	Or an animal facing down w/a tail	S: Almost like the bear but it is not dead E: Can u describe it to me as u c it? S: I c it from a side like sleeping face down E: How do u c it? S: hr r the hands & the feet & the tail but bc it is face down . . . this is the head
VII	11.	W	This ll a . . . what is it called? A dissected frog	S: I c a frog bc it has its leg bent & the frog has it that way to be able to jump & dissected bc it is opened up. I saw the arms & the legs & the head I did not pay too much attention to E: & r u closing it hr to c it? S: No, it is opened up, it is dissected
	12	D6	Or an open zipper. Nothing more	S: Bc thr r small lines along all ths so ths is like the clasp & so it is open as if so opened it up forcefully E: Why forcefully?

				S: It is broken bc they did it brusquely. It looks broken bc it is wrinkled up on one side. I c it on one side & st on the other
VIII	13.	W	A wolf looking at its reflection in the water	S: Bc I looked at it like ths from ths side & it has a large body & small legs & it is standing looking down & ths is like water bc it has like lines E: What is the water? S: ths hr
	14.v	W	Or a sick heart	S: Yes E: Why does it ll a heart? S: Bc it is pink & the green part is like a cancer or st sick E: The whole blot? S: Yes, et
	15.	D4	Or some mountains	S: Ths one hr is the tallest & the others r other mountains but they r smaller E: The whole blot? S: Yes E: Tell me how u c it S: A mountain bc it is like a triangle & the lines ll boulders
IX	16.	W	Like a carnival mask	S: Yes, bc it has carnival colors . . . the vivid colors . . . and they scare me a little bc in my country whr they have the carnival the balls w/a lot of color scared me E: But a mask? S: Bc the masks had strange faces & the masks were accompanied by a lot of noise, a lot of music, & they scared me E: But how do u c it? S: These r the eyes (white on green) & these r the holes for breathing & ths is the mouth, ths line hr
	17.v	Dd99	And on the other side like smoke that comes out of water	S: Bc ths blue part hr is like sea & the pin part is like smoke like when thr is an explosive

				E: The whole blot? S: No, only the blue part & the pink part
	18.	W	A pink tree in the forest . . . nothing more	S: Bc the green part is like a tree & ths is a stick & ths part (orange) is like the earth
X	19.	W	Like a group of different animals, a worm, a rabbit, some fish, frogs, & rats	S: The worm is the pink on hr, thn the green ones also & these blue ones r crabs & these r shrimp bc they have a lot of little legs. Fish r hr, little green & yellow bc they have a big eye & it ll they r swimming. Ths green hr ll a frog jumping & these (gray) r the rats that r fighting, they ll rats bc they have long tails hr
	20.	Dd99	On the other side a red face of a horse that is angry. Nothing else	S: ll a horse bc these r the eyes, ths hr. ths is the nose & he is angry because these r the eyebrows & bc they form a "V" it gives an angry expression

Spanish Comprehensive System Ratios, Percentages, and Derivations

R = 20   L = 0.54

$EB = 1:6.5$ $EA = 7.5$ $EBPer = 6.5$
$eb = 4:3$ $es = 7$ $D = 0$
               $Adj\ es = 7$ $Adj\ D = 0$

$FM = 4:$ $C' = 2$ $T = 0$
$m = 0:$ $V = 1$ $Y = 0$

$FC:CF+C = 2:5$ $COP = 0$ $AG = 3$
Pure C = 1   Food = 0
$SumC':WSumC = 2:6.5$ Isolate/R = 0.50
$Afr = 0.67$ $H:(H)Hd(Hd) = 0:2$
$S = 3$ $(HHd):(AAd) = 1:1$
$Blends:R = 3:20$ $H+A:Hd+Ad = 7:7$
$CP = 0$

			P = 3		Zf = 14	3r+(2)/R = 0.25
	a:p = 3:2	Sum6 = 4	X+% = 0.40		Zd = +7.5	Fr+rF = 1
	Ma:Mp = 1:0	Lv2 = 1	F+% = 0.43	W:D:Dd = 14:3:3		FD = 1
2AB+Art+Ay = 0		WSum6 = 10	X−% =0.25	W:M =14:1		An+Xy = 1
	M− = 0	Mnone = 0	S−% = 0.00	DQ+ = 7		MOR = 3
			Xu% = 0.30	DQv = 0		

SCZI = 1	DEPI = 6*	CDI = 2	S-CON = 6	HVI = No	OBS = No

Spanish Projective Data: Interpretative Statements

1. (DEPI) C. manifests symptoms of affective disruption.
2. (EB, EBPer) C.'s emotions usually dictate her actions.
3. (V, FD) C.'s introspection yields distinctly negative thoughts.
4. (FC:CF+C) C. expresses her emotions freely.
5. (S) C. is predisposed to expect the worst.
6. (# Blends) C. tends to take a straightforward approach to processing stimuli.
7. (Color-Shading Blend) C. can be overwhelmed by the intensity of her feelings, especially in emotionally complex situations.
8. (Afr) C. is ready as anyone to become involved in emotional situations.
9. (Adj. D, CDI, EA, Adj es, V, T) At face value, C.'s capacity for control and stress tolerance appears normal. However, it is possible that she can be so flooded by her emotions that she may think or act in unpredictable ways. Her painful introspection seems to be a prominent challenge to her tolerance of stress.
10. (Fr, Egocentricity Index, MOR) C. appears to protect herself using narcissistic defenses. When these defenses fail, her low self-esteem can precipitate depression, mood fluctuations, and dysfunction.
11. H:(H)Hd(Hd) C.'s self-image is based on identifications with idealized figures.
12. (FQ—Content) C.'s minus responses have themes of forceful intrusion, clinical scrutiny, illness, and broken heartedness. These themes suggest profound sadness, and abuse and/or abusiveness, alongside a capacity for child-like imagination or playfulness.
13. (Movement Content, (2) Content) These responses have themes of predation, anger, hiding, and playfulness.
14. (T, H Content, AG, Isol) C. experiences less need for closeness than most people. She is socially isolated.
15. (AG) C. tends to be aggressive and ready to defend herself against getting hurt in social interactions.
16. (P, X + %, FQ—freq. in color cards) C. can react unpredictably, especially when she is feeling emotional.
17. (W:D:Dd, W:M, Zd) C. is highly motivated when solving problems. Her tendency to gather more information than she needs when problem solving leads her to be confused.
18. (WSUM6) C.'s thinking tends to be illogical.
19. (TAT) C. has high regard for the family unit, especially the sanctity of the relationship between husband and wife.

20. (TAT) C. believes in hiding feelings that she thinks are unacceptable, and strives to present a happy façade.

21. (TAT) C. believes in a spirit world whose inhabitants can assert a protective influence over the living.

22. (TAT) C. is unsure about the reality of her perceptions of herself, others, and her relationships. However, she believes that she has been betrayed, and she feels foolish, weak, and stupid.

English Thematic Apperception Test Stories

Card 2. OK. This story takes place somewhere in Ohio and what has happened before is this couple lived on a farm and the wife was twice the age of the husband and the wife had a really hard time getting pregnant, she was having a lot of miscarriages and the husband was getting frustrated. He was the good looking youthful and very hard working man who only wanted a child in life and it was the one thing his wife couldn't give him. His neighbor was a 16-year-old shy, pretty girl. Everyday she would pass by and see him working on the field and wonder why he was so unhappy. One day she finally decided to have a conversation with him in which he asked her, I mean told her, that he had wanted, he had been watching her, too, and was in love with her and asked her if she would be the mother of that child he wanted. So the young girl agreed and fell in love with the man and eventually really became pregnant, so one day as she passed by the farm again she looked out and saw the man's wife and she was 7 months pregnant . . . the wife was 7 months pregnant. Enraged that this man had lied to her and had tricked her into also having his child, the young girl ran up to the woman and beat her to death with her school books. When the man saw what happened, he grabbed the girl and with tears rolling down his eyes exclaimed, "That lady was my Mom, not my wife!" and the man never spoke to the young girl ever again. Oh, and his wife, she eventually had 3 kids and they lived happily ever after. (How did the girl feel after he didn't speak to her?) She lost her mind and took it out on the kid she eventually had. (How did the wife feel?) He never told her.

Card 5. OK. There was this teenage girl who lived with her grandma and the grandmother was really strict. So the girl stuck to the rules, but she was always sad; so one day she decided to rebel and didn't come home 'til 4 a.m. The grandmother was sleeping when she heard the door and since she assumed her granddaughter was in her room sleeping, she was scared and took out her rifle and when the granddaughter walked in half drunk, the grandmother shot her in the arm. So now like how they feel . . . well, the granddaughter learned her lesson and the grandmother felt guilty because she mistook her granddaughter for a robber, but they were both glad they were alive and that's it.

Card 7GF. Well, there was this young rich girl who was in love with a boy in her class, but he wouldn't talk to her because he thought she was spoiled. So her Mom bought her a puppy to make her feel better and her maid read her stories to cheer her up, but nothing was working, so the girl wised up and threw money at the kid and they were inseparable after that. The girl learned that money can buy a lot of things. The boy learned that you can put up with a lot of things if the price is right and the parents were just glad that their . . . that their spoiled little brat was happy.

Card 7BF. The young guy in the picture is an actor and he's playing the role of Dorian Gray and the guy behind him is his Dad and he's proud of his son because the lazy bum actually found a job and the young guy is asking his Dad for 10 bucks to take a cab to the theater where he will play his role 'cause it's an off off off Broadway production, so his Dad is saying "Hell, no" 'cause he thinks his 40-year-old son is just pathetic to still be leeching off his parents. Besides, he wanted his son to be a lawyer instead of a starving artist actor. Of course, he hands the son a 20 and the son is not ashamed. That's it.

English CS Protocol

Card	Response	Location	First Viewing	Inquiry
I	1.	W	It ll a fly. A big fly w/ ltl hands	S: Um I said tht bc it was black um it has ths 2 bumps hr tht ll eyes (Dd22), big eyes & ths ltl things ll ltl hands sticking out (D1). E: Wht mks it ll a fly? S: Ths is th back, th face is in th front th face isn't showing & umm it looked dirty & flies r supposed to be dirty. E: Wht mks it look dirty? S: th spots all over—all ths stuff around . . . tht's it
	2.	W	Yeah . . . it ll a cat's face, w/a hair ball stuck in it's mouth	S: Yeah it ll a cat bc it has a ltl nose, lk 2 triangle ears. & um his eyes (DS30) r pulled back, lk almost Asian & tht's how cats look to me & um well th hair ball hr is th mouth & th hair ball is stuck in its

				mouth (between 2 DdS29 spaces) E: wht mks it ll a hair ball? S: Bc lk tht gray stuff around it mks it ll hair sticking out E: Hair? S: Yeah, ths stuff E: wht mks it ll hair? S: It's a ltl color & it ll ltl lines
II	3.	W	It ll uh wht do you call tht . . . 2 kids praying w/blood spattered all over them.	S: Yeah, 'cuz it ll they're kneeling down & they're facing each other. E: Can you show me whr th kids are? S: (points) & they look lk they have their hands clasped in front of them (D4) & everything red in th picture is blood. E: wht mks them ll kids? S: I don't know why I said kids . . . well . . . E: wht mks them ll a person? S: Oh, a person, well bc of th nose, eyes, th lip (all in D2, profiles facing center) E: So ths red isn't blood? S: Well, thr's blood all over their face
	4.	W	It also ll uh . . . a guy w/a black face & he's scream-ing.	S: Yeah um ths gaps right hr ths r his 2 eyes (DdS30), nose (top of DS5), & ths is his mouth & it's wide open bc he's yelling (DS5), screaming & th red stuff is prob-ably blood again tht's probably why he's screaming & um . . . I don't know wht else to say.
III	5.	D1, D3	It ll a . . . lk a bull w/red eyes.	S: It ll a bull bc hr is his nose (D7) & he has 2 big nostrils (dark areas w/I D7) & tht's how bulls r supposed to be, not tht I've ever seen a bull, but . . . E: Looking out? S: Well ths r his eyes (D3) & they're red & bulls r supposed to attack when they c red . . . & his eyes r red so he must be pissed. E: Can you clarify?

				S: Well yeah ths is his face (D9, both sides), he could be smiling (top red not included in ths percept)
	6.v	D1, D3	Upside down it ll a . . . or a dog w/a red bow tie on his nose.	S: Ll a dog . . . umm . . . E: Just show me how you c it S: It had a wrinkled face & tht's wht reminds me of a dog & umm & ths would be his eyes ths dark holes (darker areas w/I D7) thr & ths thing hr is th red bow tie (D3) on his nose E: wht mks it look wrinkled? S: ths lines hr (jagged points w/i D7) create lk shadows & it creates tht illusion E: Can you clarify? S: All ths gray lines.
IV	7.	W	It ll umm . . . it ll uh . . . big foot w/a tail . . . um (turns card all around)	S: ths r his feet (D2) & they're big & I'm looking at him on his front side & ths thing right hr in th middle is his tail (D1) & since it's a lighter color it's probably behind him & umm ths r his arms & they're stretched out in th scary monster position.
	8.v	W	It also ll a bear tht's getting burned . . . tht's it.	S: Um yeah he's a bear probably bc he ll big & he's um his head is smaller so it ll you're looking up at him & bears r big so you're always looking up a them. th gray in th picture is lk um it's lk all curvy lines & stuff it mks me think he's melting & um his arms too r melting, they're lk handing down & they um his face is burned so you can't really c th features (D3).
V	9.	W	A bat.	S: Yeah, um he's gray, he's got big wings (D4) & he's got big pointy ears (points to Dd34) & ltl feet & umm he ll he's flying. We're looking at him from behind E: Why does it look tht way? S: Bc we can't c his face, only th back of his wings.

	10.	W	Or a bunny w/wings . . . no, tht's it.	S: Yeah, he could also be a bunny bc he's got big rabbit feet (D9) & they're really long & um he's got big rabbit ears (Dd34) & um he ll he's got chubby cheeks sticking out (outside of Dd30) E: Whr? S: They gray right hr. I don't know if rabbits r supposed to have big cheeks but cartoon rabbits do.
VI	11.v	D1	Ths um . . . a bear skin rug. (Looks for a while). I don't think anything else.	S: Yeah, um ths one side (covers right half of card) ll a bear's pro-file w/it's hand (Dd24), it's paw stretched out & um since thr's 2 of them it ll th bear got sliced up or stretched out. Well ths is his face (w/i D4, above Dd24 as card is held upside-down), lk half his face cut in half. Umm tht's it.
VII	12.	W	Ll a frog tht's being dis-sected.	S: Mm hum . . . um ths r its 2 legs(D1) ths r his 2 arms(Dd21) & it's lk face down & ths whole space in th middle is whr you're lk poking your fingers in & stuff E: wht mks it ll a frog? S: Probably bc th way th legs r & frogs r supposed to leap around a lot & tht's why his legs r lk tht.
	13.	W	It could also be lk umm . . . lk a map . . . a map of some country I've never seen . . . uh, tht's it.	S: Um yeah . . . bc th part inside would be water (DS7) lk some big river or st. Ths is lk water around it & um thr's a light colored out-line around everything & around th coast it's always a lighter color bc it leads into lk th water . . . it's lk th beach & I'm assuming thr's more land hr (above th card) but it's not showed.
VIII	14.	W	Like some . . . lk uh . . . lk a wolf or st looking at his reflection or um . . . his reflection in	S: Yeah, ths is th wolf (D1) ths r his 4 skinny legs & he's pink & um . . . everything under him ll water to me bc it was green (D5) & umm ths is his face & it ll it's looking down bc it's down & he's looking at st . . . & tht's his reflection.

			th water . . . uh, I don't c anything else.	
IX	15.	W	Like some- one's vomit after eating fruit loops	S: Yeah . . . um it's bc I hate fruit loops & I hate really colorful cereals . . . when I look at a lot of colors it reminds me how gross colorful cereals r & ths particular picture has tht raspberry red, lem- ony orange theme to it & it also looks really sloppy lk someone barfed it out.
	16.v	W	Upside down it ll a pink tree & it's coming out of th water.	S: Umm . . . well ths is th top of th tree & it's pink (D6) & or a big bush & ths is lk a skinny ltl trunk (D5) . . . ummm th orange stuff is lk land (D3) & th tree is coming out of st which is lighter blue tht water (D8) & th green stuff would be some forest tht it's in (D1).
X	17.	W	Um it ll a bunch of sea animals hav- ing a party.	S: OK . . . um 'cuz we got a lot of colors hr I c blue lobsters hr (D1). ths ones hr r crabs (D7) & ths r goldfish (D2) w/ big orange eyes & um th rest I have no idea wht animals they could be but they look aquatic. Um . . . bc um . . . it ll someone made ths w/water colors & I think of water & th ocean . . . I said they were having a party bc it is so colorful & they're all over th place so it ll they're dancing.
	18.v	Dd99	Upside down . . . um . . . it ll a uh . . . how do you call those? An evil lamb . . . um . . . tht's it.	S: OK . . . I'm excluding all ths stuff . . . he ll a lamb bc he has a tiny ltl Y nose D3) ths ltl orange thing it it's nose, ths 2 yellow things r his eyes (D2) & they're red pupils bc he's mad & ths green thing in th middle is his eyebrows (D10) & they mk him look mean, th pink stuff is lk th wool (D9) & it's pink & it's behind him.

English Comprehensive System Data:
Ratios, Percentages, and Derivations

R = 18	L = 0.13		FC:CF+C = 5: 4	COP = 0	AG = 1
			Pure C = 1	Food = 0	
EB = 4: 7.0	EA = 11.0	EBPer= 1.8	SumC':WSumC= 7:7.0	Isolate/R =0.39	
eb = 4:10	es = 14	D = –1	Afr =0.38	H:(H)Hd(Hd)= 1: 2	
Adj es = 14	Adj D = –1		S = 4	(HHd):(AAd)= 1: 1	
			Blends:R=11:18	H+A:Hd+Ad =11: 4	
FM = 4 :	C'= 7	T = 0	CP = 0		
m = 0 :	V = 2	Y = 1			
		P = 5	Zf =14	3r+(2)/R=0.28	
a:p = 3: 5	Sum6 = 13	X+% =0.44	Zd = +1.0	Fr+rF = 1	
Ma:Mp = 2: 2	Lv2 = 5	F+% =0.50	W:D:Dd =14:1:3	FD = 4	
2AB+Art+Ay= 0	WSum6 = 47	X–% =0.33	W:M =14: 4	An+Xy = 0	
M– = 1	Mnone = 0	S–% =0.33	DQ+ = 6	MOR = 2	
		Xu% =0.17	DQv = 1		

SCZI = 5*	DEPI = 6*	CDI = 5*	S-CON = 7	HVI = No	OBS = No

English Protocols: Interpretative Statements

1. (EB) Emotion plays a large role in C.'s decision making, but she can employ an ideational approach.
2. (SUM6, SUM6 Content, M–, M—Content) C.'s thought processes are vulnerable to disorganization, which is likely to be reflected by C.'s actions and judgments.
3. (P, X + %, Xu%, X%, S – %) C.'s vulnerability to disorganization is linked to her susceptibility to affective disruption and her difficulty with perception and mediation. These troubles are pervasive and are not primarily associated with a response to anger.
4. (L, Zf, W:D:Dd, W:M) C. involves herself intensely in the processing of stimuli. Her ability to scan and process stimuli is average.
5. (es, Adj es, TAT) C.'s thinking tends to be inordinately complex.
6. (C') C. has an extreme tendency to internalize her feelings, leading to chronic anxiety and sadness.
7. (V, FD, MOR, TAT) C. engages in frequent self-reflection but detests what she sees. She is pessimistic and cynical.
8. (FC: CF + C, C Content) C. appears to be able to modulate her feelings adequately, however, she has lapses that may manifest in behavior that is potentially harmful.

9. (DEPI, eb, Shading Blends) C. is currently in a very painful depression.

10. (S) C. sustains a consistent undertone of anger that makes even routine inconveniences and compromises difficult to tolerate.

11. (Color-Shading Blends, eb, complexity of blends) C.'s emotional experiences are extremely conflictual. Her emotional responses can cause her thought processes to become overly complex, enhancing her confusion.

12. (Afr) C. avoids emotional stimuli.

13. (Fr, Egocentricity Index, MOR) C. appears to protect herself using narcissistic defenses. When these defenses fail, her low self-esteem can precipitate depression, mood fluctuations, and dysfunction.

14. C.'s self-image is based on identifications with idealized figures.

15. (Minus, MOR, and Movement Content) Themes of burning anger and fear are presented. Images of dissection and melting may reflect C.'s feeling of being torn apart by her feelings and her loss of cognitive organization.

16. (CDI) C. probably has frequent difficulty in day-to-day interpersonal interactions.

17. (a:p) C. avoids taking the initiative and evades responsibility for making decisions.

18. (COP, AG, H+(H)+Hd+(Hd), T, Isol, TAT) C. appears to have little interest in other people and is socially withdrawn. She may see relationships with others as a source of stress rather than sustenance.

19. (TAT) C.'s stories illustrate her use of loose logic.

20. (TAT) C. has some awareness that she can misjudge situations. She also knows that her confusion can lead to bad consequences.

21. (TAT) C. has violent reactions to betrayal or intrusion. She appears to feel that violence is an acceptable means of expression.

22. (TAT) C. suspects that strong feelings can drive people crazy.

23. (TAT) C. wishes to "rebel" when she feels constrained. She believes that she deserves to be punished for these transgressions.

24. (TAT) C. perceives people's identities, intentions, and personalities to be constantly shifting.

25. (TAT) Women have to earn men's love. Husbands are not expected to be faithful, especially if their wives are not "producing" (e.g., children, money).

Comparison of Spanish and English Comprehensive System Variables

Cluster[3]	Rorschach CS Variable	Spanish Value	English Value
Affect	DEPI	6	6
	EB	1:6.5	4:7.0
	EBPer	6.5	1.8
	eb	4:3	4:10
	FC:CF + C	2:5	5:4
	C	1	1
	Afr	.67	.38
	S	3	4
	Bl:R	3:20	11:18
	C-S Bl	1	2
	S-S Bl	0	1
Controls	Adj D, CDI	0, 2	−1, 5
	EA	7.5	11.0
	Adj es	7	14
	FM,C',T,V,Y	V = 1, T = 0	V = 2, T = 0, C' = 7
Self-Percept	Fr	1	1
	Ego	.25	.28
	FD	1, (V = 1)	4, (V = 2)
	H:(H)Hd(Hd)	0:2	1:2
	MOR	3	2
Interpers Percept	CDI	2	5
	a:p	3:2	3:5
	T	0	0
	H Freq	2	3
	COP, AG	0, 3	0, 1
	Isol	.50	.39
	(2) mvmnt	2	2
Mediation	L	.54	.13
	P	3	5
	X + %	.40	.44
	Xu%	.30	.17
	X − %, S − %	.25, 0	.33, .33
	# FQ−	significant	Highly significant

[3]This table loosely follows the cluster search routine determined by the Spanish protocol. Note that only the steps variables that yielded significant findings for either the Spanish or English protocol are included. Variables that are used repeatedly (e.g., Lambda) are mentioned only once, although they may be used in more than one cluster search.

Processing	Zf,	14	14
	W:D:Dd,	14:3:3	14:1:3
	W:M	14:1	14:4
	Zd	7.5	1.0
Ideation	Ma:M	1:0	2:2
	WSUM6	10	40
	# Lvl 2	1	3
	M–	0	1

Report: Synthesis of Spanish and English Comprehensive System and Thematic Apperception Test Protocols

C is a young woman whose inner world is characterized by emotional tumult and anguish. Her pain arises in part from her intensive introspection, which culminates in severe self-deprecation. C's environment is an equally loathsome place filled with hurtful people and dangerous situations. Her pain is augmented by her limited ability to interpret the feelings, actions, and intentions of others in spite of the enormous amount of effort she puts into making sense of ever-shifting realities. She is equally unable to judge the meanings of events around her, and her misinterpretations make her prone to act in ways that are unpredictable and sometimes alarming. Because she believes that her responses are appropriate, she may be bewildered by the consequences of her actions. She tries to ward off her vulnerability by projecting a harsh, cynical façade and a false air of superiority. All of these factors have led to her social isolation. She appears to have barely enough internal resources to cope with the stress she feels. She is depressed.

One means of defense against C's painful state appears to be her bilingualism. C seems to have segregated certain aspects of her personality such that her choice of language may reframe her perspective, providing a small degree of relief from her distress. Most likely, her choice of language influences the quality of her suffering but not its intensity.

The primary differences between C's protocols in Spanish and English are seen in her ability to manage her feeling states and her perceptual and interpretive capacities. When she spoke Spanish, C appeared to be a primarily affect-driven person who is guided almost exclusively by her feelings. She indicated that she openly engages in highly charged emotional situations, although she can be overwhelmed by her feeling states. She is very free in her expression of feelings and can appear to others to be child-like and excitable. Although she believes in the virtue of keeping a happy façade, her anticipation that she will be hurt often leads her to be oppositional and combative. C's ability to perceive events accurately while engaged in Spanish is challenged by her tendency to "go with her gut" while at the same time trying to evaluate thoroughly all cues in her environment. It is possible that she comes to rather quick, emotionally based conclusions and then tries to assemble the "big picture" using all information at her disposal to justify her conclusion. At these times, her interpretation of details would be predetermined by her conclusion, and she must employ strained logic to make all the pieces of her experience fit together.

In contrast, when engaged in English, C appeared to be quite hesitant to engage in emotional situations. She is probably perceived by others as being aloof and untouchable. Yet, hidden under her façade lies chronic anger, dark depression, and self-hatred. She describes her internalized affect in her percept of "a cat's face with a hairball stuck in its mouth." This image suggests that C imagines she might choke on her feelings. It is important to note that while engaged in Spanish, her percept of the same stimulus was a smiling cat playing with a ball of hair. Her regard for emotionality, her self, and her experience of dependence and disclosure are conveyed by her percept of "someone's vomit after eating fruit loops . . . when I look at a lot of colors it reminds me how gross colorful cereals are . . . it also looks really sloppy like someone barfed it out."

Moreover, C's English percepts suggest a greater amount of confusion and complexity in both thinking and feeling than do her Spanish responses. Her thinking tends to be overly elaborate and based in her own private logic. C.'s explanations of events may seem implausible to others due to her idiosyncratic reasoning. Nevertheless, C. is more interested in engaging in cognitive stimuli in English, suggesting a lack of awareness of how her intense cognitive involvement may derail her. Further, she is more likely to allow her thoughts to play a part in her choices in English than in Spanish. C is likely to be regarded as unconventional; however, this characteristic seems to be more pronounced in her Spanish protocol. It is possible that her responses while engaged in Spanish may be nonnormative due to her cultural background.

C's protocols in English and Spanish most likely reflect the cultural contexts in which she learned those languages. With some exceptions, her projective stories in Spanish show respect for family life, faith in the afterlife and the supernatural, loyalty to family members, and a belief that one should not be a burden to others. In contrast, her stories in English have themes of abusive family relationships, disrespect for authority figures, misbehavior, emotional and physical violence, and materialism. It is reasonable to postulate that this assault on traditional Hispanic values is more comfortably delivered in English.

In terms of the defensive use of language, C may prefer to move to an English mindset when she feels she has overindulged in affect or wishes to express attitudes that are counter to traditional Colombian mores. Conversely, she may move to Spanish when her thinking is a burden, she needs to express herself more freely, or she wishes to renew her connection with her family's tradition. In this way, she can temporarily escape from the stress of the moment, although her solution cannot ultimately resolve her suffering.

CONCLUSION

An individual's protocols in English and Spanish were analyzed using the Rorschach CS cluster search method and qualitative interpretations of the TAT. The resulting report demonstrated how the emphasis of interpretations may vary according to the language of administration of these instruments.

ACKNOWLEDGMENTS

I am grateful to the Society for Personality Assessment for their help in funding the study that produced the data discussed here. I also wish to thank Barry Ritzler, Rhiannon Allen, and Paul Ramirez for their invaluable input into the design of the study. I am especially indebted to the many administrators and coders who worked so hard gathering and scoring data, especially Ysa Nunez, Richard Rapp, Tania Serrata, and Glorianna Valls. I also thank Sarai Batchelder for her help with statistical analysis, Chris Nutini and Glorianna Valls for lending their translation skills, and Brian Levine and Jorge Pina for their help in recruiting participants at the Postgraduate Center and the Hispanic Psychoanalytic Studies Center.

11

A Filipino American Assessee

Ailsa Aguilar-Kitibutr
San Bernardino Valley College, Colton, CA

Filipino immigrants come from various regions of the Philippines, a country comprised of a number of islands. The regions into which the island archipelago is grouped are called Luzon, Visayas, and Mindanao. Filipinos from each region take pride in a bond among their *kababayan* or compatriots, which melds them together through their own language or dialect and unique cuisine.

The Filipino immigrants' erstwhile regional experiences have been enriched by commonly held cultural values and a national language called Pilipino. Pilipino and English languages are taught from kindergarten to college, whereas graduate level uses English only as the medium of instruction. A number of Filipino immigrants may have been instructed in English only. It is not uncommon, however, for Filipino immigrants to speak Tagalog, the conversational form of Pilipino, which is more often interspersed with some English.

Filipino immigrants trace their ancestral forebears from a mixture of the Malay, the Indonesians, and the aborigines of the regions. In addition, they have been exposed to other cultural influences before they came to the United States. The Spanish influence, for instance, has permeated into their cultural fabric since Spain colonized the Philippines for almost three and a half centuries, which subsequently led to the conversion of most Filipinos into the Roman Catholic faith. Likewise, the Chinese and the

Americans have influenced the Filipinos historically. Thus, Filipino immigrants bring into the United States a unique cultural orientation that has been imbued with influences from peoples who came to the Philippines to either colonize, trade, or build diplomatic ties. They settled in the United States in the hopes of having a brighter future and a better life. Having come from different regions and socioeconomic backgrounds as well as possessing varying educational experiences, linguistic abilities, and unique immigration experiences, they are not spared from acculturative stress as they adjust to the dominant host culture.

Since 1965, there has been a surge of Filipino immigration into the United States making Filipino Americans one of the largest immigrant groups (Lassiter, 1998; Sustento-Seneriches, 1997). In 2000, the population of this ethnic group registered at 1.9 million (U.S. Bureau of Census, 2002). In California alone, this immigrant population showed an 81% increase since 1990 (Berg, Rodriguez, de Guzman, & Kading, 2001). The group that came during this period is the fourth wave of immigrants comprised mostly of well-educated professionals who have had a fairly sophisticated exposure to urbanization and world cultures. They left the Philippines for financial and political reasons (Sustento-Seneriches, 1997).

Historically, Filipino slaves and workers came to the United States in 1763 through the Spanish galleon trades. In 1903, the first wave of immigrants came. They were on sponsorship by the American government to receive education in the United States. The second wave labored in Hawaii, the West Coast, and Alaska as farm and cannery workers. The third wave of immigrants consisted of soldiers and their families who fought with the Americans in World War II (Berg, Rodriguez, de Guzman, & Kading, 2001; Sustento-Senriches, 1997). At present, Filipino Americans may appear to blend very well with their new environment and often look assimilated despite difficulties and conflicts in adjustment (Cimmarusti, 1996).

CULTURAL VALUES

Filipino American values have been generally characterized as family centered and collectivist in perspective (Cimmarusti, 1996; Lassiter, 1998; Sustento-Seneriches, 1997). Whatever the wave of immigration under which the Filipino immigrants entered this country, they all bear within their psyche the importance of family. Responsibility toward nuclear and extended families is accorded premium value, giving rise to a collectivist orientation and a self-concept of which the family is the frame of reference. Personal interests and accomplishments are relegated to the service of the family.

Higher expectations of responsibility are placed on parents, older siblings, and male members of the family. Education is seen as means for upward mobility, engaging parents to make sacrifices for the sake of their children's education. Also, immigration into the United States is perceived as a privilege and a way to help relatives in the Philippines. Hence, it is common among naturalized Filipino Americans to file an immigration petition for the rest of family or send some financial assistance to relatives in the Philippines.

Respect for elders, roles, and authority are upheld. Respectful gestures, such as taking the hand of the relative and putting it on the forehead of the greeter (*pagmamano*), or kissing their cheek, or nodding one's head in deference and recognition of another's status or age are common practices. Addressing elders and strangers with words such as *po* (for more formal use) or *ho* (in less formal usage) is regarded as a distinctive mark for being well mannered.

In interpersonal relationships, respect is likewise strongly observed. Identification with the group engenders conformity in Filipino Americans, making it important to be modest and be hospitable and pleasant to others. *Pakikisama* (social harmony and hospitality), *bayanihan* (solidarity with and support for compatriots), *amor propio* (sense of dignity and word of honor in social transactions), *utang na loob* (deep sense of gratitude), *hiya* (recognition of shame for imposing on others), or *walang hiya* (being shameless) are social mores that moderate interaction.

Blood kinship is not the only source of social support for the Filipino immigrants. Trusted friends are welcome into the family circle and become part of the extended family. These friends may also be chosen to assume the role of adopted relatives or as godparents for wedding or baptismal sponsorships.

Most Filipino immigrants value spirituality, which is outwardly expressed in their religious practices. To a greater extent, religious faith influences their motivation and their attributions of achievement and good fortune. In handling the demands of living, they also rely on their abilities, problem-solving skills, financial resources, and social support. At times, they may subscribe to other culturally acceptable ways of thinking to cope with vicissitudes of life. These are *bahala na* (come what may) and fatalism (if it is bound to happen, it will) or being cursed or punished as explanations for one's life circumstances.

Handling acculturation and acculturative stress, defining one's ethnic identity, establishing gainful employment, managing problems of daily living, and securing quality of life confront Filipino Americans as they carve their niche in the American society. They perceive and negotiate reality from their own unique cultural perspective and values while being affected by all the ecological systems that impinge on them.

HANDLING ASSESSMENT DATA FROM FILIPINO AMERICAN CLIENTS

Low-inference interpretation of test data based on norms from Euro-American standardization groups may not indicate an approximation of Filipino Americans' psychological functioning because cultural orientation status and personality characteristics are closely intertwined. Even as Filipino Americans undergo varying levels of acculturation, they perceive experiences from their own unique understanding of reality. Thus, it is necessary to apply cultural knowledge when interpreting assessment findings.

The use of moderator variables as corrections for interpretation of data gathered from imposed etic measures of personality as well as considerations given toward the assessee's subjective meaning of experiences imbued with individual worldview and culture lends an emic perspective to assessments (Dana, 1993). Assessor use of other cultural measures and application of knowledge of Filipino culture to moderate test interpretation can facilitate a multiculturally sensitive assessment for Filipino Americans.

Several steps are proposed for preparation of psychological reports sensitive to Filipino American culture. These are gathering behavioral observation of the assessee, applying knowledge of Filipino culture to moderate interpretation of results, conceptualizing hypotheses about the assessee, confirming hypotheses from all available data, and organizing the report from the least to the most pronounced psychological deficits (Dana, Aguilar-Kitibutr, et al., 2002).

Behavioral observations such as the assessee's motivation, approach toward test taking, rapport with the examiner, and cultural mannerisms, among others, are gathered for collateral information about the examinee. Identification of elevated elements of test data based on available norms and adjusting interpretation through the application of the assessor's cultural knowledge about the predominant Filipino American worldviews, beliefs, and values follow. Then, hypotheses about the assessee are formed and are tested against the themes and descriptions that have become highlighted in view of all the data gathered. The result features an organized, culturally sensitive report that needs to be examined by the assessee for confirmation. The report bespeaks of a culturally competent approach to handling assessment data.

CULTURAL INFORMATION MEASURES

The Who Are You (WAY) elicits 20-item responses to the question "Who am I?" to get a glimpse of the uniquely concrete ways the assessee perceived the self. The AVS consists of 36 value statements answerable by a 7-point Likert scale ranging from 1 (*strongly disagree*) to 7 (*strongly agree*) measures the pervasive values subscribed by the test taker. Cronbach's alpha values for the scale's reliability ranged from .81 to .83 (Kim et al., 1999).

The FAAS (Advincula, 1999) contains 75 items that measure Anglo orientation, Filipino orientation, and Filipino values on a 6-point scale ranging from 1 (*strongly disagree*) to 6 (*strongly agree*) and provides data on the assessee's acculturation status. The FAAS has high reliability with alpha values ranging from .91 to .97. The Kataguchi compiled Sentence Completion Test (Sofue, 1979) consists of 30 sentence stems to examine the assessee's dominant themes of concerns. These cultural moderators are applied to the assessment data gathered from the Rorschach, the TAT, and the MMPI–2 to prevent culturally irrelevant and discriminatory profiling of ethnic assessees (Dana, 2000a). These commonly accepted etic measures have not been empirically validated for their construct applicability to cultures other than the Euro-American (Dana, 1998e, 2000d, 2001b).

In the psychological report that follows, each item response to the WAY and the AVS were examined and summarized. Also, the identification of Anglo and Filipino orientations were categorized through percentile scores from the FAAS. The name of the assessee was changed to protect his identity.

PSYCHOLOGICAL REPORT

Test Behavior and Background Information

Edwin is a 49-year-old Filipino immigrant married to a 40-year-old Filipino, and they have a six-year-old daughter. He works as an engineer in an electronics company, whereas his wife works as a nurse. Edwin was enthusiastic to take the tests. Most of the time, he was spontaneous and eager to provide responses. At times, he paused, turned some cards several times, and engaged in reflective thought before answering.

Edwin came from a family of eight siblings, one of whom lives in New York, and the rest are in the Philippines. He and his wife came from the Visayas, the central region of the Philippines and immigrated to the United States 13 years ago. Edwin is trilingual, able to speak English, Pilipino, and Cebuano. Pilipino is the national language of the Philippines, which he learned to speak through courses taught in school, whereas Cebuano is the native language of Cebu, his hometown. Edwin is a devout Roman Catholic. He goes to church regularly, spends some hours every evening in church for prayer and adoration of the Blessed Sacrament, and observes liturgical and devotional practices always.

Tests Administered

WAY
AVS
FAAS
Sentence Completion Test (Kataguchi Stems)
Rorschach Psychodiagnostic
TAT
MMPI–2

Test Data

The WAY

1. I am a God-fearing person.
2. I love music.
3. I like playing drums.
4. I am a picky guy.
5. I am very hard to please.
6. I easily lose interest in things.
7. I like challenges.
8. I hate bragging or boasting.
9. I like competition (silent).
10. I am very sensitive.
11. I am very observant.
12. I am very flexible.
13. I hate fights and arguments.
14. I like to joke a lot.
15. I hate hurting anybody.
16. I am a very positive person.
17. I don't like to be praised.
18. I always try everything possible in order to get things I want.
19. I always give away or don't hold back if I will share something.
20. I like things fast.

Sentence Completion Test (compiled by Kataguchi)

1. *My first memory of my father* is sailing with him on the ship he was working in.
2. *When I am with my mother I feel* at ease.

3. *When I meet a man, I* tend to pay less attention to his name.
4. *My attitude toward that girl* is getting ready to give her help.
5. *Most people* are less smarter than I am.
6. *When I am ordered to do something, I* feel irritated.
7. *When I am with my father, I feel* like getting ready to do real men's job.
8. *My first memory of my mother* is asking her for some change.
9. *My attitude towards that boy* is that I'm unimpressed compared to when I was his age.
10. *When I meet a woman, I* like to think how she looks without make-up.
11. *When I am introduced to people, I* tend to think how they can be useful to me.
12. *People with authority* are not there without God's authority.
13. *When people laugh at me, I* always give them worse response.
14. *When I feel that people do not like me, I* try to make them realize that they are making a big mistake and feel regretful.
15. *When I cannot get what I want, I* just keep trying.
16. *When I am criticized by others, I* always give them worse response.
17. *When people ignore me, I* don't waste my time with them.
18. *When I find something is difficult, I* would like to take the challenge.
19. *I could not do it because* it will hurt someone.
20. *I fear* no one (person).
21. *I feel depressed when* I am helpless to help people who really need help.
22. *It was wrong for me to* be rude to somebody in the freeway.
23. *I often imagine that* I am on stage playing my drums.
24. *My greatest desire is* helping people I love with their desires.
25. *I am dissatisfied by* my resources to extend help.
26. *I worry about* not having enough resources to extend help.
27. *I feel inferior when* with nobody.
28. *I feel guilty about* turning my back on those who ask for help.
29. *I wish I could* do a lot more.
30. *What I need most* is more capability of extending assistance.

MMPI–2

Clinical Scales.   L (T = 65); F (T = 51); K (T = 51); 1Hs = 48; 2 D = 54; 3 Hy = 39; 4Pd = 36; 5Mf = 35; 6Pa = 46; 7Pt = 38; 8Sc = 54; 9Ma = 43; 0Si = 58.

Harris–Lingoes Clinical Subscales.   D2 = 76; Hy1 = 56; Hy5 = 55; Pd3 = 58; Pd4 = 57; Pa1 = 58; Sc1 = 55; Sc2 = 59; Sc4 = 60.

Social Introversion Subscale.   Si2 = 71.

Content and Special Scales.   ASP = 62; CYN = 62; R = 65.

Rorschach

Card I

1. A mask

   The whole thing . . . these are the eyes and the mouth.

2. Person being held by a bigger person who is in some kind of armor . . . being reflected in a mirror

   The person being held is in the center; the bigger person is on the left. The right side is the reflection.

Card II

3. A person in a memorial place paying homage to one of his friends by touching the big wall that has his friend's name on it; image is reflected

   The person is touching the big walls . . . praying, sometimes rubbing the wall.

4. A couple of persons pulling something that exploded

   Two persons pulling tiny bits of something that exploded.

Card III

5. A couple of poodles stepping on a seat or platform; the dogs are looking at each other

   The dogs are being trained... there are two. They are being curious at each other.

6. A dog watching himself in a mirror

Card IV

7. Okay . . . looks like me looking up while the monster is standing on top of me

   I am under him. I can see the soles of his feet. He is holding me down.

8. Pond or lake with rocks . . . there are rotten trees; their reflections are on the water

   The texture makes it look like a body of water . . . more like a swamp with lots of rotten things in it. There's a reflection of the trees.

Card V

   9. It is a butterfly on flight

The whole thing . . . it's in motion.

  10. Looks like a person wearing a costume

There's the person in the middle. The costume looks like a bird with big wings.

Card VI

  11. The middle is a river . . . very far down; there are cliffs

It's a view from a chopper as you look down. The lighter side shows depth. The river is deep.

Card VII

  12. Burmese ladies doing traditional dance

Two women . . . the hand shows the motion.

  13. A couple of a-go-go dancers

They are wearing mini skirts and boots. They are dancing and their hair is flying away.

Card VIII

  14. Looks like some kind of a tiger or an animal on top of some kind of rotting wood or rocks; the whole thing is being reflected on water

There's the tiger and there's the wood or rocks. The image is reflected.

Card IX

  15. Looks like internal organs because of the color

Green, reds . . . internal organs

Card X

  16. It's a guy wearing a costume and wearing sunglasses; he has green mustache; he looks weird and there are weird animals around him

Whole white thing is the person . . . reminds you of the hood of the Ku Klux Klan . . . The blue—sunglasses . . . the green—mustache is sticking out. The white thing is the hood.

Thematic Apperception Test

Card 1. The boy is kind of upset and depressed while watching his violin. In the past, was forced by his parents to play violin even if he did not want to. He feels sad. He likes to play the violin, but right now he is frustrated. He is not catching up to what he wants. In the future, he is thinking of ways to play the way he wants to.

Card 2. The girl is going to school. She is turning her back from her parents who are taking care of the farm. She feels she does not want to go to school. She feels guilty going to school. Her parents had hard times paying for her schooling. In the future, she is determined to pay back the suffering of her parents.

Card 3 BM. What's this? Okay. Is she a hunchback? Looks like a girl . . . a hunchback. She's feeling frustrated. She has had sufferings from her past. She looks so depressed right now; she's contemplating of suicide. The future is bleak . . . there's nothing. She doesn't look into the future anymore. That's why, she's contemplating suicide.

Card 4. A couple . . . the male looks like he is up to getting something. The female seems like she is holding back. In the past, it seems like there was somebody that startled them, causing them trouble. A man was causing them trouble. The lady holds back the man. For the future, they are determined to get out of trouble because sooner or later the man may have a physical encounter with the troublemaker.

Card 5. Okay. A lady is looking through the room. She is surprised about something unexpected. She will not stop until that thing that she wants to put in order will be in order.

Card 6. Couple of individuals . . . seems like mother and son. Mother is kind of sad about something. The son looks like he just came from some place and gave his mother an unpleasant information. It looks like some scenes in the past where there was some trouble. The son did not have good news for his mother who asked him to find out something for her. That's why she looks worried. They are discussing some ways to settle the situation.

Card 7. A court scene. There's a lawyer counseling the client about something that the client had gotten into trouble in the past. In the courtroom, they're discussing something about a situation. The court scene will go on.

Card 8. The man seems to be recalling a situation about somebody being given a cheap surgery. He himself is a physician. He is determined in the future to be able to give good service as a surgeon . . . to be able to deliver a good process of surgery.

Card 9. A bunch of people taking rest. Looks like they are on a hiking trip. Almost everyone is wearing a hat. They will continue to walk . . . looks like a long walk. They're walking towards some place.

Card 10. Another couple . . . almost like in an intimate situation. The lady seems to be sincere, while the man looks insincere. He is just up to getting something from the lady. It seems that in the past this guy is a good con artist. This lady is one of his victims. This lady will be disappointed since she will be victimized. She will be hurting. Seems like the man is using an intimate situation to get what he wants.

Card 11. This is interesting. Looks like an artist's conception of different souls . . . the unfortunate ones are going some place else. They are in a disorganized situation. The fortunate ones are traveling up; they are traveling in order, in an organized manner. There's a dragon coming out from the hole or a cave. A bunch of people running away and they are about to cross some bridge ahead. All are running away from the monster.

Card 12. There is sick person. Some other person is going to lay hands on him to pray over him and administer healing on him

Card 12 BG. A river, a boat . . . looks like an abandoned place. Either the picture is faded or the photographer is a bad one.

Card 13 MF. Another couple . . . naked lady on bed and the man is on his feet. Seems like he's regretting what he just did and the lady seems lifeless, her hands hanging down. Either he killed her or that's it . . . I don't know.

Card 13B. A little boy sitting by the doorway of what looks like an entrance to a mine. He seems to be waiting for his dad who is working inside. He is barefooted.

Card 14. Silhouette of a man in a very dark room. Looks like he's unable to get some sleep or rest. He wants to go to bed, but he is watching things outside for a while.

Card 15. A cemetery scene . . . looks like an abstract picture of a cemetery with a kind of not good-looking person paying homage to somebody.

Card 16. A guy in trouble. There is a problem. Looking down on him is a picture of Jesus telling the person He has the solution and He is the solution. There is also an art design and the person prizes it and enjoys what he has accomplished. There is a little girl who is going to school. In the future she grows up to be a beautiful girl going to college. She is not so little anymore.

Card 17. A guy from a circus and he is going up the rope to do his number.

Card 18BM. A man who does not feel well and somebody is giving him a massage around the neck and arms. He is enjoying the sensation.

Card 19. An abstract painting of a place being blown away by a strong wind. That's about it. There's not much in here.

Card 20. A person wearing a hat leaning on a lamppost. His face is shaded by a shadow; one of his hands is in his pocket. It seems like he's waiting for something or he is contemplating, passing his time by the lamppost.

CULTURAL INFORMATION PROFILE

The AVS revealed that Edwin's values are changing. He somehow adheres to Asian values. He agrees and places importance on humility, emotional self-control, and family recognition through achievement. Also, he somehow agrees to conformity to norms and filial piety, but shows disagreement toward collectivism. From the FAAS, Edwin's Anglo orientation is low, and his Filipino orientation places him in the middle range. His endorsement of Filipino values is low.

The WAY showed positive descriptions of Edwin's characteristics and interests. He is God fearing, sensitive, observant, flexible, positive, committed, and generous. He is interested in music, especially in playing drums. He has presented favorable characteristics about himself, but Edwin also mentioned his unique qualities such as "being picky, hard to please, quick to lose interest, and as one who hates bragging." He gave self-descriptions that endorsed the Euro-American values such as liking "challenges, competition, getting things he wants, and things fast."

Socially, he does not want to hurt anybody and does not hold back in sharing things with others. This is reinforced by his responses in the Kataguchi stems in which eight items dealt on his desire to help others who need help and not wanting to hurt anyone. He, however, contrasted his answers in terms of his attitude toward disagreeable social encounters such as making people realize and regret for not having liked him, giving critics an unpleasant response, and not wasting time with them. He does not feel inferior to anyone, and he fears no one.

PERSONALITY EVALUATION

Edwin is a 49-year-old Filipino who immigrated to the United States 13 years ago. He is married and has a six-year-old daughter. He is gainfully employed as an engineer in an electronics company. Edwin espouses core beliefs that bespeak of Filipino orientation (FAAS). He adheres to some Asian values such as humility, family recognition through achievement, and emotional self-control (AVS). However, he may not uphold some other Asian values such as collectivism and filial piety (AVS). Although he seems to be in transition, as his Anglo orientation is low (FAAS), it appears that Edwin has a certain leaning toward the Western values yet possesses a strong tendency to uphold his core beliefs that are uniquely Filipino.

Edwin appears to be highly sensitive to his experiences (L = .14). He may tend to uphold convictions rigidly (a:p = 8:1; MMPI L = 65). This may be influenced by his strong religious and moral upbringing (WAY). The Roman Catholic teachings are usually the guide that most Filipinos adhere to in day-to-day life. Thus, the Catholic faith is pervasive in decision making, problem solving, and handling life events.

He may not prefer situations that entail expression of feelings (Afr = .23; AVS). The Rorschach data showed that he may have a limited ability to recognize how he feels and to describe how he feels to others (SumC': WSumC = 0:1.5). This result is moderated by Edwin's culture because generally speaking, Filipinos have a great capacity to persevere in the hopes of expressing the best of themselves. Edwin's self-descriptions show how he views himself and how he wants others to perceive him (WAY #1, 10, 11, 12, 16, 18, 19). At the same time, he may have a propensity toward presenting himself as being not different or deviant from what is culturally normative. *Hiya* or shame of losing face is a strong factor that moves one to do what is culturally acceptable (Lassiter, 1995).

Edwin uses cognition to control his emotional expression (FC: CF + C = 1:1). His style of coping is introversive; thus, he relies on organizing information and thinking through situations and problems (EB = 6:1.5; EB Per = 4.0). Not expressing his emotions may not have bothered him at all considering that he values the global view of things (W: M = 7:6) and that he exudes emotional stability and is comfortable with himself (MMPI Pt = 38). Furthermore, he is satisfied with the way things are and feels no need to change these situations because he possesses adequate resources and adaptive skills to handle demands in life (D = 0; Adj D = 0). Also, he is able to solve his problems efficiently and successfully (Zd = +3.0).

He values family recognition through achievement (AVS). Additionally, he likes "challenges, competition, and things fast" (WAY). He may have prided himself on his success as an immigrant. Edwin does not present himself as self-centered or selfish as purported by the elevated score in viewing himself (Fr + rF = 5). Moreover, he describes himself as somebody whose does not hold back in sharing something with others and someone who extends resources to people he loves (WAY #19; Kataguchi stems #21, 24, 25, 26, 27, 29, 30).

Because of a marked tendency to feel responsible for family, he may have placed great demands on himself in consideration of where he is at this time and what he wants to do for his family. He is in a state of flux trying to uphold some values to which he does not totally subscribe anymore (FAAS). He values family recognition through achievement but does not agree about the importance of collectivism (AVS). However, Edwin sees himself as indebted to family (TAT Card 3), falling short of what he wants to be (TAT Card 1), and is trying hard to do his part (TAT Card 17). There is likelihood that he is probably waiting for some form of approbation from his father (TAT Card 7, 8BM, 13B; Kataguchi stem 7).

Edwin may be conflicted because of changing values and because he does not want to express openly how he feels about this situation. Culturally, social status is linked to being able to help in improving the extended family's socioeconomic standing and in maintaining family solidarity. Not helping family and relatives is regarded as *walang hiya*. *Walang hiya* or being shameless is anathema and has to be avoided by all means (Lassiter, 1995). An overriding recognition of a strong sense of indebtedness and gratitude toward family and responsibility toward those who are left in the native country are also operative here (Sustento-Seneriches, 1997).

He tries to deal with these conflicting values by not facing the extent of sacrifice it exacts on him (TAT Card 11), hoping for healing (TAT Card 12M), and by having his faith to guide him (TAT Card 16). Recognizing the sufferings in the past (TAT Card 3) and how his family in the Philippines are now (TAT Cards 19, 10), he hopes to work together with his wife and with his mother's support (TAT Cards 4, 5) to assist those he loves. Additionally, he hopes to deal with these demands by being prayerful, optimistic, and being helped by others (TAT Cards 14, 15, 20, 18BM). Edwin's cultural orientation is manifested when he regards his wife in a collaborative, egalitarian standing. His cultural orientation is also manifested in his strong reliance in his faith (Lassiter, 1995; Sustento-Seneriches, 1997).

Edwin appears to have some preoccupation with himself and his self-esteem $(3r + (2)/R = 1.19)$. This may be culturally moderated because of a marked desire to present a good and estimable image to others (Sustento-Seneriches, 1997). *Amor propio* or protecting one's sense of dignity and worth is regarded as highly important (Lassiter, 1998). Also, this may be his way of assuring himself in the midst of what he hopes to accomplish. After all, he upholds humility (AVS), and humble behavior is encouraged in daily life (Lassiter, 1995).

He has a stable sense of identity (H: (H) Hd (Hd) = 8:2). He plays the traditional masculine role (MMPI Mf = 35). Being a father, he assumes the primary authority figure as head of household (Lassiter, 1995). In the Filipino culture, men tend to exude the *machismo* in terms of taking their role seriously as a leader, as a rational and objective person, and as one who is endowed with physical strength.

He has a strong interest in others and in forming harmonious and co-operative relationships (COP = 3). This tendency speaks of his cultural orientation in which others are regarded with respect and importance and in which having smooth interpersonal relationships and social acceptance are premium values (Enriquez as cited by Sustento-Seneriches, 1997; Lassiter, 1995). Edwin, however, favors being alone or being with a small group of friends (MMPI Si = 58; Isolate/R = .31). Again, this may be culturally influenced whereby strong family ties may isolate and limit interpersonal contacts (Almirol as cited by Lassiter, 1995).

The MMPI–2 revealed a low energy level that may evidence fatigue (MMPI Ma = 43). It is possible that what he does and exacts on himself to achieve may have caused low levels of energy. However, Edwin's interests are not along the lines of active sports and other vital activities. He likes music and prefers to play his drums. This result is culturally moderated because Filipino Americans tend to have mild temperaments and may appear passive (Lassiter, 1995).

Although Edwin is in the process of reassessing his values, he appears to have adequate adaptive skills and resources necessary to direct his behavior in an effective way.

By using cultural moderators, the low affective ratio in the Rorschach was not interpreted to mean that the client had a limited ability in recognizing how he felt and describing his feelings to others. Rather, this result was culturally moderated because in the assessee's culture, Filipinos have a great capacity to persevere in the hopes of expressing the best of themselves. Likewise, the assessee's elevated egocentricity index in the Rorschach may be culturally moderated because of a marked desire to present a good and estimable image to others while remaining to be modest. In the Filipino culture, *amor propio* or protecting one's sense of dignity and worth is regarded as highly important.

This report was thoroughly endorsed by the assessee as truly reflective of his personality, functioning, conflicts, and ways of coping. The assessee confirmed the descriptions as aligned to his own self-assessment and accepted new information as relevant, meaningful, and reflective of himself within the contexts of his cultural heritage and current acculturation.

CONCLUSION

Culture is central to functioning (Dana, 1993). Without cultural moderators, Edwin could have been characterized as one with an exaggerated sense of self-importance yet depressed, pessimistic, withdrawn, alienated from his feelings and from people, and deficient in coping skills. Additionally, he would have been described as submissive, dependent, indifferent to a wide range of interests, and would have had difficulties in information processing and reality grounding. With cultural moderators, an adjusted profile emerged, which the assessee validated.

An assessor who relies on low-inference interpretation based on norms from Euro-American groups could convey bias because these norms may not be applicable to multicultural groups (Dana, 2000c). Low-inference interpretation can be corrected by using cultural information to make the report a faithful representation of the person. Only then can one have a multiculturally sensitive assessment for Filipino Americans. Pathologizing of Filipino Americans can be avoided in this manner. Understanding Filipino Americans is important to clinicians because this group has changed the fabric of the American society due to their influx into the United States in recent years.

Greek[1] Assessees (Rorschach CS)

Stamatia Daroglou[2]
Jewish Family Service of San Diego, CA

The issue I discuss in this chapter and that has been discussed in other parts of this book is whether psychological testing instruments normed in one culture can be used with people from different cultures. If the answer to this question is yes, a second question must be considered, that is, whether and how these psychological tests can be interpreted accurately taking into account cultural differences. In this chapter, I am concerned with interpretations of the Rorschach Inkblot Test using the CS with the Greek population.

Researchers have described the Rorschach as an etic instrument assessing personality structures that are similar to all cultures (Exner, 1974, 1993, 2003; Georgas & Vassiliou, 1967; Mattlar, 2004; Weiner, 2003). The way people process information, however, is learned through social interactions within a cultural context (Betancourt & Lopez, 1993; Hall & Barongan, 2002), implying that there are emic aspects of behavior and information processing specific to certain cultures. If the Rorschach is to be used in another culture, an evaluator must keep in mind two important questions: First, can the Rorschach assess emic aspects of behavior and personality? Second, if yes, are the interpretations developed from one normative group generalizable to another culture and society?

---

[1]The terms *Greeks, Greek,* and *Greece* are used instead of *Hellenes, Hellenic,* and *Hellas* respectively, as they are used more frequently in the English language and are more readily understood.

[2]The author extends appreciation to Kostas Katsavdakis, Kristen Cole, and Atara Abramsky for their helpful comments and suggestions.

When Rorschach measures, and specifically CS variables, are interpreted for Greeks, it is done so without having established that these variables are understood similarly in the two cultures. There is limited research in this area, and there are no CS norms for Greeks. The CS variables used to measure the various constructs explained with the CS may have a different psychological meaning in the culture examined. The variables are interpreted in the manner that has been useful in the American culture, but that may not be an accurate interpretation in the Greek culture. In addition, the purpose of the behavior sampled may be different in the two cultures. In sum, construct equivalence and functional equivalence are essential to understand and interpret a construct with the Greek culture.

GREEK VALUES

It is crucial to discuss values and beliefs common in the Greek culture to develop a clearer understanding of persons from Greece. The values and belief system of a person in a given environment play an essential part not only in the person's behavior but, moreover, in how the person understands and perceives the world.

In general terms, there are commonalities among cultures, or more specifically, among countries, but there are many differences as well. The unique aspects of each country make up its personality in the same manner as individual differences reflect the personality of the individual. Greece has a long history that has shaped its personality in various ways.

Greek society has been described as a collectivist one (Georgas, 1989). In other words, in the Greek society, there are stable in-groups in which people have close ties to each other. Typically, the in-group is composed of members of the extended family and friends. These groups are further described as allocentric, characterized by a person who subordinates his or her personal goals to those of others. The dominant values of the in-group focus on demonstrating concern and support for other members of the in-group. Additionally, the success of the in-group is more important than individual achievement.

The Greek value of *philotimo* is crucial to the understanding of how Greeks, by American standards, disregard their own wishes and desires if they differ from those of the in-group and accept the goals of their family. *Philotimo* is a key value in the self-concept of the Greek. Lee (1953, as cited in Vassiliou & Vassiliou, 1973) declared that one cannot know or have a positive relation with a Greek individual if he or she does not have the understanding of this value. It is understood as love of honor, honesty, respect, conscientiousness, duty, morality, and humaneness. More specifically, within the in-group, it is understood as expressed love and care for others. Moreover, it is perceived as an active interest in the other person's affairs, a readiness to help in whatever ways possible, and a constant availability to assist others (Vassiliou & Vassiliou, 1973). Greeks perceive that an outcome of operating within the value of *philotimo* is being successful and obedient.

Families in Greece, as expected from the research on collectivism (Hofstede, 1980), are closely interwoven. Georgas (1991) discussed changes in Greek values since the 1960s in relation to intrafamily acculturation with a shift toward individualism. Georgas (1991) identified specific variables that he believed to be related to the change in values in the Greek culture. First, demographics in the country have changed. Beginning in the 1970s and especially in the 1980s, many people from the provinces and small communities moved to the main cities, resulting in many social changes. Second, economic change resulted as people left their small agriculture and fishing communities behind and became involved in manufacturing, tourism, and service-oriented jobs. Third, mandatory education was increased to nine years with most students completing 12 years. Fourth, communication became more advanced and more accessible as the number of television sets increased, roads improved, and commuting between the islands became easier. Fifth, bonds within small groups in the immediate community are also changing because in the younger generations, it appears that the importance of the in-group is diminishing. Finally, there has been a movement from belonging to the extended family to the acceptance of simply the nuclear family. The extended family, with its hierarchical roles in which the father is the head of the family and all members assist in the raising of the children, is changing to the urban/nuclear family in which the mother has more of a sole role in raising the children.

The results of Georgas' study (1991) are of great interest. Georgas (1991) found that within this change from the collectivist in-group type family to the urban nuclear family, some of the values of the collectivist families are retained and some are transformed to more individualistic values. In urban areas, the rejection of hierarchical roles was more evident, specifically the rejection of the father as the authority figure. In rural areas, the parents still maintained the hierarchical roles; however, the children deviate in that they do not accept the father as the head of the family who makes all the decisions. Interestingly, the daughters were the ones who challenged mostly the notion of the hierarchical roles. Georgas (1991) explained this finding as related to the sons having less to lose, as they are the heirs to the authority figure role. Nonetheless, the rejection of the hierarchical roles in the Greek family is evident in Georgas' (1991) research. Georgas (1991) hypothesized that the next stage is the father's fear that the children are disobedient, resulting in a decline of the bond in the family. This decline in turn, according to Georgas (1991), will lead to a decline in the bonds of the extended family and an imminent fading of key values in the culture. As an example, the key value of *philotimo* had in the past bound members of the in-group together; however, with the loss of the bond with the extended family and even within the nuclear family, the role that *philotimo* plays in the lives of Greeks is not as substantial as it once was.

In another study examining the shift from collectivism to individualism, Georgas (1989) compared university students who grew up in Athens and students who were from the Greek provinces. Georgas (1989) found that Athenians were more rejecting of hierarchical family roles than were students from the provinces. The participants from the provinces appeared to possess values more embedded in the in-group and Georgas (1989) concluded that the values of the extended family system and the in-group in small communities are too deeply embedded to change within the four years that students stay at the university.

Furthermore, Georgas (1989) noted the shift in the acceptance of *philotimo*. This key collectivist value of the Greek communities is still functional in the extended family system. However, the Athenian students in Georgas' (1989) sample did not include in their description and understanding of *philotimo* the responsibility of taking care of extended family members. This obligation is a key concept implied in *philotimo*, and its exclusion is exemplary of the shift in values from collectivist to individualist.

Even with a shift in typical values of a collectivist society, the family structure in Greece remains different when compared to western societies. Georgas et al. (1997) examined family bonds and family structure in several countries. Georgas et al. (1997) defined family bonds as "a multidimensional construct reflecting cognitive, emotional, and behavioral elements of the family" (p. 315). This construct is helpful in understanding the individual and the family network as well as the strength and forms of interdependence between individual and family.

Georgas et al. (1997) used a questionnaire to examine university students from five European countries comparing Greek-Cypriot and Greek students to Dutch, British, and German students. Georgas et al. (1997) found that Greek-Cypriots and Greeks had a stronger family bond than the other students. Georgas et al. (1997) concluded that the family system in Greece and Cyprus is the most important source of emotional and material support for its members. The family system is not limited only to socialization but also includes care of the elderly and financial support for adult children, which varies significantly from the family systems of the other countries. These family systems are characterized better as individualistic versus collectivistic.

Even within Greece, however, the change in values is evident as described in a study about acculturation of Greek values (Georgas, Berry, Shaw, Christakopoulou, & Mylonas, 1996). Although acculturation is defined as change in relation to two cultures, for example, change of values of a minority group within a larger host culture, the authors examined value change between generations within families and between generations within one culture. The participants for this study were Greeks, Greek Canadians, and Greek natives in the Netherlands and in Germany.

Beliefs and values are transformed in many cultures to fit the developing conditions of each country. One of the ways to explain the change in beliefs in Greece is to understand the chaotic history. The chances of survival increased when Greek people adjusted to what was happening around them. For example, millennial identities were transformed in character and demography when there was an influx of Slavs and Albanians into the Greek peninsula during the seventh and eighth centuries A.D. (Smith, 1994). The Greek-speaking people were forced to the coasts and the islands. Thus, cultural representations shifted not only with what symbols the historical change is represented but also with what geographical symbols are seen and used. Smith (1994) also discussed the shift from paganism to Orthodoxy. This modification in traditional beliefs and mores increased the chances of survival for the Greeks at the time. Greeks, as do all groups, continue to modify their values to fit the times.

PSYCHOLOGICAL ASSESSMENT IN GREECE

Studies in psychological assessment in Greece are very limited. The psychological tests currently used are mere translations of U.S. assessment tools with no available Greek norms. However, there is an effort to validate assessment tools in Greece, especially for the assessment of intelligence (Alexopoulos, 1979; Alexopoulos, Haritos-Fatouros, Sakkas, Skaltsas, & Vlachos, 2000; Georgas, Vassiliou, & Katakis, 1971; Haritos-Fatouros, 1963; Petrogiannis, Bardos, & Randou, 1999).

Unfortunately, the personality assessment arena lacks studies with Greek samples. An additional dilemma is that of the few studies conducted, most used samples from Athens or larger cities and excluded samples from rural areas. In 1967, Georgas and Vassiliou conducted the only study concerning the Rorschach. The MMPI has been translated into Greek and has been used since 1977 (Kokkevi, 1996; Manos, 1985). Coss (1999) studied false positives in the Rorschach and the MMPI–2 with a sample of Greek Americans.

Georgas and Vassiliou (1967) administered the Rorschach test to 200 adults from Athens in an attempt to develop norms for Greece. Georgas and Vassiliou used the Beck scoring system. Georgas and Vassiliou examined whether the Rorschach test can be used with this culture or whether certain unique characteristics of the Greek people exist. At the time this study was conducted, Athens represented 23% of the population in Greece; thus, potential differences between Athenians and individuals from the provinces were not examined. Georgas and Vassiliou reported that even though there is an emphasis in the difference of the Greek from the American in cross-cultural research, their examination of the Athenian sample suggests that the Rorschach examines personality characteristics similar to people from all cultures.

The change in societal values between the cities and the provincial areas in Greece is evident. It is imperative that studies in psychological assessment not only include persons from various SES and educational levels in the cities but that rural areas are included in the population samples. Conclusions cannot be generalized to the entire Greek population if the samples are restricted, as it is assumed that there are considerable differences between the industrialized cities and the provincial areas with respect to societal values.

Limitations of the studies conducted thus far in Greece led Daroglou and Viglione (2002) to compile a Greek reference sample for the CS that included participants from urban and provincial areas of Greece. The participants in the sample varied in SES, occupation, and years of education. Some of the CS variables for the Greek sample were consistent with the CS norms; however, differences were also observed. The variables that had a lower frequency mean in the Greek sample included R, Blends, M, T, SumC, WsumC, Afr, EA, es, XA, WDA, X+, and Popular responses. The variables that had a higher frequency than the CS norms were Dd, C', Y, X – %, and Wsum6. Furthermore, Daroglou and Viglione found symbols that frequently appeared in the Greek protocols that were representative or rather typical of the Greek culture such as the two-headed eagle, specific tree types, islands, and sea animals.

A subsequent study compared Greeks and Euro-Americans on interpersonal relatedness using 11 CS variables (Daroglou, 2003). The two samples were matched case by case on gender, age, and education level. Many similarities were observed between the two samples. However, some CS variables differed and were contradictory to what would be expected according to the Greek cultural values. When controlling for productivity, motivational level, and psychopathology, the Greek sample appeared on the Rorschach as expected through the cultural values and this suggested that Greeks have close interpersonal relationships, have realistic impressions of others, and generally engage in collaborative activities with others more so than the Euro-Americans of the study. In addition, a small sample of older Greeks with a mean of 4.88 years of education was compared to the rest of the Greeks and Euro-Americans. The findings suggested generational differences and corroborated the idea that the societal, political, and historical changes in the last half century have brought about changes in values, beliefs, and traditions within the Greek population. Daroglou concluded that the Rorschach can be utilized with Greeks and identified some of the variables, i.e., the perceptual thought index, which have to be controlled or calibrated to account for cultural variation. If such adjustments to the cultural values of Greece are ignored, an evaluator is likely to overpathologize the Greek person.

CASE PRESENTATIONS

I present four cases to bring to life the theoretical findings discussed previously and to guide evaluators with interpretive statements. I administered the Rorschach according to CS standards in the Greek language as part of a research project in Greece during the summer of 2001. The Rorschach Interpretation Assistance Program (RIAP), fourth version (Exner & Weiner, 2001), was used to calculate the quantitative data. In addition, the interpretive hypotheses provided by RIAP were reviewed and compared to the writer's interpretive hypotheses. It is imperative, however, to bear in mind that conclusions about an individual should not be made with data from one psychological instrument alone. Moreover, the reader is reminded that some of the following interpretations are offered with respect to single CS variables as examples that possibly include cultural components; however, this is not suggested when writing a psychological report, which would consider several CS variables in combination.

Sofia[3]—A Woman From the Provinces

Sofia is a 58-year-old married Greek woman. She is a housewife and assists with farming. In addition, she worked for approximately nine years as a factory worker. Sofia completed the sixth grade. She was born in a small village in rural Greece where she currently lives. When asked whether she ever had mental health problems, she reported experiencing grief issues after the recent death of her parent. She also reported that she suffers from rheumatoid arthritis. She produced a protocol with 28 responses and Lambda of 1.33; she gave three Popular responses and had three Blends. Segments of the Structural Summary are presented in Table 12.1.

An evaluator adhering to standard CS interpretations would hypothesize that this woman has low frustration tolerance and difficulty producing psychological resources to cope but that she would do well in structured situations. However, even though she can pay attention to detail and synthesize information well, she is unlikely to use much thought

---

[3]The names for the cases presented are ficticious.

Table 12.1
Structural Summary Segments—Sofia

EB	4:1.0	COP	0	XA%	0.71
Eb	6:3	AG	0	WDA%	0.73
EA	5.0	GHR:PHR	5:2	X – %	0.29
Es	9	a:p	5:5	S–	1
EBPer	N/A	Food	0	P	3
D	–1	H	7	X + %	0.36
AdjD	–1	PureH	5	Xu%	0.36
FM	4	PER	0	Zf	13
M	2	Isolation	0.18	W:D:Dd	6:16:6
SumC'	1	Ma:Mp	1:3	W:M	6:4
SumV	1	2AB + Art + Ay	0	Zd	–0.5
SumT	0	MOR	0	PSV	0
SumY	1	Sum6	3	DQ+	10
FC: CF + C	2:0	Level 2	0	DQv	0
Pure C	0	WSum6	9	3r + (2)/R	0.36
SumC':WsumC	1:1.0	M–	1	Fr + rF	0
Afr	0.56	Mnone	0	FD	0
S	2			An + Xy	0
Blends:R	3:28			H:(H) + Hd + (Hd)	5:2
CP	0				

in the decision-making process. She may be aware of unmet needs and may be worried that others will decide her destiny. Her approach to life is avoidant or escapist. Although Sofia has adequate reality testing, she may perceive others and events in a more unusual way. She may be self-critical. She is comfortable in social situations but has difficulty in her relationships with others, possibly keeping such relationships superficial, as she is emotionally reserved. Sofia will most likely not have the capacity to form close and intimate relationships with others.

An evaluator who bears Sofia's culture in mind could hypothesize that a Greek woman from the rural areas with limited education and in this age group, even though having the cognitive capacity to make decisions, would wait for the husband or the father to make such decisions. Further, it is likely that this woman would look up to authority and would expect the authority figure to provide structure—whether it is the male figure in the family or perhaps in the case of the Rorschach administration, the examiner. An approach to life that is rather avoidant or passive may be considered pathological in some individualist cultures, but in the Greek society, it appears to be more adaptive. Thus, Sofia may have psychological resources to be flexible and adaptive in her society.

The historical facts and the concept of *Kismet* may be significant to consider in interpreting the results. Sofia was born during World War II and lived the first years of her childhood through civil war during which time Greece was in a state of pandemonium. This may help to explain her reluctance to make decisions and the need for structure. Faced with ambiguous situations, as with the Rorschach, Sofia may have been more careful not to confront authority. Sofia was born and raised by the border of Greece and her parents and grandparents were refugees from East Thrace. Greeks that came from East Thrace and Asia Minor commonly use the concept of *Kismet* explained as fate or destiny that has control over one's life. An imported word from the Turkish language, *Kismet* is omnipotent, and one cannot change what life holds for them but can only face it with courage.

Some of the symbols that Sofia used may be commonly seen or thought of in the Greek culture but are unusual when compared to the CS norms. A mythological snakelike monster with many heads, for example, Lernaia Ydra, as seen by Sofia on card X, D1 area and warranting Form Quality unusual in the CS, may be a more common response with Greeks because Greek mythology is taught and used frequently and widely in Greece. Thus, it is not unlikely that a woman with limited education uses it in everyday language.

Sofia gave many Animal responses (A = 9, (A) = 3, Ad = 1), not as unusual for farmers, people living in rural areas, and those raising animals. Interestingly, many of the animal responses were snakes, a symbol of evil in Greek culture and implying the theme of imminent danger. Sofia also produced a T-less protocol. As Sofia is part of a collectivist culture, she may not experience the same need for closeness as compared to people from individualistic cultures. It is possible that Sofia experiences the closeness described with T within her in-group, and thus, such need might not be expressed through the Rorschach. Further, interactions within Sofia's in-group are likely seen as important and positive, but it is possible that interactions outside her in-group would be viewed as less cooperative and suspicious, which may clarify the CS interpretations regarding her interpersonal relationships.

In summary, Sofia is a 58-year-old woman from the provinces who appears to be adaptive in her society, as she expects the authority figures to provide structure in her life and is rather careful to confront authority. Sofia is aware that destiny has control over her life, which may be an acceptance of the value of *Kismet*. She appears to not experience the same need for closeness when compared to people from individualistic cultures, which is common in her culture. Sofia views interactions with people from outside her in-group not positively in comparison to her interactions with family members and close friends.

George—A Man From the Provinces

George is a 32-year-old Greek man raised in rural Greece where he lived for most of his life. He attended the university for five years and earned an agricultural degree. He never married and lives at home with his family

TABLE 12.2
Structural Summary Segments—George

EB	1:2.0	COP	0	XA%	0.88
Eb	5:2	AG	0	WDA%	0.92
EA	3.0	GHR:PHR	6:1	X – %	0.12
Es	7	a:p	5:1	S–	0
EBPer	N/A	Food	1	P	8
D	–1	H	7	X + %	0.62
AdjD	0	PureH	3	Xu%	0.27
FM	2	PER	0	Zf	16
M	3	Isolation	0.23	W:D:Dd	10:15:1
SumC'	2	Ma:Mp	0:1	W:M	10:1
SumV	0	2AB + Art + Ay	2	Zd	–3.0
SumT	0	MOR	0	PSV	1
SumY	0	Sum6	0	DQ+	10
FC: CF + C	2:1	Level 2	0	DQv	0
Pure C	0	WSum6	0	3r+(2)/R	0.31
SumC':WsumC	2:2.0	M–	0	Fr + rF	1
Afr	0.44	Mnone	0	FD	4
S	1			An + Xy	1
Blends:R	3:26			H:(H) + Hd + (Hd)	3:4
CP	0				

where he has lived most of his life with the exception of his college years, the two-year mandatory military service, and two subsequent years where he worked and lived in Athens. He reported that he has never experienced mental health concerns. He was a volunteer research participant when the Rorschach was administered. George produced a 26-response Rorschach protocol with a Lambda of 1.36, eight Popular responses, three Blends, and elevations on the CDI and HVI. Segments of the Structural Summary are presented in Table 12.2.

Adhering to standard CS interpretations, the evaluator would report that George functions better in a structured environment. In the absence of structure, he does not allow himself time to think through decisions and prefers to come to conclusions quickly. The test data suggest that George has limited psychological resources to cope with stress. In addition, the stress he currently experiences is most likely caused by situational factors. Although George has good reality testing and understands and interprets events in a conventional manner, he presents with a hypervigilant style and is suspicious of others. Furthermore, he is inflexible in reconsidering beliefs or situations resulting in George presenting himself as a closed minded person. He is aware that his needs are not always being met and that others or events have control over what happens to him. However, George can adjust and be adaptive in modulating his emotional world even though his approach in dealing with feelings is intellectual. George is introspective, lacks self-esteem and self-confidence, but has some narcissistic qualities suggesting that his narcissism may be compensating for his self-esteem. If his environment does not validate his achievements, he may become frustrated and negativistic. George has limited capacity to form close attachments with others. His interpersonal relationships are likely superficial, as he will avoid demands that he may not be able to manage.

When interpreting the test data with consideration for George's Greek culture, one would keep in mind that George is a man from the provinces, which may render him a person upholding the traditional values of the Greek society, a plausible explanation of his rigidity to reevaluate beliefs and values. However, George's age and the fact that he lived in the city would also suggest that he might adhere to more individualistic values. Thus, the evaluator must bear in mind that a combination of collectivist and individualist values may be present and that the Rorschach interpretations may have to be calibrated in such a way as to include a combination of such values. The task may appear easier because the assumption that many of the standard CS interpretations will hold true is kept in mind; however, it may be exactly the contrary, as there is not a clear and defining line of what values may be more traditional for George and what values have been incorporated into more of an individualistic lifestyle. The evaluator with a case such as George's, not having a clear dividing line of what might be collectivist and/or individualist, is more prone to flawed and contradictory interpretations.

The Rorschach administration procedure is a new experience for George and is not part of his cultural landscape. This new experience may be anxiety provoking and combined with his limited tolerance for ambiguity may have added or even prompted the situational stress he is experiencing. George grew up and lives in the same province as Sofia, and he too is a descendant of refugees from East Thrace. As such, the idea of having a certain destiny that he cannot change may be present as in the case of Sofia and may influence his perception that others exert control over his life. George is a man who lives with his parents at the age of 32, not an unusual occurrence in the culture, and he may be comfortable in his relationships within his in-group. However, the Rorschach administration procedure and this examiner were foreign to him and may have been experienced as more suspicious. Generally, George's hypervigilant style can be explained as his mistrust and weariness of unfamiliar situations and people that do not belong in his in-group. As such, his interpersonal relationships may be intimate and close with relatives and close friends but not with outsiders. Interpretations of his capacity to form close and in-depth relationships with others are similar to those of Sofia's.

George used many symbols that could have been produced by individuals his age in the American culture, making progress in communication and media more evident. Examples of such symbols are "pumpkins that Americans use for Halloween," masks of aliens from the x-files, electric guitars, and bungee jumping. He also produced symbols such as "masks they used to wear at war to scare the enemy," and although he did not specify the object of Greek heritage, it is most likely implied, as it is common to specify something from another culture and not one's own. Two of the three percepts warranting FQ– were insects, and George's education and employment are in the field of agriculture, which may be a rationale for his use of such percepts, as they are more familiar in his everyday experiences.

In brief, George, a 32-year-old Greek man from the provinces, presents with a combination of collectivist and individualistic values. He upholds traditional values, at times making him inflexible in his reevaluation of his beliefs. He may be accepting of the concept of *Kismet*, as he believes that others exert control over his life. The novel experience of the Rorschach administration may have been anxiety provoking, as he is mistrustful of unfamiliar people and situations, although he may be comfortable in his interactions with members of his in-group.

Anna—A Woman From the City

Anna is a 71-year-old married woman from Athens. Anna completed the sixth grade, worked as a dressmaker, and is now retired. She reported that she has received treatment for osteoporosis but that otherwise her health is good and that she never experienced any mental health problems. Anna produced a 19-response Rorschach protocol with a Lambda of 1.38, two Blends, seven Popular responses, and elevation on the CDI. Segments of the Structural Summary are presented in Table 12.3.

The CS trained evaluator would propose that Anna most likely leads a restricted life as a result of her efforts to keep stressors at bay, as she has limited internal resources to deal with such stressors. In all likelihood, Anna looks well adjusted in her environment, a consequence of staying within familiar state of affairs and familiar people. Anna is a thinker, she considers much information when she attempts to problem solve. This characteristic, combined with a rather avoidant and simplistic style as well as not being able to put up with much ambiguity, lead her to pass on the decision making and problem solving onto others. In addition, Anna shies away from emotionally laden situations. The test data consistently suggest that Anna has problems in her relationships with others. She relies on others and also puts aside her own needs to accommodate others. She has no close attachments to others and is socially unskilled.

The evaluator sensitive to Anna's culture would suggest that what appears to be a limitation in some cultures when a person prefers to stay

TABLE 12.3
Structural Summary Segments—Anna

EB	4:1.0	COP	0	XA%	0.95
Eb	3:1	AG	0	WDA%	0.94
EA	5.0	GHR:PHR	4:4	X–%	0.05
Es	4	a:p	2:5	S–	0
EBPer	N/A	Food	1	P	7
D	0	H	8	X+%	0.42
AdjD	0	PureH	3	Xu%	0.53
FM	2	PER	0	Zf	12
M	1	Isolation	0.58	W:D:Dd	7:9:3
SumC'	1	Ma:Mp	1:3	W:M	7:4
SumV	0	2AB + Art + Ay	1	Zd	+4.0
SumT	0	MOR	1	PSV	1
SumY	0	Sum6	2	DQ+	10
FC: CF + C	0:1	Level 2	0	DQv	0
Pure C	0	WSum6	3	3r + (2)/R	0.63
SumC':WsumC	1:1.0	M–	0	Fr + rF	0
Afr	0.46	Mnone	0	FD	1
S	0			An + Xy	0
Blends:R	2:19			H: (H) + Hd + (Hd)	3:5
CP	0				

within familiar situations and people can be regarded here as Anna's ability to function well within her familiar environment and relatives. It is not unusual, especially for a 71-year-old Greek woman, to prefer to deal with family members including extended family and avoid outsiders. The idea of staying within proximity of the family and familiar surroundings in combination with her need for structure, avoidance of emotions, and avoidance of decision making may be a result of Anna's childhood years during World War II. At the time of war, especially in larger cities such as Athens where Anna lived, food was scarce, and competition for basic provisions was high. As a result, Anna may avoid aspects of life that may remind her of the inconsistency and unstructured environment experienced during wartime. Further, these experiences may have also resulted in Anna's emotional distancing and distrust of others, especially individuals not belonging in her in-group.

Some of the symbols Anna used are typical in the Greek culture but most likely appear quite unusual to others. A very popular cartoon-like character used for Shadow Theater in Greece called *Karagiozis* was seen by Anna in the D1 area of Card III. A tree seen frequently also by others in the Greek sample in the D4 area of Card VIII was also seen by Anna. A tree in this area is coded unusual for Form Quality. The D3 area of Card IX was seen as *Kalikantzaros,* a wicked human-like creature created in the New Greek folklore. Anna saw the D3 area of Card VI as Christ. Although religious symbols were not very common in the CS sample (Daroglou & Viglione, 2002), these types of symbols were reported as a common occurrence by Georgas and Vassiliou in 1967, which would then be more consistent with Anna's age group.

Women in Anna's responses were viewed either as "broken" or wearing black clothes. In Greece, it is common that widows are dressed in all black clothing. Even though this tradition is changing, and many women return to nonblack clothing after at least one year of wearing them and being in mourning, for many people in Greece, black clothes symbolize death in the family and mourning. It is possible that Anna, at 71 years of age, has started to identify as a widow. The idea of seeing then women as broken or not whole would correspond with the idea of women associated with a husband and not being whole if alone. It may be fitting then and even expected that Anna, considering her age in regards to stage of life as well as values used by her generation, would identify as a broken women awaiting the black attire.

In summary, Anna, a 71-year-old Greek woman from Athens, prefers to deal with family members and close friends and avoids people not close to her, not an unusual occurrence within Anna's culture. Her experience during the war may have resulted in Anna's emotional distancing and distrust of others. She considers it important that women are associated with family or a husband, as the idea of interdependence is valued in her culture.

Helen—A Woman From the City

Helen is a 52-year-old divorced woman from Athens. She has completed a college education and works for a private company. She reported that she never had any serious health problems, was never hospitalized, and that she never experienced any mental health problems. She was a volunteer research participant when the Rorschach was administered. She produced a protocol with 21 responses, Lambda of 0.75, four Blends, three Popular responses, and elevation of the CDI. Segments of the Structural Summary follow in Table 12.4.

The evaluator who abides by standard CS interpretations would suggest that Helen prefers to keep stressors at a distance and leads a rather restricted life, preferring to stay within the boundaries of circumstances and people she is accustomed. Helen prefers to think things through when she tries to make a decision more so than other people, avoiding mostly any emotional involvement in the decision-making process even though she is comfortable with emotions. However, when feelings are involved, Helen will intellectualize, resulting in her presentation as emotionally reserved. Helen engages in much self-examination. In addition, Helen is

TABLE 12.4
Structural Summary Segments—Helen

EB	5:0.5	COP	1	XA%	0.90
Eb	5:2	AG	0	WDA%	0.90
EA	5.5	GHR:PHR	6:2	X−%	0.10
Es	7	a:p	4:6	S−	0
EBPer	5.0	Food	1	P	3
D	0	H	9	X+%	0.67
AdjD	0	PureH	5	Xu%	0.24
FM	5	PER	0	Zf	7
M	0	Isolation	0.14	W:D:Dd	3:17:1
SumC'	2	Ma:Mp	3:2	W:M	3:5
SumV	0	2AB + Art + Ay	1	Zd	−1.5
SumT	0	MOR	1	PSV	0
SumY	0	Sum6	0	DQ+	5
FC: CF + C	1:0	Level 2	0	DQv	0
Pure C	0	WSum6	0	3r + (2)/R	0.48
SumC':WsumC	2:0.5	M−	0	Fr + rF	0
Afr	0.75	Mnone	0	FD	3
S	0			An + Xy	1
Blends:R	4:21			H: (H) + Hd + (Hd)	5:4
CP	0				

conscious about what impact she has on others. Her consideration for and need to rely on others leads her to attend to other's needs more so than her own. However, her dependency on others combined with her emotional reservation result in her having problems in her relationships with others, rendering them more superficial and distant.

Keeping culture in mind, Helen's presentation of leading a restricted life may be very similar to Anna's with respect to the need for familiarity. The in-group in the collectivist society of Greece and the interactions among its members are valued. The relationships among members and their roles within the in-group are respected and revered. However, the relationships formed with members outside Helen's in-group may not be of importance to her and as a consequence may be avoided. Attending to other's needs is a crucial part of the key value *philotimo*. It is possible that Helen would not function well in the American society, as attaining autonomy is regarded as a necessary step for psychological well-being. However, in the Greek society, Helen's inclination to take care of other's needs, disregarding her own, is not only respected, but it is also expected of her.

Georgas and Vassiliou (1967) observed a more introversive experience balance in the Athenian sample contradicting the notion of the loud, expressive, and impulsive Greek. Georgas and Vassiliou (1967) questioned whether this behavior is a "culturally induced role performance pertaining only to the cognitive component of emotion without its affective component" (p. 37). Helen's emotional reserve could be explained in this manner. Further, a more formal approach to testing could be expected, as the examiner and the testing situation are not familiar. The emotional distance that Helen presented with would not be unusual, as it is expected to treat members not belonging to the in-group and especially authority, that is, the examiner, in a more formal and proper manner than family members. Consequently, the explanation could also be a difference in language use, as unfamiliar persons are spoken to formally and in plural.

Helen belongs to a small percentage of divorced individuals in Greece —only 5% of the Greek CS sample were divorced. As Helen is aware of the common expectation of marriage in Greece, her rather upsetting self-examination could be a result of a combination of this awareness, the comparison to others, and her thoughts and expectations about the meaning of her life at 52 years of age.

Helen, like Anna, also saw Christ in the D3 area of Card VI. In Card X, D9 area, Helen saw Italy, warranting Form Quality minus. An island in the D9 area was a very frequent response in the Greek CS sample. A further frequent response was sea animals for D7 in Card X, which was seen by Helen as well and is coded minus for Form Quality also. Although these percepts are considered unusual in the CS system, they may in fact be common for the Greeks, rendering Helen's responses more Popular and allowing her to appear more psychologically well balanced.

To sum up, Helen, a 52-year-old Greek woman from Athens, values her relationships with her family members and close friends but avoids interactions with strangers. The value of *philotimo* is apparent in Helen's presentation, as she prefers to attend to others' needs rather than her own. She appears as emotionally reserved, which may be a result of her formal approach to situations unfamiliar to her as expected in her culture. Her upsetting self-examination may be the effect of the combination of the fact that she is divorced and of her awareness of the expectations in her culture in regards to family life and marriage.

SUMMARY

Evaluators are trained to analyze and interpret psychological testing data using theories developed in Western societies. Although some of these interpretations rely on ideas that are universal, many emic aspects of behavior exist and must be interpreted within the cultural context. A number of the interpretations presented in the Greek cases, for example, were based on the idea of autonomy, especially in regards to interpersonal relationships. The evaluator has to bear in mind that interpersonal relationships and generally the family structure may look pathological, but it is compared to norms from another country. These interpretations emphasize Euro-American society values without taking under consideration that the idea of interdependence is an important value within the Greek society. Interpretations, then, appearing pathological considering what is valued in one society may be to the contrary very adaptive in the Greek society.

A brief overview of the four cases presented here reveals common themes: The values of *philotimo* and *Kismet,* the relationships within the in-group in comparison with outsiders, the formal approach to others not in the in-group, and the differences in expectations of one's self and of others depending on whether the person is functioning within the in-group.

Furthermore, it may be easier to offer interpretations of testing data when someone is either collectivist or individualist. As the Greek society is continuously changing, evaluations of persons in certain age groups and with certain background information might be difficult, as the evaluator has to tease out which cultural values are traditional and which ones have been transformed or are in the process of transformation.

I propose that when the Rorschach is administered with Greek individuals, as long as CS norms are not available for this specific population, consideration must be given to the acculturation status of the individual, as there is a shift from collectivism to individualism in Greece. The cultural values then have to be examined, and the interpretations of different variables can be adjusted to those values and expectations in the society. Following this model of interpretation should reduce flawed explanations and assumptions of an individual's personality. When a Greek American individual is being assessed, as well as any individuals of Greek heritage living in other countries such as Germany, Canada, Australia and so forth, acculturation scales should be used to gain a better understanding of the value system of the person.

In summary, the standard CS coding and variables are useful, but interpretations should be questioned and attuned to what is more fitting to the Greek culture. Greek cultural reference values can be used to adjust the CS variables, and interpretations can then be made with more certainty. Test results in conjunction with interpretations of cultural values including the Greek's approach to life can be used to assist mental health professionals in developing strategies for working effectively with members of the Greek community.

References

Abad, V., Ramos, J., & Boyce, E. (1974). A model for delivery of mental health services to Spanish-speaking minorities. *American Journal of Orthopsychiatry, 44*, 584–595.

Abe, J. S., & Zane, N. W. S. (1990). Psychological maladjustment among Asian and White American college students: Controlling for confounds. *Journal of Counseling Psychology, 37*, 437–444.

Abe-Kim, J., Okazaki, S., & Goto, S. G. (2001). Unidimensional versus multidimensional approaches to the assessment of acculturation for Asian American populations. *Cultural Diversity and Ethnic Minority Psychology, 7*, 232–246.

Abel, T. M. (1948). The Rorschach test in the study of culture. *Rorschach Research Exchange, 12*, 79–93.

Abel, T. M. (1973). *Psychological testing in cultural contexts*. New Haven, CT: College & University Press.

Acosta, F. X. (1984). Psychotherapy with Mexican Americans: Clinical and empirical gains. In J. L. Martinez, Jr., & R. H. Mendoza (Eds.), *Chicano Psychology* (2nd ed., pp. 163–189), Orlando, FL: Academic.

Acosta, F. X., & Cristo, M. H. (1981). Development of a bilingual interpreter program: An alternative model for Spanish-speaking services. *Professional Psychology, 12*, 474–482.

Adcock, C. J., & Ritchie, J. F. (1958). Intercultural use of the Rorschach. *American Anthropologist, 60*, 881–892.

Advincula, A. (1999). *Development of an acculturation scale*. Unpublished master's thesis, California State University, San Bernardino.

Akutsu, P. D., Snowden, L. R., & Organista, K. C. (1996). Referral patterns in ethnic-specific and mainstream programs for ethnic minorities and Whites. *Journal of Counseling Psychology, 43*, 56–64.

Albert, R., & Bill, D. (1990, October). *Cross-cultural communication and psychotherapy*. Workshop conducted at the meeting of the Alaska chapter, National Association of Social Workers, Anchorage, AK.

Alexopoulos, D. (1979). *Revision and standardization of the Wechsler Intelligence Scale for Children–Revised (WISC–R) for the age range 13–15 years in Greece*. Unpublished doctoral dissertaion, University of Wales, Bangor.

Alexopoulos, D., Haritos-Fatouros, M., Sakkas, D., Skaltsas, A., & Vlachos, O. (2000). Reliability and validity of the WISC–R for the age range 6 to 11 years in Greece. *Journal of the Hellenic Psychological Society, 7*(1), 35–45.

Allen, J. (1998). Personality assessment with American Indians and Alaska Natives: Instrument considerations and service delivery style. *Journal of Personality Assessment, 70,* 17–42.

Allen, J. (2002). Assessment training for practice in American Indian and Alaska Native settings. *Journal of Personality Assessment, 79,* 216–225.

Allen, J., & Dana, R. H. (2004). Methodological issues in cross-cultural and multicultural Rorschach research. *Journal of Personality Assessment, 82,* 189–206.

Allen, J., & Walsh, J. A. (2000). A construct-based approach to equivalence: Methodologies for cross-cultural/multicultural personality assessment research. In R. H. Dana (Ed.), *Handbook of cross-cultural and multicultural personality assessment* (pp. 63–85). Mahwah, NJ: Lawrence Erlbaum Associates, Inc.

Allison, K. W., Crawford, I., Echemendia, R. J., Robinson, W. I., & Knepp, D. (1994). Human diversity and professional competence: Training in clinical and counseling psychology revisited. *American Psychologist, 49,* 792–796.

Allison, K. W., Echemendia, R. J., Crawford, I., & Robinson, W. I. (1996). Predicting cultural competence: Implications for practice and training. *Professional Psychology: Research and Practice, 27,* 386–393.

Allport, G. W. (1937). *Personality: A psychological interpretation.* New York: Holt, Rinehart & Winston.

Allport, G. W., & Odbert, H. S. (1936). Trait names: A psycho-lexical study. *Psychological Monographs, 47*(1, Whole No. 211).

Altarriba, J., & Santiago-Rivera, A. L. (1994). Current perspectives on using linguistic and cultural factors in counseling the Hispanic clients. *Professional Psychology: Research and Practice, 25,* 388–297.

American Counseling Association. (1995). *Code of ethics and standards of practice.* Alexandria, VA: Author.

American Psychiatric Association. (1994). *Diagnostic and statistical manual of mental disorders* (4th ed.). Washington, DC: Author.

American Psychological Association. (1985). *Standards for educational and psychological testing.* Washington, DC: Author.

American Psychological Association. (1992). Ethical principles of psychologists and code of conduct. *American Psychologist, 47,* 1597–1611.

American Psychological Association. (1993). Guidelines for providers of psychological services to ethnic, linguistic, and culturally diverse populations. *American Psychologist, 48,* 45–48.

American Psychological Association. (2002). Ethical principles of psychologists and code of conduct. *American Psychologist, 57,* 245–251.

American Psychological Association. (2003). Guidelines on multicultural education, training, research, practice, and organizational change for psychologists. *American Psychologist, 58,* 377–402.

American Psychological Association Division 12 Presidential Task Force. (1999). Assessment for the 21st century: A model curriculum. *Clinical Psychologist, 52,* 10–15.

Anastasi, A., & Urbina, S. (1997). *Psychological testing* (7th ed.). Upper Saddle River, NJ: Prentice Hall.

Anderson, J., Moeschberger, M., Chen, M. S., Jr., Kunn, P., Wewers, M. E., & Guthrie, R. (1993). An acculturation scale for Southeast Asians. *Social Psychiatry and Psychiatric Epidemiology, 28,* 134–141.

Andronikof-Sanglade, A. (2000). Use of the Rorschach Comprehensive System in Europe: State of the art. In R. H. Dana (Ed.), *Handbook of cross-cultural and multicultural personality assessment* (pp. 329–344). Mahwah, NJ: Lawrence Erlbaum Associates, Inc.

Antonovsky, A. (1984). The sense of coherence as a determinant of health. In J. D. Matarazzo, S. M. Weiss, J. A. Herd, & N. E. Miller (Eds.), *Behavioral health: A handbook of health enhancement and disease prevention* (pp. 114–129). New York: Wiley.

Antonovsky, A. (1987). *Unraveling the mystery of health: How people manage stress and stay well.* San Francisco: Jossey-Bass.

Aponte, J. F., & Barnes, J. M. (1999). Impact of acculturation and moderator variables on the intervention and treatment of ethnic groups. In J. F. Aponte & J. Wohl (Eds.), *Psychological interventions and cultural diversity* (2nd ed, pp. 19–39). Boston: Allyn & Bacon.

Arbisi, P. A., Ben-Porath, Y. S., & McNulty, J. (2002). A comparison of MMPI–2 validity in African American and Caucasian psychiatric inpatients. *Psychological Assessment, 14,* 3–15.

Arbona, C. (1998). Psychological assessment: Multicultural or universal? *The Counseling Psychologist, 26,* 911–921.

Archer, P. A. (1987). *Using the MMPI with adolescents.* Hillsdale, NJ: Lawrence Erlbaum Associates, Inc.

Archer, P. A. (1997). *MMPI–A: Assessing adolescent psychopathology* (2nd ed.). Mahwah, NJ: Lawrence Erlbaum Associates, Inc.

Arellano, L., Huff-Musgrove, R., & Morrow, G. (2003). *Tri-City Mental Health Center Multicultural Competency Training Program.* Unpublished Manuscript.

Arnheim, R. (1951). Perceptual and aesthetic aspects of the movement response. *Journal of Personality, 19,* 265–281.

Arnold, B. R., & Matus, Y. E. (2000). Test translation and cultural equivalence methodologies for use with diverse populations. In I. Cuellar & F. A. Paniagua (Eds.), *Handbook of multicultural mental health: Assessment and treatment of diverse populations* (pp. 121–136). San Diego: Academic.

Arnold, B. R., Montgomery, G. T., Castanada, I., & Longoria, R. (1994). Acculturation and performance of Hispanics on selected Halstead–Reitan neuropsychological tests. *Assessment, 1,* 239–248.

Arredondo, P., Toporek, R., Brown, S. P., Jones, J., Locke, D. C., Sanchez, J., & Stadler, H. (1996). Operationalization of the multicultural counseling competencies. *Journal of Multicultural Counseling and Development, 24,* 42–78.

Atkinson, D. R., Maruyama, M., & Matsui, S. (1978). Effects of counselor race and counseling approach on Asian Americans' perception of counselor credibility and utility. *Journal of Counseling Psychology, 25,* 78–83.

Atkinson, D. R., Morten, G., & Sue, D. W. (1993). *Counseling American minorities: A cross-cultural perspective.* Madison, WI: Brown and Benchmark.

Avila-Espada, A. (1986). *Manual operativo para el Test de Apercepcion Tematica* [Operational manual for the Thematic Apperception Test]. Madrid, Spain: Piramide.

Avila-Espada, A. (2000). Objective scoring for the TAT. In R. H. Dana (Ed.), *Handbook of cross-cultural and multicultural personality assessment* (pp. 465–480). Mahwah, NJ: Lawrence Erlbaum Associates, Inc.

Azibo, D. A. Y. (1988). Understanding the proper and improper usage of the comparative research framework. *Journal of Black Psychology, 15,* 81–91.

Back, R., & Dana, R. H. (1977). Examiner-bias and WISC scores. *Journal of Consulting and Clinical Psychology, 45,* 500.

Back, R., & Dana, R. H. (1980). Self-help for male WISC examiners by pretest exposure to children. *Perceptual & Motor Skills, 51,* 838.

Ball, J. D., Archer, R. P., & Imhof, E. A. (1994). Time requirements of psychological testing: A survey of practitioners. *Journal of Personality Assessment, 63,* 239–249.

Barnow, V. (1963). The Rorschach test. In V. Barnow (Ed.), *Culture and personality* (pp. 239–259). Homewood, IL: Dorsey.

Barrios, B., & Hartmann, D. P. (1986). The contribution of traditional assessment: Concepts, issues, and methodologies. In R. O. Nelson & S. C. Hayes (Eds.), *Conceptual foundations of behavioral assessment* (pp. 81–110). New York: Guilford.

Bash, K. W. (1955). Einstellungstypus and Erlebnistypus: C. G. Jung and Hermann Rorschach. *Journal of Projective Techniques, 19*, 236–242.

Bass, B. A. (1982). The validity of socioeconomic factors in the assessment and treatment of Afro-Americans. In B. A. Bass, G. E. Wyatt, & G. J. Powell (Eds.), *The Afro-American family: Assessment, treatment, and research issues* (pp. 69–83). New York: Grune & Stratton.

Beck, S. J. (1950). Rorschach's test: I. Basic Processs (2nd ed.). New York: Grune & Stratton.

Behn, J. D. (1997, March). Rorschach X%: Interpretation issues from experience with multicultural populations. In R. H. (Chair), *Personality assessment practice with multicultural populations.* Symposium conducted at the midwinter meeting of the Society for Personality Assessment, San Diego, CA.

Bell, C. C. (1982). Black intrapsychic survival skills: Altered states of consciousness. *Journal of the National Medical Association, 74*, 1017–1020.

Bennett, J. M. (1986). A developmental approach to training for intercultural sensitivity. *International Journal of Intercultural Relations, 10*, 179–196.

Bennett, M. J. (1986). Modes of cross-cultural training. *International Journal of Intercultural Relations, 10*, 117–134.

Ben-Porath, Y. S. (1990). Cross-cultural assessment of personality: The case for replicatory factor analysis. In J. N. Butcher & C. D. Spielberger (Eds.), *Advances in personality assessment* (Vol. 8, pp. 27–48). Hillsdale, NJ: Lawrence Erlbaum Associates, Inc.

Ben-Porath, Y. S., Hostetler, K., Butcher, J. N., & Graham, J. R. (1989). New subscales for the MMPI–2: Social introversion (*Si*) subscale. *Psychological Assessment, 1*, 169–174.

Ben-Porath, Y. S., & Sherwood, N. E. (1993). *The MMPI–2 content component scales* (MMPI–2/ MMPI–A Test Rep. No. 1). Minneapolis: University of Minnesota Press.

Berg, J. A., Rodriguez, D. M., de Guzman, C., & Kading, V. M. (2001). Health status, health and risk behaviors of Filipino Americans. *Journal of Multicultural Nursing and Health, 7*(2), 29–36.

Berkuis, T., Cook, H., Holt, K., & Scott-Lennox, J. (1995). Ethnicity, church affiliation, and beliefs about the causal agents of health: A comparative study employing a multivariate analysis of covariance. *Health Education Research, 10*, 73–83.

Berry, J. W. (1969). On cross-cultural comparability. *International Journal of Psychology, 4*, 119–128.

Berry, J. W. (1989). Imposed etics-emics-derived etics: The operationalization of a compelling idea. *International Journal of Psychology, 24*, 721–735.

Berry, J. W., & Kim, U. (1988). Acculturation and mental health. In P. R. Dasen, J. W. Berry, & N. Sartorius (Eds.), *Health and cross-cultural psychology: Toward applications* (pp. 207–236). Newbury Park, CA: Sage.

Berry, J. W., Poortinga, Y. H., Segall, M. H., & Dasen, P. R. (2002). *Cross-cultural psychology: Research and applications* (2nd ed.). Cambridge, England: Cambridge University Press.

Berry, J. W., & Sam, D. L. (1997). Acculturation and adaptation. In J. W. Berry, M. H. Segall, & C. Kagitcibasi (Eds.), *Handbook of cross-cultural psychology* (Vol. 3, pp. 291–326). Boston: Allyn & Bacon.

Betancourt, H., & Lopez, S. R. (1993). The study of culture, ethnicity, and race in American psychology. *American Psychologist, 48*, 629–637.

Beutler, L. E., Brown, M. T., Crothers, L., Booker, K., & Seabrook, M. K. (1996). The dilemma of factitious demographic distinctions in psychological research. *Journal of Consulting and Clinical Psychology, 64*, 892–902.

Beutler, L. E., Crago, M., & Arizmendi, T. G. (1986). Therapist variables in psychotherapy process and emotions. In A. E. Bergin & S. L. Garfield (Eds.), *Handbook of psychotherapy and behavior changes* (pp. 257–310). New York: Wiley.

Beutler, L. E., & Groth-Marnat, G. (Eds.). (2003). *Integretive assessment of adult personality* (2nd ed.). New York: Guilford.

Bleuler, M., & Bleuler, R. (1935). Rorschach's inkblot test and racial psychology: Mental peculiarities of Moroccans. *Character and Personality, 4,* 97–114.

Boehm, E. (1977). Das Binder'sche Helldunkelsystem [The Bender chiaroscuro system and its theoretical basis]. *Rorschachiana, V,* 3–23.

Boey, K. M. (1985). The MMPI response pattern of Singaporean Chinese. *Acta Psychologica Sinica, 17,* 377–383.

Bourguignon, E. E., & Westerkamm Nett, E. (1955). Rorschach responses in a sample of Haitian protocols. *Journal of Projective Techniques, 19,* 117–124.

Boyer, L. B., Boyer, R. M., Dithrich, C. W., Harned, H., Hippler, A. E., Stone, J. S., & Walt, A. (1989). The relation between psychological states and acculturation among the Tanaina and Upper Tanana Indians of Alaska: An ethnographic and Rorschach study. *Ethos, 17,* 450–479.

Boyer, L. B., Klopfer, B., Boyer, R. M., Brawer, F. B., & Kawai, H. (1965). Effects of acculturation on the personality traits of older people of the Mescalero and Chiricahua Apaches. *International Journal of Social Psychiatry, 11,* 264–271.

Brandt, M. E., & Boucher, J. D. (1986). Concepts of depression in emotion lexicons of eight cultures. *International Journal of Intercultural Relations, 10,* 321–346.

Brickman, A. S., & Lerner, H. D. (1992). Barren Rorschachs: A conceptual approach. *Journal of Personality Assessment, 59,* 165–175.

Brislin, R. W. (1976). *Translation: Applications and research.* New York: Wiley.

Brislin, R. W., Lonner, W. J., & Thorndike, R. M. (1973). *Cross-cultural research methods.* New York: Wiley.

Brown, L. S. (1997). The private practice of subversion: Psychology as Tikkun Olam. *American Psychologist, 52,* 449–462.

Brown, S. (1982, May). *Native generations diagnosis and placement on the conflicts/resolution chart.* Paper presented at the annual meeting of the School of Addiction Studies, Center for Alcohol and Addiction Studies, University of Alaska, Anchorage.

Burlew, A. K., Bellow, S., & Lovett, M. (2000). Racial identity measures: A review and classification system. In R. H. Dana (Ed.), *Handbook of cross-cultural and multicultural personality assessment* (pp. 173–196). Mahwah, NJ: Lawrence Erlbaum Associates, Inc.

Burn, D. (1992). Ethical implications in cross-cultural counseling and training. *Journal of Counseling and Development, 70,* 578–583.

Butcher, J. N. (1987). *Computerized psychological assessment: A practitioner's guide.* New York: Basic Books.

Butcher, J. N. (2000). Item content in the interpretation of the MMPI–2. In J. N. Butcher (Ed.), *Clinical personality assessment: Practical approaches* (pp. 319–334). New York: Oxford University Press.

Butcher, J. N. (Ed.). (1996a). *International adaptations of the MMPI–2.* Minneapolis: University of Minnesota Press.

Butcher, J. N. (1996b). Translation and adaptation of the MMPI–2 for international use. In J. N. Butcher (Ed.), *International adaptations of the MMPI–2* (pp. 26–43). Minneapolis: University of Minnesota Press.

Butcher, J. N. (2001). A parochial perspective on cross-cultural psychology. *Contemporary Psychology, 46,* 621–622.

Butcher, J. N., Cheung, F. M., & Lim, J. (2003). Use of the MMPI–2 with Asian populations. *Psychological Assessment, 15,* 248–256.

Butcher, J. N., Nezami, E., & Exner, J. (1998). Psychological assessment of people in diverse cultures. In S. S. Kazarian & D. R. Evans (Eds.), *Cultural clinical psychology: Theory, research and practice* (pp. 61–105). New York: Oxford University Press.

Butcher, J. N., Dahlstrom, W. G., Graham, J. R., Tellegen, A., & Kaemmer, B. (1989). *MMPI–2: Minnesota Multiphasic Personality Inventory–2: Manual for administration and scoring.* Minneapolis: University of Minnesota Press.

Butcher, J., Derksen, J., Sloore, H., & Sirigatti, S. (2003). Objective personality assessment of people in diverse cultures: European adaptaptions of the MMPI–2. *Behaviour research and therapy, 41,* 819–840.

Butcher, J. N., Graham, J. R., Dahlstrom, W. G., & Bowman, E. (1990). The MMPI–2 with college students. *Journal of Personality Assessment, 54,* 1–15.

Butcher, J. N., Graham, J. R., Williams, C. L., & Ben-Porath, Y. S. (1990). *Development and use of the MMPI–2 content scales.* Minneapolis: University of Minnesota Press.

Butcher, J. N., & Han, K. (1995). Development of an MMPI–2 scale to assess the presentation of self in a superlative manner: The S scale. In J. N. Butcher & C. D. Spielberger (Eds.), *Advances in personality assessment* (pp. 25–50). Hillsdale, NJ: Lawrence Erlbaum Associates, Inc.

Butcher, J. N., & Han, K. (1996). Methods of establishing cross-cultural equivalence. In J. N. Butcher (Ed.), *International adaptations of the MMPI–2: Research and clinical applications* (pp. 44–63). Minneapolis: University of Minnesota Press.

Butcher, J. N., Lim, J., & Nezami, E. (1998). Objective study of abnormal personality in cross-cultural settings: The Minnesota Multiphasic Personality Inventory (MMPI–2). *Journal of Cross-Cultural Psychology, 29,* 189–211.

Byron, D. M. (1995). *The relationship of cultural identification to depression and alcohol use among urban American Indians.* Unpublished doctoral dissertation, California School of Professional Psychology, San Diego.

Caldwell, A. B. (1991). Commentary on the Minnesota Multiphasic Personality Inventory–2: A review. *Journal of Counseling and Development, 69,* 568–569.

Caldwell, A. (1997). Whither goest our redoubtable mentor, the MMPI/MMPI–2? In J. A. Schinka & R. L. Greene (Eds.), *Emerging issues and methods in personality assessment* (pp. 47–68). Mahwah, NJ: Lawrence Erlbaum Associates, Inc.

Camara, W. J., Nathan, J. S., & Puente, A. E. (2000). Psychological test usage: Implications for professional psychology. *Professional Psychology: Research and Practice, 31,* 141–154.

Campbell, D. T., & Fiske, D. W. (1959). Convergent and discriminant validation by the multi-trait-multimethod matrix. *Psychological Bulletin, 56,* 81–105.

Campus, N. (1976). A measure of needs to assess the stimulus characteristics of TAT cards. *Journal of Personality Assessment, 40,* 248–258.

Carbonell, S. I. (2000). An assessment practice with Hispanics in Minnesota. In R. H. Dana (Ed.), *Handbook of cross-cultural and multicultural personality assessment* (pp. 547–572). Mahwah, NJ: Lawrence Erlbaum Associates, Inc.

Carillo, C. (1982). Changing norms of Hispanic families. In E. E. Jones & S. J. Korchin (Eds.), *Minority and mental health* (pp. 250–266). New York: Praeger.

Carter, R. T. (1991). Cultural values: A review of empirical research and implications for counseling. *Journal of Counseling & Development, 70,* 164–173.

Carter, R. T. (1995). *The influence of race and identity in psychotherapy: Toward a racially inclusive model.* New York: Wiley.

Case, L., & Smith, T. B. (2000). Ethnic representation in a sample of the literature of applied psychology. *Journal of Consulting and Clinical Psychology, 68,* 1107–1110.

Castillo, R. J. (1996). *Culture and mental illness: A client-centered approach.* Pacific Grove, CA: Brooks/Cole.

Cattell, R. B. (1943). The description of personality. II. Basic traits resolved into clusters. *Journal of Abnormal and Social Psychology, 37,* 476–507.

Celano, M. P., & Tyler, F. B. (1990). Behavioral acculturation among Vietnamese refugees in the United States. *Journal of Social Psychology, 131*, 373–385.

Census, Singapore Department of Statistics. (2000). *Singapore census of population 2000*. Retrieved, February 20, 2001, from http://www.singstat.gov.sg

Chen, C., Lee, S.-Y., & Stevenson, H. W. (1995). Response style and cross-cultural comparisons of rating scales among East Asian and North American students. *Psychological Science, 6*, 170–175.

Cheung, F. M., Leung, K., Fan, R. M., Song, W. Z., Zhang, J. X., & Zhang, J. P. (1996). Development of the Chinese personality assessment inventory. *Journal of Cross-Cultural Psychology, 27*, 181–199.

Cheung, F. M., & Song, W. Z. (1989). A review on the clinical applications of the Chinese MMPI. *Journal of Consulting and Clinical Psychology, 1*, 230–237.

Cheung, F. M., Song, W. Z., & Zhang, J. (1996). The Chinese MMPI–2: research and applications in Hong Kong and the Peoples Republic of China. In J. N. Butcher (Ed.), *International adaptations of the MMPI–2* (pp. 137–161). Minneapolis: University of Minnesota Press.

Cheung, G. K., & Snowden, L. R. (1990). Community mental health and ethnic minority populations. *Community Mental health Journal, 26*, 277–291.

Childs, R. A., & Eyde, L. D. (2002). Assessment training in clinical psychology doctoral programs: What should we teach? What do we teach? *Journal of Personality Assessment, 78*, 130–144.

Chilman, C. S. (1993). Hispanic families in the United States: Research perspectives. In H. P. McAdoo (Ed.), *Family ethnicity: Strength in diversity* (pp. 141–163). Newbury Park, CA: Sage

Choi, I., Nisbett, R. E., & Norenzayan, A. (1999). Causal attribution across cultures: Variation and universality. *Psychological Bulletin, 125*, 47–63.

Church, A. T. (2000). Culture and personality: Toward an integrated cultural trait psychology. *Journal of Personality, 68*, 651–703.

Church, A. T. (2001). Personality measurement in cultural perspective. *Journal of Personality, 69*, 979–1006.

Cimmarusti, R. A. (1996). Exploring aspects of Filipino-American families. *Journal of Marital and Family Therapy, 22*, 205–218.

Clark, A. J. (1995). Projective techniques in the counseling process. *Journal of Counseling and Development, 73*, 311–316.

Clark, J. H. (1954). The interpretation of MMPI profiles of college students: Mean scores for male and female groups. *Journal of Social & Clinical Psychology, 4*, 110–113.

Clark, R., Anderson, N. B., Clark, V. R., & Williams, D. R. (1999). Racism as a stressor for African Americans: A biopsychosocial model. *American Psychologist, 54*, 805–816.

Clemence, A. J., & Handler, L. (2001). Psychological assessment on internship: A survey of training directors and their expectations for students. *Journal of Personality Assessment, 76*, 18–47.

Cohen, R. (1979). *Culture, disease and stress among Latino immigrants*. Washington, DC: Smithsonian Institution.

Comas-Diaz, L. (1993). Hispanic-Latino communities: Psychological implications. In D. W. Atkinson, G. Morten, & D. W. Sue (Eds.), *Counseling American minorities: A cross-cultural perspective* (pp. 245–263). Madison, WI: Brown & Benchmark.

Comas-Diaz, L., & Jacobsen, F. M. (2001). Ethnocultural allodynia. *Journal of Psychotherapy Practice Research, 10*, 246–252.

Comer, P. E. (1965). *Initially test structured short-term psychotherapy in a college student counseling setting*. Unpublished doctoral dissertation, West Virginia University, Morgantown.

Comer, P. E. (1974, August). *Psychological feedback and involvement via a course in oneself*. Paper presented at the meeting of the American Psychological Association, New Orleans.

Constantine, M. G. (1998). Developing competence in multicultural assessment: Implications for counseling psychology training and practice. *The Counseling Psychologist, 26,* 922–929.

Constantine, M., & Ladany, N. (2001). New visions for defining and assessing multicultural counseling competence. In J. G. Ponterotto, J. M. Casas, L. A. Suzuki, & C. M. Alexander (Eds.), *Handbook of multicultural counseling* (2nd ed., pp. 482–498). Thousand Oaks, CA: Sage.

Copeland, E. H. (1983). Cross-cultural counseling and psychotherapy: A historical perspective, implications for research and training. *Personnel and Guidance Journal, 62,* 10–15.

Copeland, E. J. (1982). Minority populations and traditional counseling programs: Some alternatives. *Counselor Education and Supervision, 21,* 197–193.

Coss, N. S. (1999). *The incidence of false positives on the Rorschach and MMPI–2 in a sample of Greek-Americans.* Unpublished doctoral dissertation, California School of Professional Psychology, Fresno.

Costantino, G., Flanagan, R., & Malgady, R. (1995). The history of the Rorschach: Overcoming bias in multicultural projective assessment. *Rorschachiana, 20,* 148–171.

Costantino, G., Malgady, R. G., & Rogler, L. H. (1988). *TEMAS (Tell-Me-A-Story) manual.* Los Angeles: Western Psychological Services.

Costa, P. T., Jr., & McCrae, R. R. (1992). *Manual for the Revised NEO Personality Inventory (NEO–PI–R) and NEO Five Factor Inventory (NEO–FFI).* Odessa, FL: Psychological Assessment Resources.

Council of National Psychological Associations for the Advancement of Ethnic Minority Interests (CNPAAEMI). (2000). *Guidelines for research in ethnic minority communities.* Washington, DC: American Psychological Association.

Cousins, S. D. (1989). Culture and self-perception in Japan and the United States. *Journal of Personality and Social Psychology, 56,* 124–131.

Craddick, R. A. (1975). Sharing oneself in the assessment process. *Professional Psychology, 6,* 279–282.

Cronbach, L. J. (1946). Response sets and test validity. *Educational and Psychological Measurement, 6,* 475–494.

Cronbach, L. J. (1949). Statistical methods applied to Rorschach scores: A review. *Psychological Bulletin, 46,* 393–429.

Cronbach, L. J., & Meehl, P. E. (1955). Construct validity in psychological tests. *Psychological Bulletin, 52,* 281–302.

Cross, T. (1992). *Organizational self-study on cultural competence for agencies addressing child abuse and neglect.* Unpublished manuscript, People of Color Leadership Institute, Center for Child Protection and Family Support, Washington, DC.

Cross, T. L., Bazron, B. J., Dennis, K. W., & Issacs, M. R. (Eds.). (1989). *Toward a culturally competent system of care. Vol I. A monograph on effective services for minority children who are severely emotionally disturbed.* Washington, DC: Georgetown University, Child Development Center, Child and Adolescent Service System Program, Technical Assistance Center.

Cross, W. E., Jr., & Vandiver, B. J. (2001). Nigrescence theory and measurement: Introducing the Cross Racial Identity Scale (CRIS). In J. G. Ponterotto, J. M. Casas, L. A. Suzuki, & C. M. Alexander (Eds.), *Handbook of multicultural counseling* (2nd ed., pp. 371–393). Thousand Oaks, CA: Sage.

Crowne, D. P., & Marlowe, D. (1960). A new scale of social desirability independent of psychopathology. *Journal of Consulting Psychology, 24,* 349–354.

Cuellar, I. (1994). *The acculturation rating scale for Mexican Americans–II scoring and interpretive program* [Software program]. (Available from PC PSYCH, P.O. Box 3960, McAllen, TX 78502).

Cuellar, I. (2000). Acculturation as a moderator of personality and psychological assessment. In R. H. Dana (Ed.), *Handbook of cross-cultural and multicultural personality assessment* (pp. 113–129). Mahwah, NJ: Lawrence Erlbaum Associates, Inc.

Cuellar, I., Arnold, B., & Maldonado, R. (1995). Acculturation Rating Scale for Mexican Americans–II: A revision of the original ARSMA scale. *Hispanic Journal of Behavioral Sciences, 17,* 275–304.

Cuellar, I., Harris, I. C., & Jasso, R. (1980). An acculturation scale for Mexican American normal and clinical populations. *Hispanic Journal of Behavioral Sciences, 2,* 199–217.

Cuellar, I., & Paniagua, F. (2000). *Handbook of multicultural mental health: Assessment and treatment of diverse groups.* San Diego, CA: Academic.

Dahlstrom, W. G. (1980). Alterned versions of the MMPI. In W. G. Dahlstrom and L. Dahlstrom (Eds.), *Basic readings on the MMPI: A new selection on personality measurement* (pp. 386–392). Minneapolis: University of Minnesota Press.

Dahlstrom, W. G. (1992). Compatability of two-point high-point code patterns from original MMPI norms to MMPI–2 norms for the restandardization sample. *Journal of Personality Assessment, 59,* 153–164.

Dahlstrom, W. G., & Gynther, M. D. (1986). Previous MMPI research on Black Americans. In W. G. Dahlstrom, D. Lachar, & L. E. Dahlstrom (Eds.), *MMPI patterns of American minorities* (pp. 24–49). Minneapolis: University of Minnesota Press.

Dahlstrom, W. G., & Tellegen, A. (1993). *Manual supplement: Socioeconomic status and the MMPI–2. The relation of MMPI–2 patterns to levels of education and occupation.* Minneapolis: University of Minnesota Press.

Dana, R. H. (1955). Clinical diagnosis and objective TAT scoring. *Journal of Abnormal and Social Psychology, 50,* 19–24.

Dana, R. H. (1956). Selection of abbreviated TAT sets. *Journal of Clinical Psychology, 12,* 36–40.

Dana, R. H. (1959a). American culture and Chinese personality. *Psychological Newsletter, 10,* 314–321.

Dana, R. H. (1959b). Proposal for objective scoring of the TAT. *Perceptual and Motor Skills, 9,* 27–43.

Dana, R. H. (1962). The validation of projective tests. *Journal of Projective Techniques, 26,* 182–186.

Dana, R. H. (1966). Eisegesis and assessment. *Journal of Projective Techniques and Personality Assessment, 30,* 215–222.

Dana, R. H. (1968a). Six constructs to define Rorschach M. *Journal of Projective Techniques and Personality Assessment, 32,* 138–145.

Dana, R. H. (1968b). Thematic techniques and clinical practice. *Journal of Projective Techniques and Personality Assessment, 32,* 202–214.

Dana, R. H. (1970). A hierarchal model for analyzing personality data. *Journal of General Psychology, 82,* 199–206.

Dana, R. H. (Chair). (1974, August). *The client as collaborator in the assessment process.* Symposium conducted at the meeting of the American Psychological Association, New Orleans.

Dana, R. H. (1975). Ruminations on teaching projective assessment: An ideology, specific usages, teaching practices. *Journal of Personality Assessment, 39,* 563–572.

Dana, R. H. (1982). *A human science model for personality assessment with projective techniques.* Springfield, IL: Thomas.

Dana, R. H. (1984a). Megatrends in personality assessment: Toward a human science professional psychology. *Journal of Personality Assessment, 48,* 563–590.

Dana, R. H. (1984b). Personality assessment: Practice and teaching for the next decade. *Journal of Personality Assessment, 48,* 46–57.

Dana, R. H. (1985). A service-delivery paradigm for personality assessment. *Journal of Personality Assessment, 49,* 598–604.

Dana, R. H. (1986). The Thematic Apperception Test with adolescents. In A. I. Rabin (Ed.), *Projective techniques for children and adolescents* (pp. 14–36). New York: Springer.

Dana, R. H. (1992a). Assessment of cultural orientation. *SPA Exchange, 2*(2), 14–15.

Dana, R. H. (1992b). A commentary on assessment training in Boulder and Vail model programs. *The Journal of Training & Practice in Professional Psychology, 6*(2), 19–26.

Dana, R. H. (1993). *Multicultural assessment perspectives for professional psychology.* Boston: Allyn & Bacon.

Dana, R. H. (1994). Testing and assessment for all persons: Beginning and agenda. *Professional Psychology: Research and Practice, 25,* 349–354.

Dana, R. H. (1995). Culturally competent MMPI assessment of Hispanic populations. *Hispanic Journal of Behavioral Sciences, 17,* 305–319.

Dana, R. H. (1996a). Assessment of acculturation in Hispanic populations. *Hispanic Journal of Behavioral Sciences, 18,* 317–328.

Dana, R. H. (1996b). *Silk purse or sow's ear? An MMPI commonground.* Unpublished manuscript.

Dana, R. H. (1996c). The Thematic Apperception Test (TAT). In C. Newmark (Ed.), *Major psychological assessment instruments* (2nd ed., pp. 166–205). Boston: Allyn & Bacon.

Dana, R. H. (1997a). Multicultural assessment and cultural identity: An assessment-intervention model. *World Psychology, 3,* 121–142.

Dana, R. H. (1997b). Thematic apperceptive testing with children and adolescents in multicultural populations. In R. H. Dana (Chair), *Projective techniques with children and adolescents.* Symposium conducted at the Fourth European Conference on Psychological Assessment, Lisbon, Portugal.

Dana, R. H. (1998a). Multicultural assessment in the United States, 1997: Still art, not yet science, and controversial. *European Journal of Personality Assessment, 14,* 62–70.

Dana, R. H. (1998b). Personality and the cultural self: Emic and etic contexts as learning resources. In L. Handler & M. Hilsenroth (Eds.), *Teaching and learning personality assessment* (pp. 325–345). Hillsdale, NJ: Lawrence Erlbaum Associates, Inc.

Dana, R. H. (1998c). Problems with managed care for multicultural populations. *Psychological Reports, 83,* 283–294.

Dana, R. H. (1998d). Projective assessment of Latinos in the United States: Current realities, problems, and prospects. *Cultural Diversity and Mental Health, 4,* 165–184.

Dana, R. H. (1998e). *Understanding cultural identity in intervention and assessment.* Thousand Oaks, CA: Sage.

Dana. R. H. (1998f, February). *Using the TAT in cross-cultural/multicultural assessment.* Paper Presented at the midwinter meeting of the Society for Personality Assessment, Boston.

Dana, R. H. (1999a). Cross-cultural and multicultural use of the Thematic Apperception Test. In M. L. Gieser & M. I. Stein (Eds.), *Evocative images: The Thematic Apperception test and the art of projection* (pp. 177–190). Washington, DC: American Psychological Association.

Dana, R. H. (1999b). Psychological assessment in the diagnosis and treatment of ethnic group members. In J. F. Aponte & J. Wohl (Eds.), *Psychological intervention and cultural diversity* (2nd ed., pp. 59–74). Boston: Allyn & Bacon.

Dana, R. H. (2000a). An assessment-intervention model for research and practice with multicultural populations. In R. H. Dana (Ed.), *Handbook of cross-cultural and multicultural personality assessment* (pp. 5–16). Mahwah, NJ: Lawrence Erlbaum Associates, Inc.

Dana, R. H. (2000b). The cultural self as locus for assessment and intervention with American Indians/Alaska Natives. *Journal of Multicultural Counseling and Development, 28,* 66–82.

Dana, R. H. (2000c). Culture and methodology in personality assessment. In I. Cuellar & F. Paniagua (Eds.), *Handbook of multicultural mental health: Assessment and treatment of diverse groups* (pp. 97–120). San Diego, CA: Academic.

Dana, R. H. (Ed.). (2000d). *Handbook of cross-cultural and multicultural personality assessment.* Mahwah, NJ: Lawrence Erlbaum Associates, Inc.

Dana, R. H. (2000e). Multicultural assessment of adolescent and child personality and Psychopathology. In A. L. Comunian & U. P. Gielen (Eds.), *Human development in international perspective* (pp. 233–258). Lengerich, Germany: Pabst Science Publishers.

Dana, R. H. (2001a). Clinical diagnosis of multicultural populations in the United States. In L. Suzuki, J. Ponterotto, & P. Meller (Eds.), *The handbook of multicultural assessment* (2nd ed., pp. 101–131). San Francisco: Jossey-Bass.

Dana, R. H. (2001b). Multicultural issues in rehabilitation assessment. In B. Bolton (Ed.), *Handbook of measurement and evaluation in rehabilitation* (3rd ed., pp. 449–469). Gaithersburg, MD: Aspen.

Dana, R. H. (2002a). Examining the usefulness of *DSM–IV*. In K. Kurasaki, S. Okazaki, & S. Sue (Eds.), *Asian American mental health: Assessment, theories, and methods* (pp. 29–46). Dordrecht, The Netherlands: Kluwer Academic.

Dana, R. H. (2002b). *Manual for multicultural competence training: Preliminary version.* Unpublished manuscript.

Dana, R. H. (2002c). Mental health services for African Americans: A cultural/racial perspective. *Cultural Diversity and Ethnic Minority Psychology, 8,* 3–18.

Dana, R. H. (2002d). Symposium introduction: Teaching methods and competence evaluation. *Journal of Personality Assessment, 79,* 195–199.

Dana, R. H. (2003a). Assessment training, practice, and research in the new millennium: Challenges and opportunities for professional psychology. *Ethical Human Sciences and Services, 5,* 127–140.

Dana, R. H. (2003b). *Manual for multicultural competence training: Revised version.* Unpublished manuscript.

Dana, R. H. (2004). A report on myself: The science and/or art of assessment. *Journal of Personality Assessment, 82,* 245–256.

Dana, R. H. (in press-a). Embedding multicultural competencies in rehabilitation psychology practice. *APA Division 22 Newsletter.*

Dana, R. H. (in press-b). Using the TAT for assessment of multicultural populations. In S. R. Jenkins (Ed.), *A handbook of clinical scoring systems for the Thematic Apperceptive Techniques.* Mahwah, NJ: Lawrence Erlbaum Associates, Inc.

Dana, R. H., Aguilar-Kitibutr, A., Diaz-Vivar, N., & Vetter, H. (2002). A teaching method for multicultural assessment: Psychological report contents and cultural competence. *Journal of Personality Assessment, 79,* 207–215.

Dana, R. H., Aragon, M., & Kramer, T. (2002). Public sector mental health services for multicultural populations: Bridging the gap from research to clinical practice. In M. N. Smyth (Ed.), *Health care in transition* (Vol. 1, pp. 15–29). Hauppauge, NY: Nova Science Publishers.

Dana, R. H., & Back, B. R. (1983). The concurrent validity of child Rorschach interpretations. *Journal of Personality Assessment, 47,* 3–6.

Dana, R. H., Bonge, D., & Stauffacher, R. (1981). Personality dimensions in Rorschach reports: An empirical synthesis. *Perceptual and Motor Skills, 52,* 711–715.

Dana, R. H., & Cocking, R. (1968). Cue parameters, cue probabilities, and clinical judgment. *Journal of Clinical Psychology, 24,* 475–480.

Dana, R. H., Dana, J., & Comer, P. (1972). Role-playing effects on Rorschach scoring and interpretation. *Journal of Personality Assessment, 35,* 415.

Dana, R. H., Erdberg, P., & Walsh, P. J. (1978, March). *The joint feedback technique: A new model for the integration of assessment findings into the treatment process.* Workshop conducted at the meeting of the Society for Personality Assessment, Tampa, FL.

Dana, R. H., & Fitzgerald, J. (1976). Educational self-assessment: A course-in-oneself. *College Student Journal, 10,* 317–323.

Dana, R. H., & Fouke, H. P. (1979). Barnum statements in reports of psychological assessment. *Psychological Reports, 44,* 1215–1221.

Dana, R. H., & Handzlik, A. (1970). Clinical judgment as fantasied identification. *Psychological Reports, 26,* 437–438.

Dana, R. H., Hinman, S., & Bolton, B. (1977). Dimensions of examinee responses to the Rorschach: An empirical analysis. *Psychological Reports, 40,* 1147–1153.

Dana, R. H., & Krauter-Willcockson, N. (1980, April). *Rorschach training demystified: Multiple sources of feedback and interpretation adequacy.* Paper presented at the meeting of the Southwestern Psychological Association, Oklahoma City, OK.

Dana, R. H., & Leech, S. (1974). Existential assessment. *Journal of Personality Assessment, 38,* 428–435.

Dana, R. H., & May, W. T. (Eds.). (1987). *Internship training in professional psychology.* New York: Hemisphere.

D'Andrea, M., & Daniels, J. (2001). Expanding our thinking about White racism: Facing the challenge of multicultural counseling in the 21st century. In J. G. Ponterotto, J. M. Casas, L. A. Suzuki, & C. M. Alexander (Eds.), *Handbook of multicultural counseling* (2nd ed., pp. 289–310). Thousand Oaks, CA: Sage.

Daroglou, S. (2003). *Greeks and European Americans: A comparative study of interpersonal relatedness using the Rorschach.* Unpublished doctoral dissertation, California School of Professional Psychology (Alliant University), San Diego, CA.

Daroglou, S., & Viglione, D. J. (2002, March). *A Rorschach Comprehensive System sample from Greece.* Paper presented at the midwinter meeting of the Society for Personality Assessment, San Antonio, TX.

Davenport, B. I. (1952). The semantic validity of TAT interpretations. *Journal of Consulting Psychology, 16,* 171–175.

Davidson, A. R., Jaccard, J. J., Triandis, H. C., Morales, M. L., & Diaz-Guerrero, R. (1976). Cross-cultural model testing of the etic-emic dilemma. *International Journal of Psychology, 11,* 1–13.

DeLeon, P. H., & VandenBos, G. R. (2000). Reflecting and leading, progress in professional practice in psychology. *Professional Psychology: Research and Practice, 31,* 595–597.

Delgado, G. (1978). *Steps to and Ecology of Mind.* New York: Ballantine.

Delgado, P., Guerrero, G., Goggin, J. P., & Ellis, B. B. (1999). Self-assessment of linguistic skills of bilingual Hispanics. *Hispanic Journal of Behavioral Sciences, 21,* 31–46.

Delvecchio Good, M.-J., & Good, B. J. (2003). Introduction. Culture in the politics of mental health research. *Culture, Medicine and Psychiatry, 27,* 369–371.

De Vos, G., & Vaughn, C. A. (1992). The interpersonal self: A level of psychocultural analysis. In L. B. Boyer & R. M. Boyer (Eds.), *The psychoanalytic study of society* (pp. 95–142). Hillsdale, NJ: The Analytic Press.

Diaz-Guerrero, R., & Diaz-Loving, R. (1990). Interpretation in cross-cultural personality assessment. In C. R. Reynolds & R. W. Kamphaus (Eds.), *Handbook of psychological and educational assessment of children: Personality, behavior, and context* (pp. 491–523). New York: Guilford.

Dick, R. W., Beals, J., Keane, E. M., & Manson, S. M. (1994). Factorial structure of the CES-D among American Indian adolescents. *Journal of Adolescence, 17,* 73–79.

Doi, T. (1973). *The anatomy of dependence.* Toyko: Kodansha International.

Doi, T. (1990). The cultural assumptions of psychoanalysis. In J. W. Stigler, R. A. Shweder, & G. Herdt (Eds.), *Cultural psychology: Essays on comparative human development* (pp. 446–453). New York: Cambridge University Press.

Domino, G. (2000). *Psychological testing: An introduction.* Upper Saddle River, NJ: Prentice Hall.

Drasgow, F., & Hulin, C. I. (1987). Cross-cultural measurement. *Interamerican Journal of Psychology, 21,* 1–24.

Duckworth, J. C. (1991). The Minnesota Multiphasic Inventory–2: A review. *Journal of Counseling and Development, 69,* 564–567.

Dyche, L., & Zayas, L. H. (1995). The value of curiosity and naivete for the cross-cultural therapist. *Family Process, 34,* 389–394.

Edwards, A. L. (1954). *Manual for the Edwards Personal Preference Schedule.* New York: Psychological Corporation.

Ekman, P. (1993). Facial expressions and emotion. *American Psychologist, 48,* 384–392.

Ellenberger, H. (1954). The life and work of Hermann Rorschach (1884–1922). *Bulletin of the Menninger Clinic, 18,* 173–219.

Ephraim, D. (1996). *El metodo Rorschach en la actualidad* [The Rorschach method at the present time]. Caracas, Venezuela: Monte Avila Editores.

Ephraim, D. (2000a). Culturally relevant research and practice with the Rorschach Comprehensive System. In R. H. Dana (Ed.), *Handbook of cross-cultural and multicultural personality assessment* (pp. 303–327). Mahwah, NJ: Lawrence Erlbaum Associates, Inc.

Ephraim, D. (2000b). A psychocultural approach to TAT scoring and interpretation. In R. H. Dana (Ed.), *Handbook of cross-cultural and multicultural personality assessment* (pp. 427–445). Mahwah, NJ: Lawrence Erlbaum Associates, Inc.

Ephraim, D. (in press). A psychocultural system for clinical practice and research. In S. R. Jenkins (Ed.), *A handbook of clinical scoring systems for Thematic Apperceptive Tests.* Mahwah, NJ: Lawrence Erlbaum Associates, Inc.

Ephraim, D., Sochting, I., & Marcia, J. (1997). Cultural norms for TAT narratives in psychological practice and research: Illustrative studies. *Rorschachiana, 22,* 13–37.

Erdberg, P. (1979). A systematic approach to providing feedback from the MMPI. In C. S. Newmark (Ed.), *MMPI research and clinical trends* (pp. 328–342). New York: Praeger.

Erdberg, P., & Shaffer, T. W. (1999, July). *International symposium on Rorschach nonpatient data: Findings from around the World I, II, III.* Symposium presented at the XVIth Congress of the International Rorschach Society, Amsterdam, The Netherlands.

Eron, L. D. (1950). A normative study of the Thematic Apperception Test. *Psychological Monographs, 64*(9, Whole No. 315).

Eron, L. D. (1953). Responses of women to the Thematic Apperception Test. *Journal of Consulting Psychology, 17,* 269–282.

Eron, L. D., Terry, D., & Callahan, R. (1950). The use of rating scales for emotional tone of TAT stories. *Journal of Consulting Psychology, 14,* 473–478.

Espin, O. M. (1987). Psychological impact of migration on Latinas. *Psychology of Women Quarterly, 11,* 489–503.

Exner, J. E., Jr. (1969). *The Rorschach systems.* New York: Grune & Stratton.

Exner, J. E., Jr. (1974). *The Rorschach: A comprehensive system.* New York: Wiley.

Exner, J. E., Jr. (1978). *The Rorschach: A comprehensive system: Vol. 2. Current research and advanced interpretation.* New York: Wiley.

Exner, J. E., Jr. (1993). *The Rorschach: A comprehensive system: Vol. 1. Basic foundations* (3rd ed.). New York: Wiley.

Exner, J. E., Jr. (2000). *Rorschach Workbook for the Comprehensive System.* (5th ed.). Asheville, NC: Rorschach Workshops.

Exner, J. E., Jr. (2002). A new nonpatient sample for the Rorschach Comprehensive System: A progress report. *Journal of Personality Assessment, 78,* 391–404.

Exner, J. E., Jr. (2003). *The Rorschach: A Comprehensive System: Vol. 1. Basic foundations and current research* (4th ed.). New York: Wiley.

Exner, J. G., & Weiner, I. B. (2001). *Rorschach Interpretation Assistance Program.* Odessa, FL: Psychological Assessment Resources.

Eysenck, H. J., & Eysenck, S. B. G. (1982). Culture and personality abnormalities. In I. Al-Issa (Ed.), *Culture and psychopathology* (pp. 277–308). Baltimore: University Park Press.

Falicov, C. (1982). Mexican Families. In M. McGoldrick, J. K. Pearce, & J. Giordano (Eds.), *Ethnicity and family therapy* (pp. 134–163). New York: Guilford.

Fantoni-Salvador, P., & Rogers, R. (1997). Spanish versions of the MMPI–2 and PAI: An investigation of concurrent validity with Hispanic patients. *Assessment, 4,* 29–39.

Fernandez-Ballesteros, R., De Bruyn, E. E. J., Godoy, A., Hornke, L. F., Laak, J. Ter, Vizcarro, C., Westhoff, K., Westmeyer, H., & Zaccagnini, J. L. (2001). Guidelines for the assessment process (GAP): A proposal for discussion. *European Journal of Psychological Assessment, 17,* 187–2000.

Finn, S. E. (1996a). Assessment feedback integrating MMPI–2 and Rorschach findings. *Journal of Personality Assessment, 67,* 543–557.

Finn, S. E. (1996b). *Manual for using the MMPI–2 as a therapeutic intervention.* Minneapolis: University of Minnesota Press.

Finn, S. E. (1996c). *Using the MMPI–2 as a therapeutic intervention.* Minneapolis: University of Minnesota Press.

Finn, S. E. (1998). Teaching therapeutic assessment in a required graduate course. In L. Handler & M. J. Hilsenroth (Eds.), *Teaching and learning personality assessment* (pp. 359–373). Mahwah, NJ: Lawrence Erlbaum Associates, Inc.

Finn, S. E., & Martin, H. (1997). Therapeutic assessment with the MMPI–2 in managed health care. In J. N. Butcher (Ed.), *Objective psychological assessment in managed health care: A practitioner's guide* (pp. 131–152). New York: Oxford University Press.

Finn, S. E., & Tonsager, M. E. (1992). Therapeutic effects of providing MMPI–2 test feedback to college students awaiting therapy. *Psychological Assessment, 4,* 278–287.

Fischer, C. T. (1986). *Individualizing psychological assessment.* Monterey, CA: Brooks/Cole.

Fones, C. S. L., Kua, E. H., Ng, T. P., & Ko, S. M. (1998). Studying the mental health of a nation: A preliminary report on a population survey in Singapore. *Singapore Medical Journal, 39,* 251–255.

Foon, A. E. (1985). Similarity between therapists' and clients' locus of control: Implications for therapeutic expectations and outcome. *Psychotherapy, 22,* 711–717.

Frank, G. (1992). The response of African Americans to the Rorschach: A review of the literature. *Journal of Personality Assessment, 59,* 317–325.

Frank, G. (1993). The use of the Rorschach with Hispanic Americans. *Psychological Reports, 72,* 276–278.

Franklin, K. W., & Cornell, O. G. (1997). Rorschach interpretation with high-ability females: Psychopathology or creative thinking? *Journal of Personality Assessment, 68,* 184–196.

French, L. (1989). Native American alcoholism: A transcultural counseling perspective. *Counseling Psychology Quarterly, 2,* 153–166.

Friedman, A. F., Lewak, R., Nichols, D. S., & Webb, J. T. (2001). *Psychological assessment with the MMPI–2.* Mahwah, NJ: Lawrence Erlbaum Associates, Inc.

Fuchs, M., & Bashshur, R. (1975). Use of traditional medicine among urban Native Americans. *Medical Care, 13,* 915–917.

Fujii, J. S., Fukushima, S. N., & Yamamoto, J. (1993). Psychiatric care of Japanese Americans. In A. C. Gaw (Ed.), *Culture, ethnicity, and mental illness* (pp. 305–345). Washington, DC: American Psychiatric Press.

REFERENCES 291

Fukuyama, M. A., & Sevig, T. D. (1999). *Integrating spirituality into multicultural counseling.* Thousand Oaks, CA: Sage.
Fuster, J. (1993). Por que T o no T, en el Rorschach? [Why T or no T in Rorschach?]. *Revista de la Sociedad Espanola del Rorschach y Metodos Proyectivos, 6,* 39–44.
Gamst, G., Dana, R. H., Der-Karabetian, A., Aragon, M., Arellano, L., & Kramer, T. (2002). Effects of Latino acculturation and ethnic identity on mental health outcomes. *Hispanic Journal of Behavioral Sciences, 24,* 479–504.
Gamst, G., Dana, R. H., Der-Karabetian, A., Aragon, M., Arellano, L., Morrow, G., & Martenson, L. (2004). Cultural competency revised: The California Brief Multicultural Competence Scale. *Measurement and Evaluation in Counseling and Development, 37,* 165–188.
Gamst, G., Dana, R. H., Der-Karabetian, A., & Kramer, T. (2000). Ethnic match and client ethnicity effects on global assessment and visitation. *Journal of Community Psychology, 28,* 547–564.
Gamst, G., Dana, R. H., Der-Karabetian, A., & Kramer, T. (2001). Asian American mental health clients: Cultural responsiveness and global assessment. *Journal of Mental Health Counseling, 23,* 57–71.
Gamst, G., Dana, R. H., Der-Karabetian, A., & Kramer, T. (2004). Ethnic match and treatment outcomes for child and adolescent mental health center clients. *Journal of Counseling and Development, 82,* 329–337.
Garb, H. N., Wood, J. M., Lilienfeld, S. O., & Nezworski, M. T. (2002). Effective use of projective techniques in clinical practice: Let the data help with the interpretation. *Professional Psychology: Research and Practice, 33,* 454–463.
Geiger, I., & Ponterotto, J. G. (1995). A framework for assessment in multicultural counseling. In J. G. Ponterotto, J. M. Casas, L. A. Suzuki, & C. M. Alexander (Eds.), *Handbook of multicultural counseling* (pp. 357–374). Thousand Oaks, CA: Sage.
Geisinger, K. F. (1988). Psychometric issues in test interpretation. In J. Sandoval, C. L. Frisby, K. L. Geisinger, J. D. Scheuneman, & J. R. Garcia. (Eds.), *Test interpretation and diversity: Achieving equity in assessment* (pp. 17–30). Washington, DC: American Psychological Association.
Geisinger, K. F. (1994). Cross-cultural normative assessment: Translation and adaptation issues influencing the normative interpretation of assessment instruments. *Psychological Assessment, 6,* 304–312.
Georgas, J. (1989). Changing family values in Greece: From collectivist to individualist. *Journal of Cross-Cultural Psychology, 20,* 80–91.
Georgas, J. (1991). Intrafamily acculturation of values in Greece. *Journal of Cross-Cultural Psychology, 22,* 445–457.
Georgas, J., Berry, J. W., Shaw, A., Christakopoulou, S., & Mylonas, K. (1996). Acculturation of Greek family values. *Journal of Cross-Cultural Psychology, 27,* 329–338.
Georgas, J., Christakopoulou, S., Poortinga, Y. H., Angleitner, A., Goodwin, R., & Charalambous, N. (1997). The relationship of family bonds to family structure and function across cultures. *Journal of Cross-Cultural Psychology, 28,* 303–320.
Georgas, J. G., & Vassiliou, V. (1967). A normative Rorschach study of Athenians. *Journal of Projective Techniques and Personality Assessment, 31*(4), 31–38.
Georgas, J. G., Vassiliou, V., & Katakis, H. (1971). The verbal intelligence of Athenians. *Journal of Social Psychology, 83,* 165–173.
Gibbs, J. T. (1985). Treatment relationships with black clients: Interpersonal vs. instrumental strategies. *Advances in Clinical Social Work.* Silver Spring, MD: National Association of Social Workers.
Gilbert, D., & Kahl, J. A. (1987). *The American class structure: A new synthesis.* Chicago: Dorsey.
Glazer, N., & Moynihan, D. P. (1976). Introduction. In D. Glazer & D. P. Moynihan (Eds.), *Ethnicity: Theory and experience* (pp. 1–26). Cambridge, MA: Harvard University Press.

Gloria, A. M., & Peregoy, J. J. (1996). Counseling Latino alcohol and other substance users/abusers: Cultural considerations. *Journal of Substance Abuse Treatment, 13,* 119–126.

Gomez-Maqueo, E. L., & Reyes-Lagunes, I. (1994). New version of the Minnesota Multiphasic Personality Inventory (MMPI–2) for Mexican college students. *Revista Mexicana de Psicologia, 11,* 45–54.

Gopinathan, S., Pakir, A., Kam, H. W., & Saravanan, V. (1998). *Language, society and education in Singapore* (2nd ed.). Singapore: Times Academic Press.

Gowri, A. (1999). *Cultural difference or deficit? Rorschach responses of Asian Indians and European Americans.* Unpublished doctoral dissertation, California School of Professional Psychology, San Diego.

Greene, R. L. (1987). Ethnicity and MMPI performance: A review. *Journal of Consulting and Clinical Psychology, 55,* 497–512.

Grimm, S. D., & Church, T. (1999). A cross-cultural study of response biases in Personality measures. *Journal of Research in Personality, 33,* 415–441.

Groth-Marnat, G. (2003). *Handbook of psychological assessment* (4th ed.). New York: Wiley.

Gurin, P., Gurin, G., Lao, R., & Beattie, M. (1969). Internal-external control in the motivational dynamics of Negro youth. *Journal of Social Issues, 3,* 29–53.

Guzman, L. P. (1993). Guidelines for treating ethnic minority clients. *Independent Practitioner, 13*(1), 22–25.

Hall, C. C. I. (1997). Cultural malpractice: The growing obsolescence of psychology with the changing U.S. population. *American Psychologist, 32,* 642–651.

Hall, G. C. N., Bansal, A., & Lopez, I. R. (1999). Ethnicity and psychopathology: A meta-analytic review of 31 years of comparative MMPI/MMPI–2 research. *Psychological Assessment, 11,* 186–197.

Hall, G. C. N., & Maramba, G. G. (2001). In search of cultural diversity: Recent literature in cross-cultural and ethnic minority psychology. *Cultural Diversity and Ethnic Minority Psychology, 7,* 12–26.

Hall, G. C. N., & Barongan, C. (2002). *Multicultural psychology.* Upper Saddle River, NJ: Pearson.

Hallowell, A. H. (1941). The Rorschach method as an aid in the study of personality in primitive societies. *Character and Personality, 9,* 235–245.

Hallowell, A. H. (1945). The Rorschach technique in the study of personality and culture. *American Anthropologist, 47,* 195–210.

Hammond, K. R., & Allen, J. M. (1953). *Writing psychological reports.* Englewood Cliffs, NJ: Prentice Hall.

Handel, R. W., & Ben-Porath, Y. S. (2000). Multicultural assessment with the MMPI–2: Issues for research and practice. In R. H. Dana (Ed.), *Handbook of cross-cultural and multicultural personality assessment* (pp. 229–245). Mahwah, NJ: Lawrence Erlbaum Associates, Inc.

Handler, L., & Potash, H. M. (1999). Assessment of psychological health: Optimism, creativity, playfulness, and transitional relatedness. *Journal of Personality Assessment, 72,* 181–184.

Haritos-Fatouros, M. (1963). *A study of the WISC applied to Greek school-children.* Unpublished master's thesis, University of London, London, England.

Harkness, A. R. (2002). Theory and measurement of personality traits. In J. N. Butcher (Ed.), *Clinical personality assessment* (pp. 24–39). New York: Oxford University Press.

Harrell, S. (1991). Pluralism, performance, and meaning in Taiwanese healing: A case study. *Culture, Medicine, & Psychiatry, 15,* 45–68.

Harris, M. (1976). History and significance of the emic/etic distinction. *Annual Review of Anthropology, 5,* 329–350.

Harris, R. E., & Lingoes, J. C. (1955, 1968). *Subscales for the MMPI: An aid to profile interpretation* [Mimeographed materials]. Department of Psychiatry, University of California at San Francisco.

Hathaway, S. R., & McKinley, J. C. (1940). A multiphasic personality schedule (Minnesota): 1. Construction of the schedule. *The Journal of Psychology, 10*, 249–254.

Hathaway, S. R., & McKinley, J. C. (1943). *The Minnesota Multiphasic Personality Inventory.* Minneapolis: University of Minnesota Press.

Hathaway, S., & McKinley, J. C. (1989). *Minnesota Multiphasic Personality Inventory (MMPI–2).* Columbus, OH: Merrill/Prentice Hall.

Hays, P. A. (2001). *Addressing cultural complexities in practice: A framework for clinicians and counselors.* Washington, DC: American Psychological Association.

Heilbrun, A. B., Jr. (1977). The influence of defensive styles upon the predictive validity of the Thematic Apperception Test. *Journal of Personality Assessment, 41*, 486–491.

Helmes, E., & Redden, J. R. (1993). A perspective on developments in assessing psychopathology: A critical review of the MMPI and MMPI–2. *Psychological Review, 113*, 453–471.

Helms, J. E. (1990). *Black and White racial identity: Theory, research, and practice.* Westfort, CT: Praeger.

Helms, J. E. (1992). Why is there no study of cultural equivalence in standardized cognitive ability testing? *American Psychologist, 47*, 1083–1101.

Henry, J. (1941). Rorschach technique in primitive cultures. *American Journal of Orthopsychiatry, 11*, 230–234.

Herkov, M. J., Gordon, R. A., Gynther, M. D., & Greer, R. A. (1994). Perception of MMPI item subtlety: Influences of age and ethnicity. *Journal of Personality Assessment, 62*, 9–16.

Herring, R. D. (1990). Nonverbal communication: A necessary component of cross-cultural counseling. *Journal of Multicultural Counseling and Development, 18*, 172–179.

Hersen, M. (Ed.). (2003). *Comprehensive handbook of psychological assessment.* Hoboken, NJ: Wiley.

Hertz, M. R. (1943). Personality patterns in adolescence as portrayed by the Rorschach inkblot method: III. The "Erlebinstypus." (A normative study). *Journal of General Psychology, 28*, 225–276.

Herzberg, E. (2000). Use of the TAT in multicultural societies: Brazil and the United States. In R. H. Dana (Ed.), *Handbook of cross-cultural and multicultural personality assessment* (pp. 447–464). Mahwah, NJ: Lawrence Erlbaum Associates, Inc.

Ho, M. K. (1987). *Family therapy with ethnic minorities.* Beverly Hills, CA: Sage.

Hoffmann, T., Dana, R. H., & Bolton, B. (1985). Measured acculturation and MMPI–168 performance of Native Americans adults. *Journal of Cross-Cultural Psychology, 16*, 243–256.

Hofstede, G. (1980). *Culture's consequences. International differences in work-related values.* Newbury Park, CA: Sage.

Holden, R. R. (1996). *Holden Psychological Screening Inventory (HPSI).* North Tonawanda, NY: Multi-Health Systems.

Holden, R. R. (2000). Are there promising MMPI substitutes for assessing psychopathology and personality? Review and prospect. In R. H. Dana (Ed.), *Handbook of cross-cultural and multicultural personality assessment* (pp. 267–292). Mahwah, NJ: Lawrence Erlbaum Associates, Inc.

Holmes, D. S. (1974). The conscious control of thematic projection. *Journal of Consulting and Clinical Psychology, 42*, 323–329.

Holt, R. E. (1978). A normative guide to the use of the TAT cards. In R. E. Holt (Ed.), *Methods in clinical psychology. Vol. 1. Projective assessment.* New York: Plenum.

Holtzman, W. H., Thorpe, J. S., Swartz, J. D., & Herron, E. W. (1961). *Inkblot perception and personality.* Austin: University of Texas Press.

Hong, G. K., Garcia, M., & Soriano, M. (2000). Responding to the challenge: Preparing mental health professionals for the new millennium. In I. Cuellar & F. A. Paniagua (Eds.), *Handbook of multicultural mental health: Assessment and treatment of diverse populations* (pp. 455–476). San Diego, CA: Academic.

Hornby, R. (1993). *Competency training for human service providers*. Mission, SD: Sinte Gleska Press.

Howard, G. S. (1991). Culture tales: A narrative approach to thinking, cross-cultural psychology, and psychotherapy. *American Psychologist, 46*, 187–197.

Huber, J. T. (1961). *Report writing in psychology and psychiatry*. New York: Harper.

Huff, R. M., & Kline, M. V. (1999). The cultural assessment framework. In R. M. Huff & M. V. Kline (Eds.), *Promoting health in multicultural populations: A handbook for practitioners* (pp. 481–499). Thousand Oaks, CA: Sage.

Hughes, C. C., & Wintrob, R. M. (1995). Culture-bound syndromes and the cultural context of clinical psychiatry. In J. M. Oldham & M. B. Riba (Eds.), *Review of psychiatry* (Vol. 14, pp. 565–597). Washington, DC: American Psychiatric Press.

Hui, C. H. (1988). Measurement of individualism-collectivism. *Journal of Research in Personality, 22*, 17–36.

Hui, C. H., & Triandis, H. C. (1989). Effects of culture and response format on extreme response style. *Journal of Cross-Cultural Psychology, 20*, 296–309.

Hui, C. H., & Yee, C. (1994). The shortened Individualism–Collectivism Scale: Its relationship to demographic and work-related variables. *Journal of Research in Personality, 28*, 409–424.

Humphrey, D. H., & Dahlstrom, W. G. (1995). The impact of changing from the MMPI to the MMPI-2 on profile configuration. *Journal of Personality Assessment, 64*, 428–439.

Ibrahim, F. A. (1985). Effective cross-cultural counseling and psychotherapy. *The Counseling Psychologist, 13*, 625–638.

Ibrahim, F. A., & Kahn, H. (1987). Assessment of worldviews. *Psychological Reports, 60*, 163–176.

Ibrahim, F., Ohnishi, H., & Sandhu, D. S. (1997). Asian American identity development: A culture-specific model for South Asian Americans. *Journal of Multicultural Counseling and Development, 25*, 34–50.

Ibrahim, F. A., Roysircar-Sodowsky, G., & Ohnishi, H. (2001). Worldview: Recent developments and needed directions. In J. G. Ponterotto, J. M. Casas, L. A. Suzuki, & C. M. Alexander (Eds.), *Handbook of multicultural counseling* (2nd ed., pp. 425–456). Thousand Oaks, CA: Sage.

Irvine, S. H., & Carroll, W. K. (1980). Testing and assessment scores across cultures: Issues in methodology and assessment. In H. C. Triandis & J. W. Berry (Eds.), *Handbook of cross-cultural psychology: Methodology* (Vol. 2, pp. 181–244). Boston: Allyn & Bacon.

Institute of Mental Health. (1998). *Woodbridge Hospital Annual Report*. Singapore: Author.

Isaacs-Shockley, M., Cross, T., Bazron, B. J., Dennis, K., & Benjamin, M. P. (1996). Framework for a culturally competent system of care. In B. A. Stroul (Ed.), *Children's mental health: Creating systems of care in a changing society* (pp. 23–40). Baltimore: Brookes.

Ivey, A. E., & Leppaluoto, J. R. (1975). Changes ahead! Implications of the Vail conference. *Personnel and Guidance Journal, 53*, 747–752.

Jackson, D. N. (1997). *The Basic Personality Inventory*. Port Huron, MI: Sigma Assessment Systems.

Jackson, L. C. (1999). Ethnocultural resistance to multicultural training: Students and faculty. *Cultural Diversity and Ethnic Minority Psychology, 5*, 27–36.

Jensen, L. C., McGhie, A. P., & Jensen, J. R. (1991). Do men's and women's worldviews differ? *Psychological Reports, 68*, 312–314.

John, O. P. (1990). The search for basic dimensions of personality: A review and critique. In P. McReynolds, J. C. Rosen, & G. J. Chelune (Eds.), *Advances in psychological assessment* (Vol. 7, pp. 1–36). New York: Plenum.

Johnson, M. E., & Lashley, K. H. (1989). Influence of Native Americans' cultural commitment on preferences for counselor ethnicity and expectations about counseling. *Journal of Multicultural Counseling and Development, 17*, 115–122.

Jones, R. (1996). *Handbook of tests and measurements for black populations* (Vols. 1–2). Hampton, VA: Cobb & Henry.

Joseph, A., & Murray, V. (1951). *Chamorro and Carolinians of Saipan.* Cambridge, MA: Harvard University Press.

Josephs, I. (1955). The problems of emotions from the perspective of psychological semantics. *Culture and Psychology, 1,* 279–288.

Kadri, Z. N. (1971). The use of the MMPI for personality study of Singapore students. *Journal of Social Clinical Psychology, 10,* 90–91.

Kalla, O., Wahlstrom, J., Aaltonen, J., Holma, J., Tuimala, P., & Mattlar, C.-E. (2004). Rorschach characteristics and comparison of first-episode psychotic patients in Finland and Spain. *Rorschachiana, 26,* 63–84.

Kamphaus, R. W., & Frick, P. (2002). *Clinical assessment of child and adolescent personality and behavior* (2nd ed.). Boston: Allyn & Bacon.

Kaplan, B. (1955). Reflections of the acculturation process in the Rorschach test. *Journal of Projective Techniques, 19,* 30–35.

Kaplan, B., & Lawless, R. (1965). Culture and visual imagery: A comparison of Rorschach responses in eleven societies. In M. E. Spiro (Ed.), *Context and meaning in cultural anthropology* (pp. 295–311). New York: Free Press.

Kazarian, S. S., & Evans, D. B. (1998). Cultural clinical psychology. In S. S. Kazarian & D. R. Evans (Eds.), *Cultural clinical psychology: Theory, research, and practice* (pp. 1–38). New York: Oxford University Press.

Kearney, M. (1975). Worldview theory and study. In B. J. Siegal (Ed.), *Annual review of psychology* (Vol. 4, pp. 247–270). Palo Alto, CA: Annual Reviews.

Keating, C. F. (1994). World without words: Messages from face and body. In W. J. Lonner & R. S. Malpass (Eds.), *Psychology and culture* (pp. 175–182). Boston: Allyn & Bacon.

Keitel, M. A., Kopala, M., & Adamson, W. S. (1995). Ethical issues in multicultural assessment. In L. A. Suzuki, P. J. Meller, & J. G. Ponterotto (Eds.), *Handbook of multicultural assessment: Clinical, psychological, and educational applications* (pp. 29–48). San Francisco: Jossey-Bass.

Kenny, D. T., & Bijou, S. W. (1953). Ambiguity of pictures and extent of personality factors in fantasy responses. *Journal of Consulting Psychology, 17,* 283–288.

Kim, B. S. K., & Abreu, J. M. (2001). Acculturation measurement: Theory, current instruments, and future directions. In J. G. Ponterotto, J. M. Casas, L. A. Suzuki, & C. M. Alexander (Eds.), *Handbook of multicultural counseling* (2nd ed., pp. 394–424). Thousand Oaks, CA: Sage.

Kim, B. S. K., Atkinson, D. R., & Yang, P. H. (1999). The Asian Values Scale: Development, factor analysis, validation, and reliability. *Journal of Counseling Psychology, 46,* 342–352.

Kim, U., & Berry, J. W. (1985). Acculturation attitudes of Korean immigrants in Toronto. In I. R. Lagunes & Y. H. Poortinga (Eds.), *From a different perspective: Studies of behavior across cultures* (pp. 93–105). Berwyn, PA: Swets North America.

Kim, U., & Berry, J. W. (Eds.). (1993). *Indigenous psychologies: Research and experience in cultural context.* Newbury Park, CA: Sage.

Kimble, G. A. (1984). Psychology's two cultures. *American Psychologist, 39,* 833–839.

Kleinberg, O. (1938). Emotional expression in Chinese literature. *Journal of Abnormal and Social Psychology, 3,* 517–520.

Kleinman, A. M. (1977). Depression, somatization, and the new cross-cultural psychiatry. *Social Science and Medicine, 11,* 3–10.

Kleinman, A. (1986). *Social origins of distress and disease.* New Haven, CT: Yale University Press.

Kleinman, A. (1988). *Rethinking psychiatry.* New York: Macmillian.

Klopfer, B., & Kelley, D. M. (1941). *The Rorschach technique.* Yonkers, NY: World Book.

Klopfer, W. G. (1960). *The psychological report: Use and communication of psychological fundings.* New York: Grune & Stratton.

Klopfer, W. G. (1983). Writing psychological reports. In C. W. Walker (Ed.), *The handbook of clinical psychology: Theory, research, and practice* (pp. 501–527). Homewood, IL: Dow Jones-Irwin.

Kluckhohn, F. R. (1960). A method for eliciting value orientations. *Anthropological Linguistics, 2*(2), 1–23.

Kluckhohn, F. R., & Strodtbeck, F. L. (1961). *Variations in value orientations.* Evanston, IL: Row Peterson.

Knapp. S., & VandeCreek, L. (2003). An overview of the major changes in the 2002 APA Ethics Code. *Professional Psychology: Research and Practice, 34,* 301–308.

Knopf, H. M. (Ed.). (1986). *The assessment of child and adolescent personality.* New York: Guilford.

Kohatsu, E. L., & Richardson, T. Q. (1996). Racial and ethnic identity assessment. In L. A. Suzuki, P. J. Meller, & J. G. Ponterotto (Eds.), *Handbook of multicultural assessment: Clinical, psychological, and educational applications* (pp. 611–650). San Francisco: Jossey-Bass.

Kokkevi, A. (1996). The Greek MMPI-2: A progress note. In J. N. Butcher (Ed.), *International adaptations of the MMPI-2* (pp. 442–447). Minneapolis: University of Minnesota Press.

Koss-Chioino, J. (1989). *Women as healers, women as patients: Mental health care and traditional healing in Puerto Rico.* Boulder, CO: Westview.

Kuhn, M. H., & McPartland, T. S. (1954). An empirical investigation of self-attitudes. *American Sociological Review, 19,* 68–76.

Kumar, S. K. K. (1986). Are Indians trans-personal in locus of control belief? *Indian Journal of Behaviour, 10*(4), 25–31.

Kurasaki, K. S. (1999). A racial identity framework for understanding psychological problems and guiding treatment among Asian and Pacific Islander Americans. In D. S. Sandhu (Ed.), *Asian and Pacific Islander Americans: Issues and concerns for counseling and psychotherapy* (pp. 91–104). Commack, NY: Nova Science Publishers.

Kwan, K.-L. K. (1999). Assessment of Asian Americans in counseling: Evolving issues and concerns. In D. S. Sandhu (Ed.), *Asian and Pacific Islander Americans: Issues and Concerns for Counseling and Psychotherapy* (pp. 229–249). Commack, NY: Nova Science Publishers.

Kwan, K.-L. K. (2000). The internal-external ethnic identity measure: Factor-analytic structures based on a sample of Chinese Americans. *Educational and Psychological Measurement, 60,* 142–152.

Kwan, K.-L. K., & Sodowsky, G. R. (1997). Internal and external ethnic identity and their correlates: A study of Chinese American immigrants. *Journal of Multicultural Counseling and Development, 25,* 51–67.

Kwang, W.-C., Chen, C.-A., Kurasaki, K., Mak, W., & Takeuchi, D. T. (2000). Factor validity of scores on a social support and conflict measure among Chinese Americans. *Educational and Psychological Measurement, 90,* 308–316.

LaFromboise, T. D., Foster, S. L. (1992). Cross-cultural training: Scientist-practitioner model and methods. *The Counseling Psychologist, 20,* 472–489.

LaFromboise, T. D., Trimble, J. E., & Mohatt, G. V. (1990). Counseling intervention and American Indian tradition: An integrative approach. *The Counseling Psychologist, 18,* 628–654.

Lai, W. M. E., & Sodowsky, G. R. (1996). Acculturation instrumentation. In G. R. Sodowsky & J. C. Impara (Eds.), *Multicultural assessment in counseling and clinical psychology* (pp. 347–354). Lincoln, NE: Buros Institute of Mental Measurements.

Lambert, W. E. (1955). Measurement of the linguistic dominance of bilinguals. *Journal of Abnormal and Social Psychology, 50,* 197–200.

Landrine, H., & Klonoff, E. A. (1994). The African American Acculturation Scale: Development, reliability, and validity. *Journal of Black Psychology, 20,* 104–127.

Lantz, H. (1948). Rorschach testing in preliterate cultures. *American Journal of Orthopsychiatry, 18,* 287–291.

La Roche, M. J., & Turner, C. (2002). At the crossroads: Managed mental health care, the ethics code, and ethnic minorities. *Cultural Diversity and Ethnic Minority Psychology, 8,* 187–198.

Lassiter, S. M. (1995). *Multicultural clients: A handbook for health care providers and social workers.* Westport, CT: Greenwood.

Lassiter, S. M. (1998). *Cultures of color in America: A guide to family, religion, and health.* Westport, CT: Greenwood.

Lee, E. (1982). A social systems approach to assessment and treatment for Chinese American families. In M. McGoldrick, J. K. Pearce, & J. Giordino (Eds.), *Ethnicity and family therapy* (pp. 527–551). New York: Guilford.

Lee, R. M., Choe, J., Kim, G., & Ngo, V. (2000). Construction of the Asian American Family Conflicts Scale. *Journal of Counseling Psychology, 47,* 211–222.

Lefcourt, H. M. (1966). Repression-sensitization: A measure of the evaluation of emotional responses. *Journal of Consulting Psychology, 36,* 444–449.

Leong, F. T. L., & Lau, A. S. I. (2001). Barriers to providing effective mental health services to Asian Americans. *Mental Health Services Research, 3,* 201–214.

Lerner, P. M. (1995). Assessing adaptive capacities by means of the Rorschach. In J. M. Butcher (Ed.), *Clinical personality assessment: Practical approaches* (pp. 317–325). New York: Oxford University Press.

Lerner, P. M. (2002, March). *Witch hunts, straw men, and the Rorschach.* Paper presented at the Society for Personality Assessment midwinter meeting, San Antonio, TX.

Levine, F. M., Sandeen, E., & Murphy, C. M. (1992). The therapist's dilemma: Using nomothetic information to answer idiographic questions. *Psychotherapy, 29,* 410–415.

Lewis-Fernandez, R., & Kleinman, A. (1994). Culture, personality, and psychopathology. *Journal of Abnormal Psychology, 103,* 67–71.

Lightsley, O. R., Jr., & Christopher, J. C. (1997). Stress buffers and dysphoria in a non-Western population. *Journal of Counseling & Development, 75,* 451–459.

Lilienfeld, S. O., Wood, J. M., & Garb, H. N. (2001, May). What's wrong with this picture? *Scientific American,* 81–87.

Lindzey, G. (1952). Thematic Apperception Test: Interpretive assumptions and related empirical evidence. *Psychological Bulletin, 49,* 1–25.

Lindzey, G. (1954). *Projective techniques and cross-cultural research.* New York: Appleton-Century-Crofts.

Lindzey, G. (1961). *Projective techniques and cross-cultural research.* New York: Appleton-Century-Crofts.

Linton, R. A. (Ed.). (1940). *Acculturation in seven American Indian tribes.* New York: D. Appleton-Century.

Lipson, J. G., Dibble, S. L., & Minarik, P. A. (1996). *Culture and nursing care: A pocket guide.* San Francisco: University of California San Francisco Nursing Press.

Locke, D. C. (1998). *Increasing multicultural understanding* (2nd ed.). Newbury Park, CA: Sage.

Loevinger, J. (1957). Objective tests as instruments of psychological theory. *Psychological Reports, 3,* 635–694

Lohr, J. M., Fowler, K. A., & Lilienfeld, S. O. (2002). The dissemination and promotion of pseudoscience in clinical psychology: The challenge to legitimate clinical psychology. *The Clinical Psychologist, 55*(3), 4–10.

Lonner, W. J., & Adamopoulos, J. (1997). Culture as antecedent to behavior. In J. W. Berry, Y. P. Poortinga, & J. Pandey (Eds.), *Handbook of cross-cultural psychology: Vol. 1. Theory and method.* Boston: Allyn & Bacon.

Lonner, W. J., & Ibrahim, F. A. (2002). Appraisal and assessment in cross-cultural counseling. In P. B. Pedersen, J. G. Draguns, W. J. Lonner, & J. E. Trimble (Eds.), *Counseling across cultures* (5th ed., pp. 335–378). Thousand Oaks, CA: Sage.

Lopez, S. R. (1989). Patient variable biases in clinical judgment: Conceptual overview and methodological consequences. *Psychological Bulletin, 108,* 1–20.

Lopez, S., & Hernandez, P. (1986). How culture is considered in evaluations of psychopathology. *The Journal of Nervous and Mental Disease, 176*(10), 175–182.

Lutz, C., & White, G. M. (1986). The anthropology of emotions. *Annual Review of Anthropology, 15,* 405–436.

Lykes, M. B. (1985). Gender and individualistic vs. collectivist notions about the self. *Journal of Personality, 53,* 356–383.

Macaranas-Sittler, N. (1986, April). *Psychological frames of reference: Cross-cultural dimensions.* Poster presented at the Southerwestern Psychological Association meeting, Ft. Worth, TX.

Mail, P. D., McKay, R. B., & Katz, M. (1989). Expanding practice horizons: Learning from American Indian patients. *Patient Education and Counseling, 13,* 91–102.

Malgady, R. G. (1996). The question of cultural bias in assessment and diagnosis of ethnic minority clients: Let's reject the Null Hypothesis. *Professional Psychology: Research and Practice, 27,* 73–77.

Malgady, R. G. (2000). Myths about the null hypothesis and the path to reform. In R. H. Dana (Ed.), *Handbook of cross-cultural and multicultural personality assessment* (pp. 49–62). Mahwah, NJ: Lawrence Erlbaum Associates, Inc.

Malgady, R. G., Rogler, L. H., & Cortes, D. E. (1996). Cultural expression of psychiatric symptoms: Idioms of anger among Puerto Ricans. *Psychological Assessment, 8,* 265–268.

Malgady, R. G., Rogler, L. H., & Costantino, G. (1987). Ethnocultural and linguistic bias in mental health evaluation of Hispanics. *American Psychologist, 42,* 228–234.

Malgady, R. G., & Zayas, L. H. (2001). Cultural and linguistic considerations in psychodiagnosis with Hispanics: The need for an empirically informed process model. *Social Work, 46,* 40–49.

Manos, N. (1985). Adaptation of the MMPI in Greece: Translation, standardization, and cross-cultural comparison. In J. N. Butcher & C. D. Spielberger (Eds.), *Advances in personality assessment* (Vol. 4, pp. 159–208). Hillsdale, NJ: Lawrence Erlbaum Associates, Inc.

Manson, S. M., Ackerman, L. M., Dick, R. W., Baron, A. E., & Fleming, C. M. (1990). Depressive symptoms among American Indian adolescents: Psychometric characteristics of the Center for Epidemiologic Studies Depression Scale (CES–D). *Psychological Assessment, 2,* 231–237.

Mao, L. M. (1992). Invitational discourse and Chinese identity. *Journal of Asian Pacific Communication, 3,* 79–96.

Marcus, H. R., & Kitayama, S. (1991). Culture and the self: Implications for cognition, emotion, and motivation. *Psychological Review, 98,* 224–253.

Marin, G., & Gamba, R. J. (1996). A new measurement of acculturation for Hispanics: The bidimensional acculturation scale for Hispanics (BAS). *Hispanic Journal of Behavioral Sciences, 18,* 297–316.

Marin, G., Gamba, R. J., & Marin, B. V. (1992). Extreme response style and acquiescence among Hispanics: The role of acculturation and education. *Journal of Cross-Cultural Psychology, 23,* 498–509.

Marin, G., & Marin, B.V. (1991). *Research with Hispanic populations.* Newbury Park, CA: Sage.

Marin, G., Sabogal, F., VanOss Marin, B., Otero-Sabogal, R., & Perez-Sable, E. J. (1987). Development of a short acculturation scale for Hispanics. *Hispanic Journal of Behavioral Sciences, 9,* 183–205.

Marks, L. I. (1998). Deconstructing locus of control: Implications for practitioners. *Journal of Counseling & Development, 76,* 251–260.

Marsella, A. J., Friedman, M. J., Gerrity, G. T., & Scurfield, R. M. (Eds.). (1996). *Ethnocultural aspects of posttraumatic stress disorder: Issues, research, and clinical applications.* Washington, DC: American Psychological Association.

Martin, J. K., & Hall, G. C. N. (1992). Thinking Black, thinking internal, thinking feminist. *Journal of Counseling Psychology, 39,* 509–514.

Mason, J. (1989). *The Cultural Competence Self-Assessment Questionnaire.* Portland, OR: Research and Training Center on Family Support and Children's Mental Health, Portland State University.

Matarrazo, J. D. (1990). Psychological assessment versus psychological testing. *American Psychologist, 45,* 999–l0l7.

Matheson, L. (1986). If you are not an Indian, how do you treat an Indian? In H. P. Lelfley & P. B. Pedersen (Eds.), *Cross-cultural training for mental health professionals* (pp. 115–130). Springfield, IL: Thomas.

Matsumoto, D. (1992). More evidence for the universality of the contempt expression. *Journal of Cross-Cultural Psychology, 16,* 363–368.

Mattlar, C.-E. (1986). Finnish Rorschach responses in cross-cultural context: A normative study. *Jyvaskyla Studies in Education, Psychology, and Social Research, 58,* Jyvaskyla, Finland: University of Jyvaskyla.

Mattlar, C.-E. (2004). Are we entitled to use Rorschach Workshop norms when interpreting the Comprehensive System in Finland? *Rorschachiana, 26,* 85–110.

Mattlar, C.-E., Carlsson, A., & Forsander, C. (1993). The issue of the popular response. *British Journal of Projective Psychology, 38,* 53–62.

Mattlar, C.-E., Forsander, C., & Maki, J. (1997). Reference values vs. norms: The distribution for the comprehensive system's constellations in two random samples of Finns. *British Journal of Projective Psychology, 42*(2), 39–45.

Mattlar, C.-E., & Fried, R. (1993). The Rorschach in Finland. *Rorschachiana, 18,* 105–125.

McCrae, R, R. (2000). Trait psychology and the revival of personality and culture Studies. *American Behavioral Scientist, 44,* 10–31.

McCrae, R. R., & Costa, P. T., Jr. (1985). Updating Norman's "adequate taxonomy": Intelligence and personality in natural language and in questionnaires. *Journal of Personality and Social Psychology, 49,* 710–721.

McCrae, R. R., & Costa, P. T., Jr. (1997). Personality trait structure as a human universal. *American Psychologist, 52,* 509–516.

McCubbin, H. I., Thompson, E. A., Thompson, A. I., & Fromer, J. (Eds.). (1998). *Resiliency in Native American and immigrant families.* Thousand Oaks, CA: Sage.

McCully, R. S. (1971). *Rorschach theory and symbolism: A Jungian approach to clinical material.* Baltimore: Williams & Wilkins.

McGee, D. P., & Clark, C. X. (1974). Critical dilemmas of Black mental health. *Journal of Black Health Perspectives, 6,* 52–58.

McGoldrick, M., Giordano, J., & Pierce, J. K. (Eds.). (1996). *Ethnicity and family therapy.* (2nd ed.). New York: Guilford.

McGoldrick, M., Pierce, J. K., & Giordano, J. (Eds.). (1982). *Ethnicity and family therapy.* New York: Guilford.

Meehl, P. E. (1945). The dynamics of "structured" personality tests. *Journal of Clinical Psychology, 1,* 296–304.

Meredith, G. M. (1967). Ethnic Identity Scale: A study in transgenerational communication patterns. *Pacific Speech Quarterly, 2,* 57–65.

Meredith, L. S., Wenger, N., Liu, H., Horada, N., & Kahn, K. (2000). Development of a brief scale to measure acculturation among Japanese Americans. *Journal of Community Psychology, 28,* 103–113.

Messick, S. (1981). Constructs and their vicissitudes in educational and psychological measurement. *Psychological Bulletin, 89,* 575–588.

Meyer, G. J. (1997). On the integration of personality assessment methods: The Rorschach and MMPI. In J. A. Schinka & R. L. Greene (Eds.), *Emerging issues and methods in personality assessment* (pp. 203–236). Mahwah, NJ: Lawrence Erlbaum Associates, Inc.

Meyer, G. J. (2001). Evidence to correct misperceptions about Rorschach norms. *Clinical Psychology: Science and Practice, 8,* 389–396.

Meyer, G. J. (2002). Exploring possible ethnic differences and bias in the Rorschach Comprehensive System. *Journal of Personality Assessment, 78,* 104–129.

Meyer, G. J., & Archer, R. P. (2001). The hard science of Rorschach research: What do we know and where do we go? *Psychological Assessment, 17,* 486–502.

Meyer, G. J., Finn, S. E., Eyde, L. D., Kay, G. G., Moreland, K. L., Dies, R. R., Eisman, E. J., Kubiszyn, T. W., & Reed, G. M. (2001). Psychological testing and psychological assessment: A review of evidence and issues. *American Psychologist, 56,* 128–165.

Meyer, G. J., Hilsenroth, M. J., Baxter, D., Exner, J. E., Jr., Fowler, J. C., Piers, C. C., & Resnick, J. (2002). An examination of Interrater reliability for scoring the Rorschach comprehensive system in eight data sets. *Journal of Personality Assessment, 78,* 219–274.

Mezzich, J. E., Kleinman, A., Fabrega, H., Jr., & Parron, D. L. (1996). *Culture and psychiatric diagnosis: A DSM–IV perspective.* Washington, DC: American Psychiatric Press.

Milliones, J. (1980). Construction of a black consciousness measure: Psychotherapeutic implications. *Psychotherapy: Theory, Research, and Practice, 17,* 175–182.

Mindess, H. (1955). Analytical psychology and the Rorschach test. *Journal of Projective Techniques, 19,* 243–252.

Miralles Sangro, F. (1997). Location tables, form quality, and popular responses in a Spanish sample of 470 subjects. *Rorschiana, 22,* 38–66.

Mirza, L. (1976). Translation and standardization of the MMPI for Pakistan. In J. N. Butcher & P. Pancheri (Eds.), *A handbook of cross-national MMPI research* (pp. 55–80). Minneapolis: University of Minnesota Press.

Molish, H. B. (1967). Critique and problems of research: A survey. In S. J. Beck & H. B. Molish (Eds.), *Rorschach's test. II: A variety of personality pictures* (pp. 335–407). New York: Grune & Stratton.

Moncher, M. S., Holden, G. W., Schinke, S. P., & Palleja, J. (1990). Behavioral family treatment of the substance abusing Hispanic adolescent. In E. L. Feindler & G. R. Kalfes (Eds.), *Adolescent behavior therapy handbook* (pp. 329–349). New York: Springer.

Montgomery, G. T., & Orozco, S. (1985). Mexican Americans' performance on the MMPI as a function of level of acculturation. *Journal of Personality Assessment, 54,* 328–342.

Morgan, W. G. (2002). Origin and history of the earliest Thematic Apperception Test pictures. *Journal of Personality Assessment, 79,* 422–445.

Morris, E. F. (2000). Assessment practices with African Americans: Combining standard assessment measures within an Africentric orientation. In R. H. Dana (Ed.), *Handbook of cross-cultural and multicultural personality assessment* (pp. 573–603). Mahwah, NJ: Lawrence Erlbaum Associates, Inc.

Muniz, J., Prieto, G., Almeida, L., & Bartram, D. (1999). Test use in Spain, Portugal, and Latin American countries. *European Journal of Psychological Assessment, 15,* 151–157.

Munley P. H., Germain, J. M., Tovar-Murray, D., Borgman, A. L. (2004). MMPI–2 profile code types and measurement error. *Journal of Personality Assessment, 82,* 179–188.

Munroe, D. (1979). Locus of control attribution among blacks and whites in Africa. *Journal of Cross-Cultural Research, 10,* 157–172.

Murray, H. A. (1938). *Explorations in personality.* New York: Oxford University Press.

Murray, H. (1943). *Thematic Apperception Test manual.* Cambridge, MA: Harvard University Press.

Murstein, B. I. (1963). *Theory and research in projective techniques.* New York: Wiley.

Myers, H. F. (1982). Research on the Afro-American family: A critical review. In B. A. Bass, G. E. Wyatt, & G. J. Powell (Eds.), *The Afro-American family: assessment, treatment and research issues* (pp. 35–68). New York: Grune & Stratton.

Narikiyo, T. A., & Kameoka, V. A. (1992). Attributions of mental illness and judgments about help-seeking among Japanese Americans and White American students. *Journal of Counseling Psychology, 39,* 363–369.

Neville, H. A., Worthington, R. L., & Spanierman, L. B. (2001). Race, power, and multicultural counseling psychology. In J. G. Ponterotto, J. M. Casas, L. A. Suzuki, & C. M. Alexander (Eds.), *Handbook of multicultural counseling* (2nd ed., pp. 257–288). Thousand Oaks, CA: Sage.

Newman, M. L., & Greenway, P. (1997). Therapeutic effects of providing MMPI-2 feedback to clients at a university counseling service: A collaborative approach. *Psychological Assessment, 9,* 122–131.

Nichols, D. S. (2001). *Essentials of MMPI-2 assessment.* New York: Wiley.

Nichols, D. S., Padilla, J., & Gomez-Maqueo, E. L. (2000). Issues in the cross-cultural adaptation and use of the MMPI-2. In R. H. Dana (Ed.), *Handbook of cross-cultural and multicultural personality assessment* (pp. 247–266). Mahwah, NJ: Lawrence Erlbaum Associates, Inc.

Nilsson, J. E., Berkel, L. A., Flores, L. Y., Love, K. M., Wendler, A. M., & Mecklenburg, E. C. (2003). An 11-year review of *Professional Psychology: Research and Practice:* Content and sample analysis with an emphasis on diversity. *Professional Psychology: Research and Practice, 34,* 611–616.

Normal, R. P. (1969). Extreme response tendency as a function of emotional adjustment and stimulus ambiguity. *Journal of Consulting and Clinical Psychology, 33,* 406–410.

Nyamathi, A., & Vasquez, R. (1995). Impact of poverty, homelessness, and drugs on Hispanic women at risk for HIV infection. In A. Padilla (Ed.), *Hispanic psychology: Critical issues in theory and research* (pp. 213–227). Thousand Oaks, CA: Sage.

Obeyesekere, G. (1985). Depression, Buddhism, and the work of culture in Sri Lanka. In A. Kleinman & B. Good (Eds.), *Culture and depression* (pp. 134–152). Berkeley: University of California Press.

Okazaki, S. (1998). Psychological assessment of Asian Americans: Research agenda for cultural competency. *Journal of Personality Assessment, 70,* 54–70.

Okazaki, S. (2000). Assessing and treating Asian Americans: Recent advances. In I. Cuellar & F. A. Paniagua (Eds.), *Handbook of multicultural mental health: Assessment and treatment of diverse populations* (pp. 171–193). San Diego, CA: Academic.

Okazaki, S., & Sue, S. (1995). Methodological issues in assessment research with ethnic minorities. *Psychological Assessment, 7,* 367–375.

Okazaki, S., & Sue, S. (2000). Implications of test revisions for assessment with Asian Americans. *Psychological Assessment, 12,* 272–280.

Olmedo, E. L. (1979). Acculturation: A psychometric perspective. *American Psychologist, 34,* 1061–1070.

O'Roark, A. M. (2002). Assessment and intervention issues in international organizational counseling. In R. L. Lowman (Ed.), *Handbook of organizational consulting psychology* (pp. 516–544). San Francisco: Jossey-Bass.

Ownby, R. L. (1997). *Psychological reports: A guide to report writing in professional psychology* (3rd ed.). New York: Wiley.

Padilla, A. M. (2001). Issues in culturally appropriate assessment. In L. A. Suzuli, J. G. Ponterotto, & P. J. Meller (Eds.), *Handbook of multicultural assessment: Clinical, psychological, and educational applications* (2nd ed., pp. 5–27). San Francisco: Jossey-Bass.

Padilla, A. M., Ruiz, R. A., & Alvarez, R. (1989). Community mental health services for the Spanish-speaking/surnamed population. *American Psychologist, 30,* 892–905.

Padilla, A. M., Wagatsuma, Y., & Lindholm, K. J. (1985). Acculturation and personality as predictors of stress in Japanese and Japanese-Americans. *Journal of Social Psychology, 125*, 295–305.

Pancoast, D. L., & Archer, R. P. (1989). Original adult MMPI norms in normal samples: A review with implications for future developments. *Journal of Personality Assessment, 53*, 376–395.

Paniagua, F. A. (1998). *Assessing and treating culturally diverse clients: A practical guide* (2nd ed.). Thousand Oaks, CA: Sage.

Paniagua, F. A. (2000). Culture-bound syndromes, cultural variations, and psychopathology. In I. Cuellar & F. A. Paniagua (Eds.), *Handbook of multicultural mental health: Assessment and treatment of diverse populations* (pp. 139–169). San Diego, CA: Academic.

Parham, T. A. (2001, January). *Cultural competence in counseling/clinical practice.* Panel 8, National Multicultural Conference and Summit II, Santa Barbara, CA.

Parham, T. A., & Helms, J. E. (1981). The influence of black students' racial identity attitude on preference for counselor's race. *Journal of Counseling Psychology, 28*, 250–257.

Park, S. E., & Harrison, A. A. (1995). Career-related interests and values, perceived control, and acculturation of Asian-American and Caucasian-American college students. *Journal of Applied Social Psychology, 25*, 1184–1203.

Pedersen, P. B. (1997). The cultural context of the American Counseling Association code of ethics. *Journal of Counseling & Development, 76*, 23–28.

Pedersen, P. B. (2002). Ethics, competence, and other professional issues in culture-centered counseling. In P. B. Pedersen, J. G. Draguns, W. J. Lonner, & J. E. Trimble (Eds.), *Counseling across cultures* (5th ed., pp. 3–27). Thousand Oaks, CA: Sage.

Pedersen, P. B., & Marsella, A. J. (1982). The ethical crisis for cross-cultural counseling and therapy. *Professional Psychology, 13*, 492–500.

Perdomo, J. (2000). *Bilingual verbal ability: A pilot study.* Unpublished manuscript.

Peterson, C. A. (1990). Administration of the Thematic Apperception Test: Contributions of psychoanalytic psychotherapy. *Journal of Contemporary Psychotherapy, 20*, 191–200.

Petrogiannis, K. G., Bardos, A. N., & Randou, E. (1999). Performance of Greek and American students on the Matrix Analogies Test: A measure of nonverbal ability. *School Psychology International, 20*, 233–238.

Phinney, J. S. (1992). The Multigroup Ethnic Identity Measure: A new scale for use with diverse groups. *Journal of Adolescent Research, 7*, 156–176.

Pinderhughes, E. (1982). Afro-American families and the victim system. In M. McGoldrick, J. J. Pierce, & J. Giordiano (Eds.), *Ethnicity and family therapy* (pp. 108–122). New York: Guilford.

Piotrowski, C. (1999). Assessment practices in the era of managed care: Current status and future directions. *Journal of Clinical Psychology, 55*, 787–796.

Piotrowski, C., Belter, R. W., & Keller, J. W. (1998). The impact of "managed care" on the practice of psychological testing: Preliminary findings. *Journal of Personality Assessment, 70*, 441–447.

Piotrowski, Z. A. (1950). A new evaluation of the Thematic Apperception Test. *Psychoanalytic Review, 37*, 101–127.

Piotrowski, Z. A. (1957). *Perceptanalysis.* New York: Macmillan.

Pires, A. A. (2000). National norms for the Rorschach normative study in Portugal. In R. H. Dana (Ed.), *Handbook of cross-cultural and multicultural personality assessment* (pp. 367–392). Mahwah, NJ: Lawrence Erlbaum Associates, Inc.

Pollack, D., & Shore, H. (1980). Validity of the MMPI with Native Americans. *American Journal of Psychiatry, 137*, 946–950.

Ponterotto, J. G. (1997). Multicultural counseling training: A competency model and national survey. In D. B. Pope-Davis & H. L. K. Coleman (Eds.), *Multicultural counseling competen-*

cies: Assessment, education and training, and supervision (pp. 111–130). Thousand Oaks, CA: Sage.

Ponterotto, J. G. (1998). Charting a course for research in multicultural counseling training. *The Counseling Psychologist, 26*, 43–68.

Ponterotto, J. G., Casas, J. M., Suzuki, L. A., & Alexander, C. M. (Eds.). (2001). *Handbook of multicultural counseling* (2nd ed.). Thousand Oaks, CA: Sage.

Ponterotto, J. G., Fuertes, J. N., & Chen, E. C. (2000). Models of multicultural counseling. In S. R. Brown & R. W. Lent (Eds.), *Handbook of counseling psychology* (3rd ed., pp. 639–669). New York: Wiley.

Ponterotto, J. G., Gretchen, D., & Chauhan, R. V. (2001). Cultural identity and multicultural assessment: Quantitative and qualitative tools for the clinician. In L. Suzuki, J. G. Ponterotto, & P. Meller (Eds.), *The handbook of multicultural assessment* (2nd ed., pp. 67–99). San Francisco: Jossey-Bass.

Ponterotto, J. G., Gretchen, D., Utsey, S. O., Stracuzzi, T., & Saya, R., Jr. (2003). The Multigroup Ethnic Identity Measure (MEIM): Psychometric review and further validity testing. *Educational and Psychological Measurement, 63*, 502–515.

Ponterotto, J. G., Rieger, B. P., Barrett, A., & Sparks, R. (1994). Assessing multicultural counseling competence: A review of instrumentation. *Journal of Counseling and Development, 72*, 316–322.

Ponterotto, J. G., & Sabnani, H. B. (1989). Classics in multicultural counseling: A systematic five-year content analysis. *Journal of Multicultural Counseling and Development, 72*, 23–37.

Pope, K. S. (1992). Responsibilities in providing psychological test feedback to clients. *Psychological Assessment, 4*, 268–271.

Pope, K. S., & Vasquez, M. J. T. (1991). *Ethics in psychotherapy and counseling: A practical guide for psychologists.* San Francisco: Jossey-Bass.

Pope-Davis, B. B., Liu, W. M., Toporek, R. L., & Brittan-Powell, C. S. (2001). What's missing from multicultural competency research: Review, introspection, and recommendations. *Cultural Diversity and Ethnic Minority Psychology, 7*, 121–138.

Prediger, D. J. (1994). Multicultural assessment standards: A compilation for counselors. *Measurement and Evaluation in Counseling and Development, 27*, 68–73.

Preli, R., & Bernard, J. M. (1993). Making multiculturalism relevant for majority culture graduate students. *Journal of Marital and Family Therapy, 19*, 5–16.

Prola, M. (1972). A review of the Transcendence Index. *Journal of Personality Asssessment, 36*, 8–12.

Radloff, L. S. (1977). A CES–D scale: A self-report scale for research in the general population. *Applied Psychological Measurement, 1*, 385–401.

Raimy, V. (Ed.). (1950). *Training in clinical psychology.* New York: Prentice Hall.

Rhee, E., Uleman, J. S., Lee, H. K., & Roman, R. J. (1995). Spontaneous self-descriptions and ethnic identities in individualistic and collectivist cultures. *Journal of Personality and Social Psychology, 69*, 142–152.

Rick, K., & Forward, J. (1992). Acculturation and perceived intergenerational differences among Hmong youth. *Journal of Cross-Cultural psychology, 23*, 85–94.

Ridley, C. R. (1995). *Overcoming unintentional racism in counseling and therapy.* Thousand Oaks, CA: Sage.

Ridley, C. R., Hill, C. L., Thompson, C. E., & Omerod, A. J. (2001). Clinical practice guidelines in assessment: Toward an idiographic perspective. In D. B. Pope-Davis & H. L. K. Coleman (Eds.), *The intersection of race, class, and gender in multicultural counseling* (pp. 191–211). Thousand Oaks, CA: Sage.

Ridley, C. R., Li, L. C., & Hill, C. L. (1998). Multicultural assessment: Reexamination, reconceptualization, and practical application. *The Counseling Psychologist, 26*, 827–910.

Ridley, C. R., Liddle, M. C., Hill, C. L., & Li, L. C. (2001). Ethical decision making in multicultural counseling. In J. G. Ponterotto, J. M. Casas, & L. A. Suzuki (Eds.), *Handbook of multicultural counseling* (2nd ed., pp. 165–188). Thousand Oaks, CA: Sage.

Ridley, C. R., Mendoza, D. W., Kanitz, B. E., Angermeier, L., & Zenk, R. (1994). Cultural sensitivity in multicultural counseling: A perceptual schema model. *Journal of Counseling Psychology, 4,* 125–136.

Ritzler, B. (2004). Cultural applications of the Rorschach, apperception tests, and figure drawings. In M. J. Hilsenroth & D. L. Segal (Eds.), *Comprehensive handbook of psychological assessment: Vol 2. Personality assessment* (pp. 573–585). New York: Wiley.

Robins, L. N., Helzer, J. E., Croughan, J., & Ratcliff, K. S. (1981). National Institute of Mental Health: Diagnostic Interview Schedule. *Archives of General Psychiatry, 38,* 381–389.

Robinson, T. L., & Ginter, E. J. (1999). Introduction to the special issue on racism. *Journal of Counseling & Development, 77,* 3.

Rogers, M. R., Hoffman, M. A., & Wade, J. (1998). Notable multicultural training in APA-approved counseling psychology and school psychology programs. *Cultural Diversity and Mental Health, 4,* 212–226.

Rogler, L., Malgady, R., & Rodriguez, D. (1989). *Hispanics and mental health: A framework for research.* Malabar, FL: Krieger.

Romero, A. J. (2000). Assessing and treating Latinos: Overview of research. In I. Cuellar & F. A. Paniagua (Eds.), *Handbook of multicultural mental health: assessment and treatment of diverse populations* (pp. 209–223). San Diego, CA: Academic.

Rorschach, H. (1942). *Psychodiagnostics: A diagnostic test based on perception* (3rd ed., B. Kronenberg & P. Lemkau, Trans.). Berne, Switzerland: Hans Huber. (Original work published in 1921)

Rosado, J. W. (1980). Important psychocultural factors in the delivery of mental health services to lower-class Puerto Rican clients: A review of recent studies. *Journal of Community Psychology, 8,* 215–226.

Ross, C. E., & Mirowsky, J. (1984). Socially-desirable response and acquiescence in a cross-cultural survey of mental health. *Journal of Health and Social Behavior, 25,* 189–197.

Rossini, E. D., & Moretti, R. J. (1997). Thematic Apperception Test (TAT) interpretation: Practice recommendations from a survey of clinical psychology doctoral programs accredited by the American Psychological Association. *Professional Psychology: Research and Practice, 28,* 393–398.

Rothke, S. E., Friedman, A. F., Dahlstrom, W. G., Greene, R. L., Arrendondo, R., & Mann, A. W. (1994). MMPI–2 normative data for the F – K index: Implications for clinical, neuropsychological, and forensic practice. *Assessment, 1,* 1–15.

Rotter, J. B. (1950). *Incomplete Sentences Blank—Adult Form.* New York: Psychological Corporation.

Rotter, J. B. (1954). *Social learning and clinical psychology.* Englewood Cliffs, NJ: Prentice Hall.

Rotter, J. B. (1966). Generalized expectancies for internal vs. external control of reinforcement. *Psychological Monographs, 80*(1, Whole No. 609).

Roysircar-Sodowsky, G., & Kuo, P. Y. (2001). Determining cultural validity of personality assessment: Some guidelines. In D. B. Pope-Davis & H. L. K. Coleman (Eds.), *The intersection of race, class, and gender in multicultural counseling* (pp. 213–239). Thousand Oaks, CA: Sage.

Roysircar-Sodowsky, G., Kwan, K.-L. K., & Pannu, R. (1995). Ethnic identity of Asians in the United States. In J. G. Ponterotto, J. M. Casas, L. A. Suzuki, & C. M. Alexander (Eds.), *Handbook of multicultural counseling* (pp. 123–154). Thousand Oaks, CA: Sage.

Roysircar-Sodowsky, G., & Maestas, M. V. (2000). Acculturation, ethnic identity, and acculturative stress: Evidence and measurement. In R. H. Dana (Ed.), *Handbook of cross-cultural and multicultural personality assessment* (pp. 131–172). Mahwah, NJ: Lawrence Erlbaum Associates, Inc.

Russell, J. A. (1991). Culture and the categorization of emotions. *Psychological Bulletin, 110,* 426–450.

Russell, J. A. (1994). Is there a universal recognition of emotion from facial expression? A review. *Psychological Bulletin, 115,* 102–141.

Sampson, E. E. (1985). The decentralization of identity: Toward a revised concept of personal and social order. *American Psychologist, 40,* 1203–1211.

Sampson, E. E. (1988). The debate on individualism: Indigenous psychologies of the individual and their role in personal and societal functioning. *American Psychologist, 43,* 15–22.

Sampson, E. E. (2000). Reinterpreting individualism and collectivism: Their religious roots and monologic versus dialogic person-other relationships. *American Psychologist, 55,* 1425–1432.

Sanchez, L. M., & Turner, S. M. (2003). Practicing psychology in the era of managed care: Implications for practice and training. *American Psychologist, 58,* 116–129.

Sandoval, M. C. (1977). Santeria: AfroCuban concepts of disease and treatment in Miami. *Social Science and Medicine, 138,* 137–151.

Saner-Yi, L., & Saner-Yu, R. (1985). Value dimensions in American counseling: A Taiwanese-American comparison. *International Journal for the Advancement of Counseling, 8,* 137–146.

Sasao, T. (1994). *Asian American cultural experience survey.* Unpublished manuscript, University of California-Santa Barbara.

Schinka, J. A., & LaLone, L. (1997). MMPI–2 norms: Comparison with a census-matched sample. *Psychology Assessment, 9,* 307–311.

Schwartz, G. E. (1984). Psychobiology of health: A new synthesis. In B. L. Hammonds & C. J. Scheirer (Eds.), *Psychology and health: The master lecture series* (Vol. 3, pp. 149–193). Washington, DC: American Psychological Association.

Schwartz, S. H., & Bilsky, W. (1987). Toward a psychological structure of human values. *Journal of Personality and Social Psychology, 58,* 550–562.

Shaffer, T. W., & Erdberg, P. (2001, March). *An international symposium on Rorschach nonpatient data: Worldwide findings.* Symposium presented at the midwinter meeting of the Society for Personality Assessment, Philadelphia, PA.

Shneidman, E. S. (1949). *The Make-A-Picture Story Test.* New York: Psychological Corporation.

Shneidman, E. S. (Ed.). (1951). *Thematic Apperception Test analysis.* New York: Grune & Stratton.

Shneidman, E. S. (1959). Suggestions for the delineation of validation studies. *Journal of Projective Techniques, 23,* 259–263.

Simons, R. C., & Hughes, C. C. (Eds.). (1985). *The culture-bound syndromes: Folk illnesses of psychiatric and anthropological interest.* Dordrecht, The Netherlands: Reidel.

Singer, J. L. (1960). The experience type: Some behavioral correlates and theoretical implications. In M. A. Rickers-Ovsiankina (Ed.), *Rorschach psychology* (pp. 223–259). New York: Wiley.

Smith, A. D. (1994). The politics of culture: Ethnicity and nationalism. In T. Ingold (Ed.), *Companion encyclopedia of anthropology: Humanity, culture, and social life* (pp. 706–733). New York: Routledge.

Smith, B. (2002, March). Scientific controversy and the Rorschach. In P. Lerner (Chair), *Reflections upon and responses to recent Rorschach criticisms.* Symposium conducted at the Society for Personality Assessment midwinter meeting, San Antonio, TX.

Smith, C., Atkinson, J. W., McClelland, D. C., & Veroff, J. (1992). *Motivation and personality: A handbook of thematic content analysis.* Cambridge, England: Cambridge University Press.

Smith, P. B., & Schwartz, S. H. (1997). Values. In J. W. Berry, M. H. Segall, & C. Kagitcibasi (Eds.), *Handbook of cross-cultural psychology: Volume 3. Social behavior and applications* (2nd ed., pp. 77–118). Boston: Allyn & Bacon.

Smith, W. H. (1978). Ethical, social, and professional issues in patients' access to psychological test reports. *Bulletin of the Menninger Clinic, 42,* 150–155.

Snowden, L. R. (2003). Bias in mental health assessment and intervention: Theory and evidence. *American Journal of Public Health, 93,* 239–242.

Sodowsky, G. R., Kuo-Jackson, P., Richardson, M. F., & Corey, A. T. (1998). Correlates of self-reported multicultural competencies: Therapist multicultural social desirability, race, social inadequacy, locus of control racial ideology, and multicultural training. *Journal of Counseling Psychology, 45,* 256–264.

Sodowsky, G. R., & Lai, E. W. M. (1997). Asian immigrant variables and structural models of cross-cultural distress. In A. Booth, A. C. Croutier, & N. Landale (Eds.), *Immigration and the family: Research and policy on U. S. immigrants* (pp. 212–234). Mahwah, NJ: Lawrence Erlbaum Associates, Inc.

Sofue, T. (1979). Aspects of the personality of Japanese, Americans, Italians and Eskimos: Comparisons using the sentence completion test. *Journal of Psychological Anthropology, 2,* 15–52.

Spielberger, C. D., Moscoso, M. S., & Brunner, T. M. (2004). Cross-cultural assessment of emotional states and personality traits. In R. K. Hambleton, C. D. Spielberger, & P. F. Merenda (Eds.), *Adapting educational and psychological tests for cross-cultural assessment.* Mahwah, NJ: Lawrence Erlbaum Associates, Inc.

Stanard, R., Sandhu, D. S., & Painter, L. C. (2000). Assessment of spirituality in counseling. *Journal of Counseling & Development, 78,* 204–210.

Stedman, J. M., Hatch, J. P., & Schoenfeld, L. S. (2001). The current status of psychological assessment training in graduate and professional schools. *Journal of Personality Assessment, 77,* 398–407.

Stein, M. I. (1948). *The Thematic Apperception Test: An introductory manual for its clinical use with adults.* Cambridge, MA: Addison-Wesley.

Stein, M. I. (1955). *The Thematic Apperception Test: An introductory manual for its clinical use with adults.* Cambridge, MA: Addison-Wesley.

Stein, M. J., Smith, M., & Wallston, K. A. (1984). Cross-cultural issues in health locus of control beliefs. *Psychological Studies, 29,* 112–116.

Stricker, L. J. (1980). "SES" indices: What do they measure? *Basic and Applied Social Psychology, 1,* 91–101.

Strickland, B. R. (2000). Misassumptions, misadventures, and the misuse of psychology. *American Psychologist, 55,* 331–338.

Sue, D. W. (1978). Worldviews and counseling. *Personnel & Guidance Journal, 56,* 458–462.

Sue, D. W., Arredondo, P., & McDavis, R. J. (1992). Multicultural counseling competencies and standards: A call to the profession. *Journal of Counseling and Development, 70,* 477–486.

Sue, D. W., Bernier, J. E., Durran, A., Feinberg, L., Pedersen, P., Smith, E. J., & Vasquez-Nuttall, E. (1982). Position paper: Cross-cultural competencies. *The Counseling Psychologist, 10,* 45–52.

Sue, D. W., & Sue, D. (1999). *Counseling the culturally different: Theory and practice* (3rd ed.). New York: Wiley.

Sue, S. (1993). Mental health issues for Asian and Pacific Islander Americans. In N. Zane, D. Takeuchi, & K. Young (Eds.), *Confronting critical health issues of Asian and Pacific Islander Americans* (pp. 266–288). Newbury Park, CA: Sage.

Sue, S. (1999). Science, ethnicity, and bias: Where have we gone wrong? *American Psychologist, 54,* 1070–1077.

Sue, S., Keefe, K., Enomoto, K., Durvasula, R. S., & Chao, R. (1996). Asian American and White college students' performance on the MMPI–2. In J. N. Butcher (Ed.), *International adaptations of the MMPI–2: Research and clinical applications* (pp. 206–218). Minneapolis: University of Minnesota Press.

Sue, S., & Sue, L. (2003). Ethnic science is good science. In G. Bernal, J. E. Trimble, A. K. Burlew, & F. T. L. Leong (Eds.), *Handbook of racial and ethnic minority psychology* (pp. 198–207). Thousand Oaks, CA: Sage.

Sue, S., & Zane, N. (1987). The role of culture and cultural techniques in psychotherapy. *American Psychologist, 42,* 37–45.

Suinn, R. M., Rickard-Figueroa, K., Lew, S., & Vigil, P. (1987). The Suinn-Lew Asian Self-Identity Acculturation scale: An initial report. *Educational and Psychological measurement, 47,* 401–407.

Sustento-Seneriches, J. (1997). Filipino American families. In E. Lee (Ed.), *Working with Asian Americans: A guide for clinicians* (pp. 101–113). New York: Guilford.

Szapocznik, J., Kurtines, W. M., & Fernandez, T. (1980). Bicultural involvement and adjustment in Hispanic-American youths. *International Journal of Intercultural Relations, 4,* 353–365.

Tait, R., DeGood, D., & Carron, H. (1982). A comparison of health locus of control beliefs in low-back patients from the U. S. and New Zealand. *Pain, 14,* 53–61.

Tallent, N. (1993). *Psychological report writing* (4th ed.). Englewood Cliffs, NJ: Prentice Hall.

Tang, M., & Fouad, N. A. (1999). The magnitude of acculturation and its impact of Asian Americans' career development. In D. S. Sandhu (Ed.), *Asian and Pacific Islander Americans: Issues and concerns for counseling and psychotherapy* (pp. 123–136. Commack, NY: Nova Science Publishers, Inc.

Teglasi, H. (1993). *Clinical use of story telling: Emphasizing the TAT with children and adolescents.* Boston: Allyn & Bacon.

Teglasi, H. (2001). *Essentials of TAT and other storytelling techniques assessment.* New York: Wiley.

Terman, L. M., & Merrill, M. A. (1973). *Stanford-Binet Intelligence Scale.* Boston: Houghton-Mifflin.

Tiemann, J. (1999). *Analysis of language-based differences on Rorschach Comprehensive System and TAT protocols of fluent bilinguals.* Unpublished doctoral dissertation, Long Island University, New York.

Tiemann, J. (2001). *An exploration of language-based personality experiences in fluent bilinguals.* Unpublished manuscript.

Tomkins, S. S. (1947). *The Thematic Apperception Test.* New York: Grune & Stratton.

Triandis, H. C. (1990). Cross-cultural studies of individualism and collectivism. *Nebraska Symposium on Motivation, 37,* 41–133.

Triandis, H. C. (1995). *Individualism and collectivism.* Boulder, CO: Westview.

Triandis, H. C., Marin, G., Lisansky, J., & Betancourt, H. (1984). Simpatia as a cultural script of Hispanics. *Journal of Personality and Social Psychology, 47,* 1363–1375.

Triandis, H. C., & Suh, E. M. (2002). Cultural influences on personality. *Annual Review of Psychology, 53,* 133–160.

Trimble, J. E., Helms, J. E., & Root, M. P. P. (2003). Social and psychological perspectives on ethnic and racial identity. In G. Bernal, J. E. Trimble, A. K. Burlew, & F. T. L. Leong (Eds.), *Handbook of racial and ethnic minority psychology* (pp. 219–275). Thousand Oaks, CA: Sage.

Trimble, J. E., & Richardson, S. S. (1983). Perceived personal and societal forms of locus of control measures among American Indians. *White Cloud Journal, 3*(1), 3–14.

Tropp, L. R., Erkut, S., Garcia Coll, C., Alarcon, O., & Vazquez Garcia, H. A. (1999). Psychological acculturation: Development of a new measure for Puerto Ricans on the U.S. mainland. *Educational and Psychological Assessment, 59,* 351–367.

Tsai, J. L., Ying, Y. W., & Lee, P. A. (2000). The meaning of "being Chinese" and "being American": Variation among Chinese American young adults. *Journal of Cross-Cultural Psychology, 31*(3), 302–322.

Tsoi, W. F. (1985). Mental health in Singapore and its relation to Chinese culture. In W. S. Tseng & D. Y. H. Wu (Eds.), *Chinese culture and mental health* (pp. 229–250). New York: Academic.

Turnbow, K., & Dana, R. H. (1981). The effects of stem length and directions on sentence completion test responses. *Journal of Personality Assessment, 44,* 27–32.

Ullmann, L. P. (1957). Productivity and the clinical use of TAT cards. *Journal of Projective Techniques, 21,* 399–403.

U.S. Bureau of Census. (2002). *Profiles of general demographic characteristics: 2000 census of population and housing.* Retrieved December 22, 2002, from http://www.census.gov/prod/cen2000/dp1/2kh00.pdf

U.S. Department of Health and Human Services. (2001). *Mental health: Culture, race, and ethnicity* (A supplement to Mental health: A report of the surgeon general). Rockville, MD: U.S. Department of Health and Human Services, Substance Abuse and Mental Health Services Administration, Center for Mental Health Services.

Utsey, S. O., Bolden, M. A., & Brown, A. L. (2001). Visions of revolution from the spirit of Frantz Fanon: A psychology of liberation for counseling African Americans confronting societal racism and oppression. In J. G. Ponterotto, J. M. Casas, L. A. Suzuki, & C. M. Alexander (Eds.), *Handbook of multicultural counseling* (2nd ed., pp. 311–336). Thousand Oaks, CA: Sage.

Van de Vijver, F. (2000). The nature of bias. In R. H. Dana (Ed.), *Handbook of cross-cultural and multicultural personality assessment* (pp. 87–106). Mahwah, NJ: Lawrence Erlbaum Associates, Inc.

Van de Vijver, F., & Hambleton, R. K. (1996). Translating tests: Some practical guidelines. *European Psychologist, 1,* 89–99.

Vane, J. R. (1981). The Thematic Apperception Test: A review. *Clinical Psychology Review, 1,* 319–336.

Vassiliou, V. G., & Vassiliou, G. (1973). The implicative meaning of the Greek concept of philotimo. *Journal of Cross-Cultural Psychology, 4,* 326–341.

Vaz, C. E. (1997). *O Rorschach: Teoria e desempenho* [Rorschach theory and practice]. Sao Paulo, Brazil: Editora Manole.

Vega, W. (1982). The Hispanic natural healer, a case study: Implications for prevention. In R. Valle & W. Vega (Eds.), *Hispanic natural support systems: Mental health prevention perspectives* (pp. 65–74). Sacramento, CA: State of California, Department of Mental Health.

Velasquez, R. J., Ayala, G. X., Mendoza, S., Nezami, E., Castillo-Canez, I., Pace, T., Choney, S. K., Gomez, F. C., Jr., & Miles, L. E. (2000). Culturally competent use of the Minnesota Multiphasic Personality Inventory–2. In I. Cuellar & F. A. Paniagua (Eds.), *Handbook of multicultural mental health: Assessment and treatment of diverse populations* (pp. 389–417). San Diego, CA: Academic.

Velasquez, R., J., Butcher, J. N., Garrido, M., & Cabiya, J. J. (1996). *Dana's culturally competent MMPI assessment of Hispanics: A case of "rounding up the usual suspects."* Unpublished manuscript.

Velasquez, R. J., Gonzales, M., Butcher, J. N., Castillo-Canez, I., Apodaca, J. X., & Chavira, D. (1997). Use of the MMPI–2 with Chicanos: Strategies for counselors. *Journal of Multicultural Counseling and Development, 25,* 107–120.

Viglione, D. J. (2002, March). Depathologizing the Rorschach: Critical corrections to false psychological interpretations. In S. D. Hickman & R. Krishnamurthy (Chairs), *Rorschach interpretation: Knowledge and practice.* Symposium conducted at the meeting of the Society for Personality Assessment, San Antonio, TX.

Viglione, D. J., & Hilsenroth, M. J. (2001). The Rorschach: Facts, fictions, and future. *Psychological Assessment, 13*, 452–471.

Vinet, E. V. (2000). The Rorschach Comprehensive System in Iberoamerica. In R. H. Dana (Ed.), *Handbook of cross-cultural and multicultural personality assessment* (pp. 345–365). Mahwah, NJ: Lawrence Erlbaum Associates.

Wallach, M. A., & Wallach, L. (1983). *Psychology's sanction for selfishness: The error of egoism in theory and practice.* San Francisco: Freeman.

Wallston, K. A., Wallston, B. S., & deVellis, R. (1978). Development of the Multidimensional Health Locus of Control (MHLC) scales. *Health Psychology Monographs, 6*(2), 160–170.

Watkins, D., Yau, J., Dahlin, B., & Wondimu, H. (1997). The Twenty Statements Test: Some measurement issues. *Journal of Cross-Cultural Psychology, 28*, 626–633.

Wechsler, D. (1939). *The measurement of adult intelligence.* Baltimore: Williams Wilkins.

Weclew, R. V. (1975). The nature, prevalence, and level of awareness of "Curanderismo" and some of its implications for community mental health. *Community Mental Health Journal, 11*, 145–154.

Weiner, I. B. (1994). The Rorschach Inkblot Method (RIM) is not a test: Implications for theory and practice. *Journal of Personality Assessment, 62*, 498–504.

Weiner, I. B. (1996). Speaking Rorschach: A test for all seasons. *Rorschachiana, 21*, 1–5.

Weiner, I. B. (1998). *Principles of Rorschach interpretation.* Mahwah, NJ: Lawrence Erlbaum Associates, Inc.

Weiner, I. B. (2000). Making Rorschach interpretation as good as it can be. *Journal of Personality Assessment, 74*, 164–174.

Weiner, I. B. (2001). Advancing the science of psychological assessment: The Rorschach Inkblot Method as exemplar. *Psychological Assessment, 13*, 423–432.

Weiner, I. B. (2003). *Principles of Rorschach interpretation.* (2nd ed.) Mahwah, NJ: Lawrence Erlbaum Associates, Inc.

Weiner, I. B. (2004). Rorschach assessment: Current status. In M. J. Hilsenroth & D. L. Segal (Eds.), *Comprehensive handbook of psychological assessment: Volume 2. Personality assessment* (pp. 343–355). New York: Wiley.

Weiner, I. B., Spielberger, C. D., & Abeles, N. (2002). Scientific psychology and the Rorschach inkblot method. *The Clinical Psychologist, 55*(4), 7–12.

Welsh, G. S. (1948). An extension of Hathaway's MMPI profile coding system. *Journal of Consulting Psychology, 12*, 343–344.

Whatley, R., Allen, J., & Dana, R. H. (2003). Ethnic differences on the MMPI: Relation of African American racial identity to MMPI scores. *Cultural Diversity and Ethnic Minority Psychology, 9*, 344–352.

Whitworth, R. H., & McBlaine, D. D. (1993). Comparison of MMPI and MMPI–2 administered to Anglo- and Hispanic-American university students. *Journal of Personality Assessment, 61*, 19–27.

Wiener, D. N. (1948). Subtle and obvious keys for the MMPI. *Journal of Consulting Psychology, 23*, 164–170.

Wiggins, J. S. (2003). *Paradigms of personality assessment.* New York: Guilford.

Willcockson, N., Dana, R. H., & Rau, T. (1981, March). *Interpretation of projective techniques: Practice effects.* Paper presented at the meeting of the Society for Personality Assessment, San Diego, CA.

Wong, O. C., & Piran, N. (1995). Western biases and assumptions as impediments in counseling traditional Chinese clients. *Canadian Journal of Counseling, 29*, 107–119.

Wood, J. M., Garb, H. N., Lilienfeld, S. O., & Nezworski, M. T. (2002). Clinical assessment. *Annual Review of Psychology, 53*, 519–543.

Wood, J. M., Nezworski, M. T., Garb, H. N., & Lilienfeld, S. O. (2001a). The misperception of psychopathology: Problems with the norms of the Comprehensive System for the Rorschach. *Clinical Psychology: Science and Practice, 8*, 350–373.

Wood, J. M., Nezworski, M. T., Garb, H. N., & Lilienfeld, S. O. (2001b). Problems with the norms of the Comprehensive System for the Rorschach: Methodological and conceptual considerations. *Clinical Psychology: Research and Practice, 8,* 397–402

Woodcock, R. W., & Muñoz-Sandoval, A. F. (1993). *Woodcock-Muñoz Language Survey Comprehensive Manual.* Chicago: Riverside.

Wuts, G. (2002). *A preliminary validation study of the psychometric properties of selected scales of the MMPI–2 with English speaking Singaporeans.* Unpublished doctoral dissertation, California School of Professional Psychology, Alliant University, San Diego.

Wylie, R. (1974). *The self-concept* (Vol. 1). Lincoln: University of Nebraska Press.

Wylie, R. (1989). *Measures of the self-concept.* Lincoln: University of Nebraska Press.

Yang, K. S., & Bond, M. H. (1990). Exploring implicit personality theories with indigenous or imported measures. *Journal of Personality and Social Psychology, 58,* 1087–1095.

Ying, Y.-W., Akutsu, P. D., Zhang, X., & Huang, L. N. (1997). Psychological dysfunction in Southeast Asian refugees as mediated by Sense of Coherence. *American Journal of Community Psychology, 25,* 839–859.

Zalewski, C., & Greene, R. L. (1996). Multicultural usage of the MMPI–2: Clinical, psychological, and educational applications. In L. A. Suzuki, P. J. Meller, & J. G. Ponterotto (Eds.), *Handbook of multicultural assessment* (pp. 77–114). San Francisco: Jossey-Bass.

Zane, N. (1993). An empirical examination of loss of face among Asian Americans. In R. Carter (Ed.), *Ninth annual cross-cultural winter roundtable proceedings* (pp. 1–6). New York: Columbia University.

Zane, N., & Mak, W. (2003). Major approaches to the measurement of acculturation among ethnic minority populations: A content analysis and an alternative research strategy. In G. Marin, P. Balls Organista, & K. M. Chun (Eds.), *Acculturation: Advances in theory, measurement, and applied research* (pp. 39–60). Washington, DC: American Psychological Association.

Zane, N., & Yeh, M. (2002). The use of culturally-based variables in assessment: Studies on loss of face. In K. S. Kurasaki, S. Okazaki, & S. Sue (Eds.), *Asian American mental health: Assessment methods and theories* (pp. 123–138). New York: Kluwer Academic.

Zheng, Y.-P., Lin, K.-M., Takeuchi, D., Kurasaki, K. S., Wang, Y., & Cheung, F. (1997). An epidemiological study of neurasthenia in Chinese Americans in Los Angeles. *Comprehensive Psychiatry, 38,* 249–259.

Zubin, J. (1950). Test construction and methodology. In R. E. Harris (Ed.), *Recent advances in diagnostic psychological testing: A critical summary* (pp. 99–120). Springfield, IL: Thomas.

Author Index

Subject Index